# The Sexually Abused Male

# The Sexually Abused Male

*Prevalence, Impact, and Treatment*

*Volume 1*

*Edited by*
Mic Hunter

Lexington Books
*An Imprint of Macmillan, Inc.*
New York

Maxwell Macmillan Canada
Toronto

Maxwell Macmillan International
New York   Oxford   Singapore   Sydney

Lexington Books
An Imprint of Macmillan, Inc.
866 Third Avenue, New York, N.Y. 10022

Maxwell Macmillan Canada, Inc.
1200 Eglinton Avenue East
Suite 200
Don Mills, Ontario M3C 3N1

Macmillan, Inc. is part of the Maxwell Communication Group of Companies.

Printed in the United States of America

printing number
2   3   4   5   6   7   8   9   10

*6-1-92- 1550949*

*Library of Congress Cataloging-in-Publication Data*

The sexually abused male / edited by Mic Hunter.
    p.     cm.
  Includes indexes.
  Contents: v.  1.  Prevalence, impact, and treatment—v.  2.  Application of
treatment strategies.
    ISBN 0–669–21518–X (v. 1 : alk. paper).—ISBN 0–669–25005–8 (v. 2 :
alk. paper)
    1.  Sexually abused children—Mental health.   2.   Adult child sexual abuse
victims—Mental health.   3.   Psychotherapy.   4.   Child molesting—Social
aspects.   5.   Boys—Mental health.   6.   Men—Mental health.
    [DNLM:  1.   Child Abuse, Sexual—psychology.   2.   Child Abuse, Sexual—
rehabilitation.   3.   Men—psychology.   4.   Sex Offenses—prevention &
control.   5.   Sex Offenses—psychology.   WA 320 S5195]
RJ507.S49S49      1990 *Vol. |*
616.85′83—dc20
DNLM/DLC
for Library of Congress                                                    90-6352
                                                                            CIP

*To the staff of the Gestalt Institute of the Twin Cities and the trainees of the two-year Intensive Postgraduate Training Program, class of 1990, for their support during this project.*

# Contents

# Preface

I t is the last decade of the twentieth century, and yet here I am sitting down to write the introduction to a book about sexual abuse. I am aware of being sad. I live in a society that considers itself civilized but allows and even encourages the abuse of its young. We have only recently had the courage to acknowledge this fact. As I look at my bookshelves, I am reminded that most of the publications that address sexual abuse in any detail have been available only within the past ten years, and the few that focus on males have been released within the past three years.

Sexual abuse does not occur in a vacuum. The societal view of sexual abuse affects everyone associated with it: the victim, his family, the offender, the legal system, the treatment provider, and the community as a whole. The standards of the society determine who is viewed as a victim and who is not, who is ignored and who obtains treatment, and even what type of treatment is available. Therefore, it is imperative that the cultural factors that lead to the underidentification and treatment of male victims of sexual maltreatment be addressed.

Part I begins with Jim Struve's historical overview of the factors in Western society that continue to play an important role in determining our model for understanding sexual abuse. Building on this broad foundation, James Trivelpiece narrows the focus with a look at how current American popular culture reflects the beliefs of the society and continues to reinforce numerous myths about sexual abuse. Fran Sepler further clarifies the societal problems facing maltreated males with a description of how the beliefs of the culture lead to shortcomings in the current victim advocacy movement.

Building on the foundation provided by the first three chapters, Part II focuses on the prevalence and impact of sexual abuse. Anthony Urquiza and Lisa Keating describe the complexities of attempting to determine the prevalence of the sexual maltreatment of males. Dr. Urquiza also joins Maria Capra in providing a review of the studies addressing the effects of sexual abuse on males. Peter Olson presents the results of his study on the long-term effects of childhood sexual abuse using the Minnesota Multiphasic Personality

Inventory (MMPI). Paul Gerber offers two case studies to illustrate the process of moving from victim to offender. And Jane Gilgun completes this part on a more hopeful note with her discussion of the factors associated with a reduced likelihood of becoming a perpetrating adult.

Part III on assessment begins with Mark Evans's chapter on crisis intervention. Carolyn Levitt follows with a description of the medical aspects of assessment, and Paul Gerber provides a format for a structured assessment interview. The lack of information concerning the existence and behavior of female offenders has reduced our ability to identify male victims and led to the underestimation of the prevalence of male victims. Charlotte Kasl addresses the topic of female offenders from a feminist standpoint and discusses the importance of ending the taboo prohibiting our awareness of the existence of female-perpetrated sexual abuse. Ruth Mathews, Jane Matthews, and Kate Speltz provide some much-needed information about female sexual offenders.

The task of this first volume is to heighten skilled helpers' awareness of the cultural factors that can prevent accurate identification and assessment of sexually maltreated males and that reduce the effectiveness of therapeutic techniques. Volume 2 is dedicated to the application of this increased awareness in treatment settings. The authors provide practical, effective strategies for the difficult task of facilitating healing in men who have been sexually maltreated.

At the beginning of this preface, I said that I am sad that the need for such a book exists. At the same time, I am also happy and proud. I am happy that there are people willing to speak out against the horror of sexual abuse. It is a cry of protest that is long overdue. I also am happy that so many women and men are concerned about male survivors. My pride comes from being associated with the people who contributed their knowledge and time to make sure this book became a reality. The authors completed their chapters in spite of conference deadlines, graduate school commitments, coast-to-coast relocations, the trials of setting up a private practice, a death in the family, personal issues related to their own recovery from sexual abuse, major illness, surgery, moving in with a new partner, adopting a child, formulating wedding plans, and being the spouse of a veterinary school student. They have always believed in the value of this project, and I have always believed in them.

# Part I
# Cultural Factors
# Affecting Males

# 1

# Dancing with the Patriarchy: The Politics of Sexual Abuse

*Jim Struve*

For too long, the collective consciousness of contemporary Western society has promoted an idyllic image of the family as a safe haven in an otherwise turbulent, violent, and unsafe world. Closer examination of the nuclear family, however, provides considerable evidence that this unit of social organization is actually a fertile environment for deadly aggression.

Nationally, more than two million cases of child abuse were reported during 1986 alone. That number included more than 314,000 cases of sexual abuse (American Humane Association 1986). The actual number of children who are being abused is probably significantly larger than the number of reported cases. Underreporting is especially true for incidents of sexual abuse, which are generally shrouded in secrecy. For example, a nationwide survey of 2,627 adults interviewed with assurances of anonymity was published by the *Los Angeles Times* on August 25, 1985. Twenty-two percent of those people interviewed acknowledged that they had been sexually abused during their childhood (Finkelhor, Hotling, Louis, and Smith 1990).

A problem such as sexual abuse that, conservatively, affects between 20 and 30 percent of the American population must not be ignored. Despite the frequency of sexual abuse, however, few children feel the safety or support that allows them to disclose their experience. The 1985 *Los Angeles Times* poll indicated that fewer than half of those people who had been victimized told anybody. Ten percent of those people who acknowledged their abuse said that they did not disclose their sexual molestation because they did not consider their abuse to be serious. Seventy percent of those who did disclose their victimization reported that no effective follow-up action occurred.

Most authorities now agree that at least one of every five girls will be sexually abused before the age of eighteen (Russell 1986). There is less agreement on the prevalence with which boys are sexually abused, but a growing number of clinicians who work with sexual abuse are discovering that males probably are sexually victimized just as frequently as females (Dimock 1988;

Lew 1988; Struve 1989; Hunter 1990). It is important to remember that available statistics probably reflect a significant discrepancy between reported and actual frequency of sexual abuse. Because social norms do not actively encourage the identification and reporting of sexual victimization involving males, statistics tend to reflect fewer incidents than actually occur.

In general, American society encourages a collective denial that children are the victims of sexual exploitation. Unfortunately, it remains the exception rather than the rule that reported incidents of child sexual abuse are believed and responded to appropriately. As I will discuss later, existing laws in most jurisdictions make it even more difficult to prosecute when the alleged victim is male, thereby further discouraging people from reporting cases involving males.

## Defining the Issue

The research that has been conducted to facilitate our understanding of child sexual abuse has been limited in scope. Theories that have been postulated to explain sexual abuse have tended to focus on dysfunctional family dynamics, stress on the family unit, intergenerational patterns within specific families, or individual psychopathology. Most of these theories have proven to be of limited value in promoting a thorough understanding of the problem or in generating effective treatment interventions.

Most discussions of child sexual abuse focus on presenting symptoms and methods for clinical intervention. Demographic or statistical data are highlighted to clarify prevalence rates and high-risk populations; emotional or behavioral indicators are offered to facilitate the identification of victims; techniques and strategies for therapeutic treatment are documented to promote healing and recovery; vignettes and testimonials are chronicled to emphasize the human pain and trauma that afflict survivors of sexual abuse. Occasionally, presentations of child sexual abuse will include a footnote to acknowledge that this problem occurs within a larger sociopolitical context.

This chapter is based on the premise that the sociopolitical context is more than just an ancillary factor. Rather, it is the essential factor requiring intervention if we are to end the sexual maltreatment of children in our society. This chapter seeks to reverse our usual field of vision, as the context in which child sexual abuse occurs is examined as foreground rather than background.

The information and analysis presented in this chapter are only a beginning and are intended to catalyze further dialog and research. It is hoped that readers will gain a greater understanding of the social and political dynamics that create such a fertile environment for the continued phenomenon of child sexual abuse.

## Examining the Context

As a beginning point, it is essential to acknowledge that this problem actually reflects a major social disorder that is more pervasive and complex than isolated family units that become dysfunctional or particular individuals who demonstrate psychopathology. The very fabric of our society is designed to perpetuate this problem while encouraging denial that any serious problem exists.

Reports of traumatic sexual experiences during childhood have been successfully silenced for years in one or a variety of ways. We have all heard adages such as the following:

Children are inclined toward fantasies; they are not credible because they cannot be consistent and truthful about events.

Adult reports of childhood sexual abuse are the product of a hysterical personality.

The home is a sacred domain; allowing children to make allegations against a parent threatens the sanctity of the family.

Unwitting adults sometimes fall victim to the seductive energies of promiscuously inclined children.

Until recently, authorities failed to acknowledge physical or sexual abuse of children as inappropriate and, therefore, deserving of intervention on behalf of victims. U.S. laws have historically been more progressive in protecting our domesticated animals than our children. A century ago, there was an American Society for the Prevention of Cruelty to Animals, but there was no such organization for children. The first recorded protective intervention for a child was accomplished in the early 1870s in New York City through the use of an animal protection law (Kempe and Helfer 1972).

In 1874, as a direct result of that case, New York City established the nation's first society for the Prevention of Cruelty to Children, which provided the initial framework for child protective services. Similar societies were gradually initiated in other cities throughout the United States and Europe. A primary thrust of these early efforts to address the maltreatment of children actually focused more on implementing child labor laws to counteract the negative repercussions of the Industrial Revolution than on the dangers of abuse within domestic settings.

Consequently, despite this flurry of activity in the late nineteenth century on behalf of children who were physically mistreated, the needs of children who were sexually abused were never similarly acknowledged. Within a relatively brief span of time, even efforts to advocate for children who were physically abused fell out of vogue. Throughout most of the twentieth century, reports of the physical and sexual abuse of children have largely been minimized and disregarded.

It was not until the early 1960s that serious attention to child abuse again emerged. The current wave of interest in the physical and sexual abuse of children was catalyzed by C. Henry Kempe, a physician who proposed the term *battered child syndrome* to focus professional and public attention on the large number of children who sustain nonaccidental injuries (Kempe 1968).

Also emerging from the social consciousness of the 1960s were a number of assertive and articulate women who provided strong leadership by speaking out about their own sexual victimization as adults or children. The rape crisis movement of the 1960s focused public attention beyond issues of physical abuse and provided an opportunity for a beginning of the child sexual abuse movement (Russell 1975; Millett 1969; Brownmiller 1975).

Most of the advocacy efforts regarding child sexual abuse have been limited to legislative change. Some important reforms have thereby been achieved. For example, in 1973 the U.S. Congress passed the Child Abuse Prevention and Treatment Act, establishing a national center to provide supportive services related to the identification and treatment of child abuse. By the mid-1970s, most states had passed legislation to establish the framework for child protective service agencies with legal mandates to intervene on behalf of children who were physically or sexually abused.

These legislative reforms have not successfully challenged or changed the basic conditions of the larger social and political order, however, and few inroads have been made in addressing the problem in a meaningful way. For example, protective service agencies have achieved very minimal success in accomplishing their goal of protecting children. Limited funding has been allocated by local, state, and federal governments, resulting in too few and poorly trained staff. Very few legislative bodies have adequately defined forms of child abuse or established laws that govern conduct related to physical or sexual assault, thereby restricting protective service interventions on behalf of children.

Religious values that promote the sanctity of the home and the family also have discouraged concerned citizens and professionals from "intruding" into the private life of a child or parent, even when there is suspicion that a child is being abused. In fact, many of the more fundamentalist religious denominations focus so rigidly on fortifying the inviolability of the family as a prescribed entity that concerns for the safety and well-being of individual members within that defined unit may be disregarded.

Modern-day social agencies have been besieged by increased threats of litigation and decreased financial support from funding sources. As a result, the policies of many private and public social service agencies have begun to reflect a greater emphasis on protecting the health liability of the agency than on protecting the lives of the human beings served by that agency.

Even today, most graduate training programs do not offer courses devoted to disseminating information or training related to any aspect of child abuse. Those few professionals who are exposed to this issue are usually indoctrinated to treat the presenting symptomatology of the victim "objectively" and to avoid the "distractions" of the sociopolitical context in which the victimization occurred.

Although many services exist in the area of child abuse, there is no cohesive political analysis of this problem. Advocates within the child sexual abuse movement have displayed an alarming collective silence regarding the social or political factors that contribute to this problem. Consequently, little energy has been devoted to promoting a potent and activist movement to effect social and political change that is necessary to confront the maltreatment of children. The leaders of the child sexual abuse movement have been delinquent in their failure to mobilize a public outcry against the low priority and the limited resources given to protecting our children.

Instead, leaders within the field have been absorbed with gaining respectability, and they have generally not encouraged working alliances with more activist social change organizations. Most of the literature in the field of child sexual abuse has remained highly reductionist in nature, thereby avoiding many of the macro-level, fundamental political issues intertwined with this problem.

This apolitical perspective differs from the battered women's and rape crisis movements, in which considerable attention has been focused on challenging those aspects of society that contribute to the continued existence of battering and rape. Early leaders of the battered women's movement provided a means to understand this issue from a perspective other than victim pathology. Their successful effort to shift the focus away from victim pathology is instructive (see, for example, Martin 1976; Walker 1970; Dobash and Dobash 1979).

For years, professionals grappled unsuccessfully with how to understand and prevent the physical battering of a woman by her husband or partner. The standard question asked by professionals focused on the (female) victim: "Why doesn't she leave?" That question was based on numerous theoretical models and treatment interventions designed to resolve the problems of battering by treating the "victim's pathology." Advocates of battered women, many of whom had been physically assaulted themselves, eventually confronted the professional establishment and posed an important reframing of the question. Quite simply, by shifting the focus from the victim to the (male) perpetrator, the primary question then became "Why does he hit?" A different reality was thus introduced. In this reality, battering was no longer defined as victim pathology but as the responsibility of the batterer.

With a focus more appropriately on factors of accountability involving the perpetrator, it quickly became necessary to address the societal context of male aggression. In short, advocates for battered women have finally been able to shift society's attention to the larger social context, in which we are required to acknowledge that the use of violence by males is actually sanctioned.

Unfortunately, advocates working to end the physical and sexual abuse of children have failed to address the underlying social and political dimensions of this issue. Whereas battered women were able to undertake networking that helped to coalesce a political movement, as a class children are disenfranchised and powerless. It is very difficult, if not impossible, for children who are sexually abused to communicate with one another. Therefore, individual children with shared experiences remain isolated. Children also do not have the right to vote and do not have easy access to leaders in the important decision-making institutions of our society (Finkelhor 1984).

The sexual abuse of children cannot be adequately addressed without acknowledging the fundamental political and social dimensions that govern our society. In the current societal structure, children are denied the avenues to advocate for their own needs. Therefore, adults must be willing to speak on behalf of children. Such secondhand advocacy tends to have less urgency and is more vulnerable to being abandoned or discounted. Furthermore, existing social norms create a climate that fosters the sexual abuse of children. The social norm that sanctions the victimization of females in general has promoted the problem of the sexual exploitation of women. However, the social norm that prescribes males as dominant creates an opportunity for males to internalize an experience of their own sexual victimization in ways that are dysfunctional. For example, many men who were victimized as children learn to overcompensate for the vulnerability and shame they feel by adopting hypermasculine roles. Those men who choose to recognize their membership in an oppressor class may experience a cognitive dissonance between their dominant status on the one hand and their victimization on the other.

## Defining Sexual Abuse

To address the social and political dimensions of sexual abuse, it is important to have a working definition of the term. Unfortunately, the definition of abusive behavior toward children is still vague to many professionals and to most laypeople. The term *sexual abuse* refers to any sexual assault or sexual exploitation of a child or adolescent by an adult. Also included is any sexual interaction between two minors if there is at least three years' age difference or if there is a perceived significant difference in power between the victim and the offender. Included in this definition are genital stimulation, fondling, oral sex, vaginal or anal penetration, voyeurism, exhibitionism, pornography, and prostitution.

Sexual abuse is an issue of power and control, not love and intimacy. It is important to recognize that power and control frequently become eroticized in our culture. Implicit in the definitions of gender for most contemporary Western societies is the concept of male dominance and female submission. Dominance stirs sexual excitement in many men, thereby eroticizing relationships that are based on power and control. The sexual abuse of a child is not an issue of unbridled lust. Rather, it reflects a disrespect of boundaries between adult and child. Child sexual victimization is one example of the outcome of such eroticized dominance, and both male and female children are vulnerable to this kind of abuse of power and control.

An essential ingredient in sexually abusive behavior is a general lack of empathy by the adult for the child's stage of development and abilities. Additionally, the adult places the satisfaction of his or her own needs above those of the child. In so doing, the essence of child sexual abuse becomes clear: the exploitation of a child for the purpose of satisfying an adult.

In many ways, the basic fabric of our society creates a high-risk situation for the sexual abuse of children. While the stated norms of our social and political institutions impose taboos on the sexual exploitation of children, the underlying norms by which our society operates actually ignore or minimize the importance of those taboos. As long as these operational norms remain an undercurrent, their power is mysterious and the prevailing social environment actually sanctions the continued sexual abuse of children.

## The Norms of Sexual Abuse

It is important to identify and examine the underlying norms that provide a social framework for the sexual abuse of children. The four basic norms that create a context for such abuse are chattel property, learned helplessness, sexual entitlement, and shroud of secrecy.

### Chattel Property

The norm of chattel property is based on the concept that men have ownership of their wives and parents have ownership of their children. Perceiving a wife or child as property provides a justification for controlling him or her. Women and children in our society are encouraged to be passive, thereby conditioning them to accept a position of being controlled. In fact, strong negative social sanctions are focused on women and children who choose not to be passive. Strong women are perceived and labeled as "aggressive" and "hostile," while strong children are perceived and labeled as "defiant" and "rebellious."

Our society overvalues control. Therefore, having a compliant child is often offered as proof of parental efficacy. It is easy to justify actions that might hurt a child in the name of discipline or as being for the good of the child. We are all familiar with the parental adage "It hurts me more than it hurts you," which frequently accompanies harsh physical punishment of a child by an adult. Teaching a child to be absolutely obedient is actually grooming him or her for victimization.

Enforced compliance discourages a child from thinking for himself or herself, from distinguishing a "good touch" from a "bad touch," from questioning any kind of authority, and from exercising independent judgment regarding the right to say no if one's personal boundaries are violated by another person who is perceived as having more power or authority.

Within our culture, the concept of chattel property is most readily embodied as male privilege. Members of society are conditioned to believe that men, by birth, have the privilege to control. This is especially prevalent—and dangerous—in the commonly held belief among men that they are guaranteed the right of sex on demand. Male privilege, when applied to the arena of human sexuality, creates the framework for a pervasive rape mentality. Unfortunately, many males who have been sexually abused also hold deep convictions of male privilege. Males who have been sexually victimized are more likely to be at greater risk for engaging in sexually offending behaviors if they also hold strong beliefs about male privilege.

*Learned Helplessness*

Learned helplessness is the ability to accept one's position of passivity in relationship to those who are defined as being more dominant, to such a degree that a person experiences psychological paralysis. Complicated psychosocial dynamics create a tapestry of factors that contribute to the emotional experience of learned helplessness. Lenore Walker, in her work with battered women, has pioneered in elaborating these dynamics (Walker 1970). Many women and children in our society function in this state of learned helplessness. For example, children are economically, legally, and socially dependent on their parents. When a child's safety is threatened, he or she may have no options for a safe haven. Obviously, few children have the economic resources or the skills and maturity to live independently.

Much progress has been made during recent years in promoting a more open discussion of the realities of child abuse. The enactment of child abuse reporting laws and the emergence of service providers who are willing to address the difficult issues presented by this social problem represent an enormous change. Nonetheless, such progress is still small compared to the magnitude of the problem. And there remain vast inconsistencies among those institutions—courts, mental health centers, and social service agencies—that are entrusted to deal with this problem.

Underlying these inconsistencies is a basic dilemma that is created in the face of information that challenges male privilege. When confronted with conflicting information presented by an adult and a child, most adults are conditioned to believe the adult rather than the child. Police, the courts, and social service agencies frequently are unable to provide the necessary protections or resources needed to ensure a child's safety. Religious institutions generally promote the sanctity of the family above all else, and many mental health professionals support efforts to keep the family together at any cost—both of which minimize protecting an individual child when measured against protecting the family as a unit.

Therefore, most children are faced with powerlessness when confronted with personal harm from a trusted adult. Such powerlessness in the face of repeated trauma over an extended period of time create global feelings of numbing, passivity, and impotence, represented by a general sense that one is helpless to exercise free choice or to pursue alternatives in most life situations. "People who feel helpless really believe that they have no influence over the success or failure of events that occur to them" (Walker 1970, 48).

### Sexual Entitlement

This is the belief that sex is a privilege for the dominant person in any relationship and an obligation for the person who is nondominant. The dominant status of adult males in our society translates into the commonly held belief that men deserve to have their sexual desires met. Perceiving sex to be a privilege for the person(s) who exercises power and control creates an atmosphere in which sex really becomes perceived as an inherent right for whoever is dominant. Adult males are socialized to believe that it is their prerogative to have sex on demand, and for many adults, the privilege of power and control blurs the boundaries between adult and child. The multimillion-dollar industries of pornography and prostitution promote the norm of sex for sale and depict women (and frequently children) as objects to be used to satisfy sexual urges. In fact, the marketing of sex is so pervasive that it is estimated that upward of one million children may be involved in pornography and prostitution in the United States alone (Alexander 1987).

### Shroud of Secrecy

This norm is the operational premise that sexual information is dangerous. Powerful elements of our culture perceive sex as dangerous and corrupting. Therefore, considerable energy is spent to maintain a shroud of secrecy over all aspects of sexuality. Global secrecy contributes to a pervasive society-wide anxiety about sexuality. We have strong social norms that discourage most people, but especially women and children, from discussing sexuality or from seeking any kind of valid information related to sexuality. Such a restrictive atmosphere creates an environment of confusion, distortion, and fear.

## Defining Patriarchy

These four dynamics are fundamental to the sexual abuse of children. To understand the complexities of child sexual abuse, it is necessary to identify and name the sources of these dynamics. No problem can be understood or resolved unless it is named. For too long, it has seemed dangerous to acknowledge that these basic dynamics underlying sexual abuse have their origin in the patriarchy.

*Patriarchy* has remained one of those shadowy and highly charged concepts that is seldom used because of its ability to unleash polarized emotions. Few books or articles define patriarchy or explain the concepts and dynamics of a patriarchal system.

*Webster's Ninth New Collegiate Dictionary* (1988) defines patriarchy as follows: "Social organization marked by the supremacy of the father in the clan or family, the legal dependence of wives and children, and the reckoning of descent and inheritance in the male line." This definition is superficial and restrictive. It suggests that patriarchy has been ended or will be ended by legal reforms that extend basic civil rights to women. In essence, however, such legal reforms merely reshape the nature of patriarchy. Although many civil rights have been achieved for women and children during the past century, patriarchy remains as strongly entrenched as ever in American society.

Gerda Lerner, in her book *The Creation of Patriarchy,* offers a more expansive framework in which to view patriarchy that helps to clarify why the larger social systems have resisted fundamental change in the face of reforms:

> *Patriarchy* in its wider definition means the manifestation and institutionalization of male dominance over women and children in the family and the extension of male dominance over women [and children] in society in general. It implies that men hold power in all the important institutions of society and that women [and children] are deprived of access to such power. It does *not* imply that women [and children] are either totally powerless or totally deprived of rights, influence, and resources. (Lerner 1986, 239)

The very essence of patriarchy is "the assumption that men own and have the right to control the bodies, labor, and minds of women [and children]" (Bleier 1984, 164). Patriarchy prescribes that the basic organization of society is formulated by men. Evidence of this may be seen in the fact that those professions that warrant the highest status in terms of money and power remain largely the domain of males and that as women enter a profession, its status becomes lower. A fundamental premise of patriarchy is that men have the power to define and control the laws, ideas, values, and scholastic systems of a society, including the sexual values and behaviors of the society. Women and children are thereby relegated to a subordinate status in all aspects of the society.

It should be noted, however, that any person who fails to conform to the standards and norms set by those in power is relegated to a subordinate status. For example, men who are gay, Hispanic, or black or who in some other way fail to conform to the established norms are denied equal access to power and resources.

In workshops I have facilitated with a colleague, Judy Pohl, on the topic of the politics of sexual abuse, participants have been asked to brainstorm the values, beliefs, and norms that they generally associate with the word *patriarchy*. Some of these random responses become very poignant and potent when they are organized into the following conceptual groupings:

> Powerful men are assumed to have ownership over women, children, and other men who are perceived to be weaker and less powerful. This becomes possible because of an exaggerated value of males and the devaluation of women and children. Men are assumed by birthright to have access to power and control.

> Males are defined as being logical and rational; females and children are defined as being illogical and irrational; logic and rationality are defined as more powerful, therefore elevating males to superiority over females and children.

> Male reality is assumed to be superior. Therefore, blind obedience to male reality is institutionalized in the legal and educational norms of society. Because male reality is unable to incorporate the concept of men as victims, no avenues are provided for males to express victimization experiences if they occur.

> Physical strength and beauty are perceived to be greater than emotionality. Therefore, domination and machismo are given elevated value, and equality is replaced by assumptions that somebody must be in charge. Such a hierarchical form of social organization implies that somebody will be controlled by those who exercise their privilege of being in charge. This hierarchy creates a natural context for the emergence of classism and sets the stage for the internalized oppression of members of society who are defined as being of lower status. Institutionalized racism and homophobia further help to define the social order and limit access to power and control.

> Religious verification is provided in support of the dominance of males. Biblical passages are used to define the natural order of the universe:

Males are strong and females are weak; adults are powerful and children must be obedient to such power; the role of victim is glamorized. God is portrayed as a white male, and men are believed to be divinely invested with their role as spiritual leaders.

Money acquires a special value in a capitalist society, and the worth of an individual becomes measured by his or her ability to earn money. Such a value system makes it possible for money to become a vehicle for gaining power, and eventually money becomes equated with power.

Men inherently need and deserve sex. Because men are perceived to be powerless to control their sexual desires, it is the responsibility of women and children to set limits regarding the sexual advances of men. Women and children who fail to set such limits are labeled "seductive," whereas attempts to impose such limits on men defy and challenge male authority and the prevailing order.

Sex sells. Money and power allow access to sex. The social hierarchy of male control contributes to a vast network of pornography in which women and children are exploited for the pleasure and enjoyment of more dominant members of society. Because males are conditioned to idolize rough and forceful sex, pornography frequently links images of violence and submission with sex. Feminine or youthful victims are pursued and conquered, usually by men who are more powerful.

It is important to stress that male control is not merely theoretical. Examination of the holders of power and control in the important institutions that shape our society reveal the day-to-day reality of patriarchy. Most influential religious leaders (and all Catholic priests) are male. Historically, most physicians and psychiatrists have been male. Most judges are male. Most lawmaking bodies—state legislatures and the U.S. Congress—are male dominated. Most American political leaders, and all our presidents, have been male.

Although limited public attention to the problem of sexual abuse is relatively recent, there is actually a long history of social and legal sanctions that have permitted, and sometimes encouraged, the abuse of children. For example, during the seventeenth and eighteenth centuries B.C., vast expanses of territory were conquered and brought under the control of the Babylonian Empire. In approximately 1750 B.C., Hammurabi, the king of Babylon, compiled and amended all the existing laws of the diverse ethnic and cultural groupings that had been assimilated into the empire into a comprehensive code that established the parameters for appropriate and inappropriate, legal and illegal behaviors (Lerner 1986).

Because males controlled the pen, these laws primarily reflected the needs, concerns, and realities of men. The Code of Hammurabi is a significant development because it provided the first instrument whereby men legally codified reality as their own, with the life experiences of women and children existing only in relationship to male reality. Institutions, rules, and regulations were created to guarantee the appropriation and proprietorship by men of a particular woman's sexuality and of her children (O'Brien 1981, 154). Through the use of laws, a hierarchy could be enforced: Men control women, and parents control children.

The codification of rules and regulations led to the creation of social and political institutions to enforce and promote the norms of the powerful. Men were the holders of power because of their access to knowledge and information. A study of historic and contemporary jurisprudence offers an interesting insight into the ramifications of the codification of power and control into laws that govern any given society. It is unclear exactly how many different laws were contained in the Hammurabic Code, but 73 of the 282 laws that have been discovered through archaeological searches deal with subjects related to marriage and sexual matters. These laws were generally more severely restrictive of females than of males. For example, under this ancient set of laws (Code 157), mother-son incest was punishable by death for both parties, while a father who raped his daughter was punished only by banishment from the city (Code 154) (Lerner 1986).

Early laws pertaining to sexual offenses demonstrated a definite bias in favor of men in positions of power and control. Most rape laws historically have incorporated principles that make it the responsibility of the victim to prove that she or he resisted the assault. According to Jewish law, a rapist was required to marry his victim, and divorce was not allowed in such situations (Deut. 22:28–29).

Historically, children have been victimized by mutilation practices, often involving sexual organs. The circumcision of males has been practiced as a religious rite throughout history and remains one of the most common surgical procedures today, despite its questionable value. Castration traditionally has been an acceptable practice, with the eunuch playing an important role in certain societies. Until relatively recently, the Chinese practiced the ancient tradition of binding the foot of girls. Within classical Roman society, the *Patria Postestas* allowed a father the privilege to sell, present for sacrifice, murder, or otherwise dispose of his child (Radbill 1974). The Roman Law of the Twelve Tables, which modified the *Patria Postestas,* forbade bringing up deformed children and imposed the restriction that a father could sell a son only three times.

By the sixteenth century, many of the legal sanctions against rape and incest in England had eroded considerably, as the legal age of consent for females had been lowered to six years old (Robbins 1959). In Victorian England, the age of consent for females was twelve years old, although a child younger than eight years old was denied the opportunity to give evidence against a man who had sexual contact with her, as the law stated that she was too young to understand the legal oath (Crow 1972). Throughout history, legal sanctions related to rape and incest have focused almost exclusively on females as the victims. The absence of laws that recognize the need to protect male children at any age is indicative of the historical belief that males should be immune from the necessity of such safeguards.

In this country, the courts in Massachusetts adopted the Mosaic Law in 1646, imposing a penalty of death on unruly children; Connecticut passed a similar law in 1651 (Radbill 1974). Current laws in most U.S. states continue to reflect the biases of patriarchial norms. Activist lawyer Catherine MacKinnon advocates that the state is based on male reality and the "law sees and treats women [and children] the way men see and treat women [and children]" (MacKinnon 1983, 644). Consequently, the laws to protect children from physical and sexual victimization are generally vague and frequently inadequate or antiquated. Current legal channels severely limit the availability of women and children to challenge male violations of their sexuality, and it is exceedingly difficult for a male to find any legal avenue to initiate a challenge if he is sexually violated. Although there are a few exceptions, most jurisdictions enforce the prevailing norms of a male reality.

The criminal code of the State of Georgia offers one example of how little reform actually has been achieved. Under present-day Georgia law, only a female can be raped (chapter 26–2001); only a female can be seduced (chapter 26–2005); incest is limited to sexual intercourse (chapter 26–2006); statutory rape is restricted to sexual intercourse with a female under the age of fourteen years old (chapter 26–2018); and child molestation is legally a concern only when the child is less than fourteen years of age (chapter 26–2019).

In addition to being antiquated, these statutes create a legal collage rife with inconsistencies and contradictions. For example, under these Georgia statutes, an adult male could be prosecuted for taking pornographic photos of a fifteen-year-old girl but not for engaging in "consensual" sexual intercourse with that same child if she were not a biological or steprelative. Similarly, an adult female could be prosecured under the criminal code of Georgia for fondling a thirteen-year-old boy but not for engaging in "consensual" sexual intercourse with a fifteen-year-old if he were not related by birth or marriage.

A review of the laws and policies in most jurisdictions will make clear that historically we have been much more concerned with protecting the rights of the alleged sexual offender than with ensuring the safety of the victim and more concerned with defending the integrity of the family as an institution than with promoting the safety and security of our children. Evidence of this tendency can be seen in the fact that laws protecting adults from false allegations and ensuring that the constitutional freedoms of the alleged offender are not restricted are much more clearly defined than are laws protecting child victims. Feminist writer Evan Stark argues that contemporary laws and the social service agencies that are established to ensure compliance with those laws generally seem to "function today as a reconstituted or extended patriarchy, defending the family form 'by any means necessary'" (Stark, Flitcraft, and Frazier 1979, 464), including overlooking violence against children within a family system.

Many men participate in the patriarchy by aspiring to modern-day images of masculinity and manhood, most of which revere male power and control. All too often masculinity is linked with sexualized images of power and control. Kate Millett, one of the early leaders of the feminist movement, insightfully notes that "patriarchal societies typically link feelings of cruelty with sexuality, the latter often equated both with evil and with power" (Millett 1969, 44).

These linkages are reflected in the images that are portrayed in our contemporary media:

> Witness our valorization of Rambo reflexes (passionate violence marshaled in the face of personal injustice); Schwarzenegger sentiments (technically precise violence with merciless execution); the Eastwood ethic (Dirty Harry's cool violence in the name of the state as antihero); Bronson brutality (vigilante violence directed against 'social refuse,' usually young black and Latino men); and Norris nuances (stylized violence with strong xenophobia). (Dyson 1989, 55)

Such media portrayals of men and women shape our imagery of gender, with male heroes consistently depicted as big, independent, powerful, having sexual prowess, and being smarter than and more important than other characters. Women and children are generally cast as being small, dependent, powerless, sexually ignorant or inexperienced, and less intelligent and less important than their male counterparts.

"The very existence of rape [and child sexual abuse] and its commonness, the ready availability of aggressive pornography, the constant portrayal in books, films, and television of men *taking* women [or children] cannot help but create a consciousness that links manhood and virility with mastery, appropriation, and force" (Bleier 1984, 185). Many women, and those men who do not inherently subscribe to the values of machismo, believe that the only way they can acquire power is to endorse the values and behaviors of patriarchy. However, many of these same women and peripheralized men find that participation in the patriarchy leads to further victimization because entry into the inner sanctums of the male world requires them to deny or abandon their inherent femininity (which is viewed as inferior) and to incorporate into their identity images of masculinity (which are viewed as superior).

Prevailing research indicates that as many as 30 percent of all children may be affected by sexual abuse (Bagley et al. 1984; Landis 1956). The collective silence and apathy of most men concerning the issues of rape and child sexual abuse is deafening. Although a large number of men in our society are fathers, most men are generally apathetic about child sexual abuse. This topic is rarely of either academic or active concern to any modern-day American male, except those few men whose careers bring them face to face with the issue. Even then, male will exert considerable energy to avoid dealing with this issue.

Even fewer men have focused any attention on understanding patriarchy. Consequently, it is difficult to find information on its development. Anyone who attempts to conduct research on this subject will quickly discover that patriarchy is seldom referenced in the indexes of books and articles written by men.

A long tradition of interpreting patriarchy as being ahistorical and invisible has contributed to a general acceptance of patriarchy as the natural order of human social organization. Much of the information we have about the historical development of human civilization suggests that patriarchal dynamics have been a part of all social and political relationships. Throughout most of recorded history, however, historians and anthropologists have been predominantly males. Therefore, much of our knowledge of history may be limited to and biased in favor of male interpretations of events and trends. Males have tended to portray men's reality as truth and fact. Historically, the voices of minorities and of the disenfranchised have been suppressed so they could not inform others of their experiences and accomplishments. Typically, the accomplishments and experiences of women, children, and minority populations have been ignored or filtered through the biases of men who have had a vested interest in promoting or protecting the status quo.

A growing body of literature produced by women and minority authors challenges the existing knowledge and presents alternative perspectives of history. Much of this literature presents extensive historical research findings that refute many of our beliefs about the inherent superiority of white males (see, for example, Bleier 1984; Figes 1970; Lerner 1986; Walker 1983).

Much insight can be gained by examining feminist interpretations of the etiology by which men acquired a consolidation of power regarding the tools for communication. The invention of an organized system of writing that incorporated grammatical elements occurred shortly after 3000 B.C. in Sumer. Written language served an important function: It provided the first opportunity to record history. Recording, interpreting, and reinterpreting historical events provided a vehicle by which humans could survive death and create a sense of continuity from generation to generation. Those who had access to the knowledge and skills of writing were invested with the responsibilities and duties of history making. "By the time of Hammarubi's empire around 1792 B.C., all the scribes were men, and women were excluded from education and therefore the knowledge that became inseparable from independence or power" (Bleier 1984, 154).

Ultimately, knowledge and information become crucial sources of power. Because women, children, and minorities traditionally have been excluded from this exchange of information and knowledge, they have long been denied access to power and control, which has reinforced their position of inferiority and subordinance. "If knowledge is power, power is also knowledge, and a large factor in their subordinate position is the fairly systematic ignorance patriarchy imposes upon women [and children and minorities]" (Millett 1969, 42). The tendency to overlook distinct events or periods in history has contributed to the more generalized social perception that male dominance is inherent in and eternal to the human condition.

By dissecting the monolithic concept of patriarchy and identifying the distinct and essential underlying features, it becomes more apparent that our current social order is truly the product of human creation rather than the result of any predetermined destiny. Contemporary feminist writers have begun to uncover a vast body of historical information that documents the evolution of patriarchy and thereby challenges contemporary perceptions of the natural order of human civilization. To understand patriarchy and its significance in creating the sociopolitical context for child sexual abuse, it is important to examine the component features of patriarchy.

## The Essential Features of Patriarchy

Five essential features, woven together, create the tapestry of patriarchy: patrilineal descent, paternalism, male hegemony, heterosexism, and misogyny. Each of these features provides a fundamental underpinning for the clinical dynamics that create a context for the sexual abuse of children (chattel property, learned helplessness, sexual entitlement, and shroud of secrecy). It is useful to examine these five features to elaborate their historical origins and their current impact on the problem of child sexual abuse.

No single historical event provides a landmark to identify a beginning for any of these features of patriarchy. Rather, the specific origins of patriarchy are vague, in part because the underlying dynamics of patriarchal societies were already strongly entrenched by the beginning of recorded history. There do, however, seem to be specific trends or periods in history that illuminate these dynamics and that provide insight into the ways in which these dynamics have been consolidated into an increasingly prevalent, complex, and powerful force.

*Patrilineal Descent*

This dynamic can be defined as male dominance in property and property laws that guarantee the inheritance rights of sons. Judith Antonelli proposes that "patriarchy is based on the 'phallacy' that the male is creator. Man's original awe and envy of woman becomes, under patriarchy, resentment and hostility. The only way man can possess female power is through woman, and so he colonizes her, suppressing her sexuality so that it serves him rather than being the source of her power. . . . Patriarchy is indeed a male neurosis" (Antonelli 1982, 401). The "male neurosis" of patriarchy that contributes to the colonization of women is the same dynamic that leads to the domination of children through physical and sexual abuse. The fact that all children are ultimately the joint creation of a male and a female is routinely ignored by patriarchal norms and laws that grant priority to patrilineage and that promote the concept that a child is merely an extension of his or her parents rather than a human being in his or her own right.

But how did such a preoccupation with male lineage emerge? To clarify this question, it is necessary to look far back into history, to the beginning of civilization. Most historians agree that human beings initially congregated in small nomadic tribes, foraging over vast expanses of land. Most of a person's waking energy was focused on survival. There are no written records from this period of history, so attempts to define the nature of social interactions can be only speculative.

It is generally agreed, however, that survival probably required considerable cooperation and equality between all members of a tribe. It is also generally agreed that the process of human reproduction was quite mysterious to men and women. As Neumann (1959) notes, "the connection between sexuality and childbearing was . . . unknown" to primitive people (p. 11). Therefore, we have the roots of females as goddesses and overseers of humanity. In the earliest periods of history, it also appears that women were perceived to have magical powers because of the general lack of knowledge regarding the birth process.

In these ancient times, neither men nor women seemed to realize that they had an active role in helping to create life. Because children emerged from the physical bodies of women, females were generally held in high esteem, and the earliest civilization created mother-goddesses as the heavenly deities to be worshiped. Women seemed to have an exclusive role in the magical process of childbirth. There is general agreement among most archeologists and historians that people in prehistoric times had no knowledge of the man's part in the reproductive process (Stone 1976).

Archeological evidence suggests that people gradually began to shift from a nomadic life-style to sedentary settlements approximately twelve thousand years ago (Bleier 1984). Excavations of the earliest villages that were settled indicate that initially there was relative equality in the distribution of possessions and rank among women, men, and children (Bleier 1984). As people began to settle in one spot for periods of time, people were able to domesticate animals. It was through this event that people gained their first insights regarding the mysteries of human reproduction. There was, for the first time, a realization that the male had a specific role in the reproductive process. This knowledge radically transformed gender roles and provided a fundamental building block for the concept of male dominance.

> Elizabeth Fisher ingeniously argued that the domestication of animals taught men their role in procreation and that the practice of the forced mating of animals led men to the idea of [rape]. . . . More recently, Mary O'Brien built an elaborate explanation of the origin of male dominance on men's psychological need to compensate for their inability to bear children through the construction of institutions of dominance and, like Fisher, dated this 'discovery' in the period of the discovery of animal domestication. (Lerner 1986, 46)

Insights about the male role in procreation provided an important cornerstone for the concept of patrilineage. With the heightened attention to patrilineage, the status of men increased and the importance of women and girls decreased. For example, archaeological excavations from a variety of cultures and historical periods reveal a pattern of increasing wealth and social differentiation and a decline in the status of women and children (Lerner 1986).

Soon women were perceived in less magical ways. Men began to usurp the femininity power of giving birth by relegating the female to the role of being a receptacle or vessel into which the male sperm was planted—a subordinate and subservient status. During this period of evolving agrarian societies, it became critical to have a stable and ample supply of human labor. Women's reproductive capacity and the labor potential of children soon were recognized as crucial tribal resources that could be controlled by the powerful members of the tribe.

Men, who were not restricted by pregnancy and childbirth, emerged as the holders of power and the managers of tribal resources. Anthropologist Claude Levi-Strauss advocates that the exchange of women and children was the first form of trade (Levi-Strauss 1969). By transforming women and children into commodities, they could be perceived and used more as objects than as human beings. The possession of women and children increasingly gave men access to power. As men became more experienced in managing the resources of the tribe, they discovered ways to consolidate their power and control in order to promote their dominance over those members of the tribe who were less powerful.

Powerful men soon discovered the symbolic power of sexual control. The rape of women, children, and men who were perceived to be powerless became an expression of dominance and provided an effective tool for creating classes of psychologically enslaved people. Even in modern-day society, sexual assault or the threat of sexual assault is frequently used as a vehicle to control those who are perceived to be less powerful. Women learn to restrict their freedom of movement at a young age because of the potential for sexual assault. Legal incarceration had generally included the reality that sexual assault is an inevitable risk within prison culture, which sometimes serves as an effective deterrent to would-be criminals. And rape historically has been accepted to be within the rules of war, with such behavior left unpunished during war and even considered to be a privilege of conquering soldiers.

As men in ancient tribal societies became more expert in their methods of controlling those who could be conquered, warfare became more commonplace. There was a great incentive to increase power by expanding the pool of available human resources, so men became bolder about raiding other tribes and settlements to steal and capture women and children. "Small self-sufficient tribes had to relate to neighboring tribes either in constant warfare or find a way toward peaceful co-existence. Taboos on endogamy and incest structured peaceful interaction and led to alliances among tribes" (Lerner 1986, 24). Within this framework, the implementation of an incest taboo became fundamentally important for social organization (Levi-Strauss 1969).

As male power and control became increasingly linked to acquisition and control of women and children, more emphasis was placed on defining and structuring human interactions. The monogamous, or nuclear, family gained importance as a social unit and provided a greater opportunity to ensure patrilineal descent.

*Paternalism*

In a paternalistic society, the male, as head of any defined social unit, has power and ownership over all members of that unit. Many laws have been enacted throughout history to enforce the sanctity of a man's rule over his "castle":

> It is said that the first law of marriage was proclaimed by Romulus, the legendary founder of Rome (753 B.C.). . . . "This law obligated the married women . . . to conform themselves entirely to the temper of their husbands and the husbands to rule their wives as necessary and inseparable possessions." . . . It was the legal right of a husband to require that his wife obey him. She was his property and subject to whatever form of control was necessary for achieving obedience. . . . Roman husbands had the legal right to chastice, divorce, or kill their wives. (Dobash and Dobash 1979, 35–37)

By this point in history, marriage was no longer as much a holy sacrament as a civil contract that protected the private property and inheritance. Many contemporary feminists have compared marriage to feudalism, as exemplified by the injunctions included in most wedding ceremonies (Millett 1969).

Classical Greek society provided the impetus for organizing autonomous family units into a larger and more cohesive social network. Aristotelian philosphy provided the substance for the creation of a vast social order in which patriarchal values were institutionalized to create the fabric for a social state. The constructs of the state as a form of social organization reflect a hierarchical and dichotomized worldview. In essence, the state was defined and controlled by men's reality and conveniently institutionalized dominance and control over women and children.

With the evolution of the concept of the state, the monogamous family was transformed into the paternalistic family, in which the wife and children became servants of the male as head of the household. An essential dynamic of paternalistic relationships is an acceptance that the master can keep the slave(s) in ignorance of past and future alternatives. Paternalism discourages any sense of collective consciousness or collective behavior. This, in turn, diminishes the potential for an individual to understand systems in political terms.

Within such a framework, justice is both defined and enforced by the paternalistic figure. According to Aristotle, "The association of a father with his sons has the form of monarchy. . . . The ideal kingship is paternal rule. . . . The association of husband and wife is clearly an aristocracy. The man rules by virtue of merit, and . . . in conformity with his own superiority" (Thomson 1977). Furthermore, Aristotle advocates that "the wife . . . will be 'silent' before her husband, no less than the children before their father" (Newman 1973).

Greek society, as exemplified by Aristotelian philosophy, actually provides the structural framework for a social order that can ignore the exploitation of those who are considered to be of a lesser status. All too frequently throughout history, such exploitation has been achieved through sexual control of those members of society who are perceived to be inferior or weaker. This control was particularly true in Greek society: "The state represent[ed] . . . the most complete codification and institutionalization of patriarchal authority. . . . The state has continued to be . . . the means through which men have controlled . . . sexuality. Laws control access to . . . sexuality through their regulation of the degree to which rape, battering, incest and child abuse, abortion, pornography, contraception, and divorce are permitted" (Bleier 1984, 158–159).

Double standards in sexuality provide an avenue to strengthen patriarchal control. For example, in Greek society, "premarital and marital chastity were strictly enforced on women, but their husbands were free to enjoy sexual gratification from lower class women, heterae, and slaves and from young men" (Lerner 1986, 202).

Aristotelian philosophy even provided the underpinning for class dominance, as the rule of some men over other men could be justified merely by ascribing to those men some of the same qualities ascribed to women. Even today, men who are perceived to be weak or passive—that is, peripheralized males—are ascribed a strong value of inferiority and subordination. This value can easily be seen in portrayals of minority males (blacks, Hispanics, gays, and so on) as being less competent and trustworthy in positions of power.

Rational thought, usually expressed in concepts of justice and injustice, became vehicles to explain away certain aspects of the human condition. Greek society was instrumental in establishing the norm that men can think freely but must remain cautious about feelings. Western culture, emerging from the constructs of classical Greece, grants permission to men to feel powerful and angry and encourages them to perceive rationality as a feeling state. But men are discouraged from accepting responsibility, from feeling compassion, and from striving to achieve a community that is grounded in equality. The process of male socialization in our culture is a testament to the consequences of this constricted approach to the human condition.

The paternalistic values of ancient Greece have provided an important cornerstone for Western culture as it has developed through the centuries. Emerging from the advancements of the Industrial Revolution were a number of significant contributions to this ongoing development, including the strengthening of paternalistic norms.

Especially important was the concept of the male as the ultimate ruler of the family unit, which was further consolidated in the Industrial Revolution. The reorganization of society that emerged from the Industrial Revolution largely reflected male values and constructs. A division of labor in which people were assigned distinctly separate and rigidly defined roles according to functional tasks became an underpinning of most productive enterprises. Because men controlled the avenues for decision making within most industrial enterprises, they determined how any particular division of labor would occur. Therefore, the workplace became defined as a male domain.

The paternalistic family became an essential ingredient in the effective functioning of an industrialized society. Within this context, the family became essentially an economic unit. Interactions between the male head of the household and his wife and children occurred only during the nonproductive times away from the workplace. "The family was promoted as a private 'haven' to compensate for the public 'heartlessness' of the factories. A man's home had to appear to be his castle and he had to feel his new privilege of playing king to compensate for the alienation he now experienced in the workplace" (Goodrich et al. 1988, 3).

To function effectively, the paternalistic family required a division of roles among family members, defined hierarchically and maintained by the male head of the household through direct and coercive forms of authority that were granted by social, legal, and religious institutions. By defining the male as the source of control in the family unit, the ruler of his kingdom, the husband/father was elevated to a godlike status within the boundaries of the family unit. Consequently, women and children were defined as subordinate, with men as the locus of control over all events and interactions among family members.

As a general rule, the sanctity of the paternalistic family extended beyond the boundaries of the physical household. As in earlier periods of history, men continued to control the labor potentials of women and children. For example, children were widely employed in factories during the early periods of industrialization, with children as young as five years of age being required to work up to sixteen hours at a time, sometimes being prevented from leaving the factory by the use of irons riveted around their ankles. It was not until 1802 that the first child labor laws were implemented, and even these laws did not apply to children who were under the supervision of their parents.

Discipline is another important locus of control within the constructs of paternalism. For example, the rule of thumb became a part of English jurisprudence during the eighteenth century. This rule allowed a husband to beat his wife with a rod or whip as long as it was no thicker than his thumb. Although the application of this concept was focused on marital relations, it could easily be applied to paternalistic controls over children.

When necessary, violence has been sanctioned as a means of discipline.

> Social scientists have primarily conceptualized violence as a breakdown in social order in which either individuals or social structures are thought to be deviant or aberrant. [It may be more accurate] to see violence used by men against women [and children] in the family as attempts to establish or maintain a patriarchal social order. Violence is used by men to chastise their wives [and children] for real or perceived transgressions of his authority and as attempts to reaffirm and maintain a hierarchical and moral order within the family. (Dobash and Dobash 1977, 17)

Sexual segregation is an extremely pervasive approach used to support paternalism. Men are routinely granted positions of leadership and control within important institutions, with women and children provided more limited access to participation through auxiliary functions. Men have even defined which issues are primary and which are auxiliary in nature. For example, cultural norms support the home and family as a private sphere of human activity. Therefore, there are strong prohibitions against infringing on male authority within the privacy of the family, even when such authority involves the use of violence or sexual assault. But public intrusion into the home is allowed and encouraged in the form of government control of birth control, abortion, marriage, and homosexuality. Of course, the institution of government is male controlled, and laws that control the sexual behaviors of family members (such as abortion and birth control laws) are promoted as pro-family. Efforts to pass laws that restrict paternalism (such as more severe penalties for battering or child abuse) are opposed because male lawmakers perceive these restrictions as a threat to the sanctity of the family unit. The unspoken reality is that such changes threaten many fundamental aspects of male privilege.

This dichotomy has been an important factor in perpetuating the abuse of power that so often accompanies paternalism. Because of the institutionalized barriers that prevent women and children from talking about their home as anything other than a sanctuary, they have remained silent about their physical and sexual abuse (Yllo and Bograd 1988). "For the maintenance of paternalism (and slavery) it is essential to convince subordinates that their protector is the only authority capable of fulfilling their needs. It is therefore in the interest of the master to keep the slave in ignorance of his [or her] past and future alternatives" (Lerner 1986, 241).

## Male Hegemony

This is the belief that men hold the fundamental power in all the important institutions in society—military, political, and religious—and women and children are deprived access to such power. Religion is the clearest example of male hegemony. Religious constructs generally reflect collective visions of the world as people perceive and wish it to be. They also reflect the attitudes and values by which human relationships are formed. Institutionalized Christianity provides one of the most interesting and comprehensive illustrations of a worldview that has at its core the concept of male hegemony.

By the time Christianity emerged as a distinct and organized theology, religion in general had already become a male domain designed to exclude women by the existence of all-male priesthoods. Images of mother-goddesses that were so prevalent during early civilization had, by the time of classical Greece, largely been replaced by male gods. Christianity took a bold leap and declared God the Father, a single male entity, to be in charge of the human condition. The creation story in the Book of Genesis provided the basis for the final shift from mother-goddesses as the holders of universal fertility to a single all-powerful male God who incorporated all the concepts of creation and generativity.

To ensure that male hegemony was firmly established and to reduce the potential for mere mortals to challenge this image of absolute male control. Christian doctrines enhanced the image of its male deity by conceptualizing him as a trinity: God the Father, God the Son, and God the Holy Ghost. Who could date to challenge such a pervasive image of power and control?

Institutionalized Christianity has reinforced the prevailing source of power and control within patriarchal societies. A fundamental concept in Christian teachings is obedience and acceptance of one's position within social and political hierarchies. For example, religious teachings have advised parents, "He who spares the rod, hates his son; But he who loves him, disciplines him diligently" (Prov. 13:24). The laws set forth by the Ten Commandments require that all children honor and respect both their mother and their father (Exod. 20:12).

While promoting the concept of blind obedience and compliant acceptance of one's status within a hierarchy, the Christian Church has actively promoted the belief that women and children are inferior. Countless examples in the Bible support Judeo-Christian claims that women and children are less than, and therefore interior to, men. For example, through the teachings of St. Thomas Aquinas, the Church established the official position that the mother is only soil in which the father's seed grows (Tuchman 1978). The teachings of St. Augustine further defined women as slaves to their husbands, granting husbands the right to beat and abuse their wives: "It is the duty of servants to obey their masters . . . [and wives] have made a contract of servitude" (Hartley 1913, 231).

Children were relegated to an equally low status. The *Apostolic Constitutions* [officially, the *Ordinances of the Holy Apostles through Clement,* a set of ecclesiastical laws laid down by the apostles (Walker 1983)] prescribed severe physical punishment for children. Ignoring the role of mothers in the parenting process, fathers were instructed, "Do not hesitate to reprove them, chastening them with severity. . . . Teach your children the word of the Lord, straiten them even with stripes and render them submissive, teaching them from infancy the Holy Scriptures" (Laistner 1951, 31).

Christianity also had a dramatic impact on the prevailing attitudes regarding almost every aspect of sexuality. The changes in the norms concerning rape offer a dramatic example of the impact of Christianity. In the ancient world, rape was clearly defined as unjust. In Roman and Saxon societies, rapists were punished by death. The punishment for a rapist in Norman society was to cut off his testicles and gouge out his eyes. And the Byzantine code prescribed death for a rapist and required that the victim be given all the rapist's property, even if she was only a slave (Pearsall 1969; Soisson and Soisson 1977)

Christian doctrines were much more ambivalent and sometimes even contradictory. Church decrees transformed sex and sexuality into an abomination. Early Church fathers advocated that the establishment of the kingdom of God was predicated on allowing the human race to die out through universal celibacy (Lederer 1968). St Augustine taught that sexual intercourse was never without sin, even between husband and wife (Russell 1972), but under Church law, it was illegal for any wife to refuse sexual intercourse with her husband. The only exception was the Church's prohibition against marital sex on holy days (Walker 1983).

Christianity has become an important factor in sexual abuse because of its strong often contradictory messages concerning sexuality. Whereas most Christian teachings reflect the underlying norm that sex is to be repressed, many other Christian edicts actually encourage marital rape. For example, in the early years after its formation, the Catholic Church enforced laws that a wife could not accuse her husband of rape, even if he used force with accompanying brutality (Bayer 1985).

The concept of male hegemony that is incorporated into the image of a single, all-powerful male God provided the justification to unleash incredible fury on anyone who failed to conform or who challenged the authority of Christian beliefs. Early efforts in the treatment of emotional problems, which were often perceived as nonconformity, were strongly influenced by religious beliefs and often sanctioned beatings to drive out the devil.

By advocating that the laws of God supersede the laws of humans, Christian thought also has provided an escape route when men have found the prevailing social order too constricting. Fundamental Christianity's obsession with salvation and the afterlife frequently diverts the valuable energies of active believers from the important tasks at hand here on earth, such as accepting our moral responsibility to provide for the nurturance and safety of all human beings, including those who are less powerful and privileged, such as children. Frequently, divine absolution is invoked to forgive a sexual offender of violating his or her earthly responsibilities. In this framework of religious values, a norm of compliant believing is more highly valued than an ethic of human responsibility.

## Heterosexism

Heterosexism is the belief in the supremacy of heterosexuality in all social and sexual relationships, as well as the institutionalization of heterosexuality in all aspects of society to support this belief, including the use of legal, social, and religious sanctions to maintain homophobia. Heterosexism emerges as a hybrid from an overlapping of the dynamics of paternalism and male hegemony. Sexuality, especially the heterosexual structuring of consciousness and institutions, is a significant factor in the patriarchal organization that facilitates the oppression of women and children, as well as any men who deviate from the established norms and values.

Patriarchal societies are grounded in repressive and sometimes contradictory norms regarding sexuality. Religious teachings, family norms, community standards, and laws are all used to define and regulate sexual behavior. While certain aspects of an individual's sexuality is innate, a great amount of it is the product of socialization and learning.

Social norms exert considerable pressure for males and females to endorse prescribed traits. Intrinsic in these stereotypes is the concept that sexual behavior and attitudes are determined by genetics, thereby allowing only one possible mode of behavior once a person is born either male or female. Failure to conform to these sex-defined gender roles often draws considerable attention, frequently prompting ostracism, confrontation, and sometimes even threats against personal safety.

Patriarchal societies reflect very narrow and rigid definitions of gender roles. Characteristics prescribed as masculine are assigned to males, and those prescribed as feminine are assigned to females. For example, to be masculine is to be assertive, dominant, strong, powerful, virulent, and rational. "Men are to be hollow fortresses, safe from attack or loss of status from without, safe from inappropriate emotions and uncertainty from within" (Fisher 1972, 105–106). To be female is to be passive, pliable, frail, soft, tender, and intuitive.

These traits of masculinity and femininity reflect gender more accurately than they do sex, so their rigid application according to sex is often problematic. Gerda Lerner provides a helpful distinction between the concepts of gender and sex:

> Gender is the cultural definition of behavior defined as appropriate to the sexes in a given society at a given time. Gender is a set of cultural roles. It is a costume, a mask, a straightjacket in which men and women dance their unequal dance. Unfortunately, the term is used . . . as interchangeable with 'sex.' . . . Such usage is unfortunate, because it hides and mystifies the difference between the biological given—sex—and the culturally created—gender. (Lerner 1986, 238)

From this perspective, it becomes clear that the ritual of dividing males and females into two ordered and distinct divisions is a political deed. In other words, rigidly defined roles of masculine and feminine are little more than an artificial system of norms cultivated and inculcated into the collective consciousness so thoroughly that they are perceived to be innate.

Rigidly prescribing gender traits creates a context that limits and controls the range of acceptable sexual behavior. Within patriarchy, sexuality must indeed remain within an extremely narrow range. Heterosexual behaviors that conform to the prevailing norms of the dominant social and political institutions are deemed normal and are therefore acceptable. Any other sexual behaviors are defined as deviant and are opposed. For example, the Catholic Church historically has imposed strong moral sanctions to discourage any sexual activity that is not undertaken with the intent of procreation (Curran 1988).

The cultural norm of homophobia has been a common method of controlling sexuality within patriarchal societies. Homophobia is any system of beliefs that supports and promotes fear, hatred, and negative stereotypes against a person who displays affection toward another person of the same sex.

An important component of this norm is the phenomenon that homophobic individuals often exhibit an actual physiological response of fear when confronted with physical closeness or emotional intimacy in a same-sex interaction (Aguero, Bloch, and Byrne 1985). But homophobia goes beyond just the emotion of fear. Within the realities of daily living, homophobia involves the active demonstration of overt hatred and bigotry. Not only do the dominant institutions within a patriarchal society invest considerable energy and resources in cultivating homophobic fear, but those same institutions tacitly condone homophobic prejudice and discrimination.

Such fear has not been predominant throughout history. For example, Plato, in his *Symposium,* specifically equates democracy with an acceptance of homosexuality: "Wherever . . . it has been established that it is shameful to be involved in homosexual relationships . . . , this is due to evil on the part of the legislators, to despotism on the part of the rulers, and to cowardice on the part of the governed" (Boswell 1980, 51).

Plato's acceptance of a broad range of human sexuality was effectively eradicated during subsequent centuries. The influence of Christian theology has been especially significant in promoting heterosexism. Much of this theology is based on the belief that sexual behaviors that do not involve procreation are unnatural. Within this belief system, homosexuality is especially suspect, and such behavior has been criticized most forcefully as a crime against nature. The assumption that heterosexuality is the biological norm for all sexual behavior and that homosexuality is an abnormality contradicts biological data, however. Research clearly indicates that most species of animal engage in physical and sexual behaviors with same-sex partners.

Nonetheless, Christianity has been rigidly intolerant of homosexuality. In spite of strong assertions by Church leaders that opposition to this aspect of sexuality is required by divine decrees, it seems just as likely that such heterosexist beliefs are really politically inspired. Several contradictions within Christian theology offer support of this contention. Historian John Boswell notes one such contradiction:

> The very same [Christian Scriptures] which are thought to condemn homosexual acts condemn hypocrisy in the most strident terms, and on

greater authority: and yet Western society did not create any social taboos against hypocrisy, did not claim that hypocrites were "unnatural," did not segregate them into an oppressed minority, did not enact laws punishing their sin with castration or death. No Christian state, in fact, has passed laws against hypocrisy per se, despite its continual and explicit condemnation by Jesus and the church. (Boswell 1980, 7)

Whereas Jesus made no specific statement condemning homosexuality, subsequent church policies and institutional norms have become deeply entrenched in homophobia.

Ultimately, homophobia is an important tool for sexual control within a patriarchal system. This concept has traditionally been used as a weapon to facilitate social and political conformity. Throughout history, individuals who have been outspoken in challenging the norms of the status quo, who have failed to conform to the prevailing social order, or who have been especially bold in expressing creative visions have been vulnerable to being labeled "homosexual," with such a label then frequently providing a vehicle for repression. The practice of burning witches at the stake was common during many periods of history. Although there were usually many reasons why a person might be accused of being a witch, suspicion of being a homosexual was one of them. Such execution by burning is but one example of the severe consequences that historically have accompanied the label of homosexuality.

For patriarchal individuals and institutions that seek to maintain order and control, such an opportunity to label, segregate, and control becomes a crucial demonstration of authority. The message is clear that anyone who might choose to deviate from the norms of the prevailing order faces the threat of being assigned a negative label, with potentially devastating consequences.

Historically, sexuality has been a major focus for exercising such authority. Within patriarchal societies, the prescribed norms of masculine and feminine roles severely limit the potential for human intimacy. For example, male intimacy may occur within narrow boundaries, and any behavior between males that fails to adhere to the designated ground rules raises suspicions of homosexuality. "It is a tragic irony in our culture that men can only come comfortably close to each other when they are sharing a common target. As teenagers they come together in a gang or as members of a team out to 'destroy' the other team. As adults, in wartime, they have a common enemy" (Goldberg 1976, 132).

Within the constructs of patriarchy, maintaining such a narrow range of acceptable behavior regarding sexuality and intimacy becomes an important source of power and control. Alternative ways of behaving are extremely threatening because freedom of choice decreases the opportunities for control. Those who rigidly control are perhaps the most fearful of being controlled themselves. "In a patriarchal society male dominance must be maintained at all costs because the person who dominates cannot conceive of any alternative but to be dominated in turn" (Figes 1970, 50). Sexuality has become symbolic of this position. For example, the Catholic Church has rigidly advocated the missionary position as the only acceptable method to be used in sexual interactions between a man and a woman, and that position is a clear demonstration of male dominance.

A significant outgrowth of heterosexism is the linkage of power and control with sexuality. In other words, heterosexism provides a foundation for the eroticism of power and control. It promotes sexuality based on the values of dominance and submission, encouraging suspicion when it is based on mutual respect. Rape and child sexual abuse are examples of the abuse of power that becomes possible because of such an elevated sense of male entitlement regarding sexuality.

People frequently use their position of power to sexually exploit those who are less powerful. Unfortunately, there are countless examples of adults—parents, relatives, teachers, clergy, physicians, therapists, and so on—who use their role to sexually abuse another person who is entrusted to their care:

> A nationwide survey of psychiatrists, reported in May 1986, found that 6.4% of respondents acknowledged sexual contact with their patients. Three national surveys of psychologists reported a range of explicit sexual contact between male therapists and patients from 9.4% to 12.1% (2 to 3 percent of female therapists had been sexually intimate with their patients.) Social workers reported a smaller prevalence rate. (Pope and Bouhoutsos 1986, v)

Pope and Bouhoutsos report that although only 7 percent of psychotherapists acknowledged that they engaged in sexual intimacies with clients, 18 percent said that they considered engaging in such behavior. Later in their book, they report that a high percentage of those clients who were sexually abused by therapists were victims of childhood sexual molestation, therefore having already been at risk for such abuse of power. This examination of the behavior of therapists provides an alarming insight into the prevalence with which such eroticized power leads to the abuse of a client.

*Misogyny*

Misogyny is male hatred of women. In other words, male nature is held to be expressive of all humanity, while female nature is held to be different from and of less value than male human nature. The field of medicine, and particularly the specialty of psychiatry, provides many fascinating and instructive insights regarding the power of misogyny. It is interesting that while the overall impact of child physical and sexual abuse, battering, and rape on health care systems has been tremendous, the general response of health care professionals and medical institutions to these problems has been limited and fragmented.

Although women are the primary consumers of psychiatric services, men's interpretation of reality defines the nature of those services. To understand the prevalence of the male perspective, one must go back to the beginning, to Sigmond Freud. Freudian theory is based in large part on the dynamics of human sexuality.

Freud believed that children were not sexual until puberty. Therefore, as he listened to reports from his female clients about their memories of sexual incidents during their childhood, he postulated that such reports could only be the result of sexual abuse by an older adult. In his famous paper "The Aetiology of Hysteria," which he delivered to the Society for Psychiatry and Neurology in 1896, Freud stated, "I . . . put forward the thesis that at the bottom of every case of hysteria there are *one or more occurrences of premature sexual experiences"* (Masson 1984, 263). He was not, however, prepared for the negative reception of his seduction theory by the male-dominated psychiatric community.

The seduction theory was viewed as a statement of nonconformity, challenging the basic tenets of psychiatry. Freud was still young at this time, and although he was already very popular, he apparently felt that he needed acceptance to ensure his continued success. Therefore, he gave in to the political pressure from his professional peers and modified his theory. He altered his conclusions and advocated instead that sexual abuse existed only in the realm of fantasy. In other words, sexual abuse was relegated to the status of being merely hysterical fantasies of neurotic females.

There is no evidence that Freud altered his theory based on new or contradictory data from his treatment of patients. However, because Freud often relied on scientific theory, his change was widely interpreted as the result of scientific study, and his modified approach was accepted as fact.

For those who might argue that Freud was merely an innocent victim of his time, it is important to note that one of his contemporaries, John Stuart Mill, was an outspoken advocate of respecting the true integrity of females. Despite intense opposition and political pressure, Mill remained true to his conscience (Bell 1983). This clearly demonstrates that Freud did have choices other than conforming to the prevailing norms of the powerful medical establishment. Unfortunately, the ramifications of Freud's failure of conscience and courage are still painfully felt today.

Freudian analysis, and the psychiatric profession in general, has been a model of misogyny. Freud's concept of the normal human being was an adult male; females were thereby defined as being deviant human beings because they lacked a penis, and even male children were defined as inferior because their power was yet undeveloped. In both cases, the entire psyche was determined to be centered on the struggle to compensate for this deficiency.

Within the framework of psychiatry, attempts to talk about experiences and feelings that do not conform to a male-biased reality are conveniently diagnosed as distorted thinking and categorized as dysfunctional or neurotic behavior. We are all too familiar with the frequency with which incest survivors have been diagnosed as hysterical or chronically depressed and treated with medication rather than being encouraged to talk about their life experiences. Psychiatry has provided a powerful set of constructs that are a first-line defense against changes in patriarchal systems. It is important to realize that Freud actually acted as an agent of control for patriarchal standards and to understand the entrenchment of our prevailing social norms and the extent to which the status quo is able to resist change.

In many respects, the psychiatric community has used the concept of misogyny in much the same way as an incest family. Victims who disclose their history of sexual abuse are not believed and/or are punished. Over the years, much professional energy has been devoted to protecting the secret that sexual abuse is a reality. Most members of the psychiatric community who have been confronted by firsthand reports of sexual abuse have conveniently chosen to ignore this issue or to minimize its significance. The constructs of psychiatry have provided a variety of mechanisms to define the experiences of victims of sexual abuse as abnormal and dysfunctional and the behaviors of offenders as expected and justifiable. It is only recently that the true nature of Freud's original thinking has reemerged into the public awareness (Masson 1984). Yet even in the 1980s, psychiatrists who believed client reports of childhood sexual abuse continued to be viewed with suspicion and were judged to be dangerous, defiant, and nonconforming members of the psychiatric community.

Freudian theory has been a strong influence in the training of mental health practitioners. Mental health treatment resources often reflect the underlying values and premises of psychoanalytic theory. It has been very difficult for psychoanalysts to treat sexual abuse effectively because there has been no easy way to categorize victims within a disease-oriented framework and much difficulty in prescribing a cure for such victimization. To respond to sexual victimization in a manageable way, the psychiatric community has conveniently reorganized the problem to focus on the symptoms of sexual victimization as reflected in psychopathology. For example, masochism, depression, suicidal tendencies, substance abuse, borderline personality disorder, hysteria, conduct disorder, hypochondriasis, and dissociative disorder are common diagnosis assigned to sexual abuse survivors. Once diagnosed with any of these behaviors, the victim, rather than the assailant, becomes a "legitimate object of medical control" (Stark, Flitcraft, and Frazier 1979, 470).

Sexual offenders, however, traditionally have not been diagnosed in terms of psychopathology. Rather, the behaviors of male perpetrators have been interpreted as inherent in the male gender, therefore shifting responsibility back to the victim to keep such male impulses within manageable boundaries. Consequently, psychiatry has traditionally approached rape and sexual abuse as outgrowths of male lust, but contemporary research has begun to challenge these approaches. For example, Groth and Birnbaum (1980) draw the following conclusion about adult rapists, which also applies to perpetrators of child sexual abuse:

> Rape is a pseudo-sexual act, complex and multi-determined but addressing issues of hostility (anger) and control (power) more than passion (sexuality). To regard rape as an expression of sexual desire is not only an inaccurate notion but also an insidious assumption, for it results in the shifting of the responsibility for the offence in large part from the offender to the victim. (p. 2)

To understand the politics of child sexual abuse, it is critical to recognize the dynamics of patriarchy. The five essential features presented here are fundamental underpinnings that allow for the continued existence of this problem.

## Patriarchy and the Male Survivor

Many people advocate that issues related to patriarchy are relevant only to females. To the contrary, patriarchy has a significant impact regardless of a person's sex or gender. The continued prevalence of patriarchy imprisons all people, male and female, who live under its influence. Ironically, there are numerous negative repercussions even for men, including their greater social isolation and the cultural expectation that they must internalize or withhold emotions, which may account for the fact that men are likely to die earlier than women.

Male survivors remain imprisoned by patriarchy by ignoring the political realities of their sexual abuse. Their fear of losing the privileges accorded them by patriarchy (including the privilege of sexual dominance) often becomes paralyzing and contributes to denial regarding the impact of sexual abuse. Too often male survivors comply with patriarchal norms by dealing with their problems "like a man."

Anecdotal information regarding the treatment of male survivors indicates that the actual experience of trauma is connected with an incident of sexual abuse is not significantly different from males than females (Dimock 1988; Lew 1988; Strube 1989). What appears to be different in working with male survivors is the aftermath of the abuse—the ways in which males cope with their abuse experience and use treatment services to facilitate the process of their healing and recovery.

The response of male survivors reflects the values and norms by which males are socialized. In essence, patriarchy grooms males to assume a position of privilege, thereby conditioning them to be comfortable with their dominant (and oppressor) status and encouraging them to perceive the concept of victim as antithetical to maleness. Within the constructs of patriarchy, there is considerable dissonance when members of an oppressor class talk about victimization experiences. Rather than struggling with the repercussions of this dissonance, male survivors often either remain silent or identify with the oppressor and engage in sexually offending behaviors themselves.

Several specific factors distinguish the recovery efforts of male survivors from those of their female counterparts. These factors are all related to the ways in which males are socialized to be different from females, and they create a gigantic web that entangles, and frequently traps, male survivors. It is through the interplay of these factors that many male survivors maintain their allegience to patriarchy and therefore impede their own potential for recovery.

Identification of nine factors that negatively affect the recovery of male survivors illustrates the degree to which patriarchy moves from an abstract concept to a concrete reality that has a significant impact on the lives of many people. These factors are as follows:

1. A reluctance to seek treatment
2. A tendency to minimize the experience of victimization
3. Difficulty accepting shame and guilt
4. A propensity toward exaggerated efforts to reassert masculine identity
5. Difficulties with male intimacy
6. Confusion about sexual identity
7. Behavior patterns with power/control dynamics
8. A tendency to externalize feelings
9. A vulnerability to compulsive behaviors

### Reluctance to Seek Treatment

Stereotypically, men are not consumers of mental health services. Most male survivors of sexual abuse encounter considerable dissonance as they struggle to accept the reality that a man can be a victim. The stereotype that sexual victimization is less traumatic for males than for females prevents many males from seeking help. Frequently, a male survivor who presents for treatment will have been sensitized or pushed to do so by a sexual partner or friend.

### Minimization of the Experience of Victimization

Confounded by social expectations that any male can rise above his feelings and easily move beyond difficulties, many male children and adult male survivors of sexual abuse are reluctant to make a disclosure. Many males who were violated by an older adolescent or adult female fear that their disclosure will be interpreted as a rite of passage and will not be recognized as a victimization experience. When the teenage victim is a self-identified homosexual, the typical adult response is to assume that the victimization experience was merely the result of his choice of sexual orientation, which is stereotypically perceived as unfortunate. People blame the victim for his homosexuality rather than placing responsibility with the offender.

## Shame-Based Personality Dynamics

Whereas a female victim seems to focus more on feelings of having been exploited—that is, the "damaged goods" syndrome—a male victim seems to focus on feelings related to his having failed to protect himself. Much effort is generally required for the male survivor to identify his feelings and acknowledge that his physical body was violated. He must put aside the protective armor that is created by his tangential focus on the assumption that his failure to protect himself makes him less of a man. Male survivors of sexual abuse consistently report a sense of internalized anger that relates directly to their perception of having failed at their manly responsibility of inflicting serious physical harm on the offender.

## Exaggerated Efforts to Reassert Masculine Identity

Having failed to protect himself from an incident of sexual abuse may be internalized and reinforced by the social norm that assumes that a male of any age should have the ability to protect himself. The male survivor may overcompensate for his anxiety by using macho behaviors to reestablish a self-perceived strong male image. There is also a potential for intensely homophobic feelings or behaviors in reaction to sexual victimization.

## Difficulties with Male Intimacy

An intense focus on creating a strong masculine image may undermine opportunities for closeness with other men. Too often, men assume that emotional intimacy is a female behavior. The general social norm of woman hating makes it seem risky for some men to align themselves with any attributes that are considered to be feminine in nature. Fear of appearing weak, needy, or frail contributes to avoidance of intimate self-disclosures with other males. Any setting that creates intimacy with other males may evoke intense feelings of anxiety or anger, as well as a general lack of safety.

## Confusion about Sexual Identity

The male victim may assume that his failure to resist his assault is a statement of passivity, and prevailing social norms inappropriately equate passivity with homosexuality. The molester of a male child is more likely to be of the same sex (since the majority of offenders are male) than is the molester of a female child. Any self-perception of arousal or physical pleasure that was experienced during a same-sex assault may be misinterpreted by the victim as latent homosexual feelings—that is, normal male physiological responses during any sexual interaction (even during a same-sex encounter) may contrast sharply with the social message that normal sexual arousal should occur only in a male-female interaction.

## Behavior Patterns with Power/Control Dynamics

Low self-esteem related to the failure to protect oneself from victimization may contribute to hypervigilance regarding control issues. Whereas a female often becomes withdrawn because of the secrets surrounding her victimization, a male is prone to externalize his energy by rigidly controlling others.

## Externalization of Feelings

Social norms encourage a male to ignore or discount his feelings and discourage him from expressing his emotions openly. Social norms prescribe that it is okay for a man to act on emotions but dangerous to feel those same emotions. Male privilege sanctioned by the patriarchy provides a license for a man to externalize his feelings, which often includes abusing others. Consequently, male survivors who subscribe to patriarchal values have an increased risk for engaging in sexually offending behavior. The risk for such victimizing behavior is further increased when the survivor feels a sense of extreme isolation—for example, when he lacks a perceived confidant to whom he can disclose his own abuse experience or when he has an elevated fear that if he confides his secret of victimization, other people may doubt his masculinity.

## Vulnerability to Compulsive Behaviors

Men in our society are expected to be productive, but any survivor of sexual abuse experiences emotional anxiety and pain. A perceived lack of permission for men to display intense emotions may prompt some male survivors to mask feelings through product- and task-oriented activities or through rigidly repetitive behaviors. Although compulsivity about work, materialism, sex, sports, and competition are generally socially acceptable for men, such behaviors may be an indicator of distress for the male survivor. Gender biases also mask the frequency with which males are at risk for addictive behaviors regarding food. As with female survivors, males who have been sexually victimized often abuse alcohol and other chemical substances.

## Male Survivors within the Context of the Women's Movement

In many ways, the nine factors discussed in the previous section create a collage of values and attitudes—norms by which males are socialized to behave differently from females in patriarchal systems. None of these factors is biologically inherent in males; rather, they emerge from the social and political dynamics of patriarchy. Again, the importance of developing a political analysis of the problem of sexual abuse is a prerequisite to effective intervention and treatment.

How we attempt to understand these political dynamics will significantly affect the analysis that emerges. In regard to the problems of child sexual abuse, it is crucial that any political analysis incorporate concerns that are important to both male and female survivors. Especially critical is the need to avoid the potential danger that the concerns of male survivors will overshadow those of female survivors. Male survivors must always remain cognizant of their heritage in the current environment of more open discussion about child sexual abuse. They must remember that there would probably be no child sexual abuse movement if advocates within the women's movement of the 1960s had not been so outspoken about the sexual exploitation of females.

As the movement to identify and treat male survivors grows, one danger is that such a focus may shift attention away from women's victimization. That shift is one of the ways in which the system could undermine change and patriarchal values could be reasserted as opposed to being addressed in a meaningful manner. A major weapon in supporting the status quo is to foment divisiveness among proponents of social change. To overcome this potential danger, it is crucial that advocates working on issues related to male victimization remain aligned with the women's movement, for it is the power and wisdom of the feminist analysis that has provided the most important energy toward identifying the root causes of violence in our society, including those of sexual abuse.

We must not be satisfied with mere reformist changes concerning a problem that is so important to our quality of life. And we must be critical in our evaluation of changes that are achieved. There is a big difference between fundamental and superficial change. Superficial change can be offered as a narcotic to circumvent demands for fundamental change. Those who wield the power and control in our society have an investment in maintaining the status quo, and those individuals and institutions have the resources to manipulate perceptions in order to achieve a collective sense of passivity or futility regarding social change.

The American experience during World War II offers an instructive illustration of this process. Prior to the Second World War, it was generally expected that women would remain in the home in the roles of housewife and mother. The few women who did work held stereotypically defined female jobs. Suddenly the country was faced with a serious mission and a tremendous labor shortage. Government and industry combined forces to launch a large-scale and systematic media blitz to reeducate the American public that it was acceptable for women to work in factories. The norm had shifted, and it was now considered unpatriotic for women to remain at home. Government and industry even established day-care centers and child assistance programs to make it easier for women to work.

At the end of the war, large numbers of men returned home and flooded a job market that was heavily populated by females. Suddenly, the attitude of government and industry shifted, and there was an equally intense effort to persuade women to return home and resume their "rightful" duties as housewives and mothers. Day-care centers were closed and child assistance programs were eliminated to "assist" women in their transition back into the home.

As this example shows, the equal participation of women in the workplace did not reflect a fundamental change in the norms and attitudes of society. Rather, it was an expedient and superficial change in response to a specific crisis.

Similarly, it is important that the responses we formulate to the problem of child sexual abuse maintain a focus on demands for fundamental, rather than superficial sociopolitical change. Especially critical are the efforts to provide psychotherapy to survivors of sexual abuse. Traditional psychotherapy, grounded in the medical model, promotes adjustment and attempts to remain neutral and objective, an approach that is particularly problematic in dealing with a problem such as child sexual abuse. To advocate for adjustment in response to this problem is really an acceptance of psychotherapy as a covert means of social control and serves only to protect the status quo against those who would challenge it.

To be effective, psychotherapy must move beyond the rational, linear, and hierarchical interventions that are grounded in the medical model of mental illness and disease. The goal of psychotherapy must be healing and change, not adjustment and accommodation. Such a goal cannot be achieved in an environment that perpetuates the values of patriarchy but rather requires that therapy be conducted in the context of a maternal space—a psychological womb. Feminist approaches to psychotherapy offer the greatest opportunity for confronting the dynamics of patriarchy and thereby provide the widest range of possibilities for achieving significant change in response to the problem of child sexual abuse.

Feminist approaches to psychotherapy include the following (Goodrich et al. 1988):

1. The therapist's use of self as a model of human behavior, with an effort to overcome the constraints of gender stereotypes

2. Creating a process in which the use of skills such as validation, empowerment, and demystification increases the client's sense of having options for himself or herself

3. Developing an analysis of gender roles and their impact within the context of interpersonal relationships

4. Using this analysis to promote interactions that both challenge and free the client from constricted, stereotypical patterns of behavior

5. Using techniques from other schools of thought as appropriate, but with full awareness of the gender consequences of those techniques

## The Future

It is imperative that the child sexual abuse movement truly emerge as a sociopolitical movement. Efforts to address child sexual abuse will not result in significant change until such endeavors grapple with the political dimensions of this problem. Real change is not possible unless the basic attitudes, values, emotions, and socialization processes of patriarchy are confronted.

Education is a critical first step in the process of liberating our children from the oppression of sexual victimization. In this regard, prevention programs are valuable. However, such approaches are not adequate for achieving significant change. No amount of education concerning the concepts of "good touch/bad touch" or "It's okay to tell" will protect a child within an environment that keeps him or her powerless and that promotes and condones a culture of violence. Failure to examine the reality of patriarchy and the resulting politics of sexual abuse is tantamount to accepting this problem as an inherent part of our society.

If we are truly committed to ending the sexual abuse of children, we must acknowledge that such maltreatment is an integral component of our prevailing sociopolitical reality. To overcome this problem, we must try to change our future. It is essential that we move beyond the symptomatology of child abuse and struggle with the underlying issues of how to create a world without patriarchy. In so doing, we must begin to address a variety of questions that are fundamental to the interrelationship of patriarchy and sexual abuse:

To what extent can we rely on the prevailing institutions, which subscribe to patriarchal norms, to promote safety and protection from sexual victimization?

To what extent do helping professionals, within the existing norms of mental health, serve as agents for accommodation and compliance versus growth and change?

What would sociopolitical institutions look like if they were free of patriarchal norms?

What are the avenues for developing social and political policies that do not promote patriarchal norms when the individuals and institutions that currently control or decision-making processes are all so deeply rooted in patriarchy?

How do we begin the process of socializing a class of decision makers who are not rooted in patriarchy?

What would an entire society look like if it were nonpatriarchal?

To what extent can we achieve an alternative future—a future that is not rooted in the norms of patriarchy—by relying on the prevailing institutions of today?

How do we address issues related to the family as a changing institution? Specifically, if the family traditionally has been an institution deeply rooted in patriarchy, what is the role and responsibility of helping professionals in protecting the family versus their role in promoting change in the family?

As the forces of the far right as well as progressive-minded people struggle to control the destiny of the family as a social unit, how do we minimize the risk that the issue of sexual abuse will be used as a weapon in this escalating battle? Specifically, how do we counteract the growing trend to use sexual abuse laws to blame the victim, separate the rich from the poor, and ultimately reinforce patriarchal norms?

By maintaining the patriarchy, we as a society accept limitations to our growth. By choosing to give up or redefine the patriarchal system, the opportunities for change and the achievement of full personal and interpersonal potential are possible. Each of us must examine and evaluate what we are able to give up and what we are willing to gain by challenging patriarchy. Just as ignoring a child's disclosure of sexual abuse impedes his or her recovery, ignoring the reality of patriarchy impedes the elimination of this crime.

# References

Aguero, Joseph, Laura Bloch, and Donn Byrne. 1985. "The Relationship among Sexual Beliefs, Attitudes, Experience, and Homophobia." In *Homophobia in American Society: Bashers, Baiters, and Bigots,* edited by John DeCecco, 95–107. New York: Harrington Park Press.

Alexander, Priscilla. 1987. "Prostitution: A Difficult Issue for Feminists." In *Sex Work: Writings by Women in the Industry,* edited by Frederique Dellacoste, and Priscilla Alexander, 184–214. Pittsburgh: Cleis Press.

American Humane Association. 1986. *Highlights of Official Child Neglect and Abuse Reporting: 1986.* Denver.

Antonelli, Judith. 1982. "Feminist Spirituality: The Politics of the Psyche." In *Politics of Women's Spirituality,* edited by Charlene Spretnak, 399–403. New York: Anchor/Doubleday.

Bagley, R., H. Allard, N. McCormick, P, Proudoot, D. Fortier, D. Ogilvie, Q. Rae-Grant, P. Gelinas, L. Pepin, and S. Sutherland (Committee on Sexual Offenses Against Children and Youth). 1984. *Sexual Offenses Against Children.* Vol. 1. Canadian Government Publishing Centre.

Bayer, Edward. 1985. *Rape within Marriage.* New York: University Press of America.

Bell, Linda, ed. 1983. *Visions of Women.* Clifton, New Jersey: Humana Press.

Bleier, Ruth. 1984. *Science and Gender: A Critique of Biology and Its Theories on Women.* New York: Pergamon Press.

Boswell, John. 1980. *Christianity, Social Tolerance, and Homosexuality.* Chicago: University of Chicago Press.

Brownmiller, Susan. 1975. *Against Our Will: Men, Women, and Rape.* New York: Simon and Schuster.

Crow, Duncan. 1972. *The Victorian Woman.* New York: Stein & Day.

Curran, Charles. 1988. *Tensions in Moral Theology.* Notre Dame, Indiana: University of Notre Dame Press.

Dimock, Peter. 1988. Adult Males Sexually Abused as Children: Characteristics and Implications for Treatment. *Journal of Interpersonal Violence* 3 (no. 2): 203–221.

Dobash, R. Emerson, and Russel P. Dobash. 1977. "Wives: The Appropriate Victims of Marital Violence." Paper printed by the Department of Sociology, University of Stirling, Stirling, Scotland.

———. 1979. *Violence Against Wives: A Case Against the Patriarchy.* New York: Free Press.

Dyson, Michael. 1989. "Central Park Miseries." *Zeta Magazine* (July/August): 54–55.

Figes, Eva. 1970. *Patriarchal Attitudes.* New York: Stein & Day.

Finkelhor, David. 1984. *Child Sexual Abuse: New Theory and Research.* New York: Free Press.

Finkelhor, D., G. Hotling, I.A. Louis, and C. Smith. 1990. "Sexual Abuse in a

National Survey of Adult Men and Women: Prevalence, Characteristics, and Risk Factors." *Child Abuse and Neglect* 14 (no. 1): 19–28.

Fisher, Peter. 1972. *The Gay Mystique.* New York: Stein & Day.

Goldberg, Herb. 1976. *The Hazards of Being Male.* New York: Signet Books.

Goodrich, Thelma J., Cheryl Rampage, Barbara Ellman, and Kris Halstead. 1988. *Feminist Family Therapy: A Casebook.* New York: W.W. Norton.

Groth, A. Nicholas, and H. Jean Birnbaum. 1980. *Men Who Rape.* New York: Plenum Press.

Hartley, C. Gasquoine. 1913. *The Truth about Women.* New York: Dodd, Mead & Co.

Hunter, M. 1990. *Abused Boys: The Neglected Victims of Sexual Abuse.* Lexington, Massachusetts: Lexington Books.

Kempe, C. Henry. 1968. *The Battered Child.* Chicago: University of Chicago Press.

Kempe, C. Henry, and Ray Helfer, eds. 1972. *Helping the Battered Child and His Family.* Philadelphia: J.B. Lippincott.

Laistner, M.L.W. 1951. *Christianity and Pagan Culture in the Later Roman Empire.* Ithaca, New York: Cornell University Press.

Landis, J. 1956. "Experiences of 500 Children with Adult Sexual Deviants." *Psychiatric Quarterly (Supplement)* 30: 91–109.

Lederer, Wolfgang. (1968). *The Fear of Women.* New York: Harcourt Brace Jovanovich.

Lerner, Gerda. 1986. *The Creation of Patriarchy.* New York: Oxford University Press.

Levi-Strauss, Claude. 1969. *The Elementary Structure of Kinship.* Boston: Beacon Press.

Lew, Mike. 1988. *Victims No Longer: Men Recovering from Incest and Other Sexual Child Abuse.* New York: Nevraumont Publishing.

MacKinnon, C. 1983. "Feminism, Marxism, Method, and the State: Toward Feminist Jurisprudence." *Signs* 8: 635–658.

Martin, Del. 1976. *Battered Wives.* San Francisco: Glide Publications.

Masson, Jeffrey M. 1984. *The Assault on Truth: Freud's Suppression of the Seduction Theory.* New York: Farrar, Straus & Giroux.

Millett, Kate. 1969. *Sexual Politics.* Garden City, New York: Doubleday.

Neumann, Erich. 1959. *Art and the Creative Unconscious.* Princeton, New Jersey: Princeton University Press.

Newman, W.L. 1973. *Philosophy of Plato and Aristotle.* New York: Arno Press.

O'Brien, M. 1981. "Feminist Theory and Dialectical Logic." *Signs* 7: 144–157.

Pearsall, Ronald. 1969. *The Worm in the Bud.* New York: Macmillan.

Pope, Kenneth, and Jacqueline Bouhoutsos. 1986. *Sexual Intimacy between Therapist and Patient.* New York: Praeger.

Radbill, Samuel. 1974. "A History of Child Abuse and Infanticide." In *The Battered Child,* edited by Ray Helfer and C. Henry Kempe, 3–21. Chicago: University of Chicago Press.

Robbins, Russell. 1959. *Encyclopedia of Witchcraft and Demonology.* New York: Crown Publishers.

Russell, Diana. 1975. *The Politics of Rape.* New York: Stein & Day.

————. 1986. *The Secret Trauma: Incest in the Lives of Girls and Women*. New York: Basic Books.

Russell, J.B. 1972. *Witchcraft in the Middle Ages*. Ithaca, New York: Cornell University Press.

Soisson, Pierre, and Janine Soisson. 1977. *Byzantium*. Geneva, Switzerland: Editions Minerva.

Stark, E., A. Flitcraft, and W. Frazier. 1979. "Medicine and Patriarchal Violence: The Social Construction on a 'Private' Event." *International Journal of Health Services* 9: 461–493.

Stone, Merlin. 1976. *When God Was a Woman*. New York: Dial Press.

Struve, Jim. 1989. "Treatment of the Sexually Abused Male." *Ridgeview Insight* 10 (no. 2): 25–31.

Thomson, J.A.K., trans. 1977. *The Ethics of Aristotle: The Nicomachean Ethics*. New York: Penguin Books.

Tuchman, Barbara. 1978. *A Distant Mirror*. New York: Alfred A. Knopf.

Walker, Barbara. 1983. *The Women's Encyclopedia of Myths and Secrets*. San Francisco: Harper & Row.

Walker, Lenore. 1970. *The Battered Woman*. New York: Harper & Row.

Yllo, Kerst, and Michele Bograd, eds. 1988. *Feminist Perspectives on Wife Abuse*. Newbury Park, California: Sage Publications.

# 2
# Adjusting the Frame: Cinematic Treatment of Sexual Abuse and Rape of Men and Boys

*James W. Trivelpiece*

> We live in a culture that encourages us not to take our own suffering seriously, but rather to make light of it or even to laugh about it.
> —Alice Miller (1981)

Men who were raped or sexually abused as children face a unique set of problems. For men, identifying particular acts as abusive is especially difficult because men are expected to be able to protect themselves (Rogers and Terry 1984). Admitting to a situation in which they were unable to do so is tantamount to denying their masculinity. Disclosing an abusive sexual experience also is difficult. If the sexual contact was with a woman, the man's motives become suspect because men are expected to value sexual contact with women. If the unwanted sexual contact was with another male, the man is told that this contact has altered his sexual orientation (Geiser 1979). Men who have been raped or abused face another problem as well in that abuse and rape are historically defined as an act that men perpetrate against females (Finkelhor 1984).

On the other side of the equation, incest, male rape, molestation, and sexual initiation are common themes in mass-market films, which are an important source of information for society. It is the premise of this chapter that insensitive cinematic portrayals of the sexual abuse of men and boys establish negative stereotypes of male characterological and behavioral responses to abuse. These negative stereotypes may influence attitudes and perceptions of real-life men who are survivors of rape or childhood sexual abuse.

I would like to thank the following people who provided vital assistance while I was preparing this work: Ann Warrington, my wife, my lover, my best friend; David Coahran, Ph.D., who remained calm on that hot August afternoon when the hard drive malfunctioned and chopped the manuscript to bits; Frank Pelfrey, Ph.D., my supervisor, in whose heart I have been held; and Eric Jensen, Ph.D., of the University of Idaho Department of Sociology, who gave me encouragement and taught me critical thinking.

Sexual abuse of boys and male rape have only recently become known outside the clinical professions. However, a trip to the local video rental outlet or public library will turn up many films that show acts of sexual abuse and rape committed against men and boys. Paying a small fee, one may rent a videotape of films portraying women seducing boys, mothers or grandmothers in incestuous relationships with boys, men and women molesting boys, and men and women raping adult men. The films and videotapes that contain these themes are not considered pornographic. They are mass-market comedies, dramas, and adventure films. Ironically, this is considered entertainment.

Movies are expensive to produce. They are produced to earn a profit. To earn the highest profit for the production company, the film must give the audience what it wants. Jarvie (1978) delineates a theory of how movies may function for their audience, identifying the following functions of movies: identification and escape, vicarious experience, reference group socialization, status aspiration, anticipatory socialization, reinforcement of values, gratification, and legitimization.

According to Jarvie, an audience seeking identification and escape might choose a film with exciting locales and characters. Such an analysis relies on an assumption that the everyday life of the audience is tedious and thus causes viewers to seek an escape. But Jarvie also says that movies are a popular form of entertainment for many people whose lives are anything but tedious, so this explanation alone will not suffice. Audiences may watch particular films to experience vicariously events that are absent from their everyday lives. Thus, says Jarvie, moviegoers may "learn from the movies informally." The treatment of delicate themes in the movies "may or may not be exemplary, but the very act of being able to anticipate them is valuable" (p. 128).

Jarvie describes how films may meet varying needs of viewers. First, a film may serve as reference group socialization. Thus, it may attract an audience because it portrays behavior in social groups to which viewers would like to belong. A film also may serve as anticipatory socialization and may instruct individuals in lower-social-status groups how to behave in order to be accepted in higher-status groups. Status aspiration suggests that films may attract viewers by granting or removing social status from particular groups. A film may reinforce the viewers' values by portraying themes that are consonant with these values in real life. It may legitimize a particular point of view or way of life. And, finally, a film may provide gratification to viewers. Any film may play one or several roles for the audience.

Applying Jarvie's theory to films that portray sexual abuse of men and boys, one might come up with an analysis such as the following: Lighthearted comedies such as *My Life as a Dog* (1985) may gratify, entertain, and affirm the values of the audience. Films such as *Nuts* (1987) and *The Color Purple* (1985) may grant greater status and legitimize the ways of life of female incest survivors (*Nuts*) and female survivors of color (*The Color Purple*). Sexual initiation films for teenagers, such as *Weird Science* (1985) and *Class* (1983), may perform a function of status aspiration by instructing teenage boys to which groups they should aspire to belong (older teenagers who are sexually active). Sexual initiation films may provide anticipatory socialization by detailing how teenagers can enter higher-status groups ("get laid") and provide specific instructions (have an affair with an older woman because no girl your own age would sleep with "a dink like you"). And finally, although Jarvie has failed to discuss it, a film may provide subliminal learning to the audience through portrayals of particular characters' habits and status (before becoming sexually active a character may be shown dressed in unattractive clothes and as less desirable).

Applying Jarvie's analysis to a film such as *Deliverance* (1972), one can see that the film may provide the audience with a means of identification and escape. The film also may function as a form of vicarious experience. Thus, *Deliverance* may allow male viewers to experience events that are outside their everyday experience—such as being raped—and allow them to formulate plans on how to respond if they ever face the threat of rape.

The problem with these functions is that while Jarvie's theory explains how an audience responds to a film, it does not address the fact that films are constructed to sell tickets. These two issues are often at cross-purposes. The audience expects a vicarious experience that will provide instruction in solving complex life problems. It expects instruction concerning which social groups are desirable, as well as explanations of how these groups may be entered. The film is designed to entertain and sell tickets, not to serve as models of adaptive behavior. Thus, the goals of the filmmaker are quite different from the expectations of the audience. Unfortunately, the audience is often unaware of this conflict. I will discuss this problem in greater detail after reviewing the content of some pertinent films.

## A Review of Incest Films

Incest, an act that is taboo in every culture in the world, would seemingly drive crowds away from the theater, but it is a subject that appears frequently in films. Mom does it with her son in *Fists in the Pocket* (1965), which portrays a pathological family that is, among other things, incestuous. *Flesh and Blood* (1979), made for television, "shows that incest is not the end of the world" (Limbacher 1983, 652). *The Damned* (1969) contains mother-son incest, as well as many other themes, in a tale of the rise of Naziism. *Luna* (1969) casts mother and son as lovers. *Night Games* (1966) suggests mother-son incest, as well as sadomasochism and pedophilia. *My Sister, My Love* (1966) portrays a story of brother-sister incest. And *Through a Glass Darkly* (1962) portrays a schizophrenic sister in an incestuous relationship with her brother.

Mother-son incest appears as a theme in *Murmur of the Heart* (1971). Limbacher (1983) describes this film as follows: "A delightful no-holds-barred sex film by Louis Malle, in which mother sleeps with son and loves it. This movie caused a brouhaha in censorship circles because neither mother nor son are neurotic" (p. 992). The film centers on the coming of age of fifteen-year-old Laurent. In this tale, everyone—mother, father, both brothers, and others—seems interested in the young boy's sexuality. While confessing sins of "solitary vice," he is molested by an effeminate priest. Later he is taken to a brothel by his two drunken brothers, who break into his room and interrupt the session, pulling him off the prostitute. Laurent becomes ill with a heart murmur and goes with his mother to a spa for a cure. Mother's lover appears on the scene, but she suddenly breaks off the relationship. Taking her son to Bastille Day festivities, she drinks heavily. When the boy takes her back to their hotel room, they have intercourse. Mother tells the boy, "We'll remember it as a beautiful moment, one that will never be repeated."

After Mom falls asleep, Laurent storms out of the room and knocks on the door of a teenage girl who is also a guest at the hotel. He kisses her roughly, and she slams the door. He knocks on the door of another teenage girl and is welcomed in. They spend the night together. Startled by her wake-up call, he grabs his shoes and dashes barefoot back to his room, where he finds his father, brothers, and mother, who laugh at the spectacle of the boy's "coming of age."

Keyser's (1975) review of this film states that "the act is presented as a positive, indeed lovely and touching moment in his life, a stage in a natural cycle. They are beyond taking the conventions of society in which they move seriously" (p. 187). Other writers have commented on the irony in this film. Forward and Buck (1978) say that in this and other films with mother-son incest themes , incest "is generally treated lightly, like a simple love affair, that just happens to be between a mother and son" (p. 73). Haskell (1974), writing from a feminist perspective, states, "Intercourse with a real mother would be less likely to liberate into happy heterosexuality; more likely it would stunt Malle's confused, sensitive adolescent forever" (p. 288).

*Midnight Cowboy* (1968), winner of the Academy Award for Best Picture, portrays the life of a young man named Joe Buck who, as a child, has an incestuous relationship with his grandmother. As an adult, he is raped by members of his gang. Joe, a young "hunk" from Texas, travels to New York, seeking his fortune as a prostitute. His get-rich-quick scheme involves servicing wealthy matrons.

The long bus ride north allows us to get to know Joe, played by Jon Voight, who has painful and confusing flashbacks of his youth: his mother abandoning him to his grandmother; lying in bed with his grandmother and one of her lovers, the old woman embracing him; sitting on the porch with his grandmother, the two of them smiling smugly; rubbing his grandmother's shoulders, the old woman moaning with pleasure; returning to his grand-mother's home on leave from the Army and finding that she has died; making love to his girlfriend and her moaning, "You're the only one"; being found by his gang while making love to his girlfriend and the gang raping her; Joe being held down while a gang member rapes him; his girlfriend telling the police about the rape and, pointing to him, saying, "He was the one; he was the only one."

Once in New York, Joe finds that men, not women, are interested in his services. He develops a friendship with a sniveling con artist, Ratso Rizzo, played by Dustin Hoffman. Ratso offers to pimp for Joe and finally arranges an encounter with a woman they meet at a party. Joe is impotent at first, but when she insinuates that he may be gay, he forces himself on her. The film follows the dissolution of Joe's dreams and the development of his friendship with Ratso. The film ends with Ratso's death from a chronic illness.

The sexual abuse portrayed in this film is subtle, perhaps so subtle as to escape the notice of most viewers. Critics seem to have missed the theme as well. Limbacher (1983) takes no notice of the incest theme, and Foster Hirsch's (1975) review of it focuses on the latent homosexual relationship between Joe and Ratso rather than on incest.

The abuse in *Midnight Cowboy* seems contrary to most definitions of sex-ual abuse. Joe's relationship with his grandmother is sexualized, appearing stimulating to both, but there is no clear indication of the two of them having intercourse. Joe instead appears to take a role as his grandmother's lover, the two of them sleeping together and enjoying each other's touch—a typology of female-perpetrated incest noted by Forward and Buck (1978). They note that one form of mother-son incest "may entail no sexual contact at all. Mother and son may sleep in the same bed together, dress and undress together, per-haps even bathe together, but that's as far as it goes" (p. 76). The authors go on to state that although there is no overt sexual behavior between mother and son, these incest cases become ever more strained and painful as the boy enters his teenage years.

Abuse by a grandmother appears again in *Mishima: A Life in Four Chapters* (1985). This film deals with the life of the Japanese writer Yukio Mishima. The film follows his activities on the last day of his life, providing flashbacks of his earlier life interwoven with portrayals of four of his short stories. As a boy, he is kidnapped from his mother by his grandmother, who claims that he will die if left in his mother's care. The grandmother denies the boy access to his mother. The film implies a sexual relationship between the child and the grandmother. In one scene, the young boy is required to massage his grandmother's legs. She moans with pleasure, saying, "Be a good boy and rub my legs. That's wonderful! Only a good boy like you can make Grand-mother better."

In this film, the disturbance in the lead character is notable. He and the characters from his fictional works have an intensity, a turbulence, and a fascination with destruction. One story tells of a young man who must sell himself to a female gangster. In one scene, she lovingly washes his chest, then cuts his skin with a razor, saying, "Your skin is so beautiful, I just had to cut it." He responds, "For the first time, I feel I exist." Their relationship ends with a mutual suicide. She binds him and bleeds him to death, then takes poison. First, however, she says, "You must not kiss me until I am dead." The film ends with a flash of red as Mishima impales himself on his sword, committing ritual suicide. The character of Mishima is portrayed as so troubled and destructive that it is difficult to feel much empathy for him.

*Little Big Man* (1970) follows the life of Jack Crabbe as he wanders through the American frontier during the 1880s. Jack's parents are killed when he is a child, and he is adopted by an Indian tribe. Later he is "rescued" and goes to live with Minister Pendrake's family. Mrs. Pendrake, his stepmother, takes a special interest in his spirituality as well as his flesh. After a beating from the minister, who attempts to beat the devil out of the boy, Mrs. Pendrake decides on a different treatment, stating, "It is my Christian duty to give this boy a bath." He finds himself falling in love with his stepmother, but before long he finds her in the sack with Mr. Cain, the local pharmacist.

Jack leaves home, taking up with a snake oil salesman, but is tarred and feathered by his own sister. He tries his hand as a gunfighter, a businessman, a hermit, a drunk, and a scout for the cavalry, tracking his adopted people. Later in the film, we encounter Mrs. Pendrake again, this time as a prostitute. The fallen flower propositions Jack, saying, "I often had wicked thoughts about you; several times I almost gave in to temptation." Despite the sexual theme, this film is available on loan from a local public library.

What can we say about these films that present themes of female-male incest? First, there are similarities in the three characters who are portrayed as adults. They are troubled, alienated, and trapped in their own self-defeating behavior. Jack Crabbe, in *Little Big Man,* is frequently placed in situations where his alienation comes to the fore. In numerous scenes in the film, he narrowly escapes death in raids by hostile Indian tribes or the cavalry. He is shown engaging in many self-defeating behaviors, and at one point in the film is portrayed as an alcoholic.

Joe Buck, of *Midnight Cowboy,* is caught up in self-defeating behaviors as well, with only his fantasies of being a "hunk" compensating for his inadequacies. He attempts to work as a prostitute but fails miserably. Instead of becoming rich, as he planned, he loses all his possessions and is forced to live on the street.

Mishima's self-defeating behaviors appear as a result of his dissatisfaction with public response to his novels. The readers fail to grasp his philosophy. As a means of educating them, he amasses a private army and lays siege to a Tokyo police garrison. When the police cadets laugh at him, he commits suicide. Mishima is portrayed as exotic and talented but highly disturbed. He and his characters are shown in continual conflict with authority in particular and society in general.

Each of the three characters is presented as being a tragic figure with major character flaws. As with real-life male survivors who enter therapy, there is no recognition in the films that the sexual act was abusive. The films portray the victims later in life as troubled individuals but give no indication that their abusive childhood sexual experiences may be related to their dysfunction as adults. In none of the films does the man recover from the trauma. Overall, an audience viewing these three films would have a strong vicarious experience, but that experience would deliver a very sad message—that male incest survivors are a disturbed and dangerous group of people.

## A Review of Molestation Films

Child molestation appears in films in several different ways. *JoJo Dancer, Your Life Is Calling* shows the exposure of a young boy to a sexualized environment. Unwanted touching appears in *Tommy* and *Fanny and Alexander*, and *My Life as a Dog* features a young boy who is exposed to three types of molestation.

*JoJo Dancer, Your Life Is Calling* (1985), starring Richard Pryor, is the story of a black comedian recovering from a life-threatening burn suffered when a free-base pipe exploded. While on the operating table, his spirit leaves his body and examines scenes from his life. Visiting himself as a child, he finds young JoJo living with his parents and grandmother in their brothel. He befriends the prostitutes. The young boy watches as men arrive at the brothel for business. Peeking through a keyhole, JoJo sees his mother with one of her customers. Later, he sees another customer bounced out of the brothel for asking one of the girls to urinate on him and then roughed up for asking the same of the bouncer.

At one point, JoJo says, "Today at school, my teacher asked what my parents did. I lied; I didn't know what to say; I felt invisible." His adult alter-ego replies, "You did good, Joe." The film traces the rise of JoJo to stardom, his struggle with racism, and his decline into drug addiction. Throughout the film, JoJo is shown as a sad and depressed character, caught up in self-defeating behaviors. In this film, no connection is made between the molestation and JoJo's mental state.

*Fanny and Alexander* (1982) is Ingmar Bergman's rich and complex portrayal of life in a Swedish family at the turn of the century. The film, which received the Academy Award for Best Foreign Film, has been broadcast over Public Television in the United States. In *Fanny and Alexander*, Bergman's talent is in full force.

Family struggle is a central theme in this film. Alexander's father dies, and his mother is forced to remarry. A bitter conflict develops between the boy and his stepfather, a strict, religious man. Mother decides to flee her new husband, but he threatens court action that would take the children from her. Undaunted, mother has the children secreted away. In hiding, the boy meets an otherworldly character who reveals himself as Ishmael, Alexander's guardian angel. Speaking to Alexander, Ishmael says, "Perhaps we are the same person, with no limits. Perhaps we flow into each other and stream through each other." Ishmael gazes into the boy's thoughts and learns of his hatred for his stepfather. The angel decides to act, saying, "You have only one way to go, and I am with you; I merge into you. Don't be afraid; I am your guardian angel." The angel fondles Alexander. As the angel works his magic, an oil lamp overturns in the stepfather's house, and the flames quickly spread. The boy cries, "No, stop." But the angel replies, "It's too late." There are screams, the house catches fire, and the stepfather dies in the flames.

*My Life as a Dog* (1985), a Swedish comedy and winner of the Academy Award for Best Foreign Film, presents a bittersweet view of family life. In the film, Ingmar and his brother live with their mother, who is terminally ill with tuberculosis. Their father is away. The film follows the dissolution of the family and the boys' placement in new homes. In the move, Ingmar loses his one true confidant. Sickan, his dog, is put to sleep. Oddly, the film is a comedy, locating humor amid all this strife.

In the film, Ingmar is sexually abused three times. First, his older brother forces Ingmar to stick his penis in a wine bottle as a sex education demonstration for the neighborhood children. His penis gets stuck, and the bottle must be shattered. His injured penis gets bandaged as the watching children laugh. Later, while driving with his uncle, Ingmar is asked to look after an elderly, bedridden neighbor, Mr. Arvidsson. He is asked to read aloud to the old man. Mr. Arvidsson produces a catalog from beneath his pillow, and Ingmar reads the descriptions of women's undergarments as the old man leers. Near the close of the film, Ingmar develops a relationship with Britt, an older woman. She asks him to chaperone her as she poses in the nude for a randy artist, to prevent his propositioning her.

*Tommy* (1975), a rock opera by the British rock group The Who, includes a molestation scene set to music. Tommy, a deaf, dumb, and blind boy, is baby-sat by his Uncle Ernie. The uncle is a detestable character with a fetish for rubber. As the parents leave, Uncle Ernie begins his song: "Down go the bedclothes/Up with the nightshirt, and we/Fiddle about, fiddle about."

Later in the film, Tommy is sent to see the Acid Queen for his sexual initiation. In this encounter, the Acid Queen engulfs him, and he is given a druggy transfusion with giant hypodermic needles. But his deafness and blindness fail to improve. Despite the fifteen years of education and effort by the clinical community since this film was released, a recent prime-time concert of songs from *Tommy,* televised on the Fox Network, still featured the theme of molestation.

Molestation appears in other films as well. In *Rage* (1980), a convicted rapist, in the course of therapy, remembers a traumatic experience. As a child, he accompanied his father on a visit to a prostitute. Forced by his father to touch her, he developed a great deal of hostility toward women, which he acted out in rape.

*Fellini: Satyricon* (1970) shows three young men sleeping their way through the Roman Empire. Two of them compete for the affections of a young boy, who is their common lover. The fickle boy spurns both in favor of marrying an older man, a cyclops.

*A Chorus Line* (1985) includes the story of Paul, a dancer trying out for a role in a new production. The director presses Paul for information to fill in gaps in his resumé. Paul refuses to provide the missing information. Finally, Paul tells his story: As a child, he accompanied his father to Saturday matinees in the theaters of New York's Times Square. Sitting apart from his father, he was molested by other theater patrons. Paul describes his embarrassment and shame at being molested. He later begins his dancing career not on Broadway but in transvestite shows, where he plays the part of a woman.

The acts of molestation presented in the films reviewed in this section present a set of mixed messages. In *My Life as a Dog,* the three molestation incidents are played for laughs. In a recent showing in a small art theater, the audience howled with laughter when Ingmar's penis got stuck in the bottle, apparently ignoring the element of force presented by his brother. The audience howled again when Mr. Arvidsson asked the boy to read stimulating information from the catalog, again ignoring the element of force or trickery. When the boy accompanied Briit to protect her from the artist, peals of laughter again rang out as the boy became interested in Briit's body and sneaked onto the studio roof, accidentally falling through the skylight.

The scene with Uncle Ernie in *Tommy* also is presented as humorous. After the molestation scene, Tommy is shown with a shocked expression on his face, which seems to be a play for laughs as well.

The scene of Ishmael fondling Alexander in *Fanny and Alexander* elicited no laughter from the audience, nor was it designed to. As is the case with audiences in most Bergman films, they responded with all the solemnity of a congregation at church, even in the humorous parts of the film. Overall, the molestation scene passed without audience comment; they just overlooked it.

Paul's disclosure scene in *A Chorus Line* is painful to watch. The intense feelings he experienced as a boy surface in the telling but are suppressed just as quickly, as the dancer must prepare himself for the remainder of the audition. In a twist of plot, he loses his place on the cast after the grueling audition. In his victory dance, he tears a tendon in his knee and must withdraw from the production. *Rage* shows an adult telling a painful story of childhood molestation. In *JoJo Dancer,* the molestation appears lost in the flurry of trauma that the lead character discloses.

Overall, audiences viewing these films are exposed to a number of messages about molestation. These range from molestation as a humorous or neutral event in *My Life as a Dog, Fanny and Alexander, Satyricon, Tommy,* and *JoJo Dancer* to a more negative portrayal in *Rage* and *A Chorus Line.* Overall, audiences may underestimate the traumatic effects of child molestation.

## A Review of Sexual Initiation Films

Films that portray the sexual initiation of a young man by an older woman are perhaps the most popular of this genre. Although these films portray sexual acts that older women perpetrate against teenage boys, our cultural stereotypes will not allow us to say that these films portray sexual abuse. Instead, these stereotypes tell us that sexual abuse is something males do to females. Our cultural blinders come into play in mass-market films as well. The public is less tolerant of mass-market films in which a teenage girl is sexually initiated by an older man. Yet in most video rental outlets in the country, one can find films portraying the sexual abuse of boys scattered throughout the comedy and drama sections.

The behavior portrayed in these films often appears gentle, loving, and caring and certainly does not appear to be overtly abusive. As a group, these films challenge other stereotypes of sexual abuse as well. Males are shown as victims and females as perpetrators, which is contrary to our society's accepted ways of thinking. What decides the issue of sexual abuse, however, is the difference in age and power between the woman and the boy. In this society, adults have more power than children. Therefore, a child is not totally free to deny a request from an adult, even if the adult has requested sexual contact.

*The Last Picture Show* (1971) presents the complicated story of teenagers coming of age in a small Texas town and of a high-school student who sleeps with the coach's wife. *Summer of 42* (1971) tells the tale of young boys coming of age in a small New England resort community. In the course of the film, one of the teenage boys sleeps with an older married woman. This film closes as the narrator describes how the experience changed his life forever. The plot of *The First Time* (1969) revolves around three teenage boys who mistake Jacqueline Bisset for a prostitute. In *The Chapman Report* (1961), a "horny" housewife seduces a grocery boy.

*Class* (1980) presents the story of a troubled relationship between a teenage boy and a middle-age woman. In this film, Jonathan, a middle-class boy, attends prep school for his senior year. The adjustment to his new school is difficult. Because of his nervousness around girls, he is unable to get dates with coeds from the sister school. As his nervousness increases, he begins to make social blunders that threaten the social life of the entire school. Skip Burroughs, the boy's roommate, suggests that he knows the root of Jonathan's problems: "Jonathan, until you get laid, none of us are safe." Jonathan is sent to the city to lose his virginity. Claiming to be older, he goes to a singles bar. There he meets Ellen, played by Jacqueline Bisset, a gorgeous but troubled woman. She seduces him in a glass elevator, and they have a torrid romance.

Initially, Jonathan appears unready to meet the needs of a mature woman. Slowly he becomes more used to the intensity of the relationship, but his lover begins to make unrealistic demands. Complications arise when Jonathan goes home with his roommate for Christmas vacation, and he learns that his lover is Skip's mother.

After the holiday, Ellen begins telephoning Jonathan at school, jeopardizing his relationship with Skip. His grades begin to falter. He learns that his admission to college is in doubt. Jonathan and Ellen meet again at a hotel to talk and break it off. In the final scene of their relationship, Ellen confesses her real interest in him, shouting, "When I saw you in that bar, you were pathetic. You were just a fuck." The two of them then leap into the sack for one last fling.

While they are in bed, there is a knock at the door. Jonathan answers, and a group of students from his school, including Skip, rush in. Skip sees his mother in bed, confronts her, and storms out of the room.

The resolution of the film is surprising. Mother is sent away to a mental hospital, seeking a cure for her "neurotic disorder." Skip excuses Jonathan, and the two of them continue as friends. This represents a significant departure from the experiences of real-life abuse victims, many of whom are required to continue living in close contact with their perpetrators.

*Private Lessons* (1981), a film for the teenage market, portrays the sexual relations between a wealthy fifteen-year-old boy, Philly, and Miss Mallow, his housekeeper. Philly's father leaves on a business trip, instructing the boy, "You're the man of the house now. Don't do anything I wouldn't do." Miss Mallow makes her move on the boy. Soon the relationship is consummated when Miss Mallow entices Philly into her bathtub. But the relationship ends just as quickly when the housekeeper feigns death from heart failure while having intercourse with the boy. Telling Lester, his chauffeur, about Miss Mallow's demise, Philly is caught in a blackmail plot. He is told that he must come up with ten thousand dollars from his father's safe to dispose of Miss Mallow's body. After the obligatory car chase, we learn that Miss Mallow is alive but under the spell of the evil chauffeur. When the blackmail plot is exposed, Lester attempts to flee but is stopped by a detective. Searching Lester's closet, the investigator finds it filled with rubber garments and an inflatable sex doll.

The script of *Private Lessons* is filled with titillating language, double entendres, and sadomasochistic themes. Frequently, Philly is placed in situations in which he must discipline adults in his service. Men get a bad rap in the film as well. They are shown secretly engaging in their own perversions. Father calls home from a business trip and speaks to his son, who is embracing his housekeeper. On the other end of the phone, father is in bed with a young woman. Lester is into rubber and has a closetful of male pinup photos. *Private Lessons* is notable both for its exploitive themes and for the nudity and sexual situations to which the child actor was exposed during filming. A September 2, 1981 review of the film in *Variety* states, "*Private Lessons* should satisfy general audiences with its diversions of frequent nudity, softcore sex, dominant rock music score, and gags."

*Weird Science* (1985), another film for the teen market, is a silly remake of the Frankenstein legend. The film centers on Gary and Wyatt, two fifteen-year-old dweebs who manufacture a woman, Lisa, with a home computer. After a fling in the shower with their new playmate, the boys head out with her for a pub crawl. Sensing the boys' desperation, Lisa acts quickly to improve their status with their peers. She conjures up a pair of snazzy sports cars for them, parades with them around the shopping mall, and throws a party, inviting all the right kids. Gary and Wyatt cannot face the people at the party so they sneak away. They meet two teenage girls who are impressed with their style. As things get serious with the foursome, some bikers crash the party. Gary and Wyatt must assert their manhood by ordering the bikers to leave. The girls swoon, and true love comes at last. Lisa, ever the proper android, bows out of the film. This movie was recently broadcast during prime time on the Fox Network.

*Harold and Maude* (1971) is a love story that pushes the limits of human values and physiology. In this film, Harold, a teenager, finds true love with Maude, a seventy-nine-year-old free spirit played by Ruth Gordon. Harold, the misfit son of a wealthy family, has a troubled relationship with his mother, an engulfing society maven. Harold's two joys in life are attending funerals and staging elaborate mock suicides. While at a funeral, he meets Maude. The two of them fall in love, and Harold begins to loosen up. Not one for long commitments, however, Maude has other plans for herself. As Harold decorates for her eightieth birthday party, Maude takes a lethal dose of poison, preferring death to old age.

*The Tin Drum* (1979), a surrealistic parable about the rise of Naziism, is set in Poland during the 1930s. This film tells the story of Oskar, a boy who, at seven years of age, decides to stop growing. The boy's one interest in life is banging on his toy drum. When his mother dies from eating too much fish, his father hires a baby-sitter for him. Oskar's baby-sitter, a youngster herself, begins to have sex with the boy. Later, Oskar finds his father having sex with the baby-sitter. Father, surprised at the interruption, loses control, and the baby-sitter becomes pregnant. Oskar decides that the baby is his and decides to teach his own son how to stop growing.

One theme that is present in most sexual initiation films is that the sexually inexperienced male is an undesirable character. In losing his virginity, the young hero loses his undesirable traits and gains his manhood. *Weird Science* shows Gary and Wyatt troubled by self-doubt. The two also are the focus of teasing and practical jokes by their peers. As the affair with Lisa develops, they gain respect from their peers and their self-esteem improves.

In *Class,* before Jonathan has his affair with Ellen, his virginity endangers the social life of the entire school. His roommate, preparing for a masquerade party, orders Jonathan to gain experience. In an ironic twist, the roomie is dressed as Christ.

*Private Lessons* shows Philly, before his encounter with Miss Mallow, as an object of scorn. Female characters in the film frequently criticize him. In this film, Sherman, Philly's chubby friend, urges the cautious boy to hop in the sack with his housekeeper. As the story evolves, Philly becomes socially adept and receives much applause from Sherman.

Similarly, Harold's emotional reaction to his encounters with Maude appears positive. His depression, apparent before the relationship, clears. But what does she see in him? We can find the answer in the following scene: One day, the two lovers steal a young tree from a park—It was choking in the smog, says Maude—and transplant it in the forest. Similarly, Maude rescues Harold from the stifling climate of his home and, by her romancing the boy, sets him free. For decades, therapists have spoken of the healing power of relationships, but one must wonder whether this is what they had in mind.

Recalling Jarvie's (1978) description of reference group socialization as a function of film, many sexual initiation films are enough to make chills run up the spine. The message seems clear: Until a teenage boy becomes sexually active, he is an object of scorn. To achieve a higher standing among his peers, he must engage in sexual activity, which may be distasteful or risky but which is considered normal behavior.

## A Review of Rape Films

The subject of male rape was late to appear in the clinical literature, although Limbacher (1983) notes that the first male rape in a feature film was in the 1962 version of *Lawrence of Arabia*. The author states that "the act was lost on the great majority of the movie-going public because of its subtlety" (p. 37). The rape was edited out of the shorter videotaped version of the film.

Male rape appears in *Myra Breckenridge* (1970) in the guise of a physical examination performed by the vengeful Myra. Female perpetrators appear in *Fatal Attraction* (1987) and *The Graduate* (1967) as well. *Fortune and Men's Eyes* (1971) presents the brutality of rape among prisoners. *The Conformist* (1971) tells the tale of a homosexual man in fascist Italy who was raped as a boy by his chauffeur. *Short Eyes* (1977) focuses on the plight of a convicted child molester doing time in prison. Finally, when many moviegoers think of male rape, they think of *Deliverance* (1972).

*Deliverance* is an adventure film that received much critical acclaim and was nominated for three Academy Awards. It follows a series of violent incidents that occur while four men are canoeing in the mountains of Georgia. On the second day of their trip, two of the men—Ed, played by Jon Voight, and Bobby, played by Ned Beatty—encounter two mountain men who are armed. Ed is tied to a tree and cut with a hunting knife. Bobby is beaten, mounted like an animal, and, with the mountain man twisting his ear, ordered to "squeal like a pig." The squeals become more desperate as the rapist penetrates him.

At the end of the scene, the rapist, spent, stands guard while the second mountain man, eyeing Ed, says, "Looks like he's got a real pretty mouth, don't he?" Opening his fly, he moves toward Ed, who is still tied to the tree. The other two canoeists arrive at this point, and one shoots and kills the rapist. The other mountain man flees. Two other characters are killed in subsequent scenes.

At the close of *Deliverance,* Ed and Bobby must fabricate a story for the sheriff to cover up the deaths of the two mountain men. As the sheriff leaves, Bobby tells Ed, "I don't think I'll be seeing you for a while." Viewers ponder Bobby's fate. Does he overcome the trauma? Was he traumatized at all? At first, the film seems to provide few answers, but then the movie ends with a dream scene. The rapist's hand, now ghastly white, is shown floating to the surface of the water. The hand appears to be pointing, perhaps at his killer. As the terrified dreamer awakes, viewers find that the dreamer was not Bobby, the rape victim, but Ed, the one who was tied to a tree. In *Deliverance,* the greater trauma occurs not to the rape victim but to Ed, who was unable to prevent the act from occurring.

*Where's Poppa?* (1970) is a black comedy involving the antics of a senile woman, played by Ruth Gordon, and the disastrous effects of her actions on the love life of her son, a lawyer. Male rape occurs as a complication of the plot. The protagonist's brother is attacked by a group of hoodlums in the park. During the attack, he is held by the hoodlums and forced to rape a woman. The plot thickens when it becomes clear that that was no woman but a male cop patrolling the park dressed in drag. The brother is arrested.

The lawyer visits his brother in jail and explains the gravity of the situation. Things look grim indeed, but a guard approaches the cell and hands the rapist a bouquet of roses. The guard says, "You the guy who raped the cop in the park? Here, these are for you." The rapist reads the card and smiles, telling his brother, "I don't think I need your help anymore. These are from the cop I raped. 'Thank you for a wonderful evening.' He's not gonna press charges. He wants me to leave my name and phone number." The rapist, now misty-eyed, says, "No one ever sent me flowers before."

Overall, *Where's Poppa?* appears to gratify its audience, an audience that is tuned in to its cynical and sarcastic tone. The presentation of male rape is controversial from at least two perspectives. First, the rape is considered humorous. Second, the victim enjoys his rape and wants to make a date with the rapist, apparently making reference to the popular belief that males who have been raped may become homosexual. In the twisted logic supporting this stereotype, males in our society are responsible for protecting themselves. If a male fails to do so, then it is not the stereotype that is incorrect but the male victim, who is seen as less of a man. In our society, those who are less male are often labeled as homosexual.

What vicarious learning might occur from this film? Perhaps viewers learn that male rape is something to be taken lightly or that a man who is raped risks losing his manhood. In any case, this seems a strange topic for a comedy.

Two other films demand attention. Both films portray abusive sexual acts between a male and a female. In neither film are the two characters related. In both films, the male is an adult. Overall, the dynamics of the sexual experience appear to fit most closely the dynamics of acquaintance rape, but it is the male, not the female, who is raped.

*The Graduate* (1967) received Academy Award nominations for best picture, best actor, and best actress. The film was a smash hit. In a listing compiled by *Variety* in 1975, this film appeared as one of the twenty-five most financially successful films of all time. It is considered a comedy. *The Graduate* begins with Benjamin Bradshaw returning to his parents' home after a successful college career. The apple of his parents' eye, Benjamin is swept up in his alcoholic parents' social life. Fleeing one cocktail party in desperation, he is pursued by Mrs. Robinson, the wife of his father's business partner. She asks him to drive her home, and he does. Once at her house, she asks him to accompany her to her door and then inside, saying, "I don't feel safe until I get the lights on. I'm very neurotic." She offers him drinks, demanding that he stay until Mr. Robinson returns because she is afraid of being alone.

She invites him upstairs to view her daughter's portrait and then asks him to unzip her dress. To his surprise, she asks, "What are you scared of?" He says that he is not scared. She retorts, "Then why do you keep running away?" He accuses her of attempting to seduce him, and she asks, "Would you like me to seduce you? Is that what you're saying?" He tries to leave, but she demands that he bring her purse to her. He tries to leave the purse on the stairs, but she demands that he bring it to her daughter's bedroom. He places the purse on the daughter's bed. Mrs. Robinson, now naked, follows him into the room and locks the door.

Car tires squeal in the driveway, indicating that Mr. Robinson is home. Mrs. Robinson tells Benjamin, "If you won't sleep with me this time, call me up. We can make some kind of arrangement." Ben runs downstairs to the bar, arriving as Mr. Robinson enters through the front door. The older man is drunk, and he sits down to talk with Ben, advising him that he appears to be taking life too seriously and should go out and sow his wild oats.

Later, Ben phones Mrs. Robinson to arrange a meeting with her in a hotel room. When she arrives, he gets cold feet, saying, "Mrs. Robinson, I can't do this." She manipulates him, asking, "Can I ask you a personal question? Is this your first time?" Ben protests that it is not. Undaunted, she continues, "On your first time, you can expect to be a bit inadequate. Just because you're inadequate in one way doesn't mean . . ." Benjamin turns off the light and jumps into bed.

In a scene one month later, Ben and Mrs. Robinson are again at the hotel. Ben says, "Mrs. Robinson, do you think we could say a few words before hopping into bed this time?" Mrs. Robinson responds, "I don't think we have much to say to each other." The relationship declines, and Mrs. Robinson is nearly out of Ben's life when Elaine Robinson appears on the scene, just graduated from college. Ben's parents pester him to date the girl. His father says that it will be good for his business relationship with Elaine's father. Ben is terrified because Mrs. Robinson forced him to promise that he would never date her daughter. But the Bradshaws insist, and Ben must face the older woman's wrath. As the relationship between Ben and Elaine develops, Mrs. Robinson tries to end it, claiming that Ben raped her. The film ends with Ben marrying Elaine.

*Fatal Attraction* (1987) is a modern-day horror film, starring Glenn Close and Michael Douglas. The film traces a relationship that begins as a weekend affair between Dan, a lawyer, and Alex, a beautiful young woman he sees at a party and later encounters at a business meeting. After the meeting, Dan walks out into the rainy streets of New York City. Alex notices him on the street, and they talk. They decide to share a cab, but none is available. Dan suggests that they have a drink until the storm passes.

A drink becomes dinner, and over dinner Alex alludes to the possibility of their having an affair. Dan replies that he is happily married and not interested. When Dan asks why she has no date that evening, she says, "I did. I stood him up. That was the phone call I just made. . . . Does that make you feel good?" Again he puts on the brakes, bringing up his marriage and family. She says, "And you're here with a strange girl being a naughty boy." Dan responds, "I don't think having dinner is a crime, is it?" Alex retorts, "Can't say yet. I haven't made up my mind. . . . We were attracted to each other at the party; that was obvious. We're two adults; that's also obvious. Dan asks for the check, and they go to her place.

They spend the night and next day together. When he attempts to leave at the end of the day, she explodes, tearing his shirt. They argue, but he gathers up his things to leave. She approaches him with a sad expression, and he sees that she has slashed her wrists. As the days pass, she begins to harass him at work. He asks his secretary to intercept her calls, so Alex begins calling him at home in the middle of the night. He finally agrees to meet her one last time to discuss their problems. At the meeting, she announces that she is pregnant, plans to carry his baby to term, and has no intention of leaving him in peace. This is just the beginning of the horror story that follows.

The screenplay for *Fatal Attraction* is a masterpiece of ambiguity, which makes the film difficult to analyze. Who is abusing whom? Is Dan or Alex the victim? Are they in fact both "consenting adults" who understood the consequences of their actions when they entered the affair? If this is so, does that make them equally liable for their actions? To how great a degree does Alex's pregnancy influence the viewer's interpretation of the film? Would it be easier to identify the victim if Dan had lured Alex into the relationship instead of the other way around? The answer is probably yes because we are not used to seeing females as perpetrators.

Sarrel and Masters (1982) discuss a typology of females who molest adult men. One such category fits the abuse shown in these two films: "Dominant woman abuse, an aggressive sexual approach to an adult male that, without direct physical force, intimidates or terrifies the victim" (p. 119). In *Fatal Attraction* and *The Graduate,* Benjamin and Dan are raped by adult women. Although Sarrel and Masters use the term *molestation* in reference to these films, the dynamics seem to fit that of acquaintance rape. Mrs. Robinson and Alex Forrest both dominate their victims with the aggression of their approach. In both films, however, the women go on to use indirect means to carry out the seduction.

In *The Graduate,* Ben catches on to Mrs. Robinson's motives, asking her if she is trying to seduce him. She denies this, saying, "No, would you like me to seduce you?" In *Fatal Attraction,* Alex twists Dan's words. At one point, she poses a challenge to him, asking why he is having dinner with her if he is happily married. She then goes on to imply that she may be interested in spending the night with him. In a strange way, both Dan and Benjamin are set up by women who are masters of manipulation.

Three other films touch lightly on the topic of male rape. In each of these, the rapist is male. *Scum* (1979), originally made for British television, portrays the dreary life of juveniles in prison. In the course of the film, one inmate, a weak and troubled youth, is raped. Shortly after, he takes his own life by slitting his wrists. *Bad Boys* (1983) also portrays life in a prison for juveniles. In this film, the victim is killed by his attacker. And in *Come Back to the 5 and Dime, Jimmy Dean, Jimmy Dean* (1982), Cher plays a man who has undergone a sex-change operation. As the film progresses, we learn that Cher's character arrived at his decision to have surgery after being raped by another man.

Viewed as a group, perhaps the most striking characteristic of these films is the low level of sensitivity they present for the victim. In many films, male victims are shown as being at risk of becoming homosexual. In *Where's*

*Poppa?* the rape victim asks for the rapists' telephone number, apparently hoping to met him again. *Come Back to the 5 and Dime, Jimmy Dean, Jimmy Dean* presents a male rape victim who has undergone surgery to become a woman. In *The Conformist,* the lead character is homosexual because of a childhood rape (Limbacher 1983, 508).

In the films reviewed here, male rape victims are shown as having few if any emotional responses to rape. Writers from the clinical community report strong emotional reactions among male rape victims, including shock, guilt, self-blame, and depression. The male rape victims in these films do not seem that bothered. In *Deliverance,* for example, shortly after Bobby is raped, the rapist is killed. Because of the murder, the focus of the film switches from the rape to surviving the rapids on the remaining stretch of river, surviving the sniper fire, and avoiding ending up in jail for the killings. The rape becomes just one of the terrible events that must be forgotten.

In *Where's Poppa?* the rape victim describes the event as a "wonderful evening," leading viewers to doubt whether he suffered much from the rape. In *Bad Boys,* the rape victim has little time to feel anything because he is done in by his attacker. In *Scum,* the rape victim is troubled after the rape, but he was troubled before the rape as well, so the filmmaker's position remains unclear. Does he slash his wrists as a result of the rape or as a result of a pre-existing pathology? No one knows. In *The Graduate,* Benjamin is troubled by Mrs. Robinson's actions but paralyzed when with other characters in the film. The trouble he feels seems worth the sexual contact with Mrs. Robinson.

In the films reviewed here, the victimized man must not disclose the rape. In *Fatal Attraction,* the rape occurs in the context of an affair. When Dan reveals his experience to his wife, she orders him out of the house. In *The Graduate,* Benjamin's parents notice his brooding after he begins sleeping with Mrs. Robinson, but Ben refuses to talk about it. This is understandable, since he has been sleeping with the wife of his father's business partner. In *Deliverance,* the rape must be kept quiet because of the danger to the campers if the killings are discovered. Recalling Jarvie's (1978) analysis of how films function for the audience, the films described here certainly present a negative example of male victims disclosing their abuse experiences. Overall, the vicarious learning from male rape films closely resembles the experience of real-life survivors: You have not been hurt, keep quiet about what has happened to you, and if you tell, there will be no one to help you.

## Three Films about Female Survivors

Although this chapter is about the treament of male rape and abuse victims in films, three films about female survivors demand discussion. *Nuts* (1987) presents the story of Claudia Kirk, a prostitute played by Barbra Streisand. Claudia is imprisoned while awaiting a hearing to determine her mental fitness to stand trial. She is accused of stabbing one of her customers in her bathroom. Her attorney, played by Richard Dreyfuss, is fascinated as he learns more about his client, wondering how an intelligent woman from a proper family could end up as a prostitute and murderer. As the film progresses, we learn more about Claudia's relationship with her father. The child would lock herself in the bathroom, and her father would pass money under the door to bribe her into letting him in. He would bathe her prior to having sex with her. The man she stabbed in her bathroom had insisted on bathing her. Claudia murdered her client while having a flashback and is excused of the murder charges.

*The Accused* (1988) tells the tale of a rape trial. A young woman named Sarah, played by Jody Foster, is gang-raped in a tavern. Three men are accused of having raped her while many other men stood cheering them on. The defense informs the prosecution that Sarah has a criminal record, is of questionable character, and was intoxicated at the time of the rape. In the course of the trial, the charges of the three men are reduced in a plea-bargaining arrangement. Although the three are found guilty of the lesser charges, Sarah is enraged. Later, a witness of the rape begins to harass her. She confronts the female attorney who prosecuted her case, and with the now contrite attorney's aid, she files charges against the men who cheered on the rapists. She wins this case.

*The Color Purple* (1985) is the story of Celie, a black woman living in the South. Incest, poverty, racism, sexism, and domestic violence are problems with which Celie and the other women in the film must contend. As the male characters become weaker, the women become stronger. The film ends on a positive note, as Celie is reunited with her sister, who had been in Africa working as a missionary. The two of them embrace in a field of purple flowers.

Three themes are apparent in these films: relationship, insight, and forgiveness. The three films about female rape and incest victims all include a character who believes in the victim despite her problems. In *The Accused* and *Nuts,* these relationships occur with the victims' lawyers. In *The Color Purple,* these relationships occur with multiple characters, all of whom are female. Also, in films in which a female is victimized, viewers generally have more insight into the effects of the trauma on her life. In these three films, the victims' current behaviors make sense in the context of what we know about their past. The theme of forgiveness comes into play at the end of the films, as the victims receive redress for their grievances and are excused for any wrongs they may have committed.

Compare the character treatment in *The Accused, The Color Purple,* and *Nuts* with the character treatment in *Deliverance, Midnight Cowboy, JoJo Dancer,* and *Mishima.* In the films about female survivors, relationships play an important role in the healing process. In the films about male survivors, there is no similar theme. *Deliverance* ends with the severing of a relationship, as Bobby tells Ed that he does not wish to see him for a while. *Mishima* presents sadistic and troubled relationships that offer no solace to the hero. *JoJo Dancer* presents troubled and violent relationships as well. *Midnight Cowboy* focuses on the relationship between Joe and Ratso, but Ratso dies of consumption, and Joe is abandoned once again. In none of these films is there another character who offers support to the male survivor.

In the films about male abuse, viewers are given little insight into how trauma in the past may cause present dysfunction. In *Midnight Cowboy,* Joe Buck is caught up in offending behaviors. Themes of incest and rape are present in the film, but the presentation is so subtle that even professional reviewers failed to notice. With *Mishima* and *JoJo Dancer,* adult dysfunction and childhood sexual trauma are both present, but no connection is made. The films portraying male survivors focus on the pathology of the survivor, whereas in the films portraying female survivors, these characters are objects of empathy despite their pathology.

Forgiveness is not present in *Deliverance, Midnight Cowboy, JoJo Dancer,* or *Mishima.* In *Deliverance,* the film ends before there is a resolution of Bobby's trauma—that is, if we assume that he was harmed. *Midnight Cowboy* ends with Joe being abandoned once again, as has happened three times previously in the film. Joe's burden becomes heavier, not lighter. *JoJo Dancer* and *Mishima* present characters who are driven, not forgiven. Clearly, there is gender bias in the treatment of male and female victims in rape and incest films.

## Discussion

This chapter has reviewed films that portray male rape, molestation of male children, and intercourse between teenage boys and adult women. What may be said collectively of the films?

In the films of male survivors of rape and sexual abuse, there is no presentation of a recovery process. For an audience that attends films for vicarious learnings, such portrayals are crucial, and their absence represents a serious omission on the part of filmmakers. In the films reviewed here, nothing legitimizes the struggle faced by male survivors. As stated previously, films such as *Nuts, The Color Purple,* and *The Accused* legitimize issues of female survivors.

In other films reviewed here, male survivors are shown engaging in antisocial behaviors. Three films show male victims becoming perpetrators. In *Midnight Cowboy,* Joe, a survivor of both incest and rape, is shown as a prostitute. *Rage* portrays a convicted rapist who was molested as a child. *Murmur of the Heart* ends with Laurent attempting to force himself on a teenage girl. Other characters are shown with different aberrations. Oskar, in *The*

*Tin Drum,* tries to control his abusive environment by stopping his growth and remaining the size of a seven-year-old forever. He decides to pass on his strange disorder to the son that he—or possibly his father—sired. *Mishima* portrays a floridly disturbed character who has both a fascination with death and confusion regarding his sexual orientation. *Little Big Man* traces the life of Jack Crabbe before, while, and after he is bathed by his stepmother. Later in life, he is shown as being alienated from society, engaging in many self-defeating behaviors, and being severely alcoholic for a period of time. Finally, the lead character in *JoJo Dancer* is shown involved in drugs, alcohol, and wife beating. Judging from the movies, male survivors are not a nice group of people.

The films reviewed here present a distorted view of the emotional reactions of male victims of rape or sexual abuse. Research and clinical work during the past two decades have generated volumes of information regarding the rape or sexual abuse experience and its effects on the emotional life of the victim. In the films reviewed here, few emotional reactions were noted, and most that were noted failed to fit the context of emotional response patterns reported in clinical works. *Deliverance,* for example, presents the story of a brutal rape occurring to a middle-age man. As previously mentioned, the film fails to portray his emotional reactions. In *Fanny and Alexander,* Alexander's emotional reactions are not shown. With the stepfather dead, the plot can move in other directions.

Three other films present positive emotional reactions to abuse. The first is *Murmur of the Heart,* which has already been discussed. *Fellini: Satyricon* presents a precocious adolescent who is happily passed off between two male lovers. And *Where's Poppa?* portrays a male rape victim who has a positive reaction to his experience.

*Tommy* depicts some mild emotional reactions of the victim. Shortly after Tommy is molested, he is shown with a shocked expression. Not one to waste time on emotions, however, he quickly sets out to form a new church based on pinball. *Little Big Man* also shows an adolescent Jack Crabbe with a shocked expression as his stepmother bathes him. No other such reactions are shown in the film. *Mishima* portrays the lead character as a child sniffling back tears after being forced to massage his grandmother's legs. His reactions, along with those of Jack Crabbe and Tommy, are milder than would be expected.

In none of these films does the victim have more than a brief emotional reaction to the sexual abuse or rape. Emotional reactions of male victims presented in the films reviewed here are seriously distorted when compared to those of real-life victims. Real-life viewers with vulnerabilities in this area may be seriously misinformed by film treatment of male affective issues resulting from rape or sexual abuse.

Perhaps one of the most striking omissions from this group of films is a discussion of the pathology of females who seek gratification with younger men. With most of the attention in these films directed toward the dysfunction of the male character, the pathology present in the female perpetrator has remained in the background. Perhaps this is understandable because most of these films present the sexual abuse and rape as normal behavior and there can be no perpetrator if the behavior is normal. However, further analysis should be directed at this area.

In conclusion, the films reviewed here present negative role models of males who have been raped, molested, or sexually abused as children. Men are shown as having few if any emotional responses to sexual abuse. Sexual contact between teenage boys and adult women is presented as a positive experience. Male survivors of childhood abuse are presented as unlikable individuals. Teenage boys also are presented as unlikable until they engage in sexual activities, which may be painful or risky. Male rape victims are presented as being at risk of becoming homosexual. And finally, in several cases, sexual assault is presented as humorous.

The films reviewed here portray sexual acts that may be outside the mainstream of experience. If the primary function of a film is to provide gratification for the audience, then adding some spice to the mix with a few strategically placed sexual scenes should cause no harm. But what of individual viewers who purchased their tickets with other expectations or vulnerabilities? What of those members of the audience who lack insight into ways to behave in situations that are difficult or unknown to them? What of viewers who misunderstand the intent of most films and respond to one that was created to gratify the audience as if it were created to educate? This may be where things go awry.

In response to the negative stereotypes presented in these films, the clinical community may need to teach men who are recovering from sexual abuse to disregard and otherwise challenge these negative portrayals. Education on a broad scale needs to occur for the general public as well to dispel negative sterotypes. And, finally, Hollywood needs to become more sensitive about the portrayal of injured men. A man who was molested as a child or raped as an adult does not need to be traumatized again while viewing a film.

# References

Finkelhor, David. 1984. *Child Sexual Abuse: New Theory and Research*. New York: Free Press.

Forward, Susan, and Craig Buck. 1978. *Betrayal of Innocence: Incest and Its Devastation*. Los Angeles: J.P. Tarcher, Inc.

Geiser, R.L. 1979. *Hidden Victims: The Sexual Abuse of Children*. Boston: Beacon Press.

Haskell, Molly. 1974. *From Reverence to Rape: The Treatment of Women in the Movies*. Chicago: University of Chicago Press.

Hirsch, Foster. 1975. "Midnight Cowboy." In *Sexuality in the Movies,* edited by Thomas R. Atkins. Bloomington: Indiana University Press.

Jarvie, I.C. 1978. *Movies as Social Criticism: Aspects of Their Social Psychology.* Metuchen, New Jersey: Scarecrow Press.

Keyser, L. 1975. "Sex in the Contemporary European Film." In *Sexuality in the Movies,* edited by Thomas R. Atkins, 172–190. Bloomington: Indiana University Press.

Limbacher, James L. 1983. *Sexuality in World Cinema.* Metuchen, New Jersey: Scarecrow Press.

Rogers, C., and T. Terry. 1984. "Clinical Intervention with Boy Victims of Sexual Abuse." In *Victims of Sexual Aggression: Treatment of Children, Women, and Men,* edited by Irving R. Stuart and Joanne G. Greer, 91–104. New York: Van Nostrand Reinhold.

Sarrell, P., and W. Masters. 1982. "Sexual Molestation of Men by Women." *Archives of Sexual Behavior* 11: 117–131.

## Bibliography

Atkins, Thomas R. *Sexuality in the Movies.* Bloomington: Indiana University Press, 1975.

Considine, David M. *The Cinema of Adolescence.* Jefferson, North Carolina: McFarland, 1985.

Cypert, Joseph K. "Cinematic Depiction of Child Maltreatment." Master's thesis, University of Texas at Arlington, 1986.

Finkelhor, David. *A Sourcebook of Child Sexual Abuse.* Beverly Hills, California: Sage Publications, 1986.

Groth, A.N., and A. Burgess. "Male Rape: Offenders and Victims." *American Journal of Psychiatry* 137 (1980): 7.

Hunter, Mic. *Abused Boys: The Neglected Victims of Sexual Abuse.* Lexington, Massachusetts: Lexington Books, 1990.

Kaufman, Arthur. "Rape of Men and the Community." In *Victims of Sexual Aggression: Treatment of Women, Children, and Men,* edited by Irving R. Stuart and Joanne G. Greer, 156–179. New York: Van Nostrand Reinhold, 1984.

Lew, Mike. *Victims No Longer: Men Recovering from Incest and Other Sexual Child Abuse.* New York: Nevraumont Publishing Company, 1988.

Miller, Alice. *The Drama of the Gifted Child: The Search for the True Self.* New York: Basic Books, 1981.

———. *Thou Shalt Not Be Aware: Society's Betrayal of the Child.* New York: Meridian Books, 1986.

Palmer, William J. *The Films of the Seventies: A Social History.* Metuchen, New Jersey: Scarecrow Press, 1987.

Porter, Eugene. *Treating the Young Male Victim of Sexual Assault: Issues and Intervention Strategies.* Syracuse, New York: Safer Society Series, 1986.

Sender, J. "Male Rape: The Hidden Crime." *Changing Men: Issues in Gender, Sex, and Politics* no. 19 (1988): 20–21.

Stuart, Irving R., and Joanne G. Greer, eds. *Victims of Sexual Aggression: Treatment of Children, Women, and Men.* New York: Van Nostrand Reinhold, 1984.

Woods, Sally Cook, and Kathryn Self Dean. "Implications of the Findings of the Sexual Abuse of Males Research." Paper presented at the Child Welfare League of America's Southern National Conference, Gatlinburg, Tennessee, 1985.

## Filmography

*The Accused.* 1988. Jonathan Kaplan, director.

*Bad Boys.* 1983. Richard Rosenthal, director.

*The Chapman Report.* 1961. George Cukor, director.

*A Chorus Line.* 1985. Richard Attenborough, director.

*Class.* 1980. Lewis John Carlino, director.

*The Color Purple.* 1985. Steven Speilberg, director.

*Come Back to the 5 and Dime, Jimmy Dean, Jimmy Dean.* 1982. Robert Altman, director.

*The Conformist.* 1971. Bernardo Bertolucci, director.

*The Damned.* 1969. Luchio Visconti, director.

*Deliverance.* 1972. John Boorman, director.

*Fanny and Alexander.* 1982. Ingmar Bergman, director.

*Fatal Attraction.* 1987. Adrian Lyne, director.

*Fellini: Satyricon.* 1970. Frederico Fellini, director.

*The First Time.* 1969. James Nielsen, director.

*Fists in the Pocket.* 1965. Marco Belocchio, director.

*Flesh and Blood.* 1979. Made for TV, director unknown.

*Fortune and Men's Eyes.* 1971. Harvey Hart, director.

*The Graduate.* 1967. Mike Nichols, director.

*Harold and Maude.* 1971. Hal Ashby, director.

*JoJo Dancer, Your Life Is Calling.* 1985. Richard Pryor, director.

*The Last Picture Show.* 1971. Peter Bogdanovich, director.

*Lawrence of Arabia.* 1962. David Lean, director.

*Little Big Man.* 1970. Arthur Penn, director.

*Luna.* 1979. Bernardo Bertolucci, director.

*Midnight Cowboy.* 1968. John Schlesinger, director.

*Mishima: A Life in Four Chapters.* 1985. Paul Schrader, director.

*Murmur of the Heart.* 1971. Louis Malle, director.

*My Life as a Dog.* 1985. Lasse Hallstrom, director.

*Myra Breckenridge.* 1970. Michael Sarne, director.

*My Sister, My Love.* 1966. Vilgot Sjoman, director.

*Night Games.* 1966. Mai Zetterling, director.

*Nuts.* 1987. Marti Ritt, director.

*Private Lessons.* 1981. Tony Wade, director.

*Rage.* 1980. William Graham, director.

*Scum.* 1979. Alan Clarke, director.

*Short Eyes.* 1977. Robert M. Young, director.

*Summer of '42.* 1971. Roy Mulligan, director.

*Through a Glass Darkly.* 1962. Ingmar Bergman, director.

*The Tin Drum.* 1979. Volker Schlondorff, director.
*Tommy.* 1975. Ken Russell, director.
*Weird Science.* 1985. John Hughes, director.
*Where's Poppa?* 1970. Carl Reiner, director.

# 3
# Victim Advocacy and Young Male Victims of Sexual Abuse: An Evolutionary Model

*Fran Sepler*

T he founding principles of victimology are hardly relics of the past. A science and practice of only the past twenty years, the focus on victimization as a primary problem has risen meteorically on the landscape of mental health and criminal justice (Young 1986). This chapter proposes that, despite the enormous progress and huge advances of current victimology, the journey to competence is not even halfway completed. As individuals who cared passionately about the plight of female victims were forced to break through oppressive and stereotypical thinking, suffering derisive and sometimes cruel treatment and bearing the scorn of the majority, the same must now be done for male victims, particularly adolescent male victims.

## A Historical Perspective

Victim advocacy emerged from the dual political influences of the feminist movement and the civil rights movement. From a base of recognition that women who had been raped were not only victims of a physical violation but also were suffering the impact of concentrically delineated imbalances of power and equity grew a movement, a philosophy, and, later, a set of services that have gradually been applied beyond the rape of adult women to victims of crime in general (Brownmiller 1975; Barry 1979).

The theoretical foundations and operational assumptions of the rape crisis movement and the victims' rights movement have long been strongly sociopolitical in nature. It is only a recent development that more scientific and clinical findings have been applied to providing victims with respectful crisis intervention, advocacy, and short-term counseling. It is important to recognize that it was, in fact, the institutional demand for empirical research and diagnostic findings to which the victims' movement was intended to serve as a prevailing counterforce. As such, the rape crisis movement matured cloaked in the language and culture of feminism, social change, and political activism.

With an underlying goal of empowerment, the rape crisis movement sought to create and maintain a safe and supportive environment for women to join together in order to diffuse their pain, to provide and receive validation through sharing the experience of rape, and to process their anger at the individual who raped them and the society that fostered such conduct through oppressive norms. As the number of women reporting rapes grew, largely in response to the increasing visibility of the antirape movement, sexual assault programs became a source of strength and identity for rape victims. Trained advocates accompanied women through the police questioning and hospital examination and demanded dignity, respect, and responsiveness to the women's wishes. Support groups provided a safe environment to heal the wounds of victimization. Gradually, rape crisis centers expanded their services to encompass adult and then child victims of sexual assault in families.

The victim services movement grew from the efforts of women who wanted to help and empower other women, who were committed to societal change, and who strongly believed that the societal myths and misconceptions about rape (that it is provoked by the victim, that it is sexually enjoyable for the victim, and that it is largely an invention of disturbed women) are part of a larger, systematic oppression of women. Rape crisis centers and their subsequent offspring stem from the notion of a safe haven for and by women, isolated from the elements of the "second assault" wrought by an insensitive, unresponsive system (Holmes and Williams 1981).

What ultimately became apparent to individuals in the rape crisis movement was that the issues of devaluation, iatrogenic intervention, and victim blaming were not unique to women who had been raped but also applied to victims of incest and domestic violence. The ontological experience of victimization bridging personal pain and societal oppression lent itself to a paradigm of male power serving to maintain women in a submissive role, with rape and other forms of violent conduct being a primary weapon in the arsenal of oppression (Brownmiller 1975). Rather than alienating the larger culture, however, much of the programmatic structure emerging from this thinking was adapted for mainstream implementation. Many of the principles and practices pioneered by the women in rape crisis centers became generic to programs sponsored by the very criminal justice system that rape crisis centers had been developed to counteract (Herrington and Russell 1982).

## Who Are the Victims?

### The Feminization of Victimization

As rape was a feminist issue, violence, the central ideological core of rape crisis thinking about rape, came to be viewed as an exclusive province of male culture. Violence has been viewed as a manifestation of power and control, as early sexual assault manuals illustrate:

> The primary motive displayed by most convicted rapists is aggression, dominance and anger, NOT sex. Sex is used as a weapon to inflict violence, humiliation and conquest on a victim. . . .
> Sexual assault is an act of power and violence expressed through sexual aggression. (Bellinger 1986, 57)

Sexual assault has been isolated as the most serious and harmful extension of the commonplace subjection of women by men (Sanday 1981; McKinnon 1979; Russell 1974).

Increasing public and professional awareness of child sexual abuse in the 1970s presented only a small challenge to the ideological and systematic framework for victims of sex crimes. There was a remarkable surge in the number of individuals reporting incest. At first, the victims were primarily adult incest victims abused by their fathers during childhood. Often this historical reporting would be triggered by a more recent act of violence. As such cases became more familiar, it was generally accepted that father-daughter incest was a reprehensible permutation of adult rape and that the view of sexual crimes as sexual violence perpetrated by males against females could continue to serve as the prevailing frame of reference for intervention (Butler 1979; Forward and Buck 1979). As Keller (1976) notes, "Most reported cases of child sexual abuse involve adult men and young girls. When young boys are exploited, they are usually the victims of adult men. Research indicates that over 90% of offenders are male" (p. 115).

As a matter of either evolution or philosophical dogmatism, victimization, and the symptoms and responses to victimization, have been largely defined from the perspective of the adult female rape victim. The training and orientation of victim service counselors and advocates focus on the very real needs for crisis intervention, physical safety, gaining or regaining a sense of control, and dealing with the issues of shame, guilt, powerlessness, and anger, which have been found to be important in adult female rape victims' being able to integrate the victimization experience into their lives. Victims have been urged to reframe their experience and to think of themselves as survivors of an ordeal. The overall dynamics of empowerment and validation prevail as critical elements in recovery from a sexual assault. The unequivocal reinforcement of the blamelessness of the victim is accompanied by practical assistance and expression of appropriate anger.

## From Specific to Generic: The Client Pool Expands

In the early 1980s, the flurry of research on sex offenders that had been prompted by increased concern for victims of sexual abuse began to produce results. A thread that ran throughout much of the data generated concerning offenders was a history of sexual victimization.

Increasingly, treatment professionals were seeing families in which male siblings of females brought to treatment for victimization also were victims. Those dealing with adolescent males who were referred to mental health counseling due to school problems and those dealing with juvenile delinquents, as well as those providing services to mentally disabled male children, reported increasing numbers of clients who had histories of sexual abuse and assault by adults (Knopp 1985; Groth 1985).

The model for defining victimization that has been used by rape and sexual assault service providers rapidly breaks down when juvenile male victims disclose prior sexual contact with adults. Many of their stories involve repeated or prolonged sexual contact with age-mates or "seductions" by adults, without a clear sense on the part of the child that victimization had taken place. In many cases, juvenile males are known to intervenors as aggressors, and victimization is discounted or minimized in lieu of an immediate focus on the current aggressive acts. Increasingly, in fact, male victims, both juvenile and adult, are identified to the justice and mental health system as sexual aggressors rather than victims.

Unlike the programs for adult and child female victims, there has been no clearly appropriate crisis or advocacy program model developed or implemented for the unique needs of young male victims. Males have generally borne the mantel of offender in the rape crisis movement. While there have been efforts to expand the model to allow for male victims, the model itself is based on a sociopolitical assumption of a vast power differential between genders—a schism that does not close in response to a male's being victimized. Despite various attempts to accommodate male victims, rape crisis programs have often alienated, tokenized, or rejected them. An essential lack of comprehension, a high level of mistrust and suspicion, and a paucity of readily available literature results in a serious service shortfall to the young male attempting to cope with sexual abuse.

The reality is that young male victims, particularly early postpubertal males, experience the victimization from an entirely different self-view and worldview than do female victims (Jacklin and Maccoby 1974). While the youngest male victims may not be gender-specific in their response to the victimization, early socialization and the cultural rites of passage that accelerate as young males near puberty clearly create different means of cognition, perception, behavior, and sexuality. Issues of violence and control may be central, but the core of the crisis precipitated by the victimization most likely is entirely distinct from a similar victimization experienced by a female. As such, it may be unresponsive to, or further precipitated by, a program model that assumes universality when it comes to sexual victimization.

## Barriers to a Broader Model of Victimization

*Language: The Myth of the Survivor*

The subjective experience of a male victim is decidedly different from that of a female victim. In many cases, the duration and nature of sexual encounters between a male child and his perpetrator bear the external trappings of consensual contact. Like a veil, the notion of consent conceals the underlying coercion and manipulation experienced by the victim. Loss of control, or being overpowered, a familiar theme of girls and women who have been sexually abused, may be emotionally inaccessible or inapplicable to male victims. The dynamic of vulnerability lies outside the emotional vocabulary of many "normal" males. It is in terms of the very nature of sexual assault that the language and rhetoric of victim services must be assessed.

In the course of developing a model and services for sexual abuse and assault victims, the term *survivor* has been used, and receptive references to the experience, such as "being hurt" as part of the assault or "having something taken away," are common, as are general references to "feeling powerless." These seemingly innocuous terms can have tremendously confounding effects for a male victim attempting to sort out the reality of his experience. The existential reality of sexual victimization for a male victim may well be a sense of ownership and participation. Sorting out the victimization from a male perspective may include a recognition of the fact that powerlessness is less a part of the dynamic than an almost reflexive adaptation to and integration of the victimization.

Because men and boys in our society are raised and socialized with a premium emphasis on mastery of self, environment, and others, it is unlikely that when males are confronted with a situation beyond their control, they will respond by acknowledging or acceding to the powerlessness (Goldstein 1987). It also is unlikely that, upon even the remotest recollection, males will view themselves as victims in the feminine sense of the word. Rather, many, if not most, young male victims will quickly make and then reinforce the psychological, physical, or social adjustment that leads them to emulate consent or volition. The cultural and psychological framework is reinforced by adaptive behavior. Leveraging through extortive tactics, accommodating the abuse in order to resolve the dissonance of the experience, turning the victimizing experience into a perceived aggressive relationship, reenacting the behavior that victimized them against a vulnerable person, and focusing on material rewards define typical male responses to ongoing abuse.

While such accommodation is well documented in many female victims (Summit 1983), the depth of the accommodation and the intensity of the notion of mastery and control is a far more gender-specific response for male victims than female victims and should be expected. These responses, including the aggressive acting out against another, are likely responses to adolescent male victimization. They cannot be extinguished by a denial that they are a normative response to victimization, nor are they less worthy of attention, support, timely intervention, and advocacy.

When a male victim is told that he was powerless or that the abuse was a form of violence, this information is likely to reinforce a proclivity to alienation. Neither powerlessness nor violence makes sense to a male victim who has accommodated the sexual abuse by adopting a pseudoconsensual posture or by reciprocating with aggressive acts. In fact, many male victims identify themselves as quite powerful as an ongoing, sexually exploitive relationship develops and find that their first level of resolution must involve their own view of themselves as exploitive, abusive of power, and overly controlling (Finkelhor 1984). It is on these terms that male victims will more readily begin to expose their experience.

## Sexism

It is important to note that the very societal oppression that leads to a gender-specific model of victimization and victim recovery sets up the male victim accommodation described above. The expansion of functional definitions of the experience of victimization defies stereotypical assumptions about male vulnerability and the way responses to victimization should exhibit themselves. The general framework for victimization, laden with painful affect, powerlessness, shame, and self-blame, reflects a societal bias toward the female experience of victimization and casts doubt and skepticism on the manifestations of victimization that are natural for male victims.

It is ironic that stereotypic expectations of males, gender-specific child-rearing practices, and social stereotypes not only form the context for the male response to victimization but also serve to devalue, discredit, or mislabel those responses, often leading to a denial of the entire dynamic. It is, unfortunately, more comfortable to deal with an aggressive affect in terms of a female victim–male offender paradigm, in which the aggressive male victimizes the vulnerable female, than to recognize that aggression and antisocial conduct are viable and predictable male responses to victimization and that the disruption and damage is comparable to that suffered by a female victim. For individuals who have dedicated their lives to advancing the lot of the female victim, it is uncomfortable to share the notion of oppression with males who are forced and programmed to respond to victimization in this way. The capacity of professionals concerned about victims to expand their understanding of oppression is pivotal. Until these professionals can embrace and empathize with the diversity of gender responses to abuse and exploitation, the notion of an inclusive concept of victimization may be beyond our reach.

## The Outsider Inside: Conceptual Issues in Services to Male Victims

### Escaping Stereotypes

If male victims are to be adequately served in the model of advocacy, self-help, and voluntary counseling, the professionals who serve victims and the larger society face a new challenge in framing victimization and the scope of appropriate responses to it. The elimination of a male offender–female victim paradigm must be coupled with a radical broadening of the notion of victim. The male victim, if he is to be dealt with in archetypal form, looks nothing like the sympathetic, traumatized, and vulnerable victim that the public recognizes but may instead appear aggressive, violent, masterful, commanding, and threatening. These postures are the socially determined means for males to accommodate victimization, and they challenge service providers who must focus on creating new definitional and functional models for advocacy and assistance.

A victim service provider dealing with an adult female victim may devote substantial time to helping the victim get in touch with anger and rage about the abuse. Male victims, however, may present *only* anger as a generalized affect, making the process of focusing or recognizing anger a fruitless or even self-defeating exercise. Acceptance of a broader definition and conceptual framework of victimization forces significant public education and public relations requirements on victim services. It is only prudent to recognize that the extent of such requirements is likely to be staggering and, in some cases, nearly prohibitive.

### Identifying the Male Victim

In many cases, males who have been victimized view themselves as initiators or offenders. A victim service center will have little meaning to many adolescent victims who are seeing themselves more as (in ascending order of likelihood) willing participants, aggressors, offenders, delinquents, or criminals. It is imperative that those who intend to serve victims of sexual abuse approach such service by dealing with male victims in their reality. Beckoning to victims will net a response from only the small numbers of males who might benefit from intervention, and that response is most likely to be facilitated by court order or some other form of involuntary induction.

Real outreach to male victims may require broad-based educational efforts and focused education of young males. Efforts to raise public awareness of the sexual abuse of males and the form it may take, as well as to acknowledge the likely response to such victimization, will not necessarily prompt large numbers of individuals who have experienced such victimization to seek services. They do, however, provide initial information to males who may later desire assistance, particularly in response to familial problems or problems in the criminal justice system. Such outreach will elicit voluntary self-identification from some victims who may seek assistance. Crucial to this outreach is a careful construction of the language and social framework in which it is cast. As discussed earlier, much of the rhetoric that now fits the currently acceptable notion of victimization is useless at best and counterproductive at worst. The challenge of developing a new language to communicate with adolescent males about their experiences is a major challenge in beginning to engage victimized and misused males.

If reliance on police reports and criminal justice involvement is a meager source of identification of female rape and sexual assault victims, it is doubly so for male victims. Often-cited estimates of unreported incidents of sexual assault illustrate the small population of victims reached through this avenue. Nevertheless, the justice system offers many legal and practical alternatives to crime victims, and male victims also require advocacy tailored to their needs.

Given the current, primitive model of the victimization of young males, and the behavior demonstrated by many of those victims, it is likely that early intervention could be facilitated by proper queries and programmatic interventions when young males are identified as acting out in a school or recreational setting. Given the slow progress of preventive intervention being adopted as a universally accepted precept in the public schools, as well as the urgency with which new program approaches are needed, it may well be that the most effective current means available for identifying male victims will come through existing intake processes for juveniles referred for correctional or mental health intervention for aggressive or delinquent conduct.

This observation is made in appreciation of the paradox that, as current conditions stand, it is only through societal identification of an individual as a perpetrator of aggressive conduct that we can begin to identify individuals who have been victimized. It is with equal irony that it is noted that once the label of perpetrator has been affixed to an individual, the challenge for victim service providers is to justify to the criminal justice and mental health systems that the individual is in need of advocacy, victim services, and the rights and status that the law may offer an individual as a victim of a crime (restitution, compensation, services, and so on).

A strong caveat must be offered at this point to clarify any confusion that might be engendered by the notion of using correctional or penal systems to identify victims. The identification of victims within the system of identified perpetrators must be careful and highly sensitive. Not all aggressive individuals are victims—a significant number are not (Hindman 1988)—and the distinctions can sometimes be quite difficult to make. It is the task of skilled professionals to glean from the correctional populations those individuals who have been arrested for acts of aggression but whose behavior masks long, strong, and formative histories of victimization. It is the opinion of many that the aggressive conduct of any individual must be extinguished prior to dealing effectively with the underlying victimization and that differential diagnostic techniques to isolate personality disorders, psychopathy, or mental illness must be part of the outreach effort. It is incumbent upon the professionals dealing with these individuals to develop rigorous diagnostic protocols that afford the individuals the best and most responsive treatment.

## The Round Peg in the Square Hole: Two Illustrative Case Histories*

"Joe," a fourteen-year-old male of Pacific Island heritage, is the second of three children. Both his parents have a history of chronic alcoholism and have been divorced, although repeatedly reunited and reseparated, since Joe was small. Joe lives with his biological mother, who has been involved in many relationships with men who have physically and sexually abused her and her children. The mother has a circle of women friends who also are abused, often by the same men.

At age five, Joe was sexually fondled by an adolescent female baby-sitter, who was the daughter of one of his mother's friends. He reported this incident to his mother, but she did not act on the information.

Joe developed a relationship at age eleven with a postpubertal female Caucasian, with whom he reported having sexual contact. His behavior in this situation was compliant, following specific instructions and responding to demands of this much older female.

At age twelve, Joe was repeatedly sexually fondled by his maternal uncle, and at age fourteen, he was forced to perform oral sex on an adult friend of his mother's. Joe reported each of these incidents to the authorities, but no legal action was taken.

Joe was left alone with, and responsible for the care of, a seven-year-old Pacific Island female neighbor for an extended period at age fourteen. During this time, he engaged in a single act of digital penetration and attempted, but failed, penile penetration. He described his behavior as impulsive and opportunistic. It was his only assaultive behavior, and it was reported. He was immediately placed in juvenile detention and remained there through an eight-week assessment period, followed by a referral into a sexual offender treatment program, where he was confronted regarding his assaultive behavior. Joe was adjudicated as a juvenile offender.

"Sam" is a seventeen-year-old white male with a long familial history of alcoholism, family violence, and drug abuse. When Sam was ten years old,

*Thanks to Paul Gerber, M.A., of PHASE for assistance in locating these examples.

his father was sent to prison for committing aggravated assault. His mother was a chronic alcoholic who was dependent on welfare. From the time Sam was small, he was forced to participate in sexually sadistic acts, including sexual performances with multiple partners and being tied to a post while he was sexually aroused by adults. When Sam's father was imprisoned, his mother treated him as a sexual partner, expecting him to participate in a sexual relationship on a regular basis. By the time Sam was eight, he was drinking regularly. By puberty, he was chronically drunk.

Sam was identified as an antisocial personality by the multiple correctional contacts he had as a result of repeated acts of vandalism, fighting, bullying, property offenses, and alcohol-related offenses and was repeatedly held in juvenile detention for those offenses. When Sam was seventeen, a worker in a juvenile detention center identified him as a victim and recommended that he be placed in a gender-specific victim treatment program. Despite Sam's history, it took months of advocacy for this de facto advocate to convince the probation authorities and the court to allow such intervention. This occurred more than five years after his initial referral to the juvenile justice system.

*A New Model of Advocacy*

Professionals serving victims as advocates, counselors, or support persons face a huge challenge in attempting to ascertain appropriate advocacy for male victims of sexual abuse. Advocacy that deals with victimization clearly differs from the legal advocacy of the courtroom. In victim services parlance, advocacy is empowerment. It involves defining choices and options and providing information and practical support to help the victim make and implement those decisions. Traditional victim advocacy breaks down into the following areas:

1.  Legal advocacy, ensuring that a victim is fully informed of his or her rights under the law and is able to insist on compliance with those rights, as well as support and clarity throughout the justice process

2.  Medical advocacy, which incorporates assurance of respectful forensic medical care and information regarding necessary testing and treatment for a wide range of sequelae of victimization

3.  Mental health and government advocacy, ensuring that the victim is treated fairly, without prejudice and bias, and according to nonstereotypical or prejudicial standards

Functionally, the standard elements of advocacy fit for male victims as well as for female victims, but the advocate faces enormously different barriers in terms of defining both the appropriate type of advocacy and the means of providing such advocacy. At present, advocacy for young male victims of sexual assault is generally limited to advocacy for young male children who require witness preparation, medical advocacy through forensic examinations, and other child advocacy methods. No literature or practice appears to be available to define a model of service advocacy for adolescent male victims. This may be largely due to the emergence of victimization in tandem with, and often overshadowed by, aggressive conduct, which then becomes the central issue to be dealt with.

Realistically, advocacy for adolescent male victims tends to emerge from the offices of dedicated social workers; psychotherapists; an occasional enlightened probation officer; and other human services professionals who are in a position to establish a one-on-one relationship with adolescent males and who have sufficient familiarity with and credibility within the system to agitate the bending of rules, special sentencing arrangements, individual treatment options, and strong statements to the court to ensure that the adolescent is seen as a victim. The young adolescent who is incarcerated in a juvenile detention facility for a single act of molestation against a neighbor child may have a ten-year history of multiple-perpetrator sexual offenses eclipsed by that single act unless he is fortunate enough to find an advocate in the guise of a mental health professional. Even then, he may come up against the prevailing model of victimization, which defies his experience. At a tender age, this young man has turned the corner from victim to perpetrator and will receive services that deal with his conduct and controlling him rather than with the core issues at stake.

Even those young male victims who do not come to the attention of the system as perpetrators face a variety of practical barriers to service. A male with sufficient information and clarity of experience to label an experience as sexually victimizing might find little in the way of crisis intervention or support available to him. A call to a local sexual assault help line may lead to a successful intervention or might be met with suspicion and an assumption that the caller is really a perpetrator or has an ulterior motive.* This response is not a program failure on the part of rape crisis centers but a logical and natural outgrowth of the paradigm of victimization that shapes the service taxonomy.

The most pressing advocacy need is to integrate into the correctional system an office or individual who is specifically designated to ferret out and advocate for the needs of these young men. The system cries out for a discrete, system-wise individual who can penetrate traditional correctional thinking and assist in the development of individual assessments for young adolescents with histories of victimization. It is entirely insufficient to allow male victims

---

*Editor's note: This issue is further complicated by the fact that there are men who call sexual assault and other crisis help lines to talk about sexual matters and masturbate. These callers cause staff members to be hyperalert for "pervert calls," so legitimate male callers are met with caution, fear, or even anger rather than empathy and compassion.

to rely on the goodwill of an individual practitioner rather than on some sort of consolidated system of advocacy and representation.

## Conclusion

The task is daunting. Once the challenge has been accepted and a willingness to alter existing models is demonstrated, the development of a new cultural framework for male victims rests on the shoulders of those who are willing to confront the resource issues, organizational challenges, and societal attitudes that still remain as obstacles for competent and effective services to victims. I hope that this chapter will motivate those who do care about these victims to begin the preliminary tasks of creating a body of empirical literature on which to base the pioneering efforts that must be undertaken if male victims are to get the assistance they deserve.

## References

Barry, K. 1979. *Female Sexual Slavery*. Englewood Cliffs, New Jersey: Prentice-Hall.

Bellinger, D., ed. 1986. *Sexual Assault: A Statewide Problem*. Saint Paul, Minnesota: Minnesota Department of Corrections.

Brownmiller, S. 1975. *Against Our Will: Men, Women, and Rape*. New York: Simon & Schuster.

Butler, S. 1979. *Conspiracy of Silence: The Trauma of Incest*. New York: Bantam Books.

Finkelhor, D. 1984. *Child Sexual Abuse: New Research and Theory*. New York: Free Press.

Forward, S., and C. Buck. 1979. *Betrayal of Innocence*. New York: Penguin.

Goldstein, S. 1987. *The Sexual Exploitation of Children*. New York: Elsevier.

Groth, A.N. 1979. *Men Who Rape: Psychology of the Offender*. New York: Plenum Press.

Herrington, L.H., with Terry Russell. 1982. *Final Report of the President's Task Force on Victims of Crime*. Washington, D.C.: GPO.

Hindman, J. 1988. "New Insight into Adult and Juvenile Sex Offenders." *Community Safety Quarterly* 1 (no. 4): 1.

Holmes, K.A., and J.E. Williams. 1981. *The Second Assault: Rape and Public Attitudes*. Westport, Connecticut: Greenwood Press.

Jacklin, C., and E. Macoby. 1974. *The Psychology of Sex Differences*. Stanford, California: Stanford University Press.

Keller, E., ed. 1976. *Sexual Assault—A Statewide Problem: A Procedural Manual for Law Enforcement, Medical, Human Services, and Legal Personnel*. Saint Paul, Minnesota: Minnesota Department of Corrections.

Knopp, F.H. 1985. "Adolescent Sex Offenders in Vermont." Monograph distributed by the Safer Society Press, Vernon, Vermont.

McKinnon, C. 1979. *Sexual Harassment of Working Women.* New Haven, Connecticut: Yale University Press.

Russell, D. 1974. *The Politics of Rape.* New York: Stein & Day.

Sanday, P.R. 1981. "The Socio-Cultural Context of Rape." *Journal of Social Issues* 37 (no. 4): 5–27.

Summit, R. 1983. "The Child Sexual Abuse Accommodation Syndrome." *Child Abuse and Neglect* 7 (no. 2): 177–193.

Young, Marlene. 1986. "A History of the Victims' Movement in the United States." Unpublished outline for NOVA Trainers, National Organization for Victim Assistance, Washington, D.C.

# Part II
# The Prevalence and Impact of Sexual Maltreatment of Males

# 4

# The Prevalence of Sexual Victimization of Males

*Anthony J. Urquiza*
*Lisa Marie Keating*

T he sexual victimization of children has been present throughout the recorded history of mankind. As testament to this assertion, several books and articles have been written describing the manner in which children have been treated by their parents, caretakers, other adults, and more powerful peers. From both the larger perspective, the history of childhood (Aries 1962; deMause 1974), and the narrower one, the maltreatment of children throughout history (Pleck 1987; Radbill 1987; Rush 1980), we can see that the phenomenon of child maltreatment is not new. A decade ago, Rush (1980) presented a comprehensive description of the sexual victimization of children throughout history that crossed many ethnic groups, religions, civilizations, and regions. While research has been quick to identify and address problems with sexually victimized girls, there has been a significant lag in the same acknowledgment for boy victims. While there are many reasons for this lag (some of which are presented in this and other chapters) one salient issue concerns the identification of how many boys are sexually abused. It is the intention of this chapter to provide information to indicate that the prevalence of the sexual victimization of boys is a major social problem deserving immediate attention.

## Significance of Prevalence Estimation

Why is it important to know how many boys are being sexually abused? For political, legislative, and mental health reasons, the prevalence of sexual victimization is essential. From a larger perspective, the number of individuals subject to any type of violence requires careful examination. It is characteristic of social policy in the United States (and, perhaps, of other government institutions) to respond to undeniable and pervasive problems rather than to seek preventive or prescriptive means to serve its citizens (Pleck 1987). Unfortunately, in the area of family violence, child victims have little voice to alter social policy. Therefore, the voices for protection of victimized children that have the power to make political and legislative changes must come from elsewhere. This is best exemplified by the movement of pediatricians, spearheaded by C. Henry Kempe, to identify and address problems related to the physical battering of young children (Kempe et al. 1962). From the work of pediatricians receiving bruised and battered children in their offices, the seminal article by Kempe et al. was published with a brief editorial establishing the significance of abuse by asserting its frequency. Soon thereafter, Dr. Kempe received a federally funded grant to study the problem of the battered child. A 1965 national survey was conducted to determine how many children were subject to nonaccidental injuries (Gil 1970), and by 1966, all fifty states had established mandatory child abuse reporting laws (Fraser 1978). In 1973, a National Center on Child Abuse and Neglect was created.

In retracing this movement, it is clear that Dr. Kempe's publication validated a well-known societal problem and became a focal point in changing American social policy and legislation to protect children. Politicians, policymakers, social scientists, and mental health professionals need to be aware of the size of this problem in order to be equipped to deal with it.

To a certain degree, this has occurred with the sexual victimization of girls. We know and clearly recognize that girls often fall prey to molesters and that, as a consequence, they must deal with serious physical, behavioral, and psychological sequelae. This is not so clear with boys. Stereotypes about sexuality, communication, and vulnerability inherent in boys and societal views concerning the ability of boys to be sexually victimized have prevented them from acknowledging their abuse and acquiring a voice in current American social policy. One of the first steps in making a significant change in the problem of the sexual victimization of boys is the identification of the numbers of boys being abused.

Traditionally, prevalence estimates of child sexual victimization have been viewed with skepticism by social scientists, mental health professionals, and the general public. The reasons for this skepticism are well founded, since prevalence estimates vary from as low as 3 percent to as high as 65 percent (Peters, Wyatt, and Finkelhor 1986). It is difficult for readers to have much confidence in an empirically sound estimate when an apparently equally sound estimate suggests a contradictory figure. To further the justification for continued investigation of the sexual victimization of males, there needs to be greater clarity with regard to prevalence estimation. Given some fundamental methodological problems (such as differences in definition, data collection, and measures), clarity may be difficult to achieve. Therefore, the approach taken in this chapter is to provide both a description of the issues involving sexual victimization prevalence estimation (specific to male victims) and the basic data describing the number of male victims. It is hoped that sufficient information will be provided to allow the reader to draw his or her own conclusion regarding the prevalence of sexual abuse among males. It is not the intention of this chapter to make any definitive estimation of how many boys are being sexual abused.

## Issues in Methodology: Unique Problems for Male Victims

Prevalence rates for any type of phenomenon are often difficult to determine. In areas of great sensitivity, such as child sexual abuse, methodological problems seem to be exceptionally troublesome. Therefore, any presentation of prevalence of child sexual victimization requires a description of these issues. This section serves as a brief explanation of three important issues in determining prevalence that appear to influence existing prevalence studies and therefore our perception of the number of boys who have been abused.

### Underreporting

Essential to any attempt at estimating the prevalence rate of victimization with any population is the acknowledgment of unique factors that influence reporting of the abuse and variations in regional, ethnic, and gender-based definitions of abuse. In the first of these factors, reporting of the abuse, several researchers have suggested that there may be significant underreporting of the sexual victimization of males. Boys may not disclose or complain about their sexually abusive experiences as readily as do girls. This pattern has its roots in the history of childhood and the study of the sexual victimization of children. It has been suggested that before Freud could conclude that the seduction by fathers was a fantasy, he had to rid himself of his earlier theory (Rush 1980). Since "men did not complain of maternal seduction, Freud limited the 'imagined' abuse to a specific female problem" (Rush 1980, 83). Absent within this proposal is the investigation of whether boys also were abused. As we now know, even when a victim fails to acknowledge past sexual victimization to himself, it continues to affect his life and does not eliminate the need for treatment.

Although reasons for this underreporting vary, several appear to have merit. First, while rates have been inconsistent, there is a general trend toward a lower prevalence rate of sexual abuse among boys than among girls. As a result, clinicians and researchers have seen fewer cases and thus may not recognize boys and men as a population in need of investigation. Related to this, both boys and men may not enter therapy for clearly identified abuse-specific problems but may have abuse histories that are as yet undisclosed. Through a greater use of externalized expressions of distress (for example, aggressiveness, noncompliance, or defiance), abuse-specific etiologies for this distress may become clouded.

Other contributors to underreporting have been suggested by Finkelhor (1984), who suggests that boys are socialized with a male ethic of self-reliance that supports the inhibition of their disclosure of victimization. In addition, as most sexual offenders are males, concerns about homosexuality may deter males from informing others of their abuse. To disclose same-sex abuse to peers or parents might threaten a boy's developing masculinity or pose the risk of being labeled as queer. Furthermore, Finkelhor suggests that because of boys greater independence and freedom to engage in unsupervised activity, disclosure may accompany fear of loss or curtailment of this freedom.

Finally, societal definitions of abuse may differ significantly based on the gender of the victim and the gender of the offender. Ambiguity in the definition of the sexual victimization of boys, especially with the elements of coercion and the ability to provide consent (essential considerations in any sexually abusive definition), may reflect societal values that are sexually biased. Finkelhor found that families within a Boston community perceived male perpetrator–male victim abuse as less harmful than male perpetrator–female victim abuse. He attributes much of this perception to the presumption that sexual contact between boys and older persons is often initiated by the boys themselves. Thus, it may be that a lower prevalence of abuse, a tendency to underreport, and societal values about male victims may contribute to an underestimation of the seriousness of the problem of male sexual abuse. Many individuals (including male victims) may perceive sexual relationships between boys and older females as something far from abusive. This "lucky" male victim may be perceived as having the fortunate opportunity to obtain early sexual training and education. Scenarios such as this are perceived to be beneficial when the male victim is an adolescent. Although little research has been conducted on this specific aspect of the victimization of males, it is important to remember that the element of coercion and the inability to provide consent are still present. While both members of the male victim–female offender pair may perceive their sexual relationship as mutually satisfactory and desired, this does not preclude adverse consequences for the male victim.

## Definition

Inherent in determining the prevalence of sexual abuse in any population is the problematic issue of definition. As Wyatt and Peters (1986a) aptly state, "altering the definition of child sexual abuse does have an effect on prevalence rates" (p. 238). While this is not the only methodological factor that influences prevalence estimates, it is clear that a significant number of respondents are included or excluded based on what is described as abusive by the researcher and what is described as abusive by the victim.

For practical purposes, the ultimate definition of child sexual abuse lies with legal statutes determined by each state. However, even among officials mandated to enforce the law (police, district attorney, and child protective services), there are various interpretations of what constitutes child sexual abuse. Furthermore, the many types of direct service providers (social workers, psychologists, psychiatrists, teachers, and so on) also have differing opinions of what constitutes child sexual abuse. To date, no clear definition of child sexual abuse has comprehensively addressed sex, age, cultural differences, and regional differences. Given the wide range of sexual experiences (both appropriate and abusive) in which an individual may become involved during childhood and the many contexts and meanings for these experiences, it is doubtful that such a definition will ever be adopted or, if adopted, will provide any meaningful contribution to the field of family violence. Therefore, it is essential to note that problems of definition are a significant source of error in determining prevalence rates and that all stated rates are only estimates. If we acknowledge that prevalence rates are only estimates of the number of boys who have been abused, several unique male-specific factors need to be addressed.

The lack of a definition of male sexual abuse is due to many factors related to the socialization of males in our society. As discussed earlier, our society's reluctance to view males, especially adolescent males, as victims of sexual abuse influences the definition and, thus, the prevalence rates. This comes in part from a general perception among men that abuse is less serious or traumatizing to the child victim (Finkelhor 1984). Consequently, men may view their own childhood sexual experiences as less serious or traumatizing. This position has been supported by research suggesting that boys rate their sexually abusive experiences less negatively than do girls (Finkelhor 1979; Urquiza 1988). Given these perceptions of childhood sexual experiences, it may be that many men do not perceive themselves as victims. The subsample of men who define themselves as having a history of childhood sexual abuse may comprise men who have irrefutable evidence and acknowledgment of their abuse, either from others (child protective services, police, and so on) or because of the severity of the abuse itself. Men who have not perceived themselves as victims throughout their lives must, therefore, not only confront the issues involved with their past relationships but also change their thinking about "normal" sexual behavior.

One common distortion influencing the definition and perception of the abuse of men concerns victim-perpetrator age differences and victim-perpetrator gender differences. While perpetrators are usually men, it has been suggested that females may constitute a sizable portion of abusers of boys (Fritz, Stoll, and Wagner 1981; Urquiza 1988).

Many of the studies cited in this chapter define sexual abuse as a sexual experience with a partner at least five years older than the victim (Bell and Weinberg 1978; Bell, Weinberg, and Hammersmith 1981; Finkelhor 1979; Fritz, Stoll, and Wagner 1981; Kercher and McShane 1983). Although the majority of offenders may be older than their victims, this assumption ignores situations in which offenders are less than five years older than their victims. Larger children molesting smaller children, older siblings molesting younger siblings, and experimentation with slightly younger coerced children also need to be examined (Groth 1977; Johnson 1988). These different abusive relationships give older or stronger children power and dominance over younger or weaker children because of the differences in their developmental levels. For instance, a nine-year-old boy may have a male or female caretaker who is thirteen years old. Although the age difference is less than five years, the social expectation of authority given to the caretaker places him or her in a position of power. Also, characteristics such as size, strength, intelligence, and streetwise sophistication may create situations of power and dominance among children who are of similar ages.

## Data Collection

One final factor in the estimation of prevalence is the method of data collection. Currently the three dominant methods of acquiring prevalence information are telephone surveys, self-report measures (self-administered questionnaires distributed through the mail, in university classrooms, and the like), and face-to-face interviews. Each method has strengths and weaknesses that influence the accuracy and reporting of prevalence figures. Because of the similarity of issues connected with telephone surveys and self-report measures, they will be discussed together and contrasted with face-to-face interviews.

Many of the benefits of both telephone surveys and self-report measures are economical or practical, such as relatively low cost, the ability to acquire large sample sizes, and access to most geographical and socioeconomic strata (most individuals in the United States can be contacted by telephone or mail). Two important factors that affect the accuracy of child sexual abuse prevalence estimation are the level of confidentiality and the use of representative probability samples. Both telephone surveys and self-report measures give individuals the opportunity to provide information about their childhood with relative anonymity, which may (1) improve the overall representativeness of the sample and (2) enable the respondent to answer sensitive or difficult questions with greater honesty. It has been argued that it is essential to use representative samples in research involving the family (Kitson et al. 1982; Miller, Rollins, and Thomas 1982) and especially in research involving child abuse (Bradley and Lindsay 1987). Recent research has suggested that these more anonymous methods offer high response rates, validity, and reliability (Bradburn and Sudman 1979; Groves and Kohn 1979; Hochstim 1977; Sudman and Bradburn 1982). These issues may be especially important when addressing the sexual victimization of men molested during their childhood.

While no specific research has been conducted addressing gender-based differences in a willingness to discuss childhood sexual victimization, a strong argument can be made that men may be more reluctant to participate in a study in which they are required to discuss perceived weaknesses, vulnerability, and/or past sexual experiences with members of the same sex. The rationale here is that if men are assured anonymity, they may be more willing to discuss past abusive experiences. In support of this, Murphy (1987) suggests that a person responding to questions by telephone can respond honestly because "anonymity is assured, other persons cannot hear or see the questions being asked, and the respondent does not have to worry about reactions of other family members because they would have no knowledge of the topic being discussed" (p. 4). These issues support the use of both telephone surveys and self-report measures to acquire representative and valid prevalence data concerning child sexual abuse.

In direct conflict with this position, some researchers have argued that both telephone interviews and self-report measures are subject to significant distortions on the part of the subject and thus yield inaccurate results (Russell 1983; Wyatt and Peters 1986a). Extensive research by Wyatt and her associates (Peters, Wyatt, and Finkelhor 1986; Wyatt 1985; Wyatt and Peters 1986b) suggests that the only truly accurate means of acquiring sensitive information such as a sexual victimization history is through the use of a face-to-face interview. Wyatt (1987) argues that many interpersonal (researcher-subject) characteristics influence the responses of subjects when dealing with sensitive topics. While most of her research in this area deals with the acquisition of a comprehensive psychosexual history and examination of the current level of sexual functioning among women, she includes many questions about childhood sexuality and abusive experiences.

Wyatt and Peters (1986b) suggest that the length of the interview, the development of rapport, the sex of the interviewer, and the ethnic similarity of the interviewer and the subject play important roles in the subject's willingness to disclose his or her past sexual history. Their argument centers on two characteristics—(1) the subject's level of comfort and willingness and (2) the length of the interview and extent of the questioning. Subjects being asked about personal topics often require an extended period of time to feel free enough to answer completely. While it may not be the subject's intent to deceive the interviewer, his or her level of discomfort may inhibit his or her responses. In addition, since prevalence studies require adults to remember events from their childhood, many subjects may distort or deny painful, embarrassing, or unpleasant memories. Through an interview conducted in a relaxed, nonthreatening atmosphere and through extensive questioning, subjects may have greater access to early childhood sexual memories.

It is important to note that Wyatt's (1985) research has been conducted exclusively with women and that there may be significant gender-based differences in response style. It is difficult to determine whether men respond positively or negatively to face-to-face interviews, since there has been little research in this area. However, Wyatt's assertions suggest that differences in reported prevalence rates are more a reflection of the method of data collection than of the number of children who were sexually abused. This is supported by the fact that the two highest prevalence rates reported among women were based on face-to-face interviews (Russell 1983; Wyatt 1985). Russell (1983) and Wyatt (1985) reported childhood sexual abuse rates for women to be 54 percent and 62 percent, respectively. The important question is whether comparable prevalence methodology characteristics are applicable to males. If so, it may be that far more males have been sexually abused than is currently believed.

## Studies Estimating the Prevalence of the Sexual Victimization of Males

Because of the inherent difficulties of estimating prevalence, it is unreasonable to assert a definitive prevalence rate for males. Therefore, several studies are presented that include data concerning the number of males who have been sexually abused during their childhood. Along with reported prevalence rates for each study, a description of the definition and method of data collection is provided. See table 4–1 for a comparison of these studies.

One of the first published studies to cite data describing the prevalence of men's childhood sexual victimization was conducted by Bell and Weinberg in the San Francisco Bay Area (Bell and Weinberg 1978). Partially funded by the Kinsey Institute, the study was designed to investigate the development of sexual preference in males and females. Using data from a comparison group of 284 heterosexual males, Bell and Weinberg used stratified random sampling throughout the San Francisco Bay Area. They conducted face-to-face interviews with all the men in this comparison group, inquiring about a variety of sexual matters from early childhood, through adolescence, and into adulthood. Interviewers were of the same sex and ethnicity as the respondents, conducted the interviews in the homes of the respondents, and were extensively trained to administer the questionnaire. The authors provide no information concerning the amount of time spent with the subjects or the emphasis on the development of rapport.

Very few of the heterosexual men (2.5 percent) and homosexual men (4.9 percent) reported "prepubertal sexual experience with a male adult involving physical contact." It is important to note that several important aspects of this study may have influenced the reported prevalence rate. The authors identify only adult male perpetrators, omitting several types of abusive situations

## Table 4–1
## Prevalence of Male Child Sexual Abuse

| Author(s) | Population and Definition of Abuse | Prevalence Rate |
|---|---|---|
| Bell and Weinberg (1978, 1981) | 284 men in a heterosexual control group of a study of homosexuality in San Francisco; prepubertal sexual experience with a male adult involving physical contact | 2.5% |
| Finkelhor (1979) | 266 college students in New Hampshire; experience under age thirteen with a partner five or more years older or an experience between ages thirteen and sixteen with a partner at least ten years older | 8.7% |
| Finkelhor (1984) | 185 fathers of children ages six to fourteen in the Boston area; (1) experience involving physical contact with a person five or more years older prior to age seventeen that the victim termed *abuse*; (2) experience before the age of thirteen with a partner at least five years older involving physical contact that the victim termed *abuse* | 6.0% 3.2% |
| Fritz, Stoll, and Wagner (1981) | 412 psychology students at the University of Washington; a sexual encounter involving physical contact with a postadolescent individual before the subject reached puberty | 4.8% |
| Urquiza (1988) | 2,016 male students at the University of Washington; direct sexual contact (i.e., physical contact that included the victim's and/or the offender's genitals) with an adult or older child (minimum five-year age difference) prior to eighteen years of age (direct abuse group) | 17.3% |
| Murphy (1987) | 789 telephone interviews in Minnesota; adult using physical or psychological force on a person under the age of eighteen to engage in any unwanted sexual contact, such as sexual touching of the person's body or unwanted intercourse | 3.0% |
| Murphy (1989) | 777 telephone interviews in Minnesota; one or more of the following factors occurring while the child was under the age of eighteen: (1) an adult exposed himself or herself to the child; (2) an adult touched or fondled the child's breast or sexual parts of the child's body when he or she was not willing; (3) the child had to touch an adult's body in a sexual way when the child did not want to; (4) an adult sexually attacked the child or forced him or her to have sexual intercourse; (5) an adult took nude photos of the child preforming sexual acts in the adult's presence; (6) the child experienced oral or anal sex with an adult | 11.0% |

(for instance, male perpetrators who were not adults and adult or adolescent female perpetrators). Also, the samples of homosexual and heterosexual men were acquired through different methods (the homosexual sample volunteered, while the heterosexual sample was selected randomly). This makes these samples difficult to compare and suggests that the volunteer sample (homosexual) was subject to significant bias. Finally, and perhaps most importantly, the intent of this study did not specifically address childhood sexual victimization. Therefore, one could question the training of interviewers on topics specific to victimization and their sensitivity to these topics during the interviews.

In what is now a seminal investigation of child sexual abuse, Finkelhor (1979) used a sample of college students selected from several colleges and universities in the New England area. As part of this study, a self-administered questionnaire was completed by 266 males. A total of 8.6 percent of the students reported having been involved in a childhood sexual experience with someone significantly older than them. More specifically, 4.1 percent reported having had a sexual experience with an adult partner, 2.3 percent reported having had a sexual experience with an adolescent partner (minimum five-year age difference), and 2.3 percent reported having had a sexual experience with an adult while the respondent was an adolescent (minimum ten-year age difference). Therefore, sexual abuse was defined as an experience under the age of thirteen with a partner five or more years older or as an experience between the ages of thirteen and sixteen with a partner at least ten years older.

A second study by Finkelhor (1984) included 185 fathers living in the Boston area who had children ranging in age from six to fourteen years. Trained interviewers conducted the interviews, which lasted approximately one hour. Six percent of these fathers stated that they had been sexually abused during their childhood (sexual abuse was defined as physical contact with a person five or more years older prior to the age of seventeen). To compare the findings of this study with the Bell and Weinberg study (1978), Finkelhor amended his definition. Under this amended definition, 3.2 percent of these men reported being involved in a sexually abusive experience. While some of the concerns of the Bell and Weinberg study are applicable to the Finkelhor study, one additional source of bias may be present. Since only fathers who had children between the ages of six and fourteen were interviewed, this eliminated fathers of children younger or older than the target sample, and, more importantly, it eliminated men who were not fathers. It could reasonably be argued that men who were sexually abused during their childhood could have difficulty initiating, developing, and/or maintaining relationships with women. Therefore, they would not have children or would divorce and not live with their children. This could eliminate an important segment of male survivors of abuse.

Using a self-administered questionnaire, Fritz, Stoll, and Wagner (1981) collected data on 412 male and 540 female undergraduate students at the University of Washington. Students were asked to respond to a forty-five-item questionnaire. Approximately half of the items addressed "salient components of the molestation" (p. 55), such as type of molestation, frequency of given types, ages of the parties involved, relationship of the molester and victim, and form of inducement. The other half of the questionnaire gathered basic demographic information. Subjects were defined as having been sexually abused if they reported at least one sexual encounter involving physical contact with a postadolescent individual before the subject had reached puberty. A sexual encounter was defined as an instance in which physical contact of an overtly sexual nature occurred. The rate of molestation for the male sample was 4.8 percent.

This study is an excellent example of the self-administered questionnaire approach to estimating prevalence. Participation in the study was completely voluntary and was conducted anonymously, providing respondents with the opportunity to answer honestly. It is possible, however, that the men in this study failed to acknowledge or report a potentially sexually abusive experience because they did not perceive past sexual encounters as abusive, did not remember them, or had a distorted recollection of them.

In a more recent study, Urquiza (1988) received 2,016 responses to a self-administered questionnaire distributed to male undergraduate students. These students were asked to provide information about a wide range of childhood family environment experiences, endorsing the presence or absence of these experiences by responding to thirty-five childhood behavioral descriptions. Embedded in these descriptions were nine items concerning inappropriate and abusive sexual experiences (for example, "As a child, I was sexually fondled by an adult or older member of my family"). Based on responses to these nine items, the men were categorized into one of three groups: men with a history of sexual abuse in their childhood (direct abuse group), men with involvement in some type of sexually inappropriate experience that could not clearly be identified as sexual abuse (indirect abuse group), and men with no history of sexual abuse or inappropriate sexual activity (nonabuse group). Of the men who responded, 14.6 percent met the criteria for the indirect abuse group and 17.3 percent met the criteria for the direct abuse group. The author suggested this two-step classification for abuse because of the wide range of childhood sexual experiences in which an individual can be involved and the difficulty in separating abusive from nonabusive experiences. *Abuse* (direct abuse group) was defined as direct sexual contact (that is, physical contact that included the victim's and/or the offender's genitals) with an adult or older child (minimum five-year age difference) prior to eighteen years of age.

Murphy (1987, 1989) conducted two major telephone interview studies to determine the prevalence of child sexual abuse. In his first study (1987), he conducted random interviews of 789 men and women in the central Minnesota area. Interviewers inquired about respondent views on various political and social issues, then included one question about child sexual abuse (occurring midway through the eighty-seven-question interview). The single question regarding sexual abuse was preceded by a transition statement informing the respondent that he or she would be asked some questions about his or her personal and family life. Respondents were assured of their anonymity and right to refuse to respond to any item. Within this study, Murphy defined sexual abuse as an adult using psychological or physical force on a person under the age of eighteen to engage in any unwanted sexual contact such as sexual touching of the person's body or unwanted intercourse. Ten (2.8 percent) of the 357 adult males interviewed reported having been sexually abused as a child.

In a similar study, Murphy (1989) investigated the relationship between an individual's child sexual abuse history and his or her past and present sexual abuse as an adult in dating and marital relationships. Once again, subjects were recruited by random telephone calls to adults in central Minnesota. Again, the sixty-five-item survey inquired about respondent views on various political, social, and family issues. Twenty-five of the sixty-five questions dealt with family and abuse experiences. These questions occurred approximately one-third of the way through the interview and were again preceded by a transition statement informing the respondent that he or she was going to be asked some questions about his or her family and personal life. Sexual abuse was defined as an experience with one or all of the following factors while the child was under eighteen years of age: an adult exposed himself or herself to the child, an adult touched or fondled the child's breasts or other sexual parts when he or she was not willing, the child had to touch an adult's body in a sexual way when the child did not want to, an adult sexually attacked the child or forced him or her to have sexual intercourse, an adult took nude photos of the child performing sexual acts in his or her presence, or the child experienced oral or anal sex with an adult. From a total of 777 interviews completed, 11 percent of the males reported having been sexually abused as a child.

## Conclusions and Recommendations

As is evident from these research studies and the preceding discussion of the complexities of determining prevalence (especially among males), a clear assertion of the number of men who have been sexually abused during their childhood is not possible. However, this should not deter us from reviewing the existing literature and attempting to acquire a best estimate for social, political, legislative, and clinical purposes. One outcome of a review of the existing prevalence literature is the need for prevalence studies that are designed specifically to investigate childhood sexual abuse and that account for the range of response biases.

Factors such as the method of data collection and the definition of abuse affect the reported prevalence rates. The manner and degree to which these factors influence prevalence rates among males is unknown. This suggests an approach that recognizes the importance of gender-specific factors in the collection of data (disclosure, anonymity, confidentiality, and so on) and the definition of abuse. Without this recognition, prevalence studies will be unable to provide any reliable estimate concerning the number of men who have been abused. Given the work done by Wyatt (Wyatt and Peters 1986a, 1986b) and Russell (1983), it appears that most studies have seriously underestimated the number of females who experienced childhood sexual abuse. With this in mind, it is possible that many more males were sexually victimized during their childhood than we previously believed.

Without additional attention to the sexual victimization of males, we will continue to ignore this major social problem. The disclosure of the sexual victimization of males will result in greater emphasis on this experience as a source of physical, affective, and psychological distress in men. Once this source is identified, we can begin to address methods of changing and treating this problem at the individual, family, community, and societal level.

# References

Aries, P. 1962. *Centuries of Childhood: A Social History of Family Life.* New York: Vintage Books.

Bell, A., and M. Weinberg. 1978. *Homosexualities.* New York: Simon & Schuster.

Bell, A.P., M.S. Weinberg, and S.K. Hammersmith. 1981. *Sexual Preference: Its Development in Men and Women.* Bloomington: Indiana University Press.

Bradburn, N.M., and S. Sudman. 1979. *Improving Interview Method and Questionnaire Design.* San Francisco: Jossey-Bass.

Bradley, J.E., and R.C.L. Lindsay. 1987. "Methodological and Ethical Issues in Child Abuse Research." *Journal of Family Violence* 2: 239–256.

deMause, L. 1974. *The History of Childhood.* New York: Psychohistory Press.

Finkelhor, D. 1979. *Sexually Victimized Children.* New York: Free Press.

———. 1984. *Child Sexual Abuse: New Theory and Research.* New York: Free Press.

Fraser, B.G. 1978. "A Glance at the Past, a Gaze at the Present, a Glimpse at the Future: A Critical Analysis of the Development of Child Abuse Reporting Statutes." *Chicago-Kent Law Review* 54: 641–686.

Fritz, G.S., K. Stoll, and N.A. Wagner. 1981. "A Comparison of Males and Females Who Were Sexually Molested as Children." *Journal of Sex and Marital Therapy* 7 (Spring): 54–59.

Gil, D.G. 1970. *Violence Against Children: Physical Abuse in the United States.* Cambridge: Harvard University Press.

Groth, N.A. 1977. "The Adolescent Sexual Offender and His Prey." *International Journal of Offender Therapy and Compararive Criminology* 21: 249–254.

Groves, R.M., and R.L. Kohn. 1979. *Surveys by Telephone: A National Comparison with Personal Interviews.* New York: Academic Press.

Hochstim, J.R. 1977. "A Critical Comparison of Three Strategies of Collecting Data from Households." *Journal of the American Statistical Association* 62: 976–989.

Johnson, T.C. 1988. "Child Perpetrators—Children Who Molest Other Children: Preliminary Findings." *Child Abuse and Neglect* 12: 219–229.

Kempe, C.H., F.N. Silverman, B.F. Steele, W. Droegemiller, and H.K. Silver. 1962. "The Battered Child Syndrome." *Journal of the American Medical Association* 181 (September): 17–24.

Kercher, G., and M. McShane. 1984. "The Prevalence of Child Sexual Abuse Victimization in an Adult Sample of Texas Residents." *Child Abuse and Neglect* 8: 495–502.

Kitson, G.C., G.K. Sussman, R.B. Williams, B.K. Zeehandelaer, B.K. Schickmanter, and J.L. Steinberger. 1982. "Sampling Issues in Family Research." *Journal of Marriage and Family* 44: 965–981.

Miller, B.C., B.C. Rollins, and D.L. Thomas. 1982. "On Methods of Studying Marriages and Families." *Journal of Marriage and Family* 44: 853–873.

Murphy, J.E. 1987. "Prevalence of Child Sexual Abuse and Consequent Victimization in the General Population." Paper presented at the Third National Family Violence Research Conference, University of New Hampshire, Durham, July.

———. 1989. "Telephone Surveys and Family Violence: Data from Minnesota." Paper presented at the Responses to Family Violence Conference, Purdue University, West Lafayette, Indiana, January.

Peters, S.D., G. Wyatt, and D. Finkelhor. 1986. "Prevalence." In *A Sourcebook on Child Sexual Abuse,* edited by D. Finkelhor, 15–59. Beverly Hills, California: Sage Publications.

Pleck, E. 1987. *Domestic Tyranny: The Making of American Social Policy against Family Violence from Colonial Times to the Present.* New York: Oxford University Press.

Radbill, S.X. 1987. "Children in a World of Violence: A History of Child Abuse." In *The Battered Child,* 4th ed., edited by R.E. Helfer and R.S. Kempe, 3–22. Chicago: University of Chicago Press.

Rush, F. 1980. *The Best Kept Secret: Sexual Abuse of Children.* Englewood Cliffs, New Jersery: Prentice-Hall.

Russell, D.E.H. 1983. "The Incidence and Prevalence of Intrafamilial and Extrafamilial Sexual Abuse of Female Children." *Child Abuse and Neglect* 7: 133–146.

Sudman, S., and N.M. Bradburn. 1982. *Asking Questions: A Practical Guide to Questionnaire Design.* San Francisco: Jossey-Bass.

Urquiza, A.J. 1988. "The Effects of Childhood Sexual Abuse in an Adult Male Population." Doctoral dissertation, University of Washington, Seattle.

Wyatt, G. 1985. "The Sexual Abuse of Afro-American and White American Women in Childhood." *Child Abuse and Neglect* 9: 507–519.

———. 1987. "Maximizing Appropriate Populations and Responses for Sex Research." Paper presented at a conference titled "Sex and Aids." The Kinsey Institute, Bloomington, Indiana, December.

Wyatt, G., and S.D. Peters. 1986a. "Issues in the Definition of Child Sexual Abuse in Prevalence Research." *Child Abuse and Neglect* 10: 231–240.

———. 1986b. "Methodological Considerations in Research on the Prevalence of Child Sexual Abuse." *Child Abuse and Neglect* 10: 241–251.

# 5

# The Impact of Sexual Abuse: Initial and Long-Term Effects

*Anthony J. Urquiza*
*Maria Capra*

L ess than half a decade ago, Browne and Finkelhor (1986) published their seminal review of the literature on the initial and long-term effects of sexual victimization in children. At that time, they limited their review to studies that focused on female victims because "few clinical and even fewer empirical studies have been done on boys, and it seems premature to draw conclusions at this point" (p. 144). In the years since the publication of the Browne and Finkelhor article, there has been a rapid increase in published literature addressing the sexual victimization of males. In the empirical research, this increase is due to studies that have been designed specifically to address male victims (Dimock 1988; Urquiza 1988) or have clearly identified males as part of their research program (Friedrich, Urquiza, and Beilke 1986; Friedrich, Beilke, and Urquiza 1988). In the clinical literature, there has been a steady growth of reports that describe specific cases of the sexual victimization of boys (Barton and Marshall 1986; Krug 1989; Rogers and Terry 1984) and gender-based differences in the sexual victimization of children (Urquiza 1986; Pierce and Pierce 1985).

As part of this recent upsurge, there has been a developing literature on common clinical issues of victimized boys and men that has identified important therapeutic themes, some of which appear to be male specific. This review rests its clinical conclusions primarily on empirical research, but these anecdotal descriptions also may provide additional information for some readers. Several other published reviews and descriptions of sexual abuse among males are available (Everstine and Everstine 1989; Finkelhor 1984, 1986; Freeman-Longo 1986; Hunter 1990; Krieger et al. 1980; Sebold 1987).

Several factors considered in the development of this chapter are worthy of mention. Perhaps most important is the influence of the previously mentioned review of female victims by Browne and Finkelhor (1986). The present authors have attempted to use this review as a basic framework to describe the effects of sexual abuse and clarify some therapeutic issues. With this in mind, it is hoped that readers will (1) use this review as a comprehensive examination of the effects of the sexual victimization of males, (2) appreciate the basic gender differences associated with childhood sexual victimization, and (3) gain a better understanding of the gender-based differences in methods of coping with childhood sexual victimization. It is our intention that this chapter be used as a companion review to the Browne and Finkelhor article. When combined, these reviews will present a comprehensive description of the effects of sexual abuse on both males and females.

To this end, we present similar caveats in definition and selection of articles. Included in this review are studies (table 5–1) that met two definitional criteria: "(1) forced or coerced sexual behavior that is imposed on a child or (2) sexual behavior between a child and a much older person or a person in a caretaking role" (Browne and Finkelhor 1986, p. 144). Because the response of sexually victimized boys is different from that of sexually victimized girls, the clustering of effects in this chapter may be slightly different from those described by Browne and Finkelhor in their article on girls. An example of this is found in the presence of behavioral disturbances such as aggression, delinquency, and hostility, which are often demonstrated by male victims but not by female victims.

## Initial Effects of the Sexual Abuse of Boys

### Behavioral Disturbances and Aggression

One of the most common findings in the literature concerning the effects of the sexual abuse of boys is the presence of a variety of behavioral disturbances such as aggression, delinquency, and noncompliance. This should not be surprising in light of strong psychological literature showing that males tend to respond to stressful and difficult situations in a behavioral or externalizing manner (Achenbach 1978; Eme 1979). In a series of publications, Friedrich and associates (Friedrich, Urquiza, and Beilke 1986; Friedrich, Beilke, and Urquiza 1987; Friedrich, Beilke, and Urquiza 1988) and Urquiza (1986) provide substantial support for the presence of behavioral disturbances in sexually abused boys. Using the Achenbach Child Behavior Checklist (Achenbach 1978; Achenbach and Edelbrock 1983) to assess postabuse behaviors (via report from a nonabusing parent), they found that boys in their sample had scores that were significantly higher than a nonabused control group on several factors of externalized behavioral problems. In their chart review of 140 sexually victimized boys, Spencer and Dunklee (1986) report some type of behavior problem in 12 percent of the cases, although they do not identify the specific type of behavior problem.

Many other studies have identified disturbances of conduct in sexually abused children (Adams-Tucker 1982; Burgess, Groth, and McCausland 1981; Gomes-Schwartz, Horowitz, and Sauzier 1985; Pomeroy, Behar, and Stewart 1981; Tufts' New England Medical Center 1984), but they have made no distinction between male and female victims. Although these studies

**Table 5–1**
**Studies of the Effects of Sexual Abuse on Males**

| Author(s) | Source of Sample | Sample Size | Age of Respondents | Focus of Study | Comparison Group |
|---|---|---|---|---|---|
| Adams-Tucker (1982) | Child guidance clinic | M = 6 F = 23 | C | I, E | No |
| Adams-Tucker (1985) | Child guidance clinic | M = 6 F = 22 | C, Ad | I | No |
| Awad (1976) | Case study | M = 1 | C | I | No |
| Barton and Marshall (1986) | Case study | M = 1 | C | I | No |
| Dimock (1988) | Case study | M = 25 | Ad | I, E | No |
| Dixon, Arnold, and Calestro (1978) | Case study | M = 10 | C, Ad | I | No |
| Ellerstein and Canavan (1980) | Children's hospital | M = 16 F = 154 | C, Ad | I, E | No |
| Farber et al. (1984) | Medical center | F = 81 M = 81 | C | I, E | Yes |
| Finkelhor (1979) | College students | F = 530 M = 266 | Ad, A | I, E | Yes |
| Friedrich, Urquiza, and Bielke (1986) | Sexual assault center, group therapy | F = 49 M = 15 | C | I, E | No |
| Friedrich and Luecke (1988) | Case studies | M = 18 F = 4 | C, Ad | I, E | Yes |
| Fritz et al. (1981) | College students | M = 412 F = 540 | A | I, E | Yes |
| Krieger et al. (1980) | Court referred | F = 73 | C, Ad | I, E | No |
| Landis (1956) | College students | F = 726 M = 224 | A | I, E | Yes |
| Pierce and Pierce (1985) | Hot line reports | M = 25 F = 180 | C, Ad | I | Yes |
| Risin and Koss (1987) | College students | M = 2,972 | A | I, E | Yes |
| Rogers and Terry (1984) | Case studies | M = 6 | C, Ad | I, E | No |
| Showers et al. (1986) | Children's | M = 81 | C | I, E | No |
| Spencer and Dunklee (1984) | Children's | M = 140 | C | I, E | No |
| Tufts' New England Medical Center (1984) | Medical | M = 95 F = 219 | C | I, E | Yes |
| Urquiza (1988) | College students | M = 52 | A | I, E | Yes |
| Urquiza and Crowley (1986) | College students | M = 28 F = 44 | A | I, E | Yes* |

Note: F = females; M = males; C = child; Ad = adolescent; A = adult; I = intrafamilial; E = extrafamilial.
*Investigation examined sex differences.

lend support to the assertion that among the responses to the sexual victimization of boys are behavioral disturbances and aggression, it is not possible to make a definitive statement solely from these data.

Case studies appear to support the empirical literature describing behavioral disturbances in sexually abused boys. Some reported behavioral disturbances include homicidal and suicidal ideation (Dixon, Arnold, and Calestro 1978), verbal explosiveness and argumentativeness (Awad 1976), fire setting and destruction of property (Geiser and Norberta 1976), and delinquency (Bender and Blau 1937; Bender and Grugett 1952). Rogers and Terry (1984) describe the case of a ten-year-old boy who adopted "an aggressive and hostile posture toward both male and female peers" (p. 96). From a previous friendly and easygoing manner, this abused boy became involved in school fights and became increasingly argumentative, recalcitrant, and aggressive. Adams-Tucker (1985) describes three of five sexually victimized boys as using acting out as a defense mechanism.

From the available empirical and clinical literature, it appears that many sexually abused males experience some behavioral disturbance following their victimization. This is not surprising considering the overall trend for boys to express their distress over trauma in an externalized manner (Eme 1979). Of concern is the response of potentially helpful resources to these disturbances of conduct. While some victims may elicit or recruit emotional assistance and support from parents, teachers, and mental health professionals, a typical response to aggression and hostility is rejection and avoidance. It may be that actions on the part of boy victims to cope with their distress or to signal that distress to others actually deters the responses of potentially beneficial resources. These behaviors may not only limit resources to the male victim for problems specifically related to his sexual victimization but also cloud the issue of sexual victimization as the cause of, or a contributor to, these behaviors. It should be noted that not all boys respond to their abuse in this way, but both empirical and case study material suggests that common behavioral problems include aggression, destructive behavior, problems with peer relations, and argumentativeness.

## Emotional Reactions and Self-Perceptions

Finkelhor (1986) and others (Boatman, Borkan, and Schetky 1981; Porter, Blick, and Sgroi 1983) suggest that a poor self-image may be the result of the powerlessness and acquired sense of "damaged goods" experienced by the sexually abused child. Related to this is an increase in the victim's feelings of guilt, shame, difference from others, lowered self-efficacy, perception of himself or herself as a victim, and lowered self-esteem. While this idea appears to be supported in female victim populations (Courtois 1979; Herman 1981), few studies have addressed this phenomenon in male populations. Therefore, we know very little about what types of emotional reactions sexually victimized boys possess. While one argument may be that through reliance on externalizing behavior and societal attitudes regarding the expression of feelings among males, emotional distress may be very difficult to ascertain, this does not mean that boys do not have these feelings and should not deter research attempts to identify them.

Although several studies do not provide separate analyses for boys, they have indicated a wide range of emotional reactions from child victims (Friedrich, Urquiza, and Beilke 1986; Tufts' New England Medical Center 1984). Almost half of the subjects in the Friedrich and associates (1986) study had significantly elevated scores on the Internalizing Scale of the Achenbach Child Behavior Checklist. Within this broad-band scale are behaviors such as depression, somatic complaints, social withdrawal, immaturity, and obsessive-compulsive behavior.

The Tufts' New England Medical Center study assessed children with several standardized measures, including the Louisville Behavior Checklist, the Piers-Harris Self-Concept Scale, the Purdue Self-Concept Scale, and the Gotteschalk-Gleser Content Analysis Scales. The researchers examined children according to one of three age groupings: preschool children (ages four to six), school-age children (ages seven to thirteen), and adolescents (ages fourteen to eighteen). In a published article based on this study, Gomes-Schwartz, Horowitz, and Sauzier (1985) identified 17 percent of their preschool group as having "met the criteria for clinically significant pathology" (p. 505). With this same descriptor, 40 percent of the school-age group and a "relatively small" portion of the adolescent group met the criteria (p. 507). However, nearly a quarter of the adolescent group showed significant pathology on a neuroticism scale. These two empirical studies clearly indicate that emotional distress is a common response to sexual victimization whether the victim is male or female.

This case study literature provides several descriptions of male victims with problems of self-concept, self-esteem, guilt, or shame (Bender and Grugett 1952; Burgess 1978; Burgess, Holmstrom, and McCausland 1977; Symonds, Mendoza, and Harrell 1980). The clinical literature also describes several cases in which male victims have engaged in self-mutilation, suicidal ideology, or some other self-destructive behavior (Adams-Tucker 1982; Dixon, Arnold, and Calestro 1978). Rogers and Terry (1984) state that many of the boys and their families engage in denial or minimalization of the abusive experience. They cite case descriptions in which the victim or the victim's family pair minimalization with a sense of shame, disgust, or blame for the abusive incident. Spencer and Dunklee (1986) report cases of sexually abused boys who made suicide attempts, although these cases are not clearly described. While not directly descriptive of their emotional state or reaction, these empirical and clinical case studies portray a male victims who frequently engages in self-destructive behaviors, which may reflect a common response of emotional distress, and displays of guilt, shame, or a negative self-concept.

## Physical Consequences and Somatic Complaints

Many of the studies from medical centers and hospitals reflect the physical damage that can occur to boys as a result of their sexually abusive experiences (Ellerstein and Canavan 1980; Sgroi 1977; Showers et al. 1983; Spencer and Dunklee 1986). It is not the intent of this section to describe the many types of physical injuries that boys may incur from being sexually abused, but it is important to note that many boys are physically injured and that certain physical injuries may be linked to later physical consequences or psychosomatic concerns. For example, anal penetration with abrasions or lacerations may result in difficulty and pain in bowel movements. This painful defecation can upset and distort normal bowel patterns and contribute to problems with constipation or encopresis (Levine 1982).

Spencer and Dunklee (1986) report that a small proportion of the boys they reviewed also had somatic complaints, although the types of problems with this subsample were not well described. From the Tufts' New England Medical Center study, Gomes-Schwartz and associates (1985) report that the 13 percent of sexually abused preschool victims (both male and female) reported significantly more somatic complaints than the general population.

A review of clinical case studies supports the presence of physical and somatic complaints in male victims. Reported problems include sleep disturbances and nightmares (Adams-Tucker 1982; Burgess, Groth, and McCausland 1981; Dixon, Arnold, and Calestro 1978), enuresis and encopresis (Dixon, Arnold, and Calestro 1978; Geiser and Norberta 1976; Spencer and Dunklee 1986), phobias (Langsley, Schwartz, and Fairbairn 1968), and increased anxiety (Adams-Tucker 1982; Burgess, Groth, and McCausland 1981; Dixon, Arnold, and Calestro 1978).

To gain a better understanding of physical and somatic responses to sexual victimization, it might be beneficial to examine the literature addressing the health implications associated with traumatic experiences (Pennebaker and Hoover 1986). As stated earlier, one form of physical and somatic problems derives from direct physical trauma resulting from the actual abusive experience (for example, lacerations or acquisition of a sexually transmitted disease), but a less direct form of these same problems may come from inhibition as a cumulative stressor that contributes to psychosomatic disease.

Simply stated, one aspect of psychosomatic theory suggests that the inhibition of ongoing behaviors, thoughts, or feelings (that is, feelings and thoughts associated with sexual victimization) results in more frequent problems in physical health (Pennebaker 1989; Pennebaker and Susman 1988). In addition to a gender-based tendency for males not to talk freely about feelings or share problems and concerns, male victims of sexual abuse may be implicitly instructed not to demonstrate or display their vulnerability. In many cases, the expression of feelings such as guilt, shame, or powerlessness is perceived as a weakness or sign of vulnerability. It can be reasonably argued that those same societal forces that encourage males to be strong, independent, and invulnerable may contribute to inhibition and lead to problems in physical health.

### Effects on Sexuality

Another common problem identified in the literature is some type of sexual disturbance, such as inappropriate sexual behavior, sexual offenses, hypersexuality, or gender confusion. Among the empirical examinations of child sexual abuse, Friedrich and associates (1986, 1987, 1988) found that 81 percent of their subjects (both male and female victims) exhibited some type of problematic sexual ideation or behavior. More than half of the parent reporters described their children by endorsing items such as "Plays with sex parts too much" and "Thinks about sex too much," while approximately 15 percent said their children demonstrated behavior or expressed a desire to be like the opposite sex.

In a similarly designed study, Urquiza (1986) identified a greater problem with these same items in a sexual abuse population than in either a nonabused "normal" control group or a nonabused outpatient referral group. McCauley et al. (1983) reviewed charts of children admitted to an inpatient psychiatric unit who exhibited various types of sexual behavior problems. In examining a subset of children who experienced the most extreme abuse, 47 percent were involved in sexually inappropriate behavior. Conversely, of the children who exhibited the most sophisticated sexual behavior problems (intercourse, fellatio, and cunnilingus), 78 percent had a known history of sexual abuse. The authors suggest that sexual abuse (especially severe abuse) has a disinhibiting effect on children's sexual behavior.

In support of this conclusion, the Tufts study (Tufts' New England Medical Center 1984) identified problems with sex-related issues in all three age-groups (preschool, school-age, and adolescent). Friedrich and Luecke (1988) report a sample of young children referred for problems with sexual aggression. Of the fourteen boys identified as sexually aggressive, eleven had a known history of prior victimization (the abuse history for one child could not be verified).

Several researchers have suggested that early childhood sexual experiences play an important role in the development of later sexual offenses (Becker 1988; Cantwell 1988; Groth 1979; Lanyon 1986; Wenet, Clark, and Hunner 1981). An examination of juvenile sexual offenders has revealed that more than half had been victims of traumatic sexual assault (Deisher et al.

1982). Davis and Leitenberg (1987) cite several published reports of sexual victimization in the life histories of adolescent sex offenders. They conclude that "many male adolescent sex offenders have themselves been sexually victimized at an earlier age, and this might have considerable etiological significance, especially when they later seem to be reenacting these previous experiences with someone else" (p. 423). They cite several studies with varying percentages of confirmed reports of adolescent sex offenders having been sexually abused when they were younger. These percentages range from as low as 19 percent (Fehrenbach et al. 1986) to as high as 47 percent (Longo 1982).

A study of offenders conducted by Gomes-Schwartz (1984) showed that 38 percent of those studied supplied confirmed reports of having been sexually abused, with probable evidence of abuse in another 17 percent of the offenders. This is clearly depicted by Ryan (1989) in her description of a dysfunctional response cycle. She suggests that victim responses such as "patterns of denial and minimalization, power and control behaviors, irrational thinking, irresponsible decision making, retaliation fantasies, deviant sexual arousal, aggression, secrecy, and preoccupation with or reenactment of one's own victimization" (pp. 338–339) may lead from victim to victimizer.

Within clinical case studies, several authors cite a variety of sexual behavior problems in male victims. These reports center on the description of problems with sexual acting out and an exaggerated interest in sexuality and sexual material (Awad 1976; Burgess, Groth, and McCausland 1981; Dixon, Arnold, and Calestro 1978; Geiser and Norberta 1976; Langsley, Schwartz, and Fairbairn 1968; and Yates 1982). Krieger and associates (1980) describe a six-year-old sexually abused boy who exhibited sexualized behavior with both his mother and his female therapist. Rogers and Terry (1984) discuss the case of an eleven-year-old boy who displayed a dramatic behavior change from being very masculine to adopting feminine mannerisms after being severely abused.

As Finkelhor (1986) has suggested, problems with sexual issues (such as sexual ideation and attitudes and adult sexual behaviors) may result from premature exposure to sexuality. Within our society, young children do not have the emotional, cognitive, or social orientation with which to make meaning of adult sexual experiences. This leaves young children with a sense of confusion and disorientation about their abusive experiences (Rasmussen and Urquiza 1987). This may come from conflict derived from pleasurable sensations resulting from the abuse (brought about solely through a physiological response or through having sexual and/or nonsexual needs met) or from conflict about the expectation of sexual activity in relationships with others (especially cases of incest where roles and boundaries may become blurred). Societal views that sexuality should not be openly discussed and that children should not have or express sexual ideas, feelings, or fantasies or engage in sexual behavior provide little opportunity for young boys (or girls) to share their concerns or problems with others.

As adults, it is our responsibility to provide a forum for young abused boys to acquire safe and accurate information about sexuality and enable them to explore their feelings and ideas about the sexual aspects of their victimization. In this way, we can alleviate distress and confusion brought about by the sexual aspects of the abuse. As Ryan (1989) states, however, traditional insight-oriented and educational approaches may not be sufficient to prevent the development of sexual offending behavior in some children. Early identification and intervention directed specifically at issues of sexuality, power and control, reenactment of the abuse, and fantasies of retaliation may be required.

*Summary*

Based on the data described in this section, it appears that there is sufficient evidence to suggest that the sexual victimization of boys has a detrimental effect on behavior, self-concept, psychophysiological symptomatology, and psychosexual behaviors and functioning. While research suggests problematic sequelae in most of the areas identified in this chapter, two clusters of problems stand out—disturbances of conduct (for example, aggressiveness, delinquency, and acting out) and inappropriate sexual behaviors (for example, confusion about sexual issues, compulsive sexual behaviors, and sexual acting out/offending). These two problem areas serve as excellent examples of the difficulty in examining the effects of abuse on males and how they are distinct from the effects on females.

For example, as most identified perpetrators are male, an examination of the effects of abuse on male victims may need to account for problems implicit in abuse when the victim and perpetrator are of the same sex. This does not appear to be a common problem for female victims because of the relatively low reported incidence of female victim–female perpetrator abuse. Therefore, males may more commonly have to deal with issues of confusion about their sexual identity and sexual preference, both at the time of their abuse and later in their lives. This is not to suggest that males are more or less adversely affected by abuse than females. The multiplicity of factors that influence patterns of response and the adoption of coping mechanisms prevent the assertion of such a statement. However, the literature fairly conclusively demonstrates that boys have a greater difficulty than girls in adjusting to many types of stressors (Emery and O'Leary 1982; Murphy 1964; Rutter 1970).

We suggest that the investigation of sexually abused boys requires an approach that acknowledges the gender-based differences in stress, coping, adaptation, family relationships, and societal values. This is most aptly described in the boys use of externalizing behavior as an expression of distress. In contrast, girls have been identified as responding to problems in a more internalizing manner (Achenbach and Edelbrock 1983). It is not valid to say that because girls may respond to distress in more socially appropriate ways (such as crying or seeking warmth or nurturance) than boys (for example, yelling, hitting, or swearing), they have more or fewer problems as a result of abuse. But the manner in which girls express their distress may be more effective in eliciting a positive and supportive response from others. Because of boys' difficulty in expressing and communicating affect, stereotypic pressures to avoid being perceived as vulnerable, and the potential for incurring harm as a result of their distress, greater attention needs to be given to boys and their response to sexual victimization.

## Long-Term Effects of the Sexual Abuse of Boys

One of the most consistent findings in the area of child psychopathology is that early exposure to traumatic or stressful events often leads to later maladjustment. This should not be surprising when one perceives early childhood events as being building blocks for later developmental stages, achievements, and outcomes. Disruption of a young child's early home environment and his or her ability to participate in appropriate and adaptive environments and relationships increase his or her risk for later psychopathology. With this in mind, it can be expected that boys who have been sexually abused during childhood may have problems later in life.

### Depression and Somatic Disturbances

One of the most common findings in the literature concerning the long-term effects of childhood sexual abuse on males is depression. Using a symptom checklist (TSC = 33), Briere and associates (1988) found a significant difference on a subscale of depression between a sample of adults abused as children and a nonabused control group. They also report that the abused males had a higher incidence of previous suicide attempts than did the control group. In a study conducted by Urquiza and Crowley (1986), the TSC-33 was administered to address physical and/or somatic problems in a sample of adult survivors of abuse and a matched (age and ethnicity) comparison group. The authors found that in the area of depression and in a combined total symptom score, the sexually abused group showed significantly more symptoms than did the comparison group.

Symptoms of depression and other psychological problems also have been confirmed by the results of the Los Angeles Epidemiological Catchment Area study (Stein et al. 1988). This study examined the lifetime and current (prior six months) prevalence of psychological reactions to child sexual abuse. In addition, the authors assessed eleven specific psychiatric disorders among adults abused as children and nonabused adults. Reports of depression occurred in 45.2 percent of the lifetime prevalence group and in 12.5 percent of the current prevalence group. Similarly, of the psychiatric disorders reported, elevated levels of major depressive disorders were found in both the current and lifetime prevalence groups of males who had experienced child sexual abuse. Other significant emotional reactions reported included anxiety, anger, and guilt.

Several case studies support the empirical literature describing depression and other emotional reactions of male victims. Some reported emotional reactions include difficulty dealing with anger, poor self-concept and self-esteem, isolation, and depression (Bruckner and Johnson 1987; Carmen, Rieker, and Mills 1984; Lew 11988). Krug (1989) also identified depression in nearly all of his eight adult males who had been sexually abused as children by their mothers. Finally, Adams-Tucker (1982) and Dixon, Arnold, and Calestro (1978) describe several cases in which male victims engaged in suicide ideology and other forms of self-destructive behavior. Therefore, there appears to be some evidence that male victims of sexual abuse may experience emotional reactions such as depression, guilt, anger, poor self-concept, and self-destructive behaviors.

Until recently, very little attention has been paid to somatic disturbances of male victims in the empirical literature. Briere et al. (1988), using the TSC-33, examined symptomatology in adult survivors. The TSC-33 consists of five subscales: dissociation, anxiety, depression, sleep disturbance, and a scale reflective of posttraumatic stress symptoms. They report that the male victims had significantly higher scores on each of these subscales when compared to the nonabused sample.

A review of the case studies appears to support the findings that a history of childhood sexual victimization is related to the presence of somatic complaints in adulthood. Reports of increased anxiety, sleep disturbance, and nightmares have been found by several authors (Adams-Tucker 1982; Burgess, Groth, and McCausland 1981; Dixon, Arnold, and Calestro 1978; Lew 1988). Although the empirical literature is still lacking in this area, the literature does suggest the presence of depression and somatic disturbances among male victims.

## Effects on Self-Esteem and Self-Concept

Within the empirical literature, the areas of self-esteem and self-concept among sexually abused males is still in its infancy. Urquiza and Crowley (1986) examined the self-concept of abused men using the Tennessee Self-Concept Scale (TSCS). They found that the abused men tended to score significantly lower on seven of the eight clinical scales of the TSCS—identity, self-satisfaction, behavioral self, physical self, moral-ethical self, personal self, and family self—than a matched comparison group. Additionally, the men in their abused group scored significantly lower than the men in the comparison group on a score reflecting total self-concept.

Although clinical reports of poor self-esteem or poor self-concept are few, there are some indications that men who have been sexually abused have more problems in this area. Lew (1988) provides several accounts of men in therapy who identified feelings of being flawed or bad, had a negative body image, and felt guilt and shame. The aspect of poor self-esteem as a consequence of child sexual abuse also is indirectly supported by research conducted with male survivors that indicates problems with suicidal ideation and self-destructive behavior (Briere et al. 1988; Urquiza 1988). Although the evidence is scarce, there does appear to be some indication that adult male survivors of child sexual abuse have difficulty in areas of self-esteem and self-concept.

## Impact on Interpersonal Relationships

While there has been little published on interpersonal relationships in the empirical literature, the clinical literature tends to support the idea that male victims experience problems with these (Bruckner and Johnson 1987; Krug 1989; Steele and Alexander 1981). Krug (1989) examined eight case histories of males who had been sexually abused by their mothers as children. He reported that all of these men experienced difficulty maintaining an intimate, emotional, and sexual relationship with one person. These males expressed "impaired ability to relate in an intimate, sustained, and meaningful manner" (p. 116).

Bruckner and Johnson (1987) reported similar findings in their clinical population of men seeking group treatment. Difficulties with trust and intimacy were evident for all group members. Several participants avoided personal relationships altogether, and all the members stated that they "felt more comfortable expressing their emotions to women than they did to men and that they generally avoided such intimacy with other men" (p. 85). This finding may be related to the fact that most of the offenders of these adult male victims were male, thereby possibly giving these victims a sense of inferiority about their independence and masculinity, which in turn inhibited their ability to disclose their feelings to other men.

In Lew's (1988) book about the consequences of the sexual abuse of boys and approaches to treatment for adult survivors, he provides accounts of many men's histories. In reviewing these accounts, it is clear that one salient feature of all these men is difficulty in initiating, developing, and maintaining close interpersonal (that is, intimate) relationships. This aspect of adult survivors has rarely been examined in the empirical literature for either males or females. This is a notable absence, since it is often the case that adult survivors enter therapy for reasons apparently unrelated to their victimization experience (for example, marital problems, isolation and depression, or anger management). Clearly, greater attention must be paid to the possibility of a victimization history in all clients seen in therapy, but perhaps this recommendation should be more strongly made with presenting problems that relate specifically to interpersonal functioning.

## Effects on Sexuality

Another issue that appears to be quite prevalent in the literature of abused males is the presence of several problems related to sexual behaviors, among which are problems with later sexual adjustment, sexual compulsiveness, dissatisfaction with sexual relationships, lower sexual self-esteem, and sexual identity (Bell and Weinberg 1981; Cairns 1983; Finkelhor 1979; Meiselman 1978; Qualand 1985; Simari and Baskin 1984; Urquiza 1988).

To examine the effects of sexual abuse on sexual feelings and behaviors, Finkelhor (1984) created a measure called sexual self-esteem. This scale was composed of six items that explored the attitudes of current sexual feelings and activities among a sample of college students comprising 17 male and 104 female victims and a comparison group of 685 nonvictims. This measure was intended to evaluate a subject's current level of sexual satisfaction and sexual adjustment. He reported that students who had been victimized, both male and female, had lower levels of sexual self-esteem. The male victims scored significantly lower than the male nonvictims, and the female victims scored lower than the comparison group. He also noted that the male victims "revealed especially high feelings of dissatisfaction after current sexual experiences" (p. 192).

Only recently has the impact of childhood sexual abuse on later sexual identity and sexual preference been explored. Several empirical studies indicate a relationship between childhood molestation and later same-sex behavior (Bell and Weinberg 1981; Finkelhor 1979; Johnson and Shrier 1985; Rogers and Terry 1988; Simari and Baskin 1984). In their study, Bell and Weinberg (1981) found that 5 percent of their male homosexual sample had had childhood sexual experiences with adults. Similarly, Finkelhor (1979) noted from his college sample that males who had been victimized by older men during childhood were four times more likely than nonvictims to be engaged in homosexual activities. However, the male respondents who had peer same-sex experiences during their childhood were not significantly more likely to be involved in later adult homosexual activity. This suggests that an important characteristic in the development of some men's sexual preference is involvement with a much older same-sex partner/perpetrator.

A "high correlation between sexual abuse in prepubescent years and homosexual and bisexual orientation during adolescence" was identified by Johnson and Shrier (1985). Of the victimized males in their study, 25 percent reported sexual dysfunctions, compared to 5 percent of the nonvictimized males. Sixty percent of the victimized males stated that the sexual abuse had had a significant impact on their lives.

Rogers and Terry (1984) also report that male victims often exhibit behavioral changes that appear to be related to the "homoerotic" implication of the abuse. The behaviors include confusion over their sexual identity, inappropriate attempts to reassert their masculine identity, and attempts for the victim to gain mastery by overidentifying with the offender and modeling his behavior.

Finally, Simari and Baskin (1984) administered an anonymous questionnaire to fifty-four homosexual men and found that 46 percent had been incestuously victimized. They also noted that less than one-third of these men reported being homosexual before their incestuous experience. Additionally, almost half of them were dissatisfied with their gender identity.

Within the clinical case studies, several authors cite numerous problems of sexual behaviors among male victims. Such problems include sexual dysfunctions, problems with sexual adjustment and sexual identity, dissatisfaction with current sexual relationships, and sexual offenses (Becker 1988; Bruckner and Johnson 1987; Brunold 1964; Carlson et al. 1987; Dean and Woods 1985; Longo 1982; Steele and Alexander 1981).

Dimock (1988) gathered information on twenty-five of his adult male clients using case records, clinical observations, and a questionnaire. He found that several of these men displayed signs of compulsive sexual behaviors, such as a preoccupation with sexual thoughts, compulsive masturbation, sexual acts with other men in pornographic bookstores and rest rooms, and frequent and multiple sex partners. One client stated, "I was 16 and was having intercourse with a few different girls. By 17 or 18 there were some occasional prostitutes and lots of masturbating. Overall, there have been many many sex partners and frequent masturbation. I have basically done the things I always thought were masculine to do" (Dimock 1988, p. 209).

In addition, Dimock notes that these clients had masculine identity confusion in the form of either confusion regarding sexual preference or confusion regarding stereotypical male roles. Sixteen of the men had confusion about their sexual preference; eight had confusion that was defined behaviorally as "sexual activity with a partner of the sex opposite the stated sexual orientation of the victim"; three had confusion cognitively ("the inability to state one's sexual preference"); five fit into a category that included both homosexual and heterosexual men who had some questions about their sexual preference and who believed that these doubts were a direct result of having been sexually abused; and two did not engage in any sexual behavior either with males or females but agonized over the sexual preference.

Dimock also found that all of the men who were involved in either homosexual or heterosexual relationships expressed difficulty in maintaining relationship stability. Two men were separated from spouses, three men were experiencing marital problems, one homosexual man expressed his dissatisfaction and his thoughts of leaving his relationship, and several of the men said that they had been involved in relationships as adults that were abusive and that mirrored the victimization experiences they had had as children.

Similarly, Bruckner and Johnson (1987) found in their clinical observations of two groups consisting of five and six male clients, respectively, that all the men questioned their independence and masculinity. Several of them described behaviors that tended to be manifested as an avoidance of sexual activity, either by refraining from sexual activity altogether or by experiencing considerable guilt about any form of sexual behavior. Also, many of the men reported their efforts to prove their worth and adequacy strictly through sexual activity by having sex without intimacy and repeatedly using their partners to confirm their masculinity.

Krug (1989) also concluded from his eight case histories of men who had been sexually molested by their mothers that each of these men experienced difficulty in maintaining a sexual relationship with one person. He reported that 75 percent of his sample had multiple concurrent sexual partners.

There is further literature to suggest that childhood sexual abuse may be related to later sexual offending (Becker 1988; Burgess and Holmstrom 1974; Groth 1979; Groth and Burgess 1977; Longo 1982). Groth (1979) examined 348 men who were convicted of sexual assault either as rapists or as child molesters. One-third of these men appeared to have experienced some type of sexual trauma during their formative years. The predominant type of sexual victimization of the rapists was a pressure/stress situation and of the child molesters a forcible assault. Seventy percent of the rapists had been assaulted by a family member, compared to 27 percent of the child molesters. It was further reported that in comparing sexual offenders who showed an exclusive preference for children with offenders who, under acute stress, deviated from their preferred adult sexual relationships to molest a child, twice as many offenders in the former group reported having been sexually victimized. The author concluded,

> The offender's adult crimes may be in part repetitions and actings out of sexual offenses he was subjected to as a child and as such may represent a maladaptive effort to solve an unresolved early sexual trauma or series of traumas. It can be observed, especially with reference to the child molester, that his later offenses often appear to duplicate his own victimization (p. 15).

Given the review of both the empirical and clinical literature, it appears that males who have been victims of sexual abuse experience a variety of long-term sequelae that are related to their sexual behavior. It is important to recognize that issues of sexual adjustment, sexual identity, and sexual preference are of concern to victimized males and often result in perceptions of confusion and/or distress. It may not be appropriate to state that the relationship between a male's childhood sexual victimization and his later sexual behavior, feelings, or problems is causal. The complexity of an individual's psychosexual development prevents such an oversimplification. However, certain characteristics of the abuse (for example, same-sex victim-perpetrator relationship) or responses to the sexually victimized boy (for example, open and supportive discussion regarding sexuality on the part of parents) may act as mediators in later psychosexual adjustment.

### Problems with Addictive Behaviors

Within the empirical literature, it appears that victimized males experience some problems with social functioning, which is reflected especially in their involvement in substance or alcohol abuse (Stein et al. 1988; Urquiza and Crowley 1986). According to the lifetime prevalence rates, Stein and her colleagues (1988) concluded that male respondents who were abused during childhood were significantly more likely than nonabused respondents to have a higher prevalence of substance use disorder (54.4 percent versus 26.7 percent), alcohol abuse/dependence (35.7 percent versus 23.2 percent), and drug abuse/dependence (44.9 percent versus 7.8 percent). From this same study, an assessment of current problems in these areas (prior six months) suggests similar findings. The men with childhood sexual abuse histories were again significantly more likely than their nonabused counterparts to have a current substance abuse disorder.

The clinical literature also cites examples of problems with substance and/or alcohol abuse among sexually victimized males (Bruckner and Johnson 1987; Dimock 1988; Krug 1989). Sixty-three percent of the men in Krug's (1989) clinical sample were involved in some type of drug abuse. In most cases, the men reported that the drug abuse had begun during or shortly after the abuse and allowed the victim to escape his past and present situations. Similarly, Bruckner and Johnson (1987) and Dimock (1988) report on clients with substance abuse problems. Problems with addictive behaviors appear to be present in some men who were abused during childhood, although the empirical and clinical material to support this claim is meager.

### Summary

Given the presentation of the literature, it appears that several empirical studies with adult male victims of childhood sexual abuse confirm many of the long-term sequelae cited in the clinical literature. Many males who have been victimized suffer detrimental long-term effects such as depression, anxiety, and self-destructive behaviors. Problems with interpersonal relationships, especially trust and maintaining an intimate relationship, also exist. In addition, detrimental effects on sexual behaviors have been reported, back up by strong support from the clinical literature. Included among these behaviors are problems with sexual adjustment, lowered sexual self-esteem, and sexual identity. While the research presented here suggests numerous long-term sequelae, this is by no means conclusive. Further research is needed if we are to continue our attempts at understanding the long-term effects of childhood sexual abuse among males. Perhaps most important is the investigation of a host of mediating factors (such as parental support, presence of familial psychopathology, or involvement with an effective therapeutic resource) that seem to be salient in predicting later adult adjustment (Conte and Schuerman 1987).

## The Impact of the Sexual Abuse of Boys

Browne and Finkelhor's (1986) chapter addressing the effects of abuse on female victims notes that there is some controversy concerning the traumatic effects of sexual victimization (p. 163). They report that certain publications have presented an overinflated perception of the trauma induced by involvement in a sexually abusive experience, that many victims may not be traumatized, and that if they are traumatized, their distress is relatively minor. The authors clearly dismiss this assertion, offering a thorough report of the sequelae of abuse. In what may be a continuation of this same argument, it has been suggested that male victims are less susceptible to victimization and, when victimized, are not as adversely affected by it. One value of a review such as this is that through the description of the type of abuse perpetrated against boys and the victims' responses to each specific characteristic of abuse, we can better understand the distress they experience.

### Effects by Type of Abuse

Little has been written about the characteristics of abuse or the specific sequelae that result from the abuse. This is, in part, a result of the fact that only recently have sexually victimized males been empirically investigated. It also is due to the fact that males may be less responsive to inquiry regarding their victimization experience (De Young 1982; Urquiza 1988). One overriding consideration in reviewing the consequences of abuse by type of abuse is the acknowledgment that doing so perpetuates examining the abuse out of context rather than viewing the victim, the perpetrator, and the family in a set of interactive environments (Bronfenbrenner 1979; Garbarino 1982). This out of context perception can easily lead to faulty or misleading conclusions regarding the comprehensive clinical picture with an individual abuse victim or with a subtype of abuse victims (for example, males, teenagers, or ethnic minorities). As no facet of abuse occurs without many complementary facets, the perception that one characteristic of abuse is more important than another ignores the individual and interactive nature of stress and coping. Thomas (1989) provides a good example of this in her description of clients with "triple jeopardy"—child abuse, drug abuse, and ethnic minority status.

Although recent statistical methods and research have been valuable in clarifying relationships among stressors and children's responses to trauma, the complexity of these problems in real life may prevent easily understood answers (Briere 1988; Garmezy 1983; Garmezy, Masten, and Tellegen 1984; Masten and Garmezy 1985). In acknowledgment of these problems and the limitations inherent in them, and for the benefit of inquiry and to serve as a stepping-stone for further understanding regarding the victimization of males, we present the effects by type here.

## Duration of Abuse

As Browne and Finkelhor (1986) state in their review of females, it is a commonly held belief that the longer the experience goes on, the more traumatic it is to the victim. In their review, they found modest support for this assertion in most of the studies they reviewed, but several of the studies found no relationship or reported evidence to the contrary (that is, longer duration is associated with less trauma). Recent studies have provided additional support for a relationship between duration of abuse and the presence or severity of behavioral and emotional problems (Cole 1987; Urquiza 1988). The issue is more complex, however. As a factor predictive of later problems, duration may be important but not as important as other characteristics of abuse (relationship to the offender, severity of the abuse, use of force, and so on). For example, a boy who is repeatedly abused over a period of three months might reasonably be expected to have greater problems than a boy who is abused only once. However, if the boy subjected to the single incident of abuse was forcefully victimized by a trusted and emotionally close perpetrator in a manner that resulted in physical damage or harm, he may experience greater distress.

## Sex of the Offender and Relationship to the Victim

The following basic questions need to be addressed: What is the sex of the offender? Who is the offender, and what type of relationship does he or she have with the male victim? What influence do the offender's sex and relationship with the victim have on the victim? The response to the first two questions should not be surprising. Most boys (and girls) are victimized by male perpetrators who are well acquainted with them. That perpetrators are usually male and that they know their victims have been substantiated repeatedly in the literature (Condy et al. 1987; Conte, Wolf, and Smith 1987; Finkelhor 1979; Friedrich and Luecke 1988; Kendall-Tackett and Simon 1987; Showers et al. 1983; Urquiza 1988).

The literature specifically addressing or identifying sexually victimized boys strongly identifies males as the primary perpetrators. Published studies report the percentage of male perpetrators as 97 percent (Friedrich, Beilke, and Urquiza 1988), 88.9 percent (Showers et al. 1983), 86 percent (American Humane Association 1981), 66.7 percent (Urquiza 1988), and 53.3 percent (Risin and Koss 1987). Separating the abuse into three levels of severity—exhibition, fondling, and penetration—Risin and Koss (1987) identified male perpetrators in 49.3 percent, 60.9 percent, and 46.8 percent of the cases, respectively.

As many of the perpetrators are male and related to the victim, it can be expected that the relationship between the victim and the offender is best characterized as father or father figure (for example, stepfather), other adult (for example, uncle), or older male relative (for example, sibling or cousin). Urquiza (1988) found only one (2 percent) father or father figure to be an offender, with approximately one-third (30 percent) of the offenders being related to the victim. Rogers and Terry (1984) report that only 8 percent of the boys in their study were abused by a parent or parent figure. In a retrospective chart review, Ellerstein and Canavan (1980) state that 13 percent of the boys in their study were abused by a family member. Data reported by Risin and Koss (1987) describe 22.2 percent of the offenders as being related to the victim. Showers et al. (1983) report that nearly 40 percent of their male victims were abused by a family member. Finally, Friedrich, Beilke, and Urquiza (1988) identified 97 percent of the offenders studied as being related to the victim, and 94 percent of the offenders consisting of male relatives. Given this information, it appears that fathers and father figures do not account for a large proportion of offenders of boys. This is in contrast with female victims, where fathers or father figures make up a significant portion of offenders (Russell 1984; Wyatt 1985).

While many of the offenders are male and family members, several researchers report both a high number of female offenders and family acquaintances (nonfamily members) who served in some caretaking capacity. Specifically, Risin and Koss (1987) report 42.7 percent of the offenders are female, many of whom appeared to be baby-sitters, teachers, neighbors, and parents' friends. Urquiza (1988) also reports 29.4 percent of the offenders as female, most of whom were baby-sitters, teachers, and neighbors. This is not to suggest that there are many undetected female offenders but rather that, for the subgroup of male victims, there may be more female offenders than previously identified in the literature.

The relationship between the victim and the offender has been an important issue with researchers who have examined the sequelae of sexual victimization. It is commonly held that the closer the relationship, the more adverse the consequences for the victim. Therefore, a child abused by a parent or parent figure would be more distressed than a child abused by an unrelated neighborhood perpetrator (that is, given stereotypical valuing for each type of offender from the perspective of the victim).

Although Finkelhor's (1979) data support this proposition, he asserts that this "closeness principle" (pp. 101–102) may not be related to the degree of trauma. Stronger support is identified by Friedrich, Urquiza, and Beilke (1986), who found that the relationship of the child to the perpetrator was a significant factor in predicting the internalization of problem behavior by sexually abused children. This trend is supported in similar analyses with the same and alternate samples (Friedrich 1988; Friedrich, Beilke, and Urquiza 1988). It is interesting to note that in Finkelhor's study of sexually aggressive children (most of whom were male), 85 percent of the identified perpetrators were related to the victim, suggesting that abuse at the hands of an emotionally valued perpetrator may have severely disruptive effects on the child's behavior.

This notion is supported by Urquiza's (1988) research, which indicates that the relationship between the victim and offender is the second most important predictor of both adult self-concept and psychosomatic symptomatology, with the most important predictor being the use of force in the abuse.

## Use of Force or Aggression

One of the best predictors of poor adjustment to any type of victimization appears to be the use of violence or the threat of violence in the abusive experience (Helfer 1987; Koss and Harvey 1987). Many of the traumatizing elements of the sexually abusive experience—such as powerlessness, distrust, distortions in normal development, and the continuing involvement in inappropriate family/peer roles and relationships—are heightened by the use of force. To explain this pattern further, the use of force may cause a variety of physical injuries, which may require medical attention or a longer physical rehabilitation period for recovery or may result in a temporary or permanent disability in physical development or functioning. For example, Ellerstein and Canavan (1980) report some type of anal abrasion or laceration in one-third of the male victims in their study. Similarly, Spencer and Dunklee (1986) found physical injury or evidence of such injury in 68 percent of the cases they reviewed.

As stated earlier, in his retrospective investigation of adult males who were abused as children, Urquiza (1988) found that the use of force in the abuse was the best predictor of both poor self-concept and psychophysiological symptomatology. This is supported by Finkelhor (1979), who states that the use of force is one of the most important indicators of trauma among females, although he had too few cases to perform similar analyses of his male victims.

Two studies that do not provide separate analyses for boys and girls appear to support this relationship between force and a negative response. In the Tufts study (Tufts' New England Medical Center 1984), children who were subjected to forceful or coercive abusive experiences demonstrated greater hostility and more fear of aggressive behavior by others. Similarly, Friedrich, Urquiza, and Beilke (1986) identified a strong correlation between the use of force in the abusive experience(s) and both internalizing and externalizing behavior, based on parent reports on the Achenbach Child Behavior Checklist.

## Age of Victim and Age of Offender

Another important element in the assertion that boys constitute a significant portion of child sexual abuse victims and that they meet definitional criteria of abuse (that is, the inability to provide consent and the level of coercion) concerns their age when the initial incident of abuse occurred. Essentially, an argument could be made that older male children or adolescents may possess the capacity to participate in a sexual relationship and interceding is a failure to recognize their rights. For children and younger adolescents, the issue regarding the ability to provide consent is much clearer. In our society, we have societal norms and legal statutes that explicitly forbid child sexual activity (with the exclusion, for the most part, of mutual peer sexual exploration or play). The element of coercion also is clear in undesired sexual activity or sexual activity involving manipulation, threat, or force. An important facet of these issues is the age of the male victim at the time of the first victimization experience and the difference in age between the victim and the perpetrator. If a boy is an adolescent at the time of his first victimization, and if the offender is of a similar age, it might be argued that this is simply an early mutually desired sexual relationship, and the terms victim perpetrator, offender, and abuse are inappropriate.

Several studies have demonstrated that victimized boys are usually in early adolescence or younger. Risin and Koss (1987), in a retrospective examination of males, found that the first incident of victimization occurred at a mean age of 9.8 years (median age was 10 years). In a smaller study, Pierce and Pierce (1985) reported the mean age of their male victims to be 8.6 years. In another retrospective study of males, Urquiza (1988) reported a mean age of 10.29 years. Rogers and Terry (1984) note that 83 percent of the boys in their sample were under the age of 12, with 26 percent under the age of

6. In their sample of boys, Showers et al. (1983) report a mean age of 7.89 years (standard deviation was 4.09 years). Male victims in Ellerstein and Canavan's (1980) study had a mean age of 9.7 years.

In contrast, the reported mean age of offenders appears to be significantly older than the reported mean age of victims. Several studies have cited ages of perpetrators, including Urquiza (1988), with a mean age of 20.35 years (standard deviation was 9.83 years); Risin and Koss (1987), who note that most of the offenders in their study were between the ages of 18 and 20 years; and Showers et al. (1983), who do not provide a mean age but report a median age of 17 years.

With such a clear difference between the age of the victims and their perpetrators, boys should clearly be perceived as being vulnerable to abuse meeting most or all definitional criteria for sexual abuse. Most of the studies previously described identify male victims as children or young adolescents, with the mean age of their perpetrators being at least eight to ten years older. Given the young age of victims and this age difference, it should be clear that the boys described in the studies were sexually abused. But aside from the difference in age between victims and offenders, and the ages of boys at first victimization, there is a question of whether age at time of abuse has an effect on the child's response to the sexually abusive experience.

Given the limited number of studies of males, there appears to be no conclusive relationship between age at onset and impact of the abuse. No strong data (specifically with male subjects) support assertions regarding a greater impact among younger or older children. Several studies failed to find any significant relationship between age at onset and behavioral or psychological outcome variables (Friedrich, Beilke, and Urquiza 1988; Urquiza 1988). Studies using both male and female subjects also have been unable to make any clear assertions regarding the age of victim at onset of abuse and effects (Friedrich, Urquiza, and Beilke 1986; Meiselman 1978; Tufts' New England Medical Center 1984).

## Problems with the Literature

An often cited criticism in the literature is the failure to apply scientific criteria to the study of a specific population. Browne and Finkelhor (1984) note, "Most of the available studies have sample, design, and measurement problems that could invalidate their findings. The study of the sexual abuse of children would benefit greatly from some basic methodological improvements" (pp. 175–176). This assertion, being accurate for their review of sexually victimized females, may be an indicator of the current status of research concerning sexually abused boys. If the body of literature concerning female victims is still in its "infancy" (Browne and Finkelhor 1984, p. 175), the parallel body of literature concerning males may best be described as in an embryonic stage.

All of the problems inherent in the field of family violence apply to the attempt to understand male victims. Most current studies of males have relied on small samples, inhibiting the use of sophisticated statistical techniques. These samples are often biased, as the participants are recruited from clinic- or therapy-referred boys or men. This results in serious problems of self-selection, which precludes the possibility of obtaining a truly representative sample of victimized boys or men. While attempts at alleviating this problem through university or college student samples reduce the problem of self-selection, they do not eliminate the problem and may bring about a different set of confounding problems, such as distortions of memory or the denial involved in retrospective research.

Few of the studies of sexually victimized boys and men have included comparison or control groups. Because of the complexities involved in the sexual victimization of children, it is strongly suggested that studies be designed with both a group of normal controls (nonabuse, nonreferral) and a clinical comparison group (referral for some type of problem). In this way, researchers can identify unique characteristics associated with being part of a clinical group or a sexually victimized group.

As stated earlier, much of the research conducted in the area of children's responses to trauma and stress has provided valuable insight into the developmental, individual, and environmental factors that lead to recovery and adjustment. To assume that we can develop a comprehensive understanding of all victim responses to sexually abusive experiences is unreasonable. The complexity and interactive nature of the child victim, the perpetrator, the victim's family, and the victim's environment play vital roles in determining both the child's response to the abuse and the manner in which he or she adapts to the abuse. Few studies have attempted to address these types of factors in understanding the abuse of children. It may be that at this time, we are unable to apply any research paradigm to address these issues in a comprehensive and meaningful way. But this should not deter us from continuing to expand our understanding of this traumatic experience. We can benefit greatly from applying and extending current research methods to male victims of abuse. This includes acknowledging that males constitute a significant portion of sexually victimized children, incorporating both boys and men into research designs, conducting analyses that examine the unique gender differences or similarities associated with victimization, and investigating differences in victim's responses to abuse.

## Conclusion

The picture drawn from the studies described in this chapter is of a broad range of both short- and long-term negative consequences resulting from childhood sexual victimization. We have long known that the sexual victimization of girls can be physically, emotionally, and psychologically damaging. Now we should also begin to realize the type and severity of the damage that can be inflicted on male victims. While we do not fully understand much of what occurs with sexually victimized boys and their development to adulthood, there is sufficient evidence to state quite strongly that *boys are vulnerable to sexual abuse, boys can be hurt by sexual abuse,* and, when hurt, *boys often carry the pain of their victimization to adulthood.* What we now need to do is to support individual, community, and societal mechanisms that will enable boys and men to be perceived as victims, to speak of their victimization, and to seek treatment to address their victimization experiences.

It may be that, at this time, the sexual victimization of males requires primary attention in the field of child sexual abuse and in both the public and political arenas. Support for this proposition comes from the fact that significant numbers of boys are victims of sexual abuse and there is some indication that males are less willing than females to disclose sexual abuse information (De Young 1982), suggesting that the current estimate regarding the prevalence of sexual abuse among males is low. This assertion is supported by research concerning nonincarceratead sex offenders, which reports that in nonincest cases, child molesters target boys much more frequently than they do girls (Abel et al. 1987). Furthermore, males are generally less likely to seek informal (social support) or formal (therapy) assistance for their abuse-related problems. Thus, these problems may be less likely to be addressed and resolved.

In contrast to female victims, men have few role models to assist them in finding their way through the complexities of recovery. This is in part demonstrated by the numerous autobiographical accounts of women with a sexually abusive history (Allen 1980; Armstrong 1978; Bass and Thornton 1983; Brady 1979; Gallagher 1985; McNaron and Morgan 1982; Morris 1982) and the absence of similar accounts by men (Hunter 1990). Finally, while there is growing evidence that females also engage in the sexual molestation of children, the evidence also suggests that child molesters are primarily males and that many of these molesters have a history of sexual victimization themselves. By attending to male victims, we can begin to address the factors that lead to the development of sexually deviant cognitions and behaviors (Ryan 1989).

Within the development of any new area, one of the first tasks is to describe the boundaries and content of the problem. This chapter has attempted to describe some of the issues unique to male victims of childhood sexual abuse. However, this is just the first step. The task at hand is to increase our understanding of the mediators that lead to various adaptive and maladaptive outcomes and then to provide support that will lead to recovery for male victims. Garmezy (1983) identifies three broad factors that lead to more healthy adaptive outcomes in children exposed to a variety of stressful events. These are (1) the basic constitutional characteristics of the child (for example, temperament, high self-esteem, and internal locus of control); (2) a supportive family environment (warmth, nurturance, organization, and so on); and (3) a supportive individual or agency that provides a primary support system to assist the child in coping and in developing a positive model for identification. Current research suggests that the keys to recovery lie in these three factors. At this time, we need to examine these factors further as they relate to the victimization experience of young boys and begin to alter our views about the vulnerability of boys and their need for therapeutic intervention.

# References

Abel, G.G., J.V. Becker, M. Mittelman, J. Cunningham-Rathner, J.L. Rouleau, and W.D. Murphy. 1987. "Self-Reported Sex Crimes of Non-incarcerated Paraphiliacs." *Journal of Interpersonal Violence* 2 (no. 1): 3–25.

Achenbach, T.M. 1978. "The Child Behavior Profile. Part 1: Boys Aged 6 through 11." *Journal of Consulting and Clinical Psychology* 46: 478–488.

Achenbach, T., and C. Edelbrock. 1983. *Manual for the Child Behavior Checklist and Revised Child Behavior Profile.* Burlington, Vermont: Queen City Printers.

Adams-Tucker, C. 1982. "Proximate Effects of Sexual Abuse in Childhood: A Report on 28 Children." *American Journal of Psychiatry* 139 (no. 10): 1252–1256.

———. 1985. "Defense Mechanisms Used by Sexually Abused Children." *Children Today* 14 (no. 1): 8–12.

Allen, C.V. 1980. *Daddy's Girl.* New York: Wyndham Books.

American Humane Association. 1981. *National Study on Child Neglect and Abuse Reporting.* Denver: AHA.

Armstrong, L. 1978. *Kiss Daddy Goodnight.* New York: Pocket Books.

Awad, G.A. 1976. "Father-Son Incest: A Case Report." *Journal of Nervous and Mental Disease* 162 (no. 2): 135–139.

Barton, B.R., and A.S. Marshall. 1986. "Pivotal Pairings: Forced Termination with a Sexually Abused Boy." *Clinical Social Work Journal* 14 (no. 2): 138–149.

Bass, E., and L. Thornton. 1983. *I Never Told Anyone: Writings by Women Survivors of Child Sexual Abuse.* New York: Harper & Row.

Becker, J.V. 1988. "The Effects of Child Sexual Abuse on Adolescent Sexual Offenders." In *Lasting Effects of Child Sexual Abuse,* edited by G.E. Wyatt and G.J. Powell, 193–207. Beverly Hills, California: Sage Publications.

Bell, A., and M. Weinberg. 1981. *Sexual Preference: Its Development among Men and Women.* Bloomington: Indiana University Press.

Bender, L., and A. Blau. 1937. "The Reaction of Children to Sexual Relations with Adults." *American Journal of Orthopsychiatry* 7: 500–518.

Bender, L., and A. Grugett. 1952. "A Follow-up Report on Children Who Had Atypical Sexual Experiences." *American Journal of Orthopsychiatry* 22: 825–837.

Boatman, B., E.L. Borkan, and D.H. Schetky. 1981. "Treatment of Child Victims of Incest." *American Journal of Family Therapy* 9 (no. 4): 43–51.

Brady, K. 1979. *Father's Days: A True Story of Incest.* New York: Dell.

Briere, J. 1988. "Controlling for Family Variables in Abuse Effects Research: A Critique of the 'Partialling' Approach." *Journal of Interpersonal Violence* 3 (no. 1): 80–89.

Briere, J., D. Evans, M. Runtz, and T. Wall. 1988. "Symptomatology in Men Who Were Molested as Children: A Comparison Study." *American Journal of Orthopsychiatry* 58 (no. 3): 457–461.

Bronfenbrenner, U. 1979. *The Ecology of Human Development: Experiments by Nature and Design.* Cambridge: Harvard University Press.

Browne, A., and D. Finkelhor. 1984. "Initial and Long-Term Effects: A Review of the Research." In *A Sourcebook on Child Sexual Abuse,* edited by D. Finkelhor, 143–179. Beverly Hills, California: Sage Publications.

Bruckner, C., and P. Johnson. 1987. "Treatment for Adult Male Victims of Childhood Sexual Abuse." *Social Casework: The Journal of Contemporary Social Work* (February): 81–87.

Brunold, H. 1964. "Observations after Sexual Traumata Suffered in Childhood." *Excerpta Criminologica* 4: 5–8.

Burgess, A.W. 1978. "Divided Loyalty in Incest Cases." In *Sexual Assault of Children and Adolescents,* edited by A.W. Burgess, A.N. Groth, L.L. Holmstrom, and S.M. Sgroi, 115–127. Lexington, Massachusetts: Lexington Books.

Burgess, A.W., A.N. Groth, and M.P. McCausland. 1981. "Child Sex Initiation Rings." *American Journal of Orthopsychiatry* 51 (no. 1): 110–119.

Burgess, A., and L. Holmstrom. 1974. *Rape: Victims of Crisis.* Bowie, Maryland: Brady.

Burgess, A.W., L.L. Holmstrom, and M.P. McCausland. 1977. "Child Sexual Assault by a Family Member: Decisions Following Disclosure." *Victimology: An International Journal* 2 (no. 2): 236–250.

Cairns, P. 1983. *Sexual Addiction.* Minneapolis: Compcare.

Cantwell, H.B. 1988. "Child Sexual Abuse: Very Young Perpetrators." *Child Abuse and Neglect* 12: 579–582.

Carlson, S., P. Dimock, J. Driggs, and T. Westly. 1987. "Relationship of Childhood Sexual Abuse and Adult Sexual Compulsiveness in Males." Workshop presented at the First National Conference on Sexual Compulsivity/Addiction: Controversies in Definition, Etiology and Treatment, Minneapolis, May.

Carmen, E., P. Rieker, and T. Mills. 1984. "Victims of Violence and Psychiatric Illness." *American Journal of Psychiatry* 141 (no. 3): 378–383.

Cole, C.B. 1987. "The Specificity of Long-Term Effects of Sexual Abuse and Factors Mediating Outcome: A Comparison of Sexually and Physically Abused Young Adults." Unpublished doctoral dissertation, University of Washington, Seattle.

Condy, S.R., D.I. Templer, R. Brown, and L. Veaco. 1987. "Parameters of Sexual Contact of Boys with Women." *Archives of Sexual Behavior* 16 (no. 5): 379–394.

Conte, J.R., and J.R. Schuerman. 1987. "Factors Associated with an Increased Impact of Child Sexual Abuse." *Child Abuse and Neglect* 2 (no. 4): 210–211.

Conte, J.R., S. Wolf, and T. Smith. 1987. "What Sexual Offenders Tell Us about Prevention Findings." Paper presented at the Third National Family Violence Conference, Durham, New Hampshire, July.

Courtois, C. 1979. "The Incest Experience and Its Aftermath." *Victimology: An International Journal* 4: 337–347.

Davis, G.E., and H. Leitenberg. 1987. "Adolescent Sex Offenders." *Psychological Bulletin* 101 (no. 3): 417–427.

Dean, K., and S. Woods. 1985. "Implications and Findings of the Sexual Abuse of Males Research." Workshop presented at the Child Welfare League of America, Inc., Gatlinburg, Tennessee, May.

Deisher, R.W., G.A. Wenet, D.M. Paperny, T.F. Clark, and P.A. Feherenbach. 1982. "Adolescent Sexual Offense Behavior: The Role of the Physician." *Journal of Adolescent Health Care* 2: 279–286.

De Young, M. 1982. *The Sexual Victimization of Children*. London: McFarland and Co.

Dimock, P. 1988. "Adult Males Sexually Abused as Children." *Journal of Interpersonal Violence* 3 (no. 2): 203–221.

Dixon, K., E. Arnold, and K. Calestro. 1978. "Father-Son Incest: Underreported Psychiatric Problem?" *American Journal of Psychiatry* 137 (no. 7): 835–838.

Ellerstein, N.S., and W. Canavan. 1980. "Sexual Abuse of Boys." *American Journal of Diseases in Children* 134: 255–257.

Eme, R.F. 1979. "Sex Differences in Childhood Psychopathology: A Review." *Psychological Bulletin* 86 (no. 3): 574–595.

Emery, R.E., and K.D. O'Leary. 1982. "Children's Perceptions of Marital Discord and Behavior Problems of Boys and Girls." *Journal of Abnormal Child Psychology* 10: 11–24.

Everstine, D.S., and L. Everstine. 1989. *Sexual Trauma in Children and Adolescents: Dynamics and Treatment*. New York: Bruner/Mazel.

Feherenbach, P.A., W. Smith, C. Monastersky, and R.W. Deisher. 1986. "Adolescent Sexual Offenders: Offender and Offense Characteristics." *American Journal of Orthopsychiatry* 56 (no. 2): 225–233.

Finkelhor, D. 1979. *Sexually Victimized Children*. New York: Free Press.

———. 1984. *Child Sexual Abuse: New Theory and Research*. New York: Free Press.

Finkelhor, D., ed. 1986. *A Sourcebook on Child Sexual Abuse*. Newbury Park, California: Sage Publications.

Freeman-Longo, R.E. 1986. "The Impact of Sexual Victimization on Males." *Child Abuse and Neglect* 10: 411–414.

Friedrich, W.N. 1988. "Behavior Problems in Sexually Abused Children: An Adaptational Perspective." In *Lasting Effects of Child Sexual Abuse*, edited by G.E. Wyatt and G.J. Powell, 171–192. Beverly Hills, California: Sage Publications.

Friedrich, W.N., R. Beilke, and A.J. Urquiza. 1987. "Children from Sexually Abusive Families: A Behavioral Comparison." *Journal of Interpersonal Violence* 2 (no. 4): 391–402.

———. 1988. "Behavior Problems in Young Sexually Abused Boys." *Journal of Interpersonal Violence* 3: 1–12.

Friedrich, W.N., and W.J. Luecke. 1988. "Young School-Age Sexually Aggressive Children." *Professional Psychology: Research and Practice* 19 (no. 2): 155–164.

Friedrich, W.N., A.J. Urquiza, and R. Beilke. 1986. "Behavior Problems in Sexually Abused Young Children." *Journal of Pediatric Psychology* 11: 47–57.

Fritz, G.S., K. Stoll, and N.A. Wagner. 1981. "A Comparison of Males and Females Who Were Sexually Molested as Children." *Journal of Sex and Marital Therapy* 7: 54–59.

Gallagher, V. 1985. *Speaking Out, Fighting Back: Women Who Have Survived Child Sexual Abuse in the Home.* Seattle: Madrona Publishers.

Garbarino, J. 1982. *Children and Families in the Social Environment.* New York: Aldine Publishing Company.

Garmezy, N. 1983. "Stressors of Childhood." In *Stress, Coping and Development in Children,* edited by M. Rutter and N. Garmezy, 43–84. New York: McGraw-Hill.

Garmezy, N., A. Masten, and A. Tellegen. 1984. "The Study of Stress and Competence in Children: A Building Block for Developmental Psychopathology." *Child Development* 55: 97–111.

Geiser, R.L., and M. Norberta. 1976. "Sexual Disturbance in Young Children." *American Journal of Maternal Child Nursing* (May/June): 187–194.

Gomes-Schwartz, B. 1984. "Juvenile Sexual Offenders." In *Sexually Exploited Children: Service and Research Project.* Washington, D.C.: U.S. Department of Justice.

Gomes-Schwartz, B., J. Horowitz, and M. Sauzier. 1985. "Severity of Emotional Distress Among Sexually Abused Preschool, School-Age and Adolescent Children." *Hospital and Community Psychiatry* 36 (no. 5): 503–508.

Groth, N. 1979. "Sexual Trauma in the Life Histories of Rapists and Child Molesters." *Victimology: An International Journal* 4 (no. 1): 10–16.

Groth, N., and A. Burgess. 1977. "Rape: Power, Anger, and Sexuality." *American Journal of Psychiatry* 134: 1239–1243.

Helfer, R.E. 1987. "The Developmental Basis of Child Abuse and Neglect: An Epidemiological Approach." In *The Battered Child,* 4th ed., edited by R.E. Helfer and R.S. Kempe, 60–80. Chicago: University of Chicago Press.

Herman, J. 1981. *Father-Daughter Incest.* Cambridge: Harvard University Press.

Hunter, M. 1990. *Abused Boys: The Neglected Victims of Sexual Abuse.* Lexington, Massachusetts: Lexington Books.

Johnson, R., and D. Shrier. 1985. "Sexual Victimization of Boys." *Journal of Adolescent Health Care* 6: 372–376.

Kendall-Tackett, K.A., and A.F. Simon. 1987. "Perpetrators and Their Acts: Data from 365 Adults Molested as Children." *Child Abuse and Neglect* 11: 237–245.

Koss, M., and M. Harvey. 1987. *The Rape Victim: Clinical and Community Approaches to Treatment.* Lexington, Massachusetts: Stephen Greene Press.

Krieger, M.J., A.A. Rosenfeld, A. Gordon, and M. Bennett. 1980. "Problems in the Psychotherapy of Children with Histories of Incest." *American Journal of Psychotherapy* 34: 81–88.

Krug, R. 1989. "Adult Male Report of Childhood Sexual Abuse by Mothers: Case Descriptions, Motivations and Long-Term Consequences." *Child Abuse and Neglect* 13: 111–119.

Landis, J. 1956. "Experiences of 500 Children with Adult Sexual Deviants." *Psychiatric Quarterly Supplement* 30: 90–91.

Langsley, D.G., M.N. Schwartz, and R.H. Fairbairn. 1968. "Father-Son Incest." *Comprehensive Psychiatry* 9: 218–226.

Lanyon, R.I. 1986. "Theory and Treatment of Child Molestation." *Journal of Consulting and Clinical Psychology* 54 (no. 2): 176–182.

Levine, M.D. 1982. "Encopresis: Its Potentiation, Evaluation, and Alleviation." *Pediatric Clinics of North America* 29 (no. 2): 315–330.

Lew, M. 1988. *Victims No Longer: Men Recovering from Incest and Other Child Sexual Abuse.* New York: Nevraumont Publishing Co.

Longo, R.E. 1982. "Sexual Learning and Experiences among Adolescent Sexual Offenders." *International Journal of Offender Therapy and Comparative Criminology* 26: 235–241.

Masten, A.S., and N. Garmezy. 1985. "Risk, Vulnerability, and Protective Factors in Developmental Psychopathology." In *Advances in Clinical Child Psychology,* vol. 8, edited by B.B. Lahey and A.E. Kazdin, 1–52. New York: Plenum Press.

McCauley, E., P.M. Burke, J. Furukawa, and A.J. Urquiza. 1983. "Sexual Behavior Problems in Pre-pubertal Children." Unpublished manuscript, University of Washington.

McNaron, T., and Y. Morgan. 1982. *Voices in the Night: Women Speaking about Incest.* Minneapolis: Cleis Press.

Meiselman, K. 1978. *Incest: A Psychological Study of Causes and Effects with Treatment Recommendations.* San Francisco: Jossey-Bass.

Morris, M. 1982. *If I Should Die before I Wake.* New York: Dell.

Murphy, H.B.M. 1964. "Foster Home Variables and Adult Outcome." *Mental Hygiene* 48: 587–601.

Pennebaker, J.W. 1989. "Confession, Inhibition and Disease." *Advances in Experimental Social Psychology* 22: 211–244.

Pennebaker, J.W., and C.W. Hoover. 1986. "Inhibition and Cognition: Toward an Understanding of Trauma and Disease." In *Consciousness and Self-Regulation,* vol. 4, edited by R.J. Davidson, G.E. Schwartz, and D. Shapiro, 107–136. New York: Plenum Press.

Pennebaker, J.W., and J.R. Susman. 1988. "Disclosure of Traumas and Psychosomatic Processes." *Social Science Medicine* 26 (no. 3): 327–332.

Peters, S. 1988. "Child Sexual Abuse and Later Psychological Problems." In *Lasting Effects of Child Sexual Abuse,* edited by G.E. Wyatt and G.J. Powell, 101–117. Newbury Park, California: Sage Publications.

Pierce, R., and L.H. Pierce. 1985. "The Sexually Abused Child: A Comparison of Male and Female Victims." *Child Abuse and Neglect* 9: 191–199.

Pomeroy, J.C., D. Behar, and M.A. Stewart. 1981. "Abnormal Sexual Behavior in Prepubertal Children." *British Journal of Psychiatry* 138: 119–125.

Porter, F.S., L.C. Blick, and S.M. Sgroi. 1983. "Treatment of the Sexually Abused Child. In *Handbook of Clinical Intervention of Child Sexual Abuse,* edited by S.M. Sgroi, 107–146. Lexington, Massachusetts: Lexington Books.

Qualand, M. 1985. Compulsive Sexual Behavior: Definition of a Problem and an Approach to Treatment." *Journal of Sex and Marital Therapy* 11: 121–132.

Rasmussen, H.K., and A.J. Urquiza. 1988. "Confusion as a Traumagenic Dynamic of Child Sexual Abuse." Paper presented at the National Symposium of Child Victimization, Anaheim, California, April.

Risin, L.I., and M.P. Koss. 1987. "The Sexual Abuse of Boys: Prevalence and Descriptive Characteristics of Childhood Victimization." *Journal of Interpersonal Violence* 2 (no. 3): 309–323.

Rogers, C., and T. Terry. 1984. "Clinical Intervention with Boy Victims of Sexual Abuse." In *Victims of Sexual Aggression,* edited by I. Stewart and J. Greer, 91–104. New York: Van Nostrand Reinhold.

Russell, D.E.H. 1984. *Sexual Exploitation: Rape, Child Sexual Abuse, Sexual Harassment.* Newbury Park, California: Sage Publications.

Rutter, M. 1970. "The Long-Term Effects of Early Experience." *Developmental Medicine in Child Neurology* 22: 800–815.

Ryan, G. 1989. "Victim to Victimizer: Rethinking Victim Treatment." *Journal of Interpersonal Violence* 4 (no. 3): 325–341.

Sebold, J. 1987. "Indicators of Child Sexual Abuse in Males." *Social Casework: The Journal of Contemporary Social Work* 68 (no. 2): 75–80.

Seidner, A., K. Calhoun, and D. Kilpatrick. 1985. "Childhood and/or Adolescent Sexual Experiences: Predicting Variability in Subsequent Adjustment." Paper presented at the Ninety-third Annual Convention of the American Psychological Association, Toronto, Ontario, August.

Sgroi, S.M. 1977. "Kids with Clap: Gonorrhea as an Indicator of Child Sexual Assault." *Victimology: An International Journal* 2 (no. 2): 251–267.

Showers, J., E.D. Farber, J.A. Joseph, L. Oshins, and C.F. Johnson. 1983. "The Sexual Victimization of Boys: A Three-Year Survey." *Health Values* 7 (no. 4): 15–18.

Simari, C.G., and D. Baskin. 1984. "Incestuous Experiences within Lesbian and Male Homosexual Populations: A Preliminary Study." *Child Psychiatry Quarterly* 17 (no. 1/2): 21–40.

Spencer, M.J., and P. Dunklee. 1986. "Sexual Abuse of Boys." *Pediatrics* 78 (no. 1): 133–138.

Steele, B., and H. Alexander. 1981. "Long-Term Effect of Sexual Abuse in Childhood." In *Sexually Abused Children and Their Families,* edited by P.B. Mrazek and C.H. Kempe, 223–234. Oxford, Eng.: Pergamon.

Stein, J., J. Golding, J. Siegel, M.A. Burnam, and S. Sorenson. 1988. "Long-Term Psychological Sequelae of Child Sexual Abuse." In *Lasting Effects of Child Sexual Abuse,* edited by G.E. Wyatt and G.J. Powell, 135–154. Newbury Park, California: Sage Publications.

Symonds, C.L., M.J. Mendoza, and W.C. Harrell. 1980. "Forbidden Sexual Behavior among Kin: A Study of Self-Selected Respondents." In *Children and Sex,* edited by L. Constantine and F.M. Martinson, 151–162. Boston: Little, Brown.

Thomas, J.N. 1989. "Triple Jeopardy: Child Abuse, Drug Abuse, and the Minority Client." *Journal of Interpersonal Violence* 4 (no. 3): 351–355.

Tufts' New England Medical Center, Division of Child Psychiatry. 1984. *Sexually Exploited Children: Service and Research Project.* Final report for the Office of Juvenile Justice and Delinquency Prevention. Washington, D.C.: U.S. Department of Justice.

Urquiza, A.J. 1986. "Behavior Problems in Child Victims of Sexual Abuse: An Empirical Investigation." Unpublished master's thesis, University of Washington, Seattle.

————. 1988. "The Effects of Childhood Sexual Abuse in an Adult Male Population." Unpublished doctoral dissertation, University of Washington, Seattle.

Urquiza, A.J., and C. Crowley. 1986. "Sex Differences in the Long-Term Adjustment of Child Sexual Abuse Victims." Paper presented at the Third National Conference of the Sexual Victimization of Children, New Orleans, May.

Wenet, F.A., T.R. Clark, and R.J. Hunner. 1981. "Perspectives on the Juvenile Sexual Offender." In *Exploring the Relationship between Child Abuse and Delinquency,* edited by R.J. Hunner and Y.E. Walker, 145–151. Montclair, New Jersey: Allenheld, Osmun.

Yates, A. 1982. "Children Eroticized by Incest." *American Journal of Psychiatry 5:* 111–124.

# 6
# The Sexual Abuse of Boys: A Study of the Long-Term Psychological Effects

*Peter E. Olson*

The sexual abuse of children has received wide attention in the past ten years. Researchers have sought to understand the dynamics of incest and extrafamilial abuse as well as to assess the number of children involved. The vast majority of research has focused on the incidence of the problem. Furthermore, most research has involved only female victims with male perpetrators.

## Estimates of the Sexual Abuse of Boys

Estimates are that approximately 8 percent of boys are sexually abused by age fifteen (Landis 1956; Finkelhor 1980a, 1981, 1984; Bell and Weinberg 1978, 1981; Gentry, Driscoll, and Hopper 1980; Fritz, Stoll, and Wagner 1981; Nielsen 1983; Kercher and McShane 1983; Hall and Flannery 1984). This suggests that a conservative estimate of the number of molested boys in this country alone runs into the millions. Despite these numbers, there has been minimal research into the extent of childhood sexual abuse of boys, its psychological impact (both short and long term), and its treatment.

David Finkelhor (1984) was one of the first researchers to ask about the sexual abuse of boys. He believed that the lack of research on the topic of male sexual abuse was due to the public's discomfort with the topic, traditional sex roles' preclusion of males as victims, and homophobia.

## Long-Term Psychological Impact

### Anecdotal Studies

Anecdotal research and theoretical writings have suggested that there exists a pattern of psychological damage in boys who are molested in or outside of the home.

A connection has been noticed between a history of incest and psychosis in female psychiatric patients (Rosenfeld 1979; Lukianowicz 1972; Browning and Boatman 1977). Margolis (1977, 1984) presented a case study of mother-son incest leading to the boy's later psychopathology. Correlations also have been seen between childhood sexual abuse and later chemical dependence and alcoholism (Cohen and Densen-Gerber 1982; Benward and Densen-Gerber 1975; Slager-Jorné 1978).

Ginsburg (1967) found a common history of childhood sexual abuse in a study of boy and adult male prostitutes, as did Coombs (1973). Lloyd (1976) estimated that there are at least 300,000 boy prostitutes in the United States. This figure excludes young adult and adult male prostitutes.

Slager-Jorné (1978) and Mrazek (1980) have stated that two-thirds of sexually abused boys and girls suffer emotional difficulties, including guilt, depression, low self-esteem, sleep disturbances, and learning and behavioral problems. Sarrel and Masters (1982) note a postassault reaction of depression, sexual aversion, and alteration in sexual facility similar to the postrape trauma syndrome described by Burgess and Holmstrom (1974). Finkelhor and Browne (1985) describe feelings of powerlessness as a consequence of sexual abuse. In a later conceptualization, Finkelhor and Browne (1985) describe a configuration of effects of sexual abuse that seem plausibly related to the dynamic of powerlessness, leading to other emotional problems such as guilt. In addition, lowered self-esteem and a loss of life quality have been seen as a long-term effect of childhood sexual abuse.

## Research with Standardized Instruments

Several studies have been conducted on adult female victims of childhood incest using standardized instruments. Meiselman (1978) administered the Minnesota Multiphasic Personality Inventory (MMPI) to sixteen adult women with incest histories, along with a control group. Although not significantly different, the victim group tended to be slightly more disturbed emotionally and much more likely to report specifically sexual problems as adults. Meiselman expanded her study in 1980 to forty-seven subjects. The incest females differed significantly from the control group on three MMPI scales: scale 2 (*D*): T = 71; scale 4 (*Pd*): T = 79; scale 8 (*Sc*): T = 74.

Tsai, Feldman-Summers, and Edgar (1979) conducted a study to assess the psychological impact of sexual abuse on the psychosexual functioning in adult women using the MMPI and two other tests with three groups of thirty women: a group of incest women in therapy, a group of incest women not in therapy who considered themselves well adjusted, and a control group of nonvictims. The clinical incest group was significantly less well adjusted than the two other groups.

Scott and Stone (1986), studying father-daughter incest families with the MMPI, also found a difference between incest females and nonincest females.

The twenty-two victims peaked significantly on scales 4 and 8, which is similar to the results of Meiselman's 1980 study.

While much information has been collected anecdotally and from the caseloads of therapists, researchers rarely have used standardized instruments and collected data other than in a self-report, self-estimate method. Much rarer are any studies collecting standardized data on male victims of childhood sexual abuse.

The purpose of the current study was to determine whether men with histories of childhood sexual abuse differed significantly in their psychological adjustment from other men. All subjects were involved in outpatient mental health psychotherapy. Did early sexual abuse correlate with later maladjustment for men? Five scales (scales 4 through 8) of the MMPI were selected to assess psychological disturbances in the subjects.

## Method

### Subjects

Sixty-nine men were recruited for the study. All the volunteers were clients in private mental health agencies or community mental health clinics, as opposed to a rape crisis center, a hospital crisis center, or a prison. All subjects were currently involved in psychotherapy. It was hoped that the subjects would be typical clients of a mental health agency rather than a crisis center or prison population. All subjects were eighteen years of age or older. Subjects were recruited by their individual psychotherapists. The average age was 32.295 years (standard deviation, 6.072) for victims with an age range of 19 to 50; the average age for nonvictims was 35.4 years (standard deviation, 8.15) with a range of 23 to 49. The majority of subjects were Caucasian and from middle-class homes.

Victims had received an average of 55.227 months (standard deviation, 45.633) of psychotherapy in their lives (excluding chemical dependence treatment or twelve-step groups), while nonvictims had received an average of 42.44 months (standard deviation, 40.744) of psychotherapy in their lives at the time they participated in the study.

Forty-four of the subjects had experienced childhood sexual abuse prior to the age of sixteen. Thirty of the victims were victims of incest. The primary incest perpetrator was the boy's mother (61.5 percent) or the boy's father (52 percent). Thirty-one of the victims were victims of nonfamilial sexual assault as children; the most common perpetrator was a neighbor (23.81 percent).

### Instruments and Procedures

This study sought to help increase information about the sexual abuse of boys by using a standardized instrument (the MMPI).

The sixty-nine subjects took the MMPI and answered an author-written questionnaire concerning demographics and information about the sexual abuse experience. A checklist echoing the problems mentioned by sexual abuse research articles was included in the questionnaire to provide some indication of how typical the victims were and the extent to which their lives had been disturbed following the sexual abuse.

*Analyses*

Five scales of the MMPI were selected to estimate the level of psychological disturbance in the victim group compared with the nonvictim group. A multivariate analysis of variance (MANOVA) was conducted measuring the overall maladjustment of the victims in comparison with the nonvictim subjects. Were the MANOVA to be significant, it would be followed up by univariate analyses of variance (ANOVAs) to estimate each scale's contribution to the overall profile of the victims and nonvictims. These six statistical maneuvers formed the basis of the six hypotheses of this study. Stated in the null format, the hypotheses postulated that mental health outpatient psychotherapy males with a history of childhood sexual abuse would not differ from other outpatient males with no such history.

An analysis of covariance (ANACOVA) also was conducted to control for the impact of psychotherapy length on MMPI scores. There was an obvious concern that men who had received more therapy would appear healthier on the MMPI than men who had received less therapy, introducing a confounding variable into the study.

## Results

All six hypotheses were found to be significant. All six null hypotheses were therefore rejected. The victim group differed significantly from the nonvictim control group on all five scales of the MMPI as well as in the MANOVA.

The MANOVA of the five scales of the MMPI (Pd, Mf, Pa, Pt, and Sc), using victimization as the independent variable, found a highly significant Wilks' lambda $\lambda$ and $F$ statistic, with significance at $p < .00001$ (table 6–1).

**Table 6–1**
**Hypothesis 1: MANOVA of Pd, Mf, Pa, Pt, and Sc**

| Multivariate Test Statistics | | Degrees of Freedom | p |
|---|---|---|---|
| Wilks' lambda $\lambda$ | 0.40611 | | |
| F statistic | 18.42638 | 5,63 | $< .00001$ |

**Table 6–2**
**Univariate Hypotheses Results**

| Hypothesis | Scale | F test | p |
|---|---|---|---|
| Hypothesis 2 | Scale 4 | 72.472 | <.0001 |
| Hypothesis 3 | Scale 5 | 20.293 | .0001 |
| Hypothesis 4 | Scale 6 | 10.068 | .0023 |
| Hypothesis 5 | Scale 7 | 13.38 | .0005 |
| Hypothesis 6 | Scale 8 | 30.51 | <.0001 |

Since the MANOVA was significant, univariate ANOVAs could proceed. Table 6–2 shows that the victim group's scores were significantly higher than the nonvictim group's, allowing for rejection of the remaining five null hypotheses. Figure 6–1 presents the results of the hypotheses in graphic form. The data for all the clinical scales of the MMPI are expressed in table 6–3.

The term *profile* is used to describe common groups of scale configurations and the typical psychological makeup one could possibly expect in the test subject. The Welsh code is the most frequent way to present test profile results. The victim group had a Welsh code profile of 548*726"390'1/ F'-K/L?:. The nonvictim group had a mean Welsh code of 5'4728 63-901/ FK/L?.

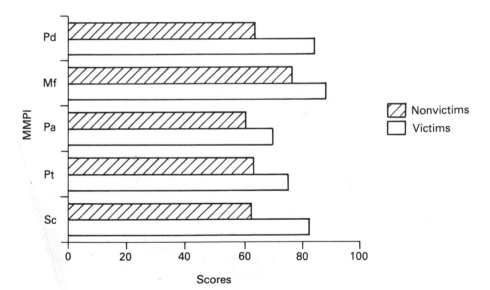

**Figure 6–1. Hypotheses Results**

**Table 6–3**
**Mean T Scores on *K*-Corrected MMPI Scales**

|            | L    | F    | K    | 1    | 2    | 3    | 4    | 5    | 6    | 7    | 8    | 9    | 0    |
|------------|------|------|------|------|------|------|------|------|------|------|------|------|------|
| Victims    | 44.4 | 72.1 | 52.1 | 59.0 | 73.4 | 66.1 | 83.9 | 87.5 | 70.2 | 75.1 | 82.0 | 61.4 | 60.6 |
| Nonvictims | 45.8 | 58.1 | 55.0 | 51.8 | 63.5 | 60.4 | 62.8 | 75.9 | 60.4 | 62.9 | 62.2 | 56.4 | 53.3 |

Figure 6–2 summarizes the differences between the sexually abused men in psychotherapy and their nonvictimized counterparts. These results include forty-four victims and twenty-five nonvictims. The ANACOVA revealed that when the impact of psychotherapy was accounted for in the MMPI scores, the differences between the victim group and the control group increased. The actual results, including the original means and adjusted means, are presented in table 6–4. Thus, even when the impact of treatment length was controlled for, the five scales of the MMPI still successfully differentiated the victims from the nonvictims with robust significance. The adjusted means are shown graphically in figure 6–3.

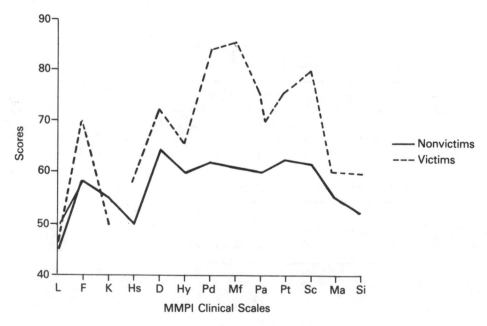

**Figure 6–2. MMPI Results**

**Table 6–4**
**Analyses of Covariance**

| | Victims | | Nonvictims | | | |
|---|---|---|---|---|---|---|
| Scale | Original Mean X | Adjusted Mean X | Original Mean X | Adjusted Mean X | F test | p |
| Pd | 83.909 | 84.07 | 62.76 | 62.477 | 74.707 | <.00001 |
| Mf | 87.455 | 87.695 | 75.88 | 75.457 | 23.044 | .00001 |
| Pa | 70.159 | 70.432 | 60.4 | 59.919 | 11.807 | .00103 |
| Pt | 75.045 | 75.375 | 62.88 | 62.299 | 15.804 | .00018 |
| Sc | 81.955 | 82.158 | 62.24 | 61.881 | 31.751 | <.00001 |

The MANOVA and five of its univariate ANOVAs were significant, refuting each of the null hypotheses. This indicates a higher psychopathology in the victim group than in the nonvictim group. When the length of treatment was controlled for using a multivariate approach with an ANACOVA, the five scales still predicted that victims would score significantly more psycho-pathologically than their nonvictim counterparts.

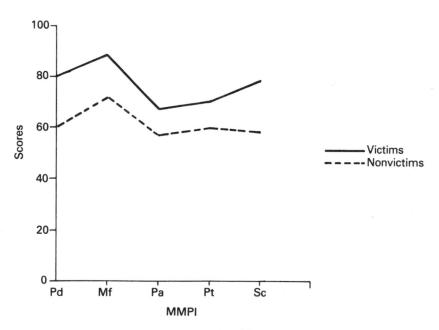

**Figure 6–3. MMPI Means Adjusted by ANACOVA**

**Table 6–5**
**Problem Checklist**

| Behavioral Problem | Victims N | Victims % | Nonvictims N | Nonvictims % | $x^2$ | $p$ |
|---|---|---|---|---|---|---|
| Chemical dependence | 26 | 59 | 8 | 32 | 4.681 | .0305 |
| Alcohol/drug abuse | 35 | 80 | 14 | 56 | 4.294 | .0383 |
| Compulsive gambling | 1 | 2 | 3 | 12 | 2.762 | .0965 |
| Compulsive sexual behavior | 33 | 75 | 5 | 20 | 19.49 | .0001 |
| Bed-wetting past age eight | 11 | 25 | 3 | 12 | 1.666 | .1928 |
| School truancy | 17 | 39 | 3 | 12 | 5.495 | .0191 |
| Poor school performance/concentration | 27 | 61 | 10 | 40 | 2.926 | .0872 |
| Illiteracy or dyslexia | 4 | 9 | 1 | 4 | .615 | .433 |
| Compulsive overworking | 27 | 61 | 8 | 33 | 4.885 | .0271 |
| Work underachievement | 30 | 68 | 11 | 44 | 3.866 | .0493 |
| Binging/purging food | 5 | 11 | 0 | 0 | 3.063 | .0801 |
| Compulsive overeating | 18 | 41 | 4 | 16 | 4.554 | .0328 |
| Anorexia/starving | 8 | 18 | 1 | 4 | 2.827 | .0927 |
| Hustling/prostituting | 6 | 14 | 0 | 0 | 3.734 | .0533 |
| Hiring prostitutes | 3 | 7 | 2 | 8 | .033 | .8556 |
| Rage | 39 | 89 | 11 | 44 | 15.918 | .0001 |
| Violence in a relationship | 16 | 36 | 6 | 24 | 1.122 | .2895 |
| Partner's violence | 21 | 48 | 4 | 16 | 6.946 | .0084 |
| Arrested | 16 | 36 | 1 | 4 | 8.993 | .0027 |
| Served time in jail | 7 | 16 | 0 | 0 | 4.426 | .0354 |
| Compulsive shoplifting | 11 | 25 | 2 | 8 | 3.013 | .0826 |
| Compulsive spending | 24 | 55 | 2 | 8 | 14.708 | .0001 |
| Self-mutilation | 11 | 25 | 1 | 4 | 4.894 | .027 |
| Compulsive relationships | 24 | 55 | 5 | 20 | 7.808 | .0052 |

## Problem Checklist

The scientific literature suggests that sexually abused people suffer from a variety of behavioral and interpersonal problems, either self-inflicted or brought on by important people in their lives. The questionnaire used a problem checklist to determine the more commonly cited problems.

Table 6–5 summarizes the list and the results. The differences between the two groups were highly significant on most of the behavioral problems in the checklist. Although the chi-square is not a highly refined test statistic, here it suggests that male victims bring an assortment of difficult problems with them into psychotherapy.

## Discussion

Is childhood sexual abuse correlated with the later development of adult personality pathology? More specific to this study, does a history of childhood sexual abuse differentiate men who suffered such abuse from other men seeking psychotherapy? This study suggests that it does to a great degree.

All six null hypotheses were rejected, revealing robustly significant differences between sexually abused men in psychotherapy and other men in therapy. The MANOVA on MMPI scales 4 through 8 revealed significance at a level of $p < .00001$ (df = 5,63). Each of the scales was significant by itself in post hoc univariate ANOVAs, in particular scales 4, 5, and 8.

The highest of the mean victim profiles was scale 5 (masculinity-femininity). The victim group with a T score of 87.5 was nearly 4 standard deviations above the norm of 50. According to Graham (1977), scale 5 suffers a second-class status compared to the other clinical scales of the MMPI due to its outmoded norms of sex role stereotyping and sexism. Nonetheless, spiking this high on the fifth scale suggests nonsubscription to traditional sex roles, passivity, or a behavior suppressor.

The second highest scale for victims was scale 4, *Pd*. This scale measures a level of rebelliousness or conflict either in the family, in society, or internally. The higher the scale, according to Duckworth and Anderson (1986), the more overt the struggle—hence the origination of the scale's first title, psychopathic deviate.

The victim group had a mean of T = 83.9, more than 3 standard deviations over the norm of 50. This suggests an intense level of conflict and lack of sync with society, possibly reflecting itself in criminal behavior, compulsions, or other antisocial characteristics. The majority of the victim literature indicates that male victims of sexual abuse struggle with acting-out behaviors, including compulsions and addictions. Scores this high can support the likelihood of such problems. The nonvictim group mean was 62.8, more than 2 standard deviations lower and much closer to societal norms. These men's conflicts are probably much more covert.

Scale 8 (*Sc*) was the third highest for the victim group. The victim group had a mean score of 81.96, compared with 62.24 for the control group. The eighth scale, formerly known as schizophrenia, measures disturbances in thinking. Duckworth and Anderson (1986) suggest that scores in the 70s and above indicate mental confusion, thinking disorders, a lack of logic, and possible chronic disorientation. This author predicted that male victims experience more mental confusion, bizarre thinking, and thought disorder than the control group and the high score on scale 8 lends support to this belief.

Duckworth and Anderson (1986) indicate that the sixth scale of the MMPI (paranoia) suggests three things:

1. Scores from 60 to 70 indicate sensitivity to interacting with others.
2. Scales over 70 suggest a suspiciousness in addition to sensitivity, as well as a flavor of self-rightousness.

The male victim group scored significantly higher than the nonvictim group at T = 70.159, indicating a higher sensitivity, or sense of paranoia, and suspiciousness of others.

Scale 7 of the MMPI, psychasthenia, describes a long-term trait (rather than a state) of anxiety. People who score high on scale 7 experience dread, omnipotence, fear of falling, limited productivity, low self-confidence, and moodiness. The victim group mean score was 75.045, 13 points higher than the nonvictim group. This suggests that the therapy victims in the study experienced trait anxiety more consistently than did the control group members. Dread, or the fear of something bad happening, may be correlated with childhood sexual abuse for men seeking psychotherapy.

## Summary of Hypotheses Results

It must be noted that this was causal-correlational research, a common research model for social research, and not laboratory research with full control of outside variables. Laboratory experimental research is not practical or ethical in research such as this. The possibility of confounding or contributing third variables is acknowledged in causal-correlational research. This was the reason for the post hoc ANACOVA controlling for treatment length as a possible covariate.

Therefore, cause and effect cannot be claimed here but merely a relationship between the experience of childhood sexual abuse and the psychological profile of men who enter psychotherapy. Childhood sexual abuse appears to be highly correlated with the later development of behavior, personality, and thinking disorders in a subject pool of men seeking psychotherapy for personal problems. The discovery in this study supports earlier anecdotal and theoretical research conducted with male victims of sexual abuse and closely resembles the research results of studies of female victims.

## Analysis of Covariance

A follow-up ANACOVA controlled for the impact of treatment length of subjects. When treatment length was controlled for, the MMPI score differences actually increased. Despite the fact that victims tended to have received thirteen months more psychotherapy than nonvictims on the average, the victims appeared more psychologically disturbed than the nonvictims in psychotherapy.

## Overall MMPI Profile Interpretation

Scoring all of the MMPI validity scales and clinical scales allows the use of Marks and Seeman's (1963) MMPI code types. MMPI results are commonly analyzed as groups of scales. (The elevation of all MMPI clinical scales for the two groups was presented in table 19 and figure 8 in chapter 4 of Marks and Seeman.) Using the Welsh elevation code, the experimental and control groups are described below.

The Welsh elevation code for the experimental group of this study is 548*726"390'1/ F'K/L?.: It fits in the 4-8-2/8-4-2/8-2-4 category of the Marks-Seeman MMPI code types.

Graham (1977) suggests that 48/84 (scales 4 and 8) persons

do not seem to fit into their environments. They are seen by others as odd, peculiar, and queer. They are nonconforming and resentful of authority and they often espouse radical religious or political views. Their behavior is erratic and unpredictable, and they have marked problems with impulse control. They tend to be angry, irritable, and resentful, and they act out in asocial ways. . . . Prostitution, promiscuity, and sexual deviation are fairly common among 48/84 individuals. Excessive drinking and drug abuse (particularly involving hallucinogens) may also occur.

[They] harbor deep feelings of insecurity, and they have exaggerated needs for attention and affection. They have poor self-concepts, and it seems as if they set themselves up for rejection and failure. They may have periods during which they become obsessed with suicidal ideation. 48/84 persons are quite distrustful of other people, and they avoid close relationships. When they are involved interpersonally, they have impaired empathy and try to manipulate others into satisfying their needs. They lack basic social skills and tend to be socially withdrawn and isolated. The world is seen as a threatening and rejecting place, and their response is to withdraw or to strike out in anger as a defense against being hurt. . . .

48/84 persons tend to harbor serious concerns about their masculinity or femininity. They may be obsessed with sexual thoughts, but they are afraid that they cannot perform adequately in sexual situations. They may indulge in antisocial sexual acts in an attempt to demonstrate sexual adequacy.

Psychiatric patients with the 48/84 code tend to be diagnosed as schizophrenia (paranoid type), asocial personality, schizoid personality, or paranoid personality. If both scales 4 and 8 are very elevated, and particularly if scale 8 is much higher than scale 4, the likelihood of psychosis and bizarre symptomatology, including unusual thinking and paranoid suspiciousness, increases. (p. 74)

The nonvictimized group was much more likely to fall within the normal range of the MMPI. The Welsh code profile for the nonvictimized control group was 5' 4728 63-901/ FK/L?. Its 2-4-7/4-7-2/7-4-2 profile suggests a contradiction, according to Dahlstrom, Welsh, and Dahlstrom (1982). Scale 4 can indicate some tendency toward impulsive action with little forethought, hurting others, and breaking social norms. But scale 7 suggests excessive concern about one's impact on others. This profile suggests that the subjects might take actions followed by guilt or remorse. Scale 2's depression could inhibit action and feed remorse. At T = 63.48, 62.76, and 62.88 for scales 2, 4, and 7, respectively, though, the scores are only slightly elevated and do not indicate severe problems.

The behavioral and maturity problems of the victimized study group, with thinking disorders likely in addition to the personality disorder, indicate a serious psychopathology. These results support the anecdotal and theoretical literature on the long-term behavioral and characterological impact of sexual abuse on boys, with the subsequent behavioral and thought disorders that seem apparent in groups interviewed: prostitutes, chemically dependent persons, juvenile delinquents, and prisoners. Victims' problems with intimacy and sexuality, noted by numerous writers (including Finkelhor 1984), are validated by the MMPI results and profile interpretation by Dahlstrom, Welsh, and Dahlstrom (1982).

A problem checklist was included in the author-designed questionnaire to reflect current concerns and beliefs in the professional literature about sexually abused boys and the long-term impact of abuse. Analysis found that the vast majority of behavioral problems listed were significantly more frequently faced by the victim group than by the nonvictim group.

The sexually abused men were significantly more likely to have struggled with compulsive behaviors such as chemical addiction and abuse, sexual acting out, compulsive spending, compulsive overworking, and compulsive overeating. They were more likely to have had problems with truancy in school and later to have been involved in criminal behavior. They also reported having been incarcerated in jail more frequently than the nonvictims.

Victims had more often spent time in their lives as prostitutes or hustlers. They reported having a great deal more trouble controlling their own rage and had experienced the violence of a relationship partner. The victims were more likely to have mutilated their bodies by cutting or burning and to have been bulimic (binging and purging) or anorexic.

Approaching the study's question of the long-term impact of sexual abuse from a different angle than the null hypotheses and the MMPI, the problem checklist found that the sexually abused men suffered from more behavioral, social, and adaptation problems than did the other men in psychotherapy.

From either an anecdotal self-report method or using valid, reliable instrumentation and comparative methodology, it was found that men who sought psychotherapy and had been sexually abused as children inside or outside their homes were far more psychologically disturbed than were other male therapy clients, even when length of treatment was controlled for.

## Conclusion

Significant energy has been put into understanding the emotional impact of sexual abuse on children. Most of the research and data collection have gone into understanding females who have been molested by their fathers and other relatives.

Vastly varying beliefs have been bandied about regarding the scars left by this childhood experience. It has been believed that boys who are molested may become prostitutes, violent felons or delinquents, child molesters, socially isolated or sexually compulsive, scholastically limited, psychotic, self-mutilating, angry, guilt ridden, depressed, or ashamed. They may experience low self-esteem or evaluate themselves as unharmed by their history. They may become sexually impotent or suffer from other sexual dysfunctions, and they may become confused about their own sexual preference or gender orientation.

Information about these boys has been scarce. Early researchers believed that no males were molested. The advent of the American feminist movement in the 1970s brought awareness about sexual abuse, but theorists developed models of understanding only for female victims and male perpetrators. The deficiency of the models has only started to be overcome so that they can accommodate the full range of child molestation experiences.

The mental health profession has needed education about the extent and long-term damage done by molestation of boys. Some men have reported facing rejection and doubt from their psychotherapists when attempting to reveal the experience.

Boys still experience shame about their abuse and deny the emotional impact on them. It is difficult to expect children or adults to estimate the impact of so socially denigrated and shameful an experience on the full development of one's life as a man. To ask people to look at their lives and estimate how an incident or life experience has prevented them from becoming better can at best produce widely varying responses. Clinicians have unfortunately held back progress in children's development in this area, but with reeducation they can help boys alleviate the shame and other negative emotions associated with their abuse.

Scientific method and personality assessments of the general subpopulation of sexually abused boys and men are needed. Recent work by Meiselman (1978, 1980) has brought professional and scientific method to the understanding of the human experience of the victimization of women. This now needs to be done for men.

Finkelhor (1979) found that emotional neglect existed in 79 percent of the families in which children suffered sexual abuse, with physical abuse in 11 percent of these cases. Swift (1977) notes, "the high rate of emotional neglect may account in part for the predominance in the literature of the theme of cooperation and/or seduction on the part of the child, and the related finding that few children defined as sexually victimized appear to suffer damaging or long-lasting effects from the experience" (p. 323).

The importance of establishing empirical evidence of the incidence of male sexual abuse and its psychological impact lies in the possibility that these children could be helped and that such evidence could prevent further damage as well as the perpetuation of abusive systems. German theorist and clinician Alice Miller (1983) has said that without recognition and rejection of the parental abuse received, the child will undoubtedly assimilate the experience into his or her personality and repeat the abuse gestures with the next generation of children—not necessarily to molest but to tolerate molestation as a normal, unfortunate, but not damaging experience, to underestimate its impact, or to be blind to one's own children's abuse.

Now we have some indication of the deep scars left and the subsequent damage done by sexual abuse in a study of a group of sexually abused men who sought psychotherapy. What remains frustrating is that despite lengthy psychotherapy, the victim group of this study continues to suffer. Their psychological profile indicates severe behavioral and cognitive problems. With information available about the impact on a wider basis, perhaps treatment can become more sophisticated, more focused, and more successful. Only with understanding can clinicians and psychologists help suffering boys and men and perhaps prevent the abuse cycle from continuing and the long-term psychological impact from going misdiagnosed and untreated.

# References

Bell, A., and M. Weinberg. 1978. *Homosexualities*. New York: Simon and Schuster.
———. 1981. *Sexual Preference: Its Development among Men and Women*. Bloomington: Indiana University Press.
Benward, J., and J. Densen-Gerber. 1975. "Incest as a Causative Factor in Antisocial Behavior: An Exploratory Study." *Contemporary Drug Problems* 4 (no. 3): 323–341.
Browning, D.H., and B.B. Boatman. 1977. "Incest: Children at Risk." *American Journal of Psychiatry* 134 (no.   ): 69–72.
Burgess, A.W., and L.L. Holmstrom. 1974. "Rape Trauma Syndrome." *American Journal of Psychiatry* 131 (no. 9): 981–986.
Cohen, F.S., and J. Densen-Gerber. 1982. "A Study of the Relationship between Child Abuse and Drug Addiction in 176 Patients." *Child Abuse and Neglect* 6: 383–387.
Coombs, N.R. 1973. "Male Prostitution: A Psychosocial View of Behavior." *American Journal of Orthopsychiatry* 44 (no. 5): 782–789.
Dahlstrom, W.G., G.S. Welsh, and L.E. Dahlstrom. 1982. *An MMPI Handbook*. Vol. 1: *Clinical Interpretation*. Rev. ed. Minneapolis: University of Minnesota.
Duckworth, J.C., and W.P. Anderson. 1986. *MMPI Interpretation Manual for Counselors and Clinicians*. Muncie, Indiana: Accelerated Developments Inc.
Finkelhor, D. 1979. *Sexually Victimized Children*. New York: Free Press.
———. 1980a. "Risk Factors in the Sexual Victimization of Children." *Child Abuse and Neglect* 4: 265–273.
———. 1980b. "Sex among Siblings: A Survey on Prevalence, Variety, and Effects." *Archives of Sexual Behavior* 9 (no. 3): 171–193.

———. 1981. "The Sexual Abuse of Boys." *Victimology: An International Journal* 6 (no. 1/4): 76–84.

———. 1984. *Child Sexual Abuse: New Theory and Research*. New York: Free Press.

Finkelhor, D., and A. Browne. 1985. "The Traumatic Impact of Child Sexual Abuse: A Conceptualization." *American Journal of Orthopsychiatry* 55 (no. 4): 530–541.

Fritz, G., K. Stoll, and N. Wagner. 1981. "A comparison of Males and Females Who Were Sexually Molested as Children." *Journal of Sex and Marital Therapy* 7: 54–59.

Gentry, C.E., R. Driscoll, and B.D. Hopper. 1980. "A Retrospective Study of Child/Adolescent Sexual Abuse." *Victimology: An International Journal* 5 (no. 204): 444–446.

Ginsburg, K.N. 1967. "The 'Meat Rack' ": A Study of the Male Homosexual Prostitute. *American Journal of Orthopsychiatry* 21: 170–185.

Graham, J.R. 1977. *The MMPI: A Practical Guide*. New York: Oxford University Press.

Hall, E.R., and P.J. Flannery. 1984. "Prevalence and Correlates of Sexual Assault Experiences in Adolescents." *Victimology: An International Journal* 9 (no. 304): 398–406.

Kercher, G., and M. McShane. 1983. "The Prevalence of Child Sexual Abuse Victimization in an Adult Sample of Texas Residents." Mimeograph, Sam Houston State University, Huntsville, Texas.

Landis, J.T. 1956. "Experiences of 500 Children with Adult Sexual Deviants." *Psychiatric Quarterly Supplement* 30: 91–109.

Lloyd, R. 1976. *For Money or Love: Boy Prostitution in America*. New York: Vanguard Press.

Lukianowicz, N. 1972. "Incest. Part 1: Paternal Incest." *British Journal of Psychiatry* 120: 301–313.

Margolis, M. 1977. "A Preliminary Report of a Case of Consummated Mother-Son Incest." *Annual Psychoanalysis* 5: 267–293.

Margolis, M. 1984. "A Case of Mother-Adolescent Son Incest: A Follow-up Study." *Psychiatric Quarterly* 53: 355–385.

Marks, P.A., and W. Seeman. 1963. *The Actuarial Description of Personality: An Atlas for Use with the MMPI*. Baltimore: Williams & Wilkins.

Meiselman, K.C. 1978. *Incest: A Psychological Study of Causes and Effects with Treatment Recommendations*. San Francisco: Jossey-Bass.

———. 1980. "Personality Characteristics of Incest History Psychotherapy Patients: A Research Note." *Archives of Sexual Behavior* 9 (no. 3): 195–197.

Miller, A. 1983. *For Your Own Good*. New York: Farrar, Strauss & Giroux.

Mrazek, D.A. 1980. "The Child Psychiatric Examination of the Sexually Abused Child." *Child Abuse and Neglect* 4: 275–284.

Nielsen, T. 1983. "Sexual Abuse of Boys: Current Perspectives." *Personnel and Guidance Journal* 62 (no. 3): 139–142.

Rosenfeld, A.A. 1979. "Incidence of a History of Incest among 18 Female Psychiatric Patients." *American Journal of Psychiatry* 136 (no. 6): 791–795.

Sarrel, P., and W. Masters. 1982. "Sexual Molestation of Men by Women." *Archives of Sexual Behavior* 11 (no. 2): 117–131.

Scott, R.L., and D.A. Stone. 1986. "MMPI Profile Constellations in Incest Families." *Journal of Consulting and Clinical Psychology* 54 (no. 3): 364–368.

Slager-Jorné, P. 1978. "Counseling Sexually Abused Children." *Personnel and Guidance Journal* 57: 103–105.

Swift, C. 1977. "Sexual Victimization of Children: An Urban Mental Health Center Survey." *Victimology: An International Journal* 2: 322–327.

Tsai, M., S. Feldman-Summers, and M. Edgar. 1979. "Childhood Molestation: Variables Related to Differential Impacts on Psychosexual Functioning in Adult Women." *Journal of Abnormal Psychology* 88: 407–417.

# 7
# Victims Becoming Offenders:
# A Study of Ambiguities

*Paul N. Gerber*

T he transition from victim to offender is a phenomenon that has generated much debate. A broad spectrum of theories have been set forth that are rooted in everything from clinical impression to emperical data (O'Brien 1989; Freund, Watson, and Dickey 1988; Hindman 1988). One empirically derived theory suggests that a significant percentage of males who were sexually abused as children will become offenders (O'Brien 1989). Moreover, the gender of the abuser will influence the selection of the gender of the next generation of victims. In other words, boys who are sexually abused by males will decidedly choose male victims when they make the transition from victim to offender. As boys and men have a growing social permission to come forward and identify themselves as victims of sexual molestation and sexual assaults, we will see an increasing number of males referred who have not acted out sexually against others in response to their victimization. This has been my clinical experience to date.

Abundantly available for more than a decade is research and theory regarding the treatment of adult male offenders. Pioneering clinical researchers such as Nicholas Groth (Groth et al. 1978) developed theories that brought us terms such as *fixated* and *regressed* as typologies for adult sex offenders.

These theories were widely subscribed to in the mental health and related fields until Abel and his associates (1987) published research findings that challenged the grouping of "regressed" offenders as overly simplistic. This was due to their discovery that purportedly regressed offenders often had large numbers of victims. Additionally, adult male sex offenders frequently had numerous paraphilias. Abel et al. (1987) found large numbers of previously undetected victims per offender, particularly among adult males who selected male children as their victims. This new data on numbers of male victims per adult offender should challenge how we have viewed data collected from victims and offenders in the past.

---

I would like to acknowledge the generous support of Dr. William N. Friedrich, Mayo Clinic, who greatly contributed to the completion of this chapter.

Our understanding of adolescent sex offenders (O'Brien 1989; Becker and Abel 1984; Davis and Leitenberg 1987), female offenders (Mathews 1989), and male victims (Porter 1986; Hunter 1990; Buckner and Johnson 1987) has increased. In light of this new body of knowledge, clinicians will have to reexamine their fondly held theories about victims and offenders. Understanding male victims is necessary, since research in the 1970s and early 1980s primarily identified females as the most frequent victim of child sexual abuse (Finkelhor 1979).

What is increasingly obvious is that there is an imbalance in the information we have about sexual normality or commonality when compared to the abundance of information on deviations or variations. Early research by pioneers such as Kinsey (1948) showed the public that among the general population, there were significant numbers of people involved in uncommon sexual behaviors. Conservative attitudes about what constitutes sexual deviation or variation is illustrative in the continued existence of sodomy laws in state statutes. This imbalance also has the potential to skew the insights of those professionals dealing with the dynamics of sexual molestation or sexual assault victims, as well as sexual offenders. The subject of sexuality in general has been slow to evolve because of the discomfort the topic causes in our society.

It would seem senseless to debate the frequency in which the transition from victim to offender occurs among boys and men. It seems more reasonable to acknowledge that according to research, it occurs with some frequency and causation is attributable to a variety of variables, such as the theory to be set forth here.

My theory is that the transition is in direct proportion to a number of variables, which include age of the victim at the onset of the abuse, duration of the abuse, and the level of trauma and arousal experienced by the victim. Those variables, based on clinical impression, are as follows:

1. The sexual abuse, either periodically or routinely, involved bizarre or ritualistic acts, particularly to the extremes of pseudoreligiosity, pseudosatanism, or satanism.

2. The sexual abuse routinely involved gross paraphilic behaviors such as urolagnia, coprophilia, clysmophilia, or sexual sadism and sexual masochism (DSM III 1987).

3. The victim was subjected to either periodic or routine threats of harm, physical injury, or violence as part of the sexual abuse scenario.

4. The victim was used to recruit other youths, and the recruits were either manipulated or coerced to participate in individual or group sexual activities. A different dynamic will exist when the sexual activities involved a more structured or commercialized form of prostitution or production of pornographic works.

5. The victim was initially induced to be sexual through a seductive, covert, presexual conditioning process. Longevity ultimately was ensured through the progressive use of subtle enticements and inducements. Additionally, the progressive use of subtle coercion or covert threats ensured long-term compliance.

6. The victim previously developed serious characterological/personality problems (conduct disorder, narcissistic personality disorder, and so on) wherein the process of internalizing and normalizing the abuse experience became representative of the victim's existing psychosexual pathology.

7. The long-term abuse experience brought the victim to a point where he was using force or violence in an attempt to resolve the interpersonal conflicts created by his own experience.

8. Through the prolonged exposure to the sexually abusive behavior, an adolescent victim became highly eroticized to the overall abuse experience or very specific aspects of certain acts. In some cases, this erotization can represent the onset of a paraphilia. The emerging paraphilia can be reinforced through fantasy paired with masturbation, but overt acts against others may not occur. Comparatively, an abuse-reactive, latency-age child may have sexual contact with peers that far exceeds age-appropriate experimental sexual behaviors expected from an individual with a naive cognitive structure. These may not represent paraphilias.

9. The victim is involved in a dysfunctional family system that may support his denial or minimization, support the protection of his offender, resist family involvement at the point of crisis intervention, or actively sabotage the ongoing therapeutic process.

10. The victim has a history of chronic substance abuse or is actively chemically dependent. Most problematic are factors that may create a poor outcome prognosis for, or a total barrier to, chemical dependence treatment. Intoxication will relate directly to a poor internal locus of control.

11. The victim was sexually abused by one or more family members and has a very passive, dependent personality, causing considerable difficulty with either a therapeutic intervention or removal from the home. Male children and adolescents left in gross family dysfunction will have little ability to benefit from outpatient psychotherapy or any other form of intervention as long as they remain within the dysfunctional nuclear family.

Generally, there seem to be two basic theories—the psychoanalytic theory and the social learning theory—as to how boys and men move from the position of victim to that of victimizer. While mental health and social service professionals often subscribe to variations of these, it is my experience that the social learning theory is more widely accepted. In either theory, the common thread is that through the abuse experience, every young victim intimately knows the process of disempowerment and dehumanization irrespective of its intensity. Even when seduced by a covert, presexual, conditioning process, each victim will have great familiarity with the passive side of a power dynamic.

Key concepts from psychoanalytic theory that are useful to our understanding of the victim's transition to offender status are fixation and the concept of ego defense mechanisms. Fixation suggests that normal development is derailed and the individual becomes stuck at one of the several stages of ego development (Erikson 1963). For example, an anally fixated individual may be either highly conforming and orderly (anal retentive) or very cruel and sadistic (anal aggressive).

Anna Freud broke new ground with her conceptualization of ego defenses, which are operations the individual uses to deal with anxiety as a result of libidinal urges (Freud 1946). Defense mechanisms have two common features: (1) they distort reality, and (2) they operate unconsciously. For example, victims may deny their victimization, or memories of it may be repressed. Victims also may identify with their victimizers and thus act out in the process of undoing their victimization. The anxiety generated by the victimization may be overwhelming, and the victim manages it compulsively via repetition compulsion that is either self-destructive (self-cutting) or other-destructive (victimization).

The social learning theory also assumes that early abuse experiences have a great potential to imprint, ultimately affecting the child or adolescent developmentally. Major factors in relation to trauma are age of onset, frequency, level of erotization, and duration.

In common with other learning-based theories, social learning theory rests on the assumption that human behavior is largely acquired and the principles of learning—for example, reinforcement—are sufficient to explain the development or maintenance of that behavior. However, social learning theory pays attention to the social context of the behavior and also believes that modeling and vicarious learning are important. This modeling of behavior and subsequent imitations by the child or adult appears similar to the process of identification discussed in the previous paragraph. A classic experiment by Bandura (1977), the developer of social learning theory, demonstrated that children who witness adult aggressive behavior are more likely to exhibit aggressive behavior in a similar context. If that holds true for physically aggressive behavior, it certainly holds true for sexually aggressive behavior.

In many instances, the victim begins to associate pleasure and arousal with abusive experiences. Arousal and pleasure can be associated with either same-sex experiences or opposite-sex experiences. Significant conflicts are often spawned by a variety of factors to include internalized societal attitudes. We learn what we experience. We practice what we learn. We become what we practice.

Although these theories clearly suggest why victims become perpetrators, they do not explain the numerous exceptions to the rule. What factors seem to mitigate against transition? There are several, many of which are relational in nature. For example, very positive affirming experiences with others in power positions can be naturally reparative, particularly when they are in close proximity to the abuse experience. Loving, balanced male role models are helpful irrespective of the gender of the person perpetrating the abuse. This is particularly true of young men age twelve or thirteen who are at the cusp of adolescence. One of the critical ingredients seems to be a healthy, supportive, intact family (Friedrich 1986). For adolescent males, entering an intimate relationship where there is some shared reality, honesty, and an age-appropriate commitment seems to provide significant balance. For children or adolescent males to be sexually functional with themselves (self pleasuring) also has a healing effect.

Conversely, the sexual abuse of a younger male child contaminates the child's naiveté. Sexual experiences that would ordinarily be spawned by age-appropriate curiosity and experimentation become more reactive in nature and tend to be a reaction to age-inappropriate stimulation and erotization. At this point, one latency-age child might foist age-inappropriate sexual experiences on an age-mate. While this has all the dynamics of offending behavior, these individuals have been referred to as abuse reactive as opposed to offenders.

Last, but certainly not least, would be the victim having a strong sense of self established prior to the abuse experience. Good ego strength will accelerate the healing process.

I have chosen two clients who provide classic illustrations of a seemingly natural progression from victim to offender.

## Case Study 1: "Nick"

The first case study involves "Nick," a client who describes sexual abuse experiences that started at age eleven and spanned seven years. His disclosure was made when he was thirty-five. In this instance, the adult offender was male. This scenario also represents relatively subtle but negative environmental conditions for the victim prior to the abuse experiences.

At the onset of the abuse, Nick was a shy, shameful, withdrawn boy. He was from a blended family with emotionally absent parents. Nick describes his family life as being checkered with personal conflict. He reports feeling separate from the family and feeling as though he did not measure up to his stepsiblings. During his latency years, he felt that his mother was extremely disapproving of him, and he recalls that he was constantly striving for approval. Nick knew that his biological father had been physically abusive to his mother and had also spent time in a penal institution. His biological father's character defects were a constant theme for discussion among family members. Nick recalls feeling profoundly embarrassed and angry about his father and somehow internalized that pain and made it his own identity. During the diagnostic interview, Nick exclaimed, "I was his kid—I hated him!"

Nick describes his mother as a strong willed and very aggressive woman who "yelled a lot when she was angry." He points out that she would "stick her neck out" for her family. Nick says that his mother has remained strong willed and assertive in his adult life but has become more of a friend and more willing to listen to him. He describes his stepfather as being very absent during his childhood and adolescence, and he experienced his stepfather as being easily embarrassed and somewhat isolated. Nick has never had a sense that he or his stepfather had any emotional bonds, but they did enjoy fishing and hunting together, which, as he describes these activities, sound like parallel play. Nick views these activities as somewhat representative of their superficial camaraderie.

Nick's knowledge about his biological father is a collage of alleged facts and reviews by other family members. Nick reports, "I heard he was bad, drank a lot, and beat my mother and I. When he almost killed her, my mother divorced him." Nick reports that during his early latency years, he met his biological father, who, initially, "tried to buy my love," and then his father disappeared from his life altogether. Nick reports that he loved his half brother and that they had a normal sibling relationship, save for Nick's internal conflicts. Nick felt some sense of being less accepted by his parents than was his brother, but his personal interactions with his brother were apparently positive. Today he reports feeling uncomfortable being around his brother because, in contrast, he feels like an inherently bad person and feels as though he has let his brother down.

Nick's stepsister is ten years his junior, and due to her age, she posed no threat to him as a child. She was the only person in the family with whom he did not become emotionally reactive. Nick felt that she was too young to be able to detect his sexual secrets. He still feels very close to her and indicates that he loves her. Now that they are adults he has concerns about how they will interact. Her maturation causes him to feel a great deal of discomfort about her judgment of what he has done.

Nick reports that his mother and stepfather are in the process of a divorce. There is no sense of loss as he explains it. Because he has been separated from the family for a significant period of time, and because he has never had a close relationship with his stepfather, the divorce has little impact on him.

Nick's earliest recollection of anything sexual being part of his life is an event that occurred at age six. He remembers kids in school talking about sex. One of the kids talked about using a vacuum cleaner to suck on his penis, which made it feel good. He experimented with a vacuum cleaner, and at the time of the experiment, his grandfather walked in on him. Nick remembers feeling strange because he knew his grandfather had seen him and then pretended that he had not.

At age eleven, Nick moved to the country. He recalls that the bathroom was not finished completely and that there were partially completed walls. There were holes around the faucets and spigot. Nick remembers feeling quite curious about seeing a female's body. His curiosity was heightened by some recent but brief exposure to pornography. He remembers peeking at his mother on two or three occasions and feeling extremely fearful that he had somehow been detected. Both the incident with the vacuum cleaner and the incidents of peeking at his mother seemed to mark the onset of a sense of secrecy and shame about sexuality.

Nick is uncertain about the time period, but he also remembers wanting to initiate sex play with children of the same age. His sense of alienation from his family affected his peer relationships, and he did not initiate or participate in any of the sex play because he feared being mocked or rejected. (Nick also remembers seeing some pornography in school that further heightened his curiosity about nudity.) He remembers several incidents of exposure to pornography between ages seven and eleven. He remembers that during this same time period, his mother would come in to say good night and he could see her body through her nightgown. This would be a trigger for his shame, and he would immediately reflect on how guilty he felt about the times he had peeked at her when she was bathing.

Nick was having problems in school at that time and recalls being held back in the sixth grade. Nick remembers feeling even more shameful about nudity at age eleven due to the early onset of puberty. Because most of his age-mates were prepubital, he was particularly shameful about his body hair and the size of his penis, which was larger than most of his peers'.

At age twelve, Nick recalls, he began learning about sex from his peers in school. At that point, the sum total of his knowledge focused on intercourse and masturbation. Not unlike other children that age, he was both misinformed and underinformed. Nick remembers being shameful about the sexual knowledge. Sex was not an open topic in his home, which somehow exacerbated all the secrecy and negativity that he already felt about his sexual experiences up to that point.

It was at or about age twelve, Nick reports, that he met Mr. Shermunds, a wealthy farmer and neighbor to his parents. He explains, "I thought he was great. When I was with him, I was somebody." At age twelve, Nick was extremely impressed with having the responsibility of driving tractors. He goes on to say that it was extremely impressive that Mr. Shermunds owned the hardware store in town. The large farm and the hardware store were symbols of his wealth and status in the community; and Nick was very conscious of this status. He recalls, "I was treated special by the store employees because I was with Mr. Shermunds."

Nick indicates that the first attempts Mr. Shermunds made to be sexual with him were masked as physical play. Although they made Nick slightly uncomfortable, it is only in retrospect that it is clear to him that they were attempts to be sexual. These initial attempts Nick describes as "grab-ass," and while there was near genital contact, there was no real overt sexual behavior.

One morning Mr. Shermunds sent Nick to the machine shed under the guise of preparing the cultivator. Nick indicates that shortly after arriving at the machine shed, Mr. Shermunds followed him in. Mr. Shermunds was a huge man, by Nick's description, exceeding 6 feet in height and weighing more than 275 pounds. Nick remembers Mr. Shermunds wrapping his arms around Nick's chest and cupping Nick's groin. Nick was very startled and uncomfortable with the situation because Mr. Shermunds's initial attempts were extremely rough. He remembers that Mr. Shermunds squeezed his penis and testicles so hard that it caused him pain. Nick remembers struggling because of his sense of shock and the tremendous physical discomfort caused by the assaultive nature of the touch.

When it became apparent to Nick that his struggles were fruitless, he stopped struggling. At that point, Nick became fearful that someone would come in and see Mr. Shermunds touching him. Nick reports that he experienced the profound discomfort and confusion that he had always felt about sexual issues. Nick was being held from behind and could not see Mr. Shermunds's face. Mr. Shermunds lightened his grasp, freeing one arm, and he heard Mr. Shermunds unzipping his own trousers. He remembers he could tell that Mr. Shermunds was playing with his own penis and that he seemed to play with it for a long period of time. Although Mr. Shermunds kept Nick's back to him, he held him so that he was angled in such a manner that he could look down and toward the rear and see Mr. Shermunds masturbating.

Nick could feel Mr. Shermunds's penis occasionally being thrust against his clothed buttocks. Mr. Shermunds also attempted to masturbate Nick by removing his penis from his trousers and pulling it and squeezing it. Nick had an erection at one point, but his penis became flaccid because of the discomfort caused by the harsh manner in which Mr. Shermunds was touching him. Nick had never experienced an orgasm, nor was he particularly clear on what an orgasm or ejaculation was. He recalls Mr. Shermunds masturbating faster and faster and then saying, "Look at this!" Nick describes Mr. Shermunds ejaculating, and he remembers that the semen "shot past me." Almost immediately following his orgasm, Mr. Shermunds released Nick and walked away. Nick remembers putting his penis back into his trousers and feeling incredibly shameful. He couldn't look at Mr. Shermunds for the rest of the day and kept blaming himself for what happened.

Nick says that he felt terribly conflicted and confused, and, ultimately, he began to blame himself for not fighting to get away. Nick reports feeling helpless to disclose his horrible secret when he first began being sexually abused by Mr. Shermunds. Already shameful, Nick remembers coming home and feeling totally consumed by shame. The sexual abuse only exacerbated his feeling of alienation within his family and his sense of feeling different from his stepsiblings. Nick reports that his sense of shame was so intense that he was afraid it was physically visible and so he would do his best to isolate himself from the family.

He felt trapped by his secret and asserts, "Mom thought it was real great that I had this job! She was very proud I was doing this for myself." He was convinced that were he to reveal the abuse, no one would believe him. Mr. Shermunds was one of the richest farmers in the county and was so highly respected that Nick saw himself as having no credibility by comparison. This imbalance of power greatly intensified his sense of hopelessness and alienation.

The morning following the first incident of abuse, Nick recalls being in the pickup truck and how differently Mr. Shermunds was acting. Nick said, "I got scared it would happen again! He parked, took his penis out, and jacked off." Mr. Shermunds then began teaching Nick how to masturbate himself as well as to masturbate him. Nick describes feeling almost compelled to withhold his orgasm, which he succeeded at doing. Nick reports being horrified by his plight. He explains, "I felt so dirty. I didn't want to touch him anymore than I had to." He remembers being repulsed by having to touch Mr. Shermunds's penis. He says, "I used my forefinger and thumb—Mr. Shermunds complained."

Nick recalls how Mr. Shermunds would coax and cajole him. Somehow Mr. Shermunds's dialogue was always that of a teacher. Nick explains, "He always talked like I wanted to learn that shit!" The mutual masturbation became nearly a daily occurrence. They would drive a short way from home and park. Mr. Shermunds would initiate the contact, and there would be mutual masturbation. When Mr. Shermunds would stop touching Nick's penis, Nick would immediately take his hand off Mr. Shermunds's penis. Nick recalls Mr. Shermunds masturbating himself to orgasm and ejaculating onto the floor of the truck. Nick says that after his ejaculation, Mr. Shermunds would immediately bring him back to the farm, where he would begin his daily chores. He and Mr. Shermunds always pretended nothing had happened.

Nick describes the tremendous shame he was experiencing, which always made him fearful that somehow his exterior would give away the emotional pain he was in. Often the mutual masturbation would occur again in the afternoon following the completion of the day's work. At that time, Nick was working six days a week and found himself constantly being molested by Mr. Shermunds.

Nick describes how repulsed he was by the odor of Mr. Shermunds's body, particularly his groin area. He remembers feeling frantic about having the odor of Mr. Shermunds's penis on his hands. Almost immediately following a sexual contact, Nick would try to find a faucet to wash his hands. Often fearful that the hand washing would seem unreasonable and obvious, he would go behind a building or wait until he was in the field, and then he would rub his hands in the dirt until he thought the smell was gone.

Nick began to masturbate himself and experienced his first ejaculation. He remembers being consumed by the sensation. He would masturbate up to seven times a day. His masturbatory behavior was compulsive in nature, and he would achieve orgasm and then immediately experience shame rather than resolution. Nick recalls that he would be working in the fields and feel driven to masturbate. He would stop the tractor, crawl underneath it, hide against the large rear wheel, and masturbate until ejaculation. His masturbatory practices were so frequent that his penis became raw. In spite of the sores on his penis, the frequent, repetitive pattern continued.

Nick indicates that his focus was purely on the sensation of orgasm. He became aware that he never wanted the pleasure of orgasm paired with assaults. Nick recalls being committed to withholding his orgasm in concert with any sexual contact with Mr. Shermunds. He explains, "I never wanted it to feel good with him. I turned my mind off!"

Nick remembers that Mr. Shermunds began to talk to him about girls. He began to press Nick for details, and Nick experienced him as being jealous. The inquiry was repetitive, and Nick says, "He grilled me on my sex life." The constant questioning made Nick more uncomfortable because he had no sexual experience except what was occurring with Mr. Shermunds. Nick said he began obsessively thinking about sex. Soon sex seemed to consume his every thought, and he began stealing "dirty" magazines from local stores.

Nick then began to involve himself in scatological phoning. He began to call women and talk to them about observing his penis and how he wanted to see their vaginas. He recalls that he desperately did want to see their vaginas. Nick says, "I wanted to say, 'Here is my address; come on over.'" Nick would masturbate while on the phone and would tell the women he was talking to that he had been peeking in their windows. He would tell them that he had been watching them bathe. Nick remembers that so many of them hung up immediately that he began to talk scatologically the moment they answered the phone. Nick memorized the phone numbers of women who would talk to him or listen to him talk "dirty." He would repeatedly call them back. Ultimately, one of the repeated calls was a "phone trap," and Nick was confronted by juvenile authorities. Nick emphatically denied making the calls. He remembers his stepfather laughing and shaking his head. The familiar shame pressed him.

Nick's compulsive sexual behaviors continued to escalate, and by age thirteen, he was masturbating in school. Immediately following school, he would go home and begin scatological phoning. At night, he would go to the housing development outside town where he began his voyeuristic behaviors. He remembers sitting outside women's homes and masturbating while he watched them. Nick says that his fantasy was that the women would pull him into one of the houses.

Acceptance by women was becoming paramount, and he says, "I remember masturbating, and when the women would pull me into the house, they would say, 'I'm glad you came.'" Nick also became involved in exhibitionist behaviors. Fearing detection, he would go to the freeway knowing that the passersby would be strangers. He would hide near a freeway fence, and when he saw a woman coming down the freeway, he would jump out of his hiding place and walk toward her car with his penis exposed. This was done in concert with masturbation.

By age fourteen, Nick reports, he had taken his exhibitionist and voyeuristic behaviors into the heart of town. He says, "I got bolder and bolder. I would knock, and if women appeared at the screen, I'd reach in and grab their breasts." Nick also continued with the scatological phoning. As Nick was nearing fifteen, he was arrested by juvenile authorities for exposing himself. There were two other arrests for obscene phone calls. Nick was sent to the Minnesota Correctional Facility at Red Wing, where he spent four to five months. He remembers that it was difficult to masturbate there, but he continued to masturbate as often as he could. There was never any discussion by any of the correctional authorities or court services personnel about Nick's sexual behavior.

Nick says that the silence reinforced his feelings of shame and secrecy, which he believed were synonymous with sex. He says that he spent those four to five months feeling frightened and shameful about correctional staff bringing the subject up. On the last day he was in Red Wing, his worst fears came to fruition. Nick states, "I had to publicly tell all the kids on the last day before I could get out." Nick remembers his probation officer publicly admonishing him and extracting a promise that he would never do it again.

At age fifteen, Nick ran away to Colorado. His deviated sexual behaviors had not subsided, and he was arrested for exposing himself to a woman there. Nick was flown home and charged with a parole violation. At this point, he was sent to a hospital for treatment. Nick refused to talk about sexuality while at the hospital. He was then placed in a foster home and describes feeling relief because he did not want to go home and experience the embarrassment of facing his family. He remembers masturbating on a daily basis in the bathroom at the foster home, but the exhibitionist and voyeuristic behaviors came to a halt because he was always being watched by his peers.

By the time Nick was sixteen, he had run away from the foster home and was sent home to live. He recalls that shortly after returning home, an agemate spent the evening at his home. When they were in the bedroom, the age-mate initiated sexual contact. Nick agreed to participate. He remembers that the boy tried to have anal intercourse with him and was unable to penetrate him. Nick, in turn, attempted anal intercourse on the other boy and was able to penetrate him. Nick recalls that the boy masturbated and ejaculated while Nick was performing anal intercourse on him. Nick did not experience an orgasm and felt extremely uncomfortable immediately following the sexual event. Shortly thereafter, Nick resumed the scatological phoning, exhibitionism, and voyeurism.

Nick also went back to work for Mr. Shermunds, who immediately picked up on the same behaviors of mutual masturbation one or two times a day. Mr. Shermunds acted dumbfounded and accusatory about Nick's sexual problems. The conflict of Mr. Shermunds's incessant sexual contact and condemnation brought a new level of anxiety into Nick's life. He reports feeling tremendously angry and would constantly abuse the farm equipment to the point where it would need major repairs. Mr. Shermunds seemed oblivious to the constant breakdowns. Nick took further liberties by coming and going from his job as he pleased. These new behaviors were temporarily tolerated by Mr. Shermunds.

Ultimately, Mr. Shermunds became very demeaning and physically abusive to Nick. He began to strike Nick about the head regularly. Nick says, "He cuffed me all the time." The hitting and criticism escalated to the point where it bothered Nick immensely. Nick remembers a particular incident of physical abuse, which he describes as "the worst experience of my life." He remembers working in a trench that Mr. Shermunds was digging with a backhoe. He recalls that Mr. Shermunds was being extremely reckless with the backhoe and that somehow he knew that Mr. Shermunds was going to hurt him. Finally, when Nick was alongside the trench, Mr. Shermunds swung the backhoe and knocked him into the trench. Although he was terribly frightened and hurt, Nick made certain not to show his pain.

Another incident with a similar impact on Nick was when Mr. Shermunds confronted him about doing a bad job of cultivating. Mr. Shermunds punished Nick by knocking him down and then laying on him. Nick says that at that time, Mr. Shermunds weighed in excess of three hundred pounds, and Nick remembers panicking. Mr. Shermunds lay motionless on top of him and said nothing. Nick describes trying to struggle but says he was consumed by fear because he was having trouble breathing and feared he might smother. When Nick is done describing the physical abuse, he exclaims, "I still flinch when I fuck up around people! I can't make mistakes around people!"

At age seventeen, Nick joined the U.S. Army, which marked a form of emancipation for him. To that date, outside of the sexual abuse, Nick had never experienced sex in a relationship. The only consensual sexual experience involved that single encounter with the male age-mate. That also proved to be a negative experience emotionally and void of physical satiation. His solitary sexual experiences through scatological phoning, exhibitionism, and voyeurism continued, as did the unhealed repetition of the shame cycle. Nick's lifelong sense of alienation, low self-worth, and isolation were interwoven with his sexuality.

Adult relationships and sexual encounters in the Army replicated his adolescent history of self-debasing behaviors and exploitation at the hands of others. Nick recalls befriending "two black guys from New York" who appealed to him because they were worldly. Ultimately, it became apparent that they were exploitive of Nick. While at Fort Benning, Georgia, Nick reports, they would go to Atlanta, and, to continue to be in their company, Nick felt obligated to pay for everything. This developed into a pattern where he felt obligated to pay no matter whose company he was in. During this period, he and the "two black guys" met two white prostitutes and one black prostitute. Nick selected the black prostitute, and they had sexual intercourse. The sexual intercourse with the black prostitute marked the first time Nick recalls experiencing an orgasm with a willing sexual partner.

Nick's pattern of self-debasing behavior continued but changed in dynamic by him attempting to ferret out "bar girls" on his own. Inevitably, he would find women who would manipulate him for drinks. He would spend his entire paycheck on drinks for them. These self-debasing behaviors left Nick in a bad emotional state, and he says, "The day after, I always felt like a chump." Nick goes on the say that his anger and frustration was so intense that he began pretending that these events never happened. His self-loathing was mixed with rage for the women who exploited him. This masochistic behavior was repetitious and replaced his other sexual behaviors. Nick indicates that he had expectations of sexual favors with each contact. Despite all the energy he spent relating to "bar girls," Nick says, disdainfully, that only once did a "bar girl" briefly masturbate him through his clothing.

Nick requested a transfer to the Air Force. He went through basic training at Lackland Air Force Base in Texas and then awaited his transfer. He remembers his Army training being more intensive and says he felt like "more of a man" than the other Air Force recruits. At that time, Nick met a woman whom he cared about. She was the first female he had ever shared his feelings with. Nick was obsessed about being sexual with this woman, but fear kept him from initiating sexual discussions. Just before moving out of Texas, while on their last date, the young woman brought up the subject of sex. She revealed that she would have been a willing sexual partner weeks earlier. Nick left that day with yet another relationship ending without any sense of sexual fulfillment or resolution.

Nick's next assignment was at Lowry Air Force Base in Denver, where he again sought out "bar girls." He continued to spend entire paychecks on these on these women, buying champagne at ten to twenty dollars a glass. Nick recalls, "It was the same denial game. I hated the whores for using me, even though I knew I was the sucker. I hated myself, too."

Nick then transferred to another Air Force base. At that point, the abated paraphilias again emerged. Nick resumed his voyeurism around motels and would masturbate in concert with his voyeurism on a nightly basis. Nick's anxiety and conflict about sexuality grew. He continued to feel frustrated by his dysfunction in relationships and angry at the women whom he had set himself up to be exploited by. It was at this point that Nick committed his first rape.

The night of the rape, he stalked a sixteen-year-old female who was cleaning up at a café. He went there to expose himself and waited outside the back door for her to come out. Nick had his erect penis in his hand, and, as she came out, he put his foot in the door and shoved her. Nick reports, "I crossed the line. I never felt that rush before." Nick says that he told himself, "I can do anything I want here."

This was a sense of power that Nick had never known. Nick told the young lady he did not want to hurt her. He took her into a vehicle and forced her to masturbate him and to perform fellatio on him. He attempted intercourse but became flaccid, which made him furious. They dressed, and he took her to a sand pit, where he forced her to get into the backseat of the vehicle. He removed her clothing and penetrated her with his penis. Nick recalls feeling terribly frustrated because "she was crying and I didn't want her to. I was getting frustrated and angry because she was crying and I didn't want her to, because I couldn't get what I wanted."

Fitting the pattern of his sexual history, Nick left the young woman without being physically satiated. He reports that he was "still rushing," and when he had driven about halfway back to the base, he broke down and began to weep. Nick says, "I couldn't believe I had done that to somebody." Nick's sense of alienation and guilt overwhelmed him, and he says, "I was afraid everybody at the base would be able to tell what I did. I couldn't look at anybody. I thought everybody could see. I was furious because I didn't get what I wanted!"

Nick reports that within five days, he went back to rape again, saying, "I wanted to get what I didn't get the first time." Nick stalked another small café and waited for the woman inside. He reports that the "rush" began while he was waiting. The predatory pattern was now being strongly reinforced with physiological responses. This time, Nick carried a knife, which he says was to scare the woman. When she came out of the restaurant, he grabbed her, showed her the knife, and took her to her car. They sat in her car, and he took her to the same sand pit. While driving, he forced her to masturbate him and perform fellatio on him. Upon arriving at the sand pit, he took the woman into the backseat, removed her clothing, and demanded intercourse.

She retorted, "Fuck you!" whereupon he forced her down to attempt intercourse. She began talking about her family, and Nick remembers screaming, "Shut up!" Nick says, "It was taking the rush away." The more the young woman talked, the greater Nick's shame became, and he remembers running from the scene.

Nick was arrested for both rapes and sentenced to two ten-year sentences to be served in a state correctional facility. Because he was so young, Nick was offered a great number of opportunities to participate in prison sex but isolated himself from the other prisoners. He masturbated to fantasies of exhibitionism and voyeurism, but his primary sexual fantasy had become that of violent rape. Nick's repertoire of sexual fantasies and experiences continued to be void of sex that was relational, romantic, or intimate.

At age twenty-five, Nick was paroled from the state correctional facility and returned to his hometown. He recalls immediately "prowling" the bars, bookstores, and video shops. Nick describes approaching a "go-go dancer" about sex, and she agreed to have sex with him. When he approached her for a second interlude, she rejected him, and he became rageful. He watched her dance, and the longer he watched her, the more rageful he became. By that time, he had been out of prison approximately two months. Nick's rage at the dancer was so intense that he knew there was a potential for him to rape. He drove toward home and made a concerted effort not to look toward the sidewalks for fear he would see a woman.

Nick was so rageful and obsessed when he finally saw a person walking along that, he reports, "I wasn't sure if the 'mark' was a male or female." He abducted the woman, yanking her into the passenger seat of the car. He reports that she was terribly frightened. Nick drove into the country to commit the rape and found himself parked near Mr. Shermunds's home. The spot was in very near proximity to the place where he had been taken by Mr. Shermund when he was an adolescent. Again, Nick forced his victim to masturbate him and to perform fellatio on him. While attempting to penetrate her vaginally, he was frantic and accidentally penetrated her anally. The woman's fear seemed so intense that Nick found himself repeating, "I won't hurt you! I won't kill you!" Nick reports having been so delusional that he took the young woman home and they checked on her children. He raped her again in her bedroom. Nick says he believed that she liked it and wanted him more. He believed she trusted him. When she went into the bathroom, Nick was struck by the reality of his crime, became consumed by shame, and ran from her house.

Nick was arrested for the rape and released on bail. While on bail, he raped another woman. According to Nick, this woman was reputed to be a "whore" and a "coke freak." The behavior pattern of the rape matched all Nick's other rapes. The woman reported the rape, but the charges were dropped because the woman allegedly lacked credibility in the community. Nick was kept in jail from then on and was ultimately sentenced to spend sixty-five months in a state correctional facility. It was at this point that Nick disclosed his life's tormenting secrets during intensive psychotherapy. This account was extracted from a formal psychosexual assessment done independently of the correctional treatment program. Today Nick is serving another term for yet another brutal rape.

## Case Study 2: "Timothy"

The second clinical study is unique in that it involves an adolescent male, "Timothy," who reports being sexually abused on several occasions during his latency years by two different adolescent females. Being a lonely and isolated youth, he found these sexual experiences extremely powerful. Ultimately, he was rejected by both girls but continued to be obsessed with his experiences.

Timothy lives in rural southern Minnesota. He describes a relatively normal family life and presents as a boy who found his family to be a source of support. He had difficulty with peer relationships, which was exacerbated by mild learning disabilities that caused him to feel further alienated in the academic setting. He reports being tormented because he was seen by his peers as a "nerd."

During his latency years, Timothy was remarkably thin, which caused him marked issues about body image and contributed to his feelings of alienation and low self-worth. Timothy describes himself as a physically unattractive child. He also felt as if he were a clumsy child with no particular talents to aid him in his struggle to win friends. Timothy's parents anguished over his isolation but felt powerless to assist him other than by assuring him that he was a worthwhile and lovable human being. Timothy reports overwhelming loneliness during his late latency years and at the onset of adolescence. This description is validated by his parents, who say that he spent endless hours playing with the lambs he had chosen as a 4-H project.

With the onset of puberty came some positive changes in his physique but also the onset of significant acne. By the time Timothy entered junior high school, his poor self-concept was so pervasive that he abandoned his efforts to connect with his peers.

At the time of his referral to treatment as an adolescent sex offender, Timothy was in a significant amount of emotional pain. The clinical team saw Timothy as a compulsive youth with a well-established paraphilia. The assessment process and psychological testing also clearly indicated clinical depression. Following a psychiatric examination, Timothy was diagnosed as having a major depressive episode and was medicated. During the course of a long and intensive assessment process, Timothy provided an in-depth sexual history. It was the first time he disclosed details about being sexually abused.

Timothy reports no recall of sexual experiences in his preschool years or early latency years. He says that at age eight, he found pornography in a paper bag in a ditch near his home. This prized possession enabled him to connect with a male age-mate who was a new neighbor. The two boys began spending a significant amount of time in the outbuildings on Timothy's farm studying the pornography.

According to Timothy, the pornography eroticized both boys, and they began experimenting with some of the same-sex behaviors that were depicted in the magazine. Initially the behavior involved viewing each other's genitalia but ultimately escalated into passive and active fellatio, passive and active anal intercourse, ditigal penetration of the rectum, and mutual fondling of the penis. Both boys also developed a curiosity about the elimination of both urine and feces and incorporated viewing of these functions into their sexual relationship. There were approximately ten incidents in which the boys were sexual with each other over a brief period of time. Their sexual relationship ended abruptly when Timothy's age-mate moved out of the area with his family.

Timothy recalls feeling secretive and shameful about the same-sex behavior. Timothy also has a distinct memory of how powerful the eroticization was, particularly when paired with having an age-mate who was there to dissipate his loneliness.

Timothy's next disclosure of a significant sexual event in his life involved sexual contact with a female baby-sitter who stayed with him and his siblings when his parents had social engagements that kept them away from home overnight. At that time, Timothy was nine and the young woman seventeen. The kids would make "forts" out of chairs and blankets. Ultimately, the baby-sitter would go inside the fort alone with Timothy. She would teach him how to rub her breasts and vulva, and in turn she would gently rub his penis. Timothy also recalls the girl saying lots of words that he knew were "dirty" and attempted to discuss other things that, to him, were nonconceptual. Eventually, Timothy came to understand they were highly sexualized conversations. This sexual abuse involved a few isolated incidents.

Timothy again reports that he was highly eroticized by the sexual contact with the older girl. Because of his loneliness, Timothy was extremely grateful for the very special attention he received in concert with the sexual behavior.

Among his many disclosures, the most difficult was the incident involving his oldest sister's friend, "Janna." Timothy says that Janna often came by to visit when his sister was not home. Timothy was twelve when this second sexually abusive scenario began. Janna reportedly took him into the basement, whereupon she induced him to undress and began to teach him about how older people have sex. During the course of approximately two months, there were five similar incidents that involved acts of fellatio, cunnilingus, and vaginal intercourse. While there was some kissing, the interaction was largely genitally focused. Timothy remembers becoming obsessed with thoughts of what had occurred to him. The marked increase of interest in Janna apparently began to unnerve the young woman. Janna began giving clear messages that their relationship was going to go back to the original status. She returned to relating to Timothy with stereotypic irritation at the presence of the younger sibling of a girlfriend. Timothy reports that his sense of rejection was profound, considering the fact that his sexual experiences with Janna constituted another oasis in his isolation from his peers.

Timothy reports the appearance of secondary sexual characteristics beginning at age thirteen and says that his experiments with masturbation were ultimately rewarded with his first sensation of orgasm, which was paired with ejaculation. At this point, Timothy's fantasies were exclusively of Janna. Timothy reports that he began masturbating twice a day, seven days a week to fantasies of Janna. His obsessive thinking about Janna involved replicating their sexual relationship, which ultimately led to his voyeuristic behaviors.

Initially, the voyeurism involved Timothy standing in the grove near Janna's home. Occasionally he was able to view her from that distance if she left the window shades up. His voyeuristic behaviors became almost nightly, and he began going into the building site. Timothy progressed until he found himself extremely close to the girl's bedroom window. At times, even after the lights were out, he would remain there, consumed with obsessive sexual thoughts. Timothy indicates that he experienced arousal each time he engaged in the voyeurism, but he did not masturbate until he returned home. Occasionally, he says, he woke up the family dog, which was always taken into the house in the evening. At first the dog's barking was frightening to him, but ultimately the thrill of avoiding detection became part of the ritual.

The fantasy that was always paired with the voyeuristic behavior was Janna peering out the window, seeing Timothy standing there, and inviting him into her bedroom. They would then become lovers as they had in the past. Timothy indicates that one evening the feeling was so overpowering that he felt compelled to enter the home and walk into her bedroom. He was convinced that upon entering her bedroom, she would invite him to lay down with her and they would be lovers again. She awakened and drove him out, and he was subsequently arrested.

Timothy continued to masturbate to thoughts of Janna after his arrest and through the adjudicatory process. Timothy's mother says that she repeatedly caught him attempting to sneak out of the house in the evening, contrary to the disciplinary sanctions the court had set. Eventually, Timothy was successful at sneaking out of the house and returning to Janna's window. Additional complaints were made, and the criminal justice system levied further sanctions against Timothy.

It was well into his sex-offender therapy that Timothy finally disclosed having been sexually abused by Janna. He did so in a flood of tears. Timothy believed his disclosure was a betrayal of Janna, the girl of his dreams, as well as of his sister, who was Janna's best friend. While it was obvious that his voyeuristic behaviors were directly linked to his having been sexually abused by two older females, those facts simply did not fit with his reality. With the support of intensive therapy, Timothy's cognitive distortions began to be reframed. He understood the pain he had caused others. Later, the grim reality of his own pain became part of his awareness. Timothy is making a fresh start in a new school.

## Dealing with the Transition from Victim to Victimizer

Once a clinician has identified the transition (Friedrich, Berliner, Urquiza, and Beilke 1986), which problem should he or she treat first? When a clinician is faced with the duality of someone who has been victimized and has transcended that identity by becoming a victimizer, what are the choices? In the mental health field, there are many different opinions on this issue. Here is yet another to add to the pile.

The most important issue is that of assessment and treatment. Shame, denial, and minimization play a part in distorting reality for the person's experiences as both a victim and an offender. It would seem reasonable to assume that if the clinician has not uncovered all of the deviant arousal, he or she cannot fully treat the individual. Conversely, there must be some caution in overpathologizing child or adolescent clients. Assuming that the transition has taken place and that the individual has been identified by way of reported criminal sexual behaviors, then the focus has been set. Simplistically, the approach is that the client must take responsibility for the pain he has caused others before he can deal with the pain others have caused him. Too often, premature focus on the client's victim history creates an atmosphere that enables avoidance or projective blame.

A formula established for adolescent offenders by the Program for Healthy Adolescent Sexual Expression creates an assessment process that incorporates a wide variety of therapeutic approaches. This process has been modified to be effective with latency-age children who are acting out sexually. The process begins with an intake that involves family members. Two clinicians meet with the entire family to get a sense of the system, as well as how the family interacts when the youth's victimizing sexual behaviors are discussed. The clinicians then separate the juvenile offender from his parents. At this juncture, the parents and child get individualized attention in a more rigorous and detailed interview format. Subsequent to or in concert with the initial intake, a variety of psychological tests are administered.

If the individual is judged to be amenable to the extended education/

assessment process, he is given an opportunity to attend four two-hour group sessions over a four-week period. This gives the clinical team an opportunity to watch the client interact with a peer group. The group has a psychoeducational format. A less obvious agenda is to observe each individual's interactions with his peers while he details his aberrant sexual behaviors and sociosexual attitudes for the group.

During this same four-week period, a primary therapist is assigned and continues to conduct rigorous individual assessment sessions, as well as two to four family therapy sessions. In the event that the client has continued to deny his offenses because of resistance or possibly because of memory problems, a variety of techniques can be used, such as hypnosis, guided imagery, additional projective testing, and, in more extreme cases, polygraph and plethysmography. At the completion of the assessment, a comprehensive treatment plan can be formulated. For an individual with patterned deviant arousal, behavior therapies will most likely be blended with cognitive therapies as part of the treatment plan.

Ultimately, the offender's own personal maltreatment experiences will arise as a natural course of assessment or therapy. (Extreme care must be taken while extracting sexual history information regarding abuse experiences. Far too often the question begs the answer.) Since offenders may overreport victimization to minimize their offenses, great care must be taken to validate the reports of abuse. When the issue is raised to be legitimately addressed and not used as manipulation, the treatment plan should be modified to address the new issues. In some settings, the offender's own victim experiences can be addressed in the offender treatment process, or the client may be transferred to a group that is specifically designed for male victims. This is particularly appropriate for clients whose offender histories are relatively brief in contrast to their victimization histories. Again, a proactive approach is prescribed if a client has appropriate ego strength and cognitive abilities.

The mental health field is divided somewhat regarding the relative importance of having the victim/perpetrator identify or uncover his abuse experiences. William Friedrich (1990) has suggested several rationales to support the need for uncovering. These fit the proactive assessment approach for adolescent male victims. By being proactive and moving quickly toward a full disclosure, the clinician can create opportunities for the client to make sense of the victimization experiences. Doing so becomes a cognitive/developmental task. Affect is then available for therapeutic change. Until that point, no anxiety exists because the client views the abuse experience being normalized. The proactive approach circumvents the fragmentation in favor of integration. Uncovering in the boundaries of the therapeutic relationship occurs in a safe context and allows for the restructuring of a more appropriate functional map of relationships. The client is allowed to view himself in a more positive light. His inappropriate cognitions are exposed and can be challenged. Trauma is frequently secretive, and disclosing the traumatic aspects of an event neutralizes the secret. This is enhanced if the family is participating in therapy and can offer a similarly safe place in the home.

Clinicians might bear in mind the unique aspects of a sexually abusive experience for males. It is apparent to me that our culture pushes male children toward early separation and individuation. The belief system seems to be that if you are male, you are powerful. To be abused as a male presumes failure and creates a dichotomy. Further, our culture believes that sexual abuse is painful and should be responded to with rage. This belief system makes it difficult to resolve the incongruities created by covert, presexual conditioning and accompanying arousal. Arousal is a particularly poignant issue for males in that, unlike females, their arousal is markedly visible. Perpetrators often remark about the dimensions of the victim's erection and related physiological responses. Additionally, the belief system is that arousal equals pleasure and pleasure equals complicity. In same-sex incidents, arousal can translate into questioning of one's sexual identity, which can ultimately spawn internalized homophobia. The myth of complicity translates being abused into an inability to self-protect and, therefore, failure as a male. This can also result in self-identification as a consenting participant.

All of these gender-specific aspects must be addressed when treating males who have been sexually abused. These issues are also germane if a latency-age boy has started acting out sexually or has clearly transcended the legal and social barriers between victim and offender.

The development of a comprehensive treatment plan that addresses the needs of individuals who have been both victims and offenders is obviously complicated. Among the many aspects needing scrutiny is the tendency to move a client toward "normalcy," a term that, by its very nature, stands in diametric opposition to the respect of individuality and personhood. At best, clients should be guided toward recognizing and accepting responsibility for their behavior, understanding the consequences of their actions for themselves and others, developing healthier ways to meet their emotional and interpersonal needs, and integrating those new skills into their lives. This task demands that the clinician have a nonprescriptive view of sexuality.

Such a philosophy was set forth by U.S. Supreme Court justice Blackmun in *Bowers* v. *Hardwick* (1981), which seems on point here. In his dissenting opinion, Justice Blackmun states,

> Only the most willfull blindness could obscure the fact that sexual intimacy is a sensitive, key relationship of human existence, central to family life, community welfare, and the development of human personality. The fact that individuals define themselves in a significant way through their intimate sexual relationships with others suggests, in a nation as diverse as ours, that there may be many right ways of conducting those relationships, and that

much of the richness of a relationship will come from the freedom an individual has to choose the form and nature of their intensely personal bonds.

## References

Abel, G.C., J.V. Becker, M. Mittleman, J. Cunningham-Rathner, J. Rouleau, and W.D. Murphy. 1987. "Self-Reported Crimes of Nonincarcerated Paraphiliacs." *Journal of Interpersonal Violence* 2 (no. 1): 3–23.

American Psychological Association. 1987. *Diagnostic and Statistical Manual of Mental Disorders,* 3d ed. (revised). Washington, D.C.: APA.

Bandura, A. 1977. *Social Learning Theory.* Englewood Cliffs, New Jersey: Prentice-Hall.

Becker, J.V., and G.G. Abel. 1984. "Methodological and Ethical Issues in Evaluating and Treating Adolescent Sexual Offenders." National Institute of Mental Health monograph (June: Grant #MH 36347, Treatment of Child Molesters).

Blackmun, J. 1986. *Bowers v. Hardwick,* 92L, 2d ed., 140–154. Saint Paul, Minnesota: West Publishing.

Bruckner, D.F., and P.E. Johnson, 1987. "Treatment for Adult Male Victims of Childhood Sexual Abuse." *Social Casework: The Journal of Contemporary Social Work* (February): 81–87.

Davis, G.E., and H. Leitenberg. 1987. "Adolescent Sex Offenders." *Psychological Bulletin* 101 (no. 3): 417–427.

Erikson, E. 1963. *Childhood and Society,* 2d ed. New York: W.W. Norton.

Finkelhor, D. 1979. *Sexually Victimized Children.* New York: Free Press.

Freud, A. 1967. *Ego and the Mechanisms of Defense,* vol. 2 (revised). Madison, Connecticut: International Universities Press.

Freund, K., R. Watson, and R. Dickey. 1988. "Does Sexual Abuse in Childhood Cause Pedophilia?" Joint study of the Department of Behavioral Sexology and the Forensic Division, Clarke Institute of Psychiatry, Toronto, Ontario, Canada.

Friedrich, W.N., R.L. Beilke, and A.J. Urquiza. 1987. "Behavior Problems in Young Sexually Abused Boys: A Comparison Study." *Journal of Interpersonal Violence* 2 (no. 1): 3–23.

Friedrich, W.N., L. Berliner, A. Urquiza, and R. Beilke. 1986. "Brief Diagnostic Group Treatment of Sexually Abused Boys: A Comparison Study." *Journal of Interpersonal Violence* 3 (no. 3): 331–343.

Friedrich, W.N., and W.J. Leucke. 1988. "Young School-Age Sexually Aggressive Children." *Professional Psychology: Research and Practice* 19 (no. 2): 155–164.

Friedrich W.N., A.J. Urquiza, and R. Beilke. 1986. "Behavior Problems in Sexually Abused Young Children." *Journal of Pediatric Psychology* 11 (no. 1): 47–57.

Groth, N.A., A.W. Burgess, H.J. Birnbaum, and T.S. Gray. 1978. "A Study of the Child Molester: Myths and Realities." *LAE Journal of the American Criminal Justice Association* 41 (no. 1): 17–23.

Hindman, J. 1988. "New Insight into Adult and Juvenile Sex Offenders." *Community Safety Quarterly* 1 (no. 4): 1.

Hunter, M. 1990. *Abused Boys: The Neglected Victims of Sexual Abuse.* Lexington, Massachusetts: Lexington Books.

Kinsey, A.C., W.B. Pomeroy, and C.E. Martin. 1948. *Sexual Behavior in the Human Male.* Philadelphia: Saunders.

Masters, W.H., V. Johnson, R.C. Kolodny. 1982. *Sex and Human Loving.* Boston: Little, Brown and Co.

Mathews, R., J. Mathews, and K. Speltz. 1989. *Female Sexual Offenders: An Exploratory Study.* Orwell, Vermont: Safer Society Press.

National District Attorneys Association. "Research Disputes Assumptions about Child Molesters." *NDAA Bulletin* 7 (no. 4): 1–3.

O'Brien, M.J. 1989. *Characteristics of Male Adolescent Sibling Incest Offenders: Preliminary Findings.* Orwell, Vermont: Safer Society Press.

Porter, E. 1986. *Treating the Young Male Victim of Sexual Assault: Issues and Intervention Strategies.* Syracuse, New York: Safer Society Press.

# 8
# Factors Mediating the Effects of Childhood Maltreatment

*Jane F. Gilgun*

Generalizations about the effects of sexual abuse on male children are difficult to make. Male sexual abuse victims are largely unknown, unidentified, and underresearched. Everyday observation, clinical experience, and the limited research available, however, suggest that most, if not all, male victims have some characteristics and behaviors in common but vary widely in others. In addition, men not known to have been sexually abused as children sometimes display behaviors associated with the effects of childhood sexual abuse.

When boys are sexually abused, their sexuality usually is affected. Sexual and gender identity issues related to the sexual abuse of male children include fears about being homosexual (Dimock 1988; Gilgun and Reiser, in press; Nasjleti 1980; Vander Mey 1988); gender identity confusion (Burgess 1985); feelings of inadequacy as a male and fears of being effeminate (Cotton and Groth 1984; Pierce and Pierce 1985; Rogers and Terry 1984); sexual compulsion, sexual addiction, and hypersexuality (Carnes 1983; Gilgun 1988; Jones 1986; Rogers and Terry 1984; Yates 1982); and avoidance of sexual activity (Bruckner and Johnson 1987; Gilgun and Reiser, in press; Johnson and Shrier 1985). Some male victims experience all of these outcomes, while others struggle with one or two. As far as we know, some individuals may not have sexual problems, but this may be relatively rare.

Serious violent and criminal acts also have been associated with childhood sexual abuse and other maltreatment. Some male victims become rapists (Groth and Birnbaum 1979; Wolf 1985), child molesters (Davis and Leitenberg 1987; Finkelhor 1986; Groth 1983; Justice and Justice 1979; Longo 1982), and murderers (Gilgun 1988), although most do not.

This chapter was originally presented at the annual conference of the National Council on Family Relations, New Orleans, November 3–6, 1989. Support for this research was through the Minnesota Agricultural Experiment Station, the Saint Paul Foundation, First Bank Saint Paul, the Mardag Foundation, Edwards Memorial Trust, F.R. Bigelow Foundation, Minneapolis Star and Tribune/Cowles Media Company, and the St. Paul Companies.

While research has linked this range of outcomes to the effects of child-hood sexual abuse, a significant proportion of known molesters, rapists, and men with other sexual problems are not known to have been sexually abused as children (Davis and Leitenberg 1987; Finkelhor 1986; Gilgun 1988). These men, however, experienced other forms of childhood maltreatment. Such findings suggest that psychological damage, or damage to the self-system, may underlie the effects of all forms of childhood maltreatment (Erickson and Egeland 1987; Starr, MacLean, and Keating 1989). Underlying psychological damage may be linked to a variety of outcomes, some of which are related to sexuality and others of which are not.

For the child, maltreatment may represent a serious blow to a sense of the self as being worthy of consideration, love, and respect. Children leave the experience of abuse with questions about their own self-worth. They may have a sense that they are fundamentally defective. These questions about the self can lead to self-rejecting attitudes and severe psychological distress (Kaplan, Robbins, and Martin 1983). Attempts at coping with distress result in a range of behaviors, from adaptive and life-enhancing, such as going into therapy or confiding in a trusted person, to maladaptive, such as alcohol or drug abuse, gambling, and physical violence.

Boy victims may be less likely than girl victims to confide in others about both their abuse experiences and other emotionally laden topics (Gilgun 1989a, 1989b). The prescriptions and restrictions of the male gender role tend to associate disclosure of personal issues, especially issues suggesting that the male could not take care of himself, with weakness and lack of manliness. For example, sexually assaulted boys and men tend not to disclose because of these prescriptions (Pierce and Pierce 1985; Rogers and Terry 1984). If childhood maltreatment leads to severe psychological distress, which seems to be the case, then individuals who do not work through issues related to child-hood maltreatment continue to experience severe distress. This distress can affect their functioning in many ways and may lead to a higher risk for antiso-cial behavior (Gilgun 1988).

Accounting for the range of outcomes associated with the sexual abuse of boys has important theoretical, clinical, and practical implications. As the preceding discussion shows, boys who have been sexually abused exhibit a wide range of behaviors that may be related to their abuse experience. What accounts for the differences in outcome? In addition, some adolescents and adults who are not known to have been sexually abused develop behaviors similar to those of men who have been sexually abused. What accounts for this?

The present research explored these questions using the grounded theory approach of Glaser and Strauss (1967). The grounded theory approach is par-ticularly well suited to delineating poorly understood areas and provides procedures for concept and hypothesis development (Gilgun 1989a; Knafl and Webster 1988). A conceptual framework based on the theory of developmental psychopathology, social support, resilience, and protective mechanisms guided the analysis.

## The Conceptual Framework

### Developmental Psychopathology

Developmental psychopathology is the study of the origins and course of maladaptive behaviors (Sroufe and Rutter 1984). Traditional approaches to psychopathology are based on a disease model and focus on symptoms, pathology, and prognosis. The framework provided by developmental psychopathology directs the researcher or clinician to look for factors that protect against negative adult outcomes as well as factors that might lead to maladaptive behaviors. An emerging field of study, developmental psychopathology brings attention to the study of resilience and protective mechanisms as well as to the study of vulnerability, risk, stress, and coping (Anthony and Cohler 1987; Cicchetti 1987; Masten and Garmezy 1985; Sroufe and Rutter 1984).

### Social Support

Previous research provides some clues to the nature of the mechanisms related to differential effects of child sexual abuse. Social support may mediate the short- and long-term effects of abuse and neglect in childhood. For example, researchers have found that social support helps children work through the immediate effects of child sexual abuse (Adams-Tucker 1985; Conte and Schuerman 1987). In relationship to long-term effects, social support also has been identified in the lives of individuals who survive childhood abuse and neglect without major signs of cognitive, sexual, or psychosocial disturbances (Conte 1985; Kaufman and Zigler 1987; Main and Goldwyn 1984; Wyatt and Mickey 1987). Fraiberg, Adelson, and Shapiro (1975) hypothesized that being in touch with the memories and pain of maltreatment in childhood provides a powerful deterrent against repeating abusive acts in adolescence and adulthood. Keeping in touch with memories and pain are associated with the presence of confidants in the lives of individuals who are maltreated in childhood. The one factor that appears to break the cycle of physical abuse is social support (Egeland, Jacobvitz, and Sroufe 1988). Having someone in whom to confide and who is supportive appears to be important in helping individuals overcome the effects of childhood maltreatment (Gilgun 1988).

## Resilience and Protective Mechanisms

The ideas of resilience and protective mechanisms from developmental psychopathology fit with and add to previous child maltreatment research. Resilience, which Murphy (1987) defines as recovery from adversity, is a quality found in individuals who, despite difficult childhoods, manage to work through adversity and achieve good peer relationships, respectable academic records, and successful work histories (Werner and Smith 1982). Researchers have identified several factors associated with resilience. These factors are called protective mechanisms. The underlying factor of protective mechanisms is human relationship. Secure attachments in infancy and early childhood are thought to provide the foundation for later relationships and for the development of personal attributes that lead to continued successful adaptation (Bowlby 1973; Cicchetti 1987; Egeland, Jacobvitz, and Sroufe 1988). Personal attributes stemming primarily from supportive relationships have been identified as protective mechanisms. Both Cicchetti (1987) and Masten present an extended discussion of personal attributes, which include positive self-concept and sensitivity to the internal states of the self and of others. A supportive environment enhances the development of personal attributes, and a harsh, negative environment can undermine their development.

## Vulnerability

Vulnerability refers to a predisposition or susceptibility to negative developmental outcomes (Masten and Garmazey 1985). Persons become vulnerable through troubled interpersonal relationships (particularly in childhood), harsh and negative environments, genetic factors as in the development of some types of mental illness, and accidents of the environment, such as through birth complications and separations in war. In the present discussion, childhood sexual abuse is conceptualized as a vulnerability factor, which, in interaction with other factors, some poorly understood and unknown, lead to differential outcomes, some of which are relatively mild and some of which lead to violent and criminal behavior.

## Childhood Maltreatment

In the present research, childhood maltreatment includes physical abuse, sexual abuse, emotional abuse, physical neglect, emotional neglect, and neglect of sex education. An extended discussion of the definitions of these terms may be found in Gilgun (1988).

For this study, child sexual abuse was defined as both covert and overt. Covert sexual abuse refers to seductive looks, talk, and behavior that sexualizes the child and makes him an object of sexual gratification for a person who has power over him. In covert abuse, there is no physical contact between the child and the perpetrator, although the child's personal and psychological boundaries are repeatedly invaded. In overt abuse, the child is the object of a more powerful person's sexual gratification, and, in addition to sexualizing the child and being psychologically invasive, the perpetrator has sexual contact with the child. In both forms of sexual abuse the child does not give consent or is unable to give consent because of age. Through the sexual abuse, the child is placed in a powerless position, is used for the sexual gratification of another, and experiences severe psychological and emotional distress as a result of this experience.

## Methods

This chapter is based on intensive, life history interviews conducted for an average of twelve hours per subject over six or more interview sessions. Thirty-four men, twenty-three of whom were victims of child sexual abuse, made up the sample. All experienced one or more forms of childhood maltreatment. Of the sexually abused men, nine had no criminal history, seven were child molesters, five were rapists, and one was an armed robber. The eleven nonsexually abused men included seven child molesters, two rapists, and two murderers and attempted murderers. Two of the rapists also were murderers or attempted murderers. Thus, the sample contained men with a variety of developmental outcomes. Sources of the sample were community-based treatment programs, maximum and medium security prisons, and self-help groups.

All subjects were in treatment at the time of the interview. This may bias the sample in unknown ways. The research, however, probes deeply into sensitive areas, and it was important to ensure that each subject had a supportive environment to help him deal with memories and feelings that the research might provoke.

The sample was not random, another source of potential bias. The information generated by the grounded theory approach, however, is not meant to be generalized to all persons for all time. Rather, the findings of grounded theory take the forms of patterns. If one individual displays a particular pattern, then this is a finding. If ten individuals display the same pattern, this, too, is a finding. It is not ever known whether a particular pattern will be found in a succeeding case. The patterns developed in one case are matched to the patterns discovered in the succeeding case. When the previously constructed pattern does not match the pattern found in the case under investigation, the previous construction is modified to fit the new data. When a pattern can be shown to apply to a wide range of cases, this new information can make some claim to breadth of applicability. Usually the pattern has many branches, and the data are presented in the forms of branching figures.

The interviews were tape-recorded and transcribed. The transcriptions were content analyzed with the help of Ethnograph, a computer program (Seidel, Kjolseth, and Clark 1985). The interviews were designed to be noncoercive and respectful of the subjects' freedom of choice to answer or not answer questions as they were posed (Gilgun 1989b). The noncoercive nature of the interview process was an attempt to recognize the sensitive nature of the research and to protect individuals from sharing information they might not be ready to share. The author was the sole interviewer.

## Results

The results show that mediators and not the fact of being sexually abused by itself affect the outcome of being sexually abused. The research identified both positive and negative mediating factors. Positive factors increased the likelihood that subjects would not develop criminal and violent behaviors, although subjects still had milder negative effects. These factors probably can be considered factors protective against the highly negative effects of being sexually abused. The positive factors were the presence of confidants and other supportive persons in the abused child's life. These individuals were sometimes family members but also persons outside the family. Sometimes they were peers, and often they were older persons in positions of authority, such as youth group leaders, parents of friends, and employers. The supportive persons were primarily men, but some of the subjects reported meaningful relationships with same-age girlfriends and older women.

Negative factors appeared to interact with, and intensify the effects of, sexual abuse when the subject had no confidants or supportive persons. The entire sample reported some, and sometimes all, of these factors. When subjects had confidants, they did not commit major antisocial acts such as rape, child molestation, murder, and attempted murder. The negative factors included being sexualized through overt or covert sexual abuse or both, using sexual behavior (usually masturbation) to cope with psychological distress beginning by age twelve or thirteen, and being physically abused. These factors alone did not differentiate men who were violent from men who were not.

What differentiated men who committed violent, criminal acts from those who did not was the presence or absence of confidants. When men had confidants, they did not exhibit criminal and violent behaviors, even in the presence of major negative factors. In other words, many men in this sample suffered severe forms of abuse and neglect, but if they had confidants and other supportive persons, they did not rape, molest children, or commit other violent, nonsexual acts.

When the outcome was rape, sexual abuse of children, or physical violence, several factors interacted. Men who committed rape reported the following patterns: physical abuse, the absence of confidants and supportive persons, and developmental milestones reached within generally accepted norms. Two of the eight men who committed rape were not sexually abused as children. Four of these men became sexually compulsive by age eighteen, meaning they masturbated one or more times daily for the purpose of relieving emotional tension.

When the outcome was sexual abuse of children, multiple factors also were involved: lack of confidants, sexualized environment, being sexualized, and early onset of sexual behavior. Seven of the men who molested children had not themselves been sexually abused. These men began to use masturbation and various forms of sexual molestation in preadolescence or early adolescence.

Men who were physically but not sexually violent experienced child physical abuse, psychological abuse, and various types of neglect. Two of these three men were sexually abused in childhood or adolescence. Two of these men used masturbation and sexual intercourse as a way of coping with stress, but this behavior did not begin until well into adolescence.

Figures 8–1, 8–2, and 8–3 show the patterns discovered in the lives of the men in the sample. These figures show all the possible outcomes reported by the subjects under three conditions: being sexually abused only, being physically abused only, and being sexually and physically abused. Not every subject reported all of the outcomes. For example, sexual identity was an issue for nineteen of the subjects. The self as defective was found in the accounts of all the subjects, a result most likely linked to subjects' experience of childhood maltreatment in various forms. These figures represent tentative patterns that need further validation but that are supported by the data produced by the present research.

Figure 8–1 represents developmental patterns in the lives of the men who were sexually and physically abused. Nineteen subjects experienced these conditions. As this figure shows, in the presence of protective mechanisms such as supportive persons, outcomes were relatively benign, even when the men experienced sexualization. The term *sexualization* is in the process of being defined, and it is a construct developed in the present research. Sexualization means that the individual tends to cope with emotional stress through some type of sexual behavior. At the mild end of sexualizing behavior, the following behaviors were discovered in the research:

1. The tendency to view other people, often both men and women, as persons who will be demanding of sex, which the subject feels he must give

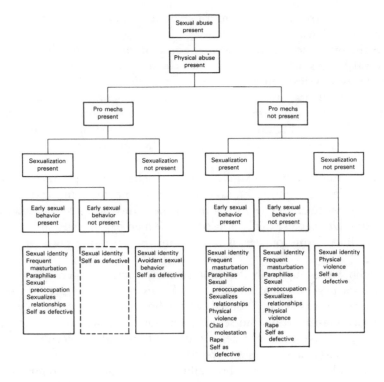

Note: Pro mechs = protective mechanisms; – – –· = not present in sample.

**Figure 8–1. Outcomes for Which Boys Are At Risk When Sexual and Physical Abuse Are Present**

2. Masturbation several times a day as a tension-reduction strategy
3. Use of pornography to distract the self from emotional tension
4. Preoccupation with sexual thoughts and fantasies
5. Exhibitionism and voyeurism

Eight of the nineteen subjects represented in figure 8–1 exhibited these behaviors. In the absence of supportive persons, outcomes were strongly negative and included rape, sexual molestation, physical violence, and murder.

Figure 8–2 represents developmental patterns when subjects were not sexually abused but were physically abused. Seven men are represented in this figure: four molesters, two rapists, and one attempted murderer. As the figure shows, all the outcomes present in figure 8–1 also are present in figure 8–2 except for rape, which is not present in figure 8–2. Not all the rapists had

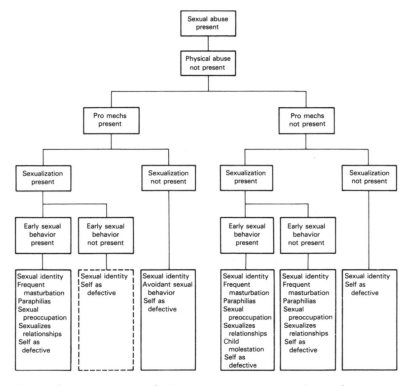

Note: Pro mechs = protective mechanisms; ‐ ‐ ‐ · = not present in sample.

**Figure 8–2. Outcomes for Which Boys Are At Risk When Sexual Abuse Is Present and Physical Abuse Is Absent**

been sexually abused. Four of the men represented in figure 8–2 were molesters but were not sexually abused as children. For the men in this sample, rape is associated with being physically abused during childhood, lack of protective mechanisms, and developmental milestones attained at normative times. Sexually compulsive behaviors, such as using masturbation as a tension-reduction strategy, may or may not be present in the behavior of men who rape.

Figure 8–3 represents developmental patterns in the lives of men who were not sexually abused and who experienced child physical abuse. Six men represented this pattern. Three of the men were molesters, two were rapists, and one was convicted of attempted murder. None of these subjects reported supportive persons. Two men in the sample, both molesters, were neither physically nor sexually abused. Neither of them had confidants. There were no men in the sample who were not sexually abused and were physically abused and who had confidants or other supportive persons.

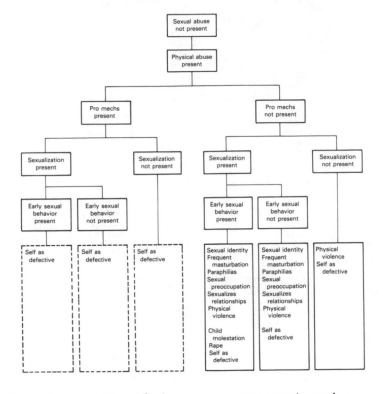

Note: Pro mechs = protective mechanisms; − − −· = not present in sample.

**Figure 8–3. Outcomes for Which Boys Are At Risk When Sexual Abuse Is Absent and Physical Abuse Is Present**

## Discussion

The effects of the child sexual abuse of boys are associated with various outcomes. Some of these outcomes are criminal, and others are painful to the individual but not criminal. The effects of sexual abuse appear to be mediated by the environment. In an environment where the individual receives positive support, the outcomes are relatively benign. When the individual can find no one in whom to confide and who accepts him, he may be at high risk for violent sexual behavior.

All of the behaviors found in men who were sexually abused as children also were found in men who were not sexually abused as children. Such a finding leads to the speculation that sexual abuse brings about psychological injury that may be similar to that brought about by other forms of childhood maltreatment. Men who have been sexually abused, however, may be more likely to use sexual behaviors as a tension-reducing mechanism.

The men in this study who were not sexually abused but were maltreated in other ways sought ways to cope with their psychological distress. When they used sexual behavior as a tension-reduction strategy, they appear to have stumbled on this as a solution to their psychological distress. Masturbation, child molestation, and rape represent forms of sexualized tension-reducing behaviors. The two rapists who were not sexually abused fit this pattern. A twenty-one-year-old man with no history of being sexually abused but who appeared to be psychologically injured through physical and psychological abuse began masturbating at sixteen when he discovered violent pornography. He became preoccupied with rape fantasies. Within a year, he began to rape women. He said he experienced a great sexual, physical pleasure in looking at violent pornography and fantasizing about rape and masturbating to those fantasies. A second rapist told a similar story.

The patterns discovered in the present research were meant to be applied to individual clinical situations and to be used as guidelines for treatment and prevention programs. In clinical work, for example, the patterns discovered in the present research can be compared to the patterns in a clinical case. If the patterns do not match, then the clinician can change those patterns to fit the case. Individuals, therefore, are not forced to fit into some preformulated pattern. The patterns of the present research are meant to illuminate poorly understood phenomena, but they are not meant to dictate what the clinician should find.

This research highlights the importance of helping maltreated boys to talk about, grapple with, and come to terms with their maltreatment. Supports found naturally in the environments of some boy victims may have helped to mitigate the most drastic of outcomes. This research challenges primary prevention and treatment programs to replicate within their programs the natural supports found in the lives of some subjects. Forcing clients to talk about their maltreatment will only replicate the coercion and abuse they have already experienced and probably will not promote healing. Using a noncoercive method and allowing clients to tell their stories under conditions in which they feel safe will likely lead to healing (Gilgun 1989b). The men in this sample who did talk about their painful experiences did so of their own free choice.

This study is retrospective, and such studies have been questioned because of possible flaws in subject recall (Yarrow, Campbell, and Burton 1970). As Cohler (1988) points out, however, the most important method for studying human development may be the subjectively constructed narrative. It is through the subjectivity that persons create meaning and coherence in their lives. In addition, if the subjects in the present study distorted, repressed, or omitted important aspects of their lives, it is not likely that every subject will distort in exactly the same way. This type of error is more likely to be distributed in a random or a haphazard way. Using multiple subjects interviewed over multiple session also provides reliability and validity checks.

This research has discovered developmental patterns related to the effects of childhood sexual abuse on boy victims. Perhaps the most salient findings to emerge are the following

1. Psychological harm underlies all forms of maltreatment.

2. Individuals attempt to cope with the consequent psychological distress, and this coping may take sexual forms, regardless of whether the person had been sexually abused.

3. Whether the coping leads to alleviation of the distress or leads to antisocial acts such as rape and molestation depends on the availability of environmental supports.

4. The presence of confidants and other supportive persons appears to be associated with more benign outcomes.

5. Men who have not been sexually abused often have outcomes similar to those found in men who have been sexually abused.

There is, therefore, reason to be optimistic that boys who have been sexually abused can overcome the effects of the abuse. The fewer the environmental supports for these boys, however, the higher the risk for dangerous acting out. Conversely, the more supportive the environment, the less likely it is that the boy will be at risk for highly adverse outcomes.

## References

Adams-Tucker, C. 1985. "Defense Mechanisms Used by Sexually Abused Children." *Children Today* 14: 9–12, 34.

Anthony, E.J., and B.J. Cohler. 1987. *The Invulnerable Child.* New York: Guilford.

Bowlby, J. 1973. *Attachment and Loss: Separation, Anxiety, and Anger.* Vol. 2. New York: Basic Books.

Bruckner, D., and P. Johnson. 1987. "Treatment for Adult Male Victims of Childhood Sexual Abuse." *Social Casework:* 81–87.

Burgess, A.W. 1985. "Sexual Victimization of Adolescents." In *Rape and Sexual Assault,* edited by A.W. Burgess, 123–138. New York: Garland.

Carnes, P. 1983. *Out of the Shadows.* Minneapolis: CompCare.

Cicchetti, D. 1987. "Developmental Psychopathology in Infancy: Illustrations from the Study of Maltreated Youngsters." *Journal of Consulting and Clinical Psychology* 55: 837–845.

Cohler, B.J. 1988. "The Human Studies and the Life History." *Social Service Review* 62: 552–575.

Conte, J.R. 1985. "The Effects of Sexual Abuse on Children: A Critique and Suggestions for Future Research." *Victimology* 10: 110–130.

Conte, J.R., and J.R. Schuerman. 1987. "Factors Associated with an Increased Impact of Child Sexual Abuse." *Child Abuse and Neglect* 11: 201–211.

Cotton, D.J., and A.N. Groth. 1984. "Sexual Assault in Correctional Institutions: Prevention and Intervention." In *Victims of Sexual Aggression,* edited by I.R. Stuart and J.G. Greer, 127–155. New York: Academic Press.

Davis, G.E., and H. Leitenberg. 1987. "Adolescent Sex Offenders." *Psychological Bulletin* 101: 417–427.

Dimock, P. 1988. "Adult Males Sexually Abused as Children." *Journal of Interpersonal Violence* 3: 203–221.

Egeland, B., D. Jacobvitz, and A.L. Sroufe. 1988. "Breaking the Cycle of Abuse." *Child Development* 59: 1080–1088.

Erickson, M.R., and B. Egeland. 1987. "A Developmental View of the Psychological Consequences of Maltreatment." *School Psychology Review* 16: 156–168.

Finkelhor, D. 1986. *A Sourcebook on Child Sexual Abuse.* Newbury Park, California: Sage Publications.

Fraiberg, S., E. Adelson, and V. Shapiro. 1975. "Ghosts in the Nursery: A Psychoanalytic Approach to the Problems of Impaired Mother-Child Relationships." *Journal of the American Association of Child Psychiatry* 14: 387–421.

Gilgun, J.F. 1988. "Factors Which Block the Development of Sexually Abusive Behavior in Adults Abused and Neglected in Childhood." Paper presented at the First National Conference on Male Victims and Offenders, Minneapolis, October 27–28.

———. 1989a. "Discovery-Oriented, Qualitative Methods Relevant to Longitudinal Research on Child Abuse and Neglect." Paper presented at the Research Forum on the Issues in the Longitudinal Study of Child Maltreatment, Toronto, October 14–18.

———. 1989b. "Freedom of Choice and Research Interviewing in Child Sexual Abuse." In *Social Work Processes,* 4th ed., edited by B.R. Compton and B. Galaway, 358–369. Chicago: Dorsey.

———. In press. "Hypothesis Generation in Social Work Research." *Journal of Social Service Research.*

Gilgun, J.F., and E.R. Reiser. In press. "Sexual Identity Development among Men Sexually Abused as Children." *Families in Society* (formerly *Social Casework*).

Glaser, B.G., and A.L. Strauss. 1967. *The Discovery of Grounded Theory.* New York: Aldine.

Groth, A.N. 1983. "Treatment of the Sexual Offender in a Correctional Institution." In *The Sexual Aggressor: Current Perspectives in Treatment,* edited by J.G. Greer and I.R. Stuart, 160–176. New York: Van Nostrand Reinhold.

Groth, A.N., and H.J. Birnbaum. 1979. *Men Who Rape: The Psychology of the Offender.* New York: Plenum Press.

Johnson, R., and D. Shrier. 1985. "Sexual Victimization of Boys." *Journal of Adolescent Health Care* 6: 372–376.

Jones, D.P.H. 1986. "Individual Psychotherapy for the Sexually Abused Child." *Child Abuse and Neglect* 10: 377–385.

Justice, B., and R. Justice. 1979. *The Broken Taboo: Sex in the Family.* New York: Human Sciences Press.

Kaplan, H.B., C. Robbins, and S.S. Martin. 1983. "Antecedents of Psychological Distress in Young Adults." *Journal of Health and Social Behavior* 24: 230–244.

Kaufman, J., and E. Zigler. 1987. "Do Abused Children Become Abusive Parents?" *American Journal of Orthopsychiatry* 57: 186–192.

Knafl, K.A., and D. Webster. 1988. "Managing and Analyzing Qualitative Data: A Description of Tasks." *Western Journal of Nursing Research* 10: 195–218.

Longo, R.E. 1982. "Sexual Learning and Experience among Adolescent Sexual Offenders." *International Journal of Offender Therapy and Comparative Criminology* 26: 235–241.

Main, M., and M. Goldwyn. 1984. "Predicting Rejection of Her Infant from Mother's Representation of Her Own Experience: Implications for the Abused-Abusing Intergenerational Cycle." *Child Abuse and Neglect* 8: 203–217.

Masten, A.S., and N. Garmezy. 1985. "Risk, Vulnerability, and Protective Factors in Developmental Psychopathology." In *Advances in Clinical Child Psychology,* vol. 8, edited by B.V. Lahey and A.E. Kazdin, 1–52. New York: Plenum Press.

Murphy, L. 1987. "Further Reflections on Resilience." In *The Invulnerable Child,* edited by E.J. Anthony and B.J. Cohler, 84–105. New York: Guilford.

Nasjleti, M. 1980. "Suffering in Silence: The Male Incest Victim. *Child Welfare* 59: 269–276.

Pierce, R., and L.H. Pierce. 1985. "The Sexually Abused Child: A Comparison of Male and Female Victims." *Child Abuse and Neglect* 9: 191–199.

Rogers, C.M., and T. Terry. 1984. "Clinical Intervention with Boy Victims of Sexual Abuse." In *Victims of Sexual Aggression,* edited by I.R. Stuart and J.G. Greer, 91–104. New York: Academic Press.

Seidel, J.V., R. Kjolseth, and J.A. Clark. 1985. *The Ethnograph.* Littleton, Col.: Qualis Research Associates.

Sroufe, L.A., and M. Rutter. 1984. "The Emergence of Developmental Psychopathology." *Child Development* 55: 17–29.

Starr, R.H. Jr., D.J. MacLean, and D.J. Keating. 1989. "Life-span Developmental Outcomes of Child Maltreatment." Paper presented at the Research Forum on Issues in the Longitudinal Study of Child Maltreatment, Toronto, October 15–18.

Vander, Mey, B.J. 1988. "The Sexual Victimization of Male Children: A Review of Previous Research." *Child Abuse and Neglect* 12: 61–72.

Werner, E., and R.S. Smith. 1982. *Vulnerable but Invincible.* New York: McGraw-Hill.

Wolf, S.C. 1985. "A Multi-Factor Model of Deviant Sexuality." *Victimology* 10: 359–374.

Wyatt, G.E., and M.R. Mickey. 1987. "Ameliorating the Effects of Child Sexual Abuse." *Journal of Interpersonal Violence* 2: 403–414.

Yarrow, M.R., J.D. Campbell, and R.V. Burton. 1970. "Recollections of Childhood: A Study of the Retrospective Method." *Monographs of the Society for Research in Child Development* 35 (no. 5).

Yates, A. 1982. "Children Eroticized by Incest." *American Journal of Psychiatry* 139: 482–485.

# Part III
# Assessment Issues

# 9

# The Needs of a Blue-Eyed Arab: Crisis Intervention with Male Sexual Assault Survivors

*Mark C. Evans*

T he English leader of the Bedouin Rebellion in Arabia, T.E. Lawrence, paid close attention to men in crisis. A sexual assault survivor himself at the hands of the Turks, he well understood such pain. Many have linked his assault to his later order for the slaughter of seven hundred retreating Turkish soldiers in Syria (Lawrence 1938).

Some of the men associated with Lawrence, such as the Ageyl tribesmen, kept their own counsel and unburdened themselves of pain through their fierceness toward others. The Bedu of Hejaz shared everything, from food to fear, in tightly knit groups. The British were different; they were called blue-eyed Arabs. For all their efforts, men like Lawrence did not fit in. In response, they tended to share only one close friendship, a bond with one man as alike as possible: "'Holding together', they called it: a war-time yearning to keep within four ears such thoughts as were deep enough to hurt" (Lawrence 1938, p. 642).

We do not know in whom Lawrence confided after his sexual assault or how he coped with the personal crises that most likely followed. We do know that many men who survive rape carry their hurt to the grave. Today the telephone line leads to agencies that better understand a man's suicide or drug addiction. It may lead to a rape crisis center with therapists or counselors who clearly understand the needs of the female sexual assault survivor but not those of the male survivor. In a world of unequal risk and reward, our society appears to teach boys and girls different lessons about crises. Silence in the face of pain is but one of the lessons.

Just as Lawrence found that men under stress may never disclose their emotional wounds, those who care about the recovery of male survivors sometimes see only rare opportunities to address sexual assault issues, making crisis intervention with the adult male survivor a challenging situation.

The effects of gender socialization are addressed in this chapter, as are effective techniques for intervening with men who have survived sexual assault. Basic issues of male survival are discussed in other chapters, and basic descriptions of crisis theory are available in a number of excellent books. Only particular issues facing male sexual assault survivors in crisis are addressed here.

## Gender Socialization of the Coping Process

Crisis results when an individual's ability to cope with problems is diminished. This coping ability, called dynamic homeostasis, is a kind of equilibrium while running the maze of life issues. When this "balance in motion" is lost, problems often appear insurmountable, and activities as diverse as work, leisure, contemplation, and grieving simply stop. Dan, a thirty-six-year-old rape survivor, explains the effects:

> One day was worse than the rest. Not the day it happened, I just mean one day I woke up paralyzed. I couldn't seem to get dressed for work. I called my boss and lied. I just sat there on the bed . . . my heart was racing to beat the band. I'd say I was paralyzed but there wasn't a goddamn thing wrong with me. I felt like such a coward. (Personnal communication to the author, April 1989)

Crisis intervention consists of those steps taken to interrupt the survivor's disequilibrium, ease anxieties and tension that contribute to the situation, and increase the survivor's empowerment to cope with life's problems.

Dan's words show us that a crisis, while often precipitated by a specific event such as a sexual assault, may come on any given day and appears to have many causes. For instance, it is not unusual for a serious coping issue to be overshadowed by day-to-day barriers that, if overcome, leave the survivor with the strength necessary to confront even the most serious issues without necessarily encountering a crisis point (Gambe and Getzel 1989).

While it is important to investigate the stressors that precipitate a crisis (Mulvey and Dohrenwend 1983), it is equally important to examine the effects of gender socialization in the evolution of survivor crisis so that interveners may be especially aware of them. While the body of research in these areas remain small, a number of particular gender differences have been investigated, and the recognition of them may be important to understanding men in crisis.

### Lack of Anticipation

Posttraumatic stress disorders are the result of events "outside the normal human experience" (American Psychiatric Association 1980, 247), and the reduced perception of potential assault by men makes this even more so (Riger and Gordon 1983). This reduced perception of risk also contributes significantly to posttraumatic shock (Bart 1987).

*Lack of License to Express Feelings*

It has long been recognized that the expression of fear or vulnerability are important to postrape recovery (Katz and Mazur 1981). Recent studies have shown that most men do not yet feel free to express these feelings. In an examination of men and the grieving process, Scully (1985) found that gender conditioning of men to act as protectors or providers specifically inhibited their ability to address issues in the grieving process. Another study of disabled men (Skord and Schumacher 1982) not only linked gender socialization to the inhibition of expression but also described masculinity as one handicapping condition among disability issues.

*Validation through Physical Injury*

Harm to the body of a sexual assault survivor has been seen as a validation of resistance for women (Brownmiller 1975), but little study of the psychic effects of physical harm to male survivors has been conducted. A study by Anne Hoiberg and Brian McCaughey (1984) in a similar area may help clarify the relationship. Hoiberg and McCaughey studied 723 men aboard two U.S. Navy ships that collided at sea. They found that, three years after the accident, the highest percentage of men who required separation from the service or psychiatric hospitalization were those who were evacuated but uninjured after the collision. As this study indicates, gender socialization may produce in the male survivor a stronger need for physical symptomatology in order to feel self-approval for his reaction to the traumatic event.

*Self-Definition of a Crisis*

Those men who are the most in need of psychological support tend to be the most fearful. One researcher (Whitaker 1987) found that men were significantly more likely to cause personal harm or even commit suicide than to seek crisis intervention. While the socialization of men may promote violence as a more acceptable option in crisis situations, a recent English study suggests that a key blocking mechanism in male crisis recognition is a lower internal-attentiveness level for personal distress (O'Brien 1988). This indicates that a male survivor may not view himself as in crisis until it can no longer be denied.

Jerome Frank suggests that men in crisis suffer demoralization and alienation, pushing away the first persons who seek to help them because they remain in denial (Frank 1972). This sequence not only explains the strong denial found among male rape survivors but also has implications for crisis intervention. Even a male survivor who expresses understanding of rape trauma needs to be sounded out as to his view of the situation and his perception of crisis, as it has been observed that men who seek counseling are often more assertive without a matching increase in their insight regarding their personal crises (Dua and McNall 1987). A variety of self-assessment tools are available. Some, such as the Symptom Check List–90 (Steer 1983), are quite structured, but it is possible to assess the survivor's self-perception of crisis through less structured interviews, including telephone crisis intervention formats.

## Loss of Power

Women are often socialized to recognize, if not accept, positions of powerlessness and victimization (Brownmiller 1975). Male socialization, in contrast, has fostered a deep-held belief in personal power tested by the inevitability of conflict (May 1986). Loss of power can, in and of itself, constitute a crisis for men. Coupled with other issues, it can be lost in the shuffle as more apparently vital needs are addressed. When this happens, gender identity and coping skills can be seriously threatened (Lorensen 1985).

## Emphasis on Action

Male survivors may recognize the full extent of the rape trauma and be prepared to address it. Here, again, gender socialization affects the way in which men respond. Men often seek action when they need to seek attitude. Paul Schurman (1987) argues that men's privileged position and freedom of action actually inhibit the changing of harmful attitudes. The ability of helpers to equate attitude changes (for example, seeing sexual assault as violence and not sex) with action may be one of our most challenging and vital functions in crisis intervention (Washington 1982).

## Lack of Information

Men have been particularly prone to gender and rape myths, but few studies have addressed the reasons for this. Substituting lack of information or myths with accurate information would appear to be relatively straightforward, but it is not. A Minneapolis program addressing rape attitudes found a lack of empathy and sensitivity for sexual assault survivors, as well as a serious misunderstanding of the facts surrounding sexual assault. Preprogram and postprogram surveys uncovered a significant resistance on the part of male participants to accept new information on rape issues. Not only did education prove ineffective in changing attitudes, but researchers also found that other information avenues, such as personally knowing a rape victim or attending church on a regular basis, made no difference in attitudes regarding rape (Borden, Karr, and Caldwell-Colbert 1988). While survival may promote acceptance of information by men, it is clear that denial of the occurrence of rape is as pervasive as denial of its effects.

## Processing of Emotion

Just as male survivors may lack permission to express emotion or knowledge regarding the emotional impact of the assault, they also may process what emotions they do feel in ways that are altered by their perceived gender role. The three most prevalent emotions expressed after sexual assault—anger, fear, and guilt—may have different foci for male survivors.

Anger, while the least socially acceptable response for female survivors (Brownmiller 1975; Burgess and Holmstrom 1979), is the most acceptable for men, and, in circumstances often found in sexual assaults, anger is expected to be both intense and retribution centered (Zumkley 1982). The unacceptability of an anger-based solution may create for the survivor a problem for which there is no solution, which promotes a crisis. Reporting the assault, which has been found to be an effective anger-based response for female survivors, does not appear to be as effective for men, who often express feelings of a loss of control and powerlessness once retribution is left to the legitimate authorities. In some cases, unresolved anger resulting from child sexual assault has been linked to the fear of male survivors that they will become offenders as adults, a position in which they would seek to vent their rage and regain power through the victimization of others (Vander May 1988).

Fear is another emotion that is expressed in ways that are influenced by gender socialization. While male survivors do not always express fear of the assailant, it has been my experience in twenty-eight consecutive intake interviews that the fear of increased vulnerability was readily expressed. The vulnerability, while admitted, is often balanced with retributional or other psychic but not practical coping responses. A focus on the external effects of fear has been noted with other types of male posttraumatic stress survivors (Brown 1984) and may result in crisis management that centers on one-for-one solutions to problems such as heightened fear but that does not address that fear or provide solutions that decrease anxiety or increase feelings of competence or mastery.

Guilt for male sexual assault survivors is actually a double burden in that the survivor not only blames himself for his own assault but also takes responsibility for his impaired ability to cope afterward. Just as male power is a social creation, the perception that males cannot be raped without their consent is a pervasive perception resulting from gender socialization (Smith, Pine, and Hawley 1988). A male survivor's lack of information and perception of emotion can make his recovery difficult. Such difficulty in regaining and retaining personal control can produce guilt (Washington 1982).

The conflict between gender mythology and true gender identity, say some researchers, runs so deep and is so central to the male identity that it may defy recognition by the survivor (May 1986). The guilt of a male rape survivor may center on the event itself ("If only I hadn't gone to his car with him . . ."), but it also may be the precipitator of the crisis, the leding edge of a downward spiral in which the ideal man, who cannot be raped, and the real man, who has, grips the survivor with a force that can be felt but not expressed (Jacobson 1975).

Factors such as lack of anticipation, lack of license to express feelings, the need for validation through physical injury, the impaired self-definition of crisis, the loss of power, an emphasis on action, lack of information, and gender-bound processes for emotion shape the posttraumatic responses of male rape survivors and promote crisis.

Clinicians involved in crisis intervention should take these and other gender-related factors into account when choosing a method and course for intervening, thereby better detecting signs that a male's coping techniques are becoming inadequate.

## Precipitators for Seeking Crisis Intervention

A crisis is the temporary mastery of anxiety over coping skills. The less defined anxiety, the more likely it is that the precipitator for a male survivor to seek crisis intervention will consist of a physical, medical, or interpersonal concern. These concerns will be addressed later in this chapter, but first I will discuss what role these concerns have in the survivor's decision to seek crisis intervention.

### Men's Barriers to Outcry

Gender socialization creates a bevy of inhibitors in men who consider seeking emotional support after rape. Such socialization is recognized as a factor in the underreporting of male sexual assault (Howard 1984; Burgess and Holmstrom 1985). The helper who will encounter male survivors needs to understand the effects of this socialization, which include a reluctance to use support networks, a limited use of disclosure opportunities, and the tendency to introduce concerns that can be addressed cognitively rather than emotionally. Leo, a nineteen-year-old rape survivor, expresses his concerns in this area:

> If I had my way, I wouldn't have told anybody. When you ask me, 'Hey did I tell some friend of mine or somebody in my family?' you oughta imagine what's gonna happen if I go sit down with them and say, 'Your Leo is still your Leo but his ass belongs to the man who scared him into taking down his pants.' You ask stupid questions, for a man. You're lucky I talk to you 'cause nobody else is gonna ever here this boy's story. (Personal communication to the author, April 1989)

Leo brings up a number of attitudinal inhibitors to male outcry. He feels that he cannot talk to close friends or family without changing their conception of him as a person who can protect himself against harm. He thinks that others will believe that he must have agreed to have sex with his attacker, since "men cannot be raped." Mistaking the aggression of rape for sexual preference, Leo also may fear being labeled a homosexual, a fear that speaks to his own heterosexism/homophobia as well as that of his community and society.

We also must consider institutional inhibitors to outcry by male survivors such as Leo. They may choose to contact a therapist or mental health counseling organization. This could be challenging even in the largest communities. The Rape Crisis Program of Houston, for instance, identified only sixty-seven therapists who specialize in sexual assault intervention as having significant experience with male survivors (Houston Area Women's Center 1988). Most of these therapists actually concentrate on the needs of adolescent and adult incest survivors using treatment styles that are applied to survivors of both genders. The outlook in smaller communities, with fewer therapeutic options and comparatively lower male outcry rates, is even dimmer.

Other male survivors face, as Leo did, the prospect of calling a rape crisis center. The understandable orientation of almost all such centers to female survivors of sexual assault may contribute to the extremely low numbers of males who contact these agencies. Even rape crisis agencies are not universal, and men trying to understand their rape survival may find crisis intervention only through a general crisis hot line, a state family issues agency, or even a drug abuse program.

This leads to an important point regarding the outcry of male survivors. The person's gender and individual characteristics, as well as the institutional barriers to men's disclosure of rape, are so numerous that, as Leo warns us, male survivors may never disclose their assaults or, if they do, may make few attempts to disclose them. The male survivor's choice of crisis intervener may, therefore, be much more pivotal than the female survivor's choice.

One way in which we can provide more effective intervention to the male survivor is to be prepared for the issues that may be raised and the way in which they will be presented. Here again, gender socialization has some effect on the male survivor.

While crises develop for male survivors of rape in an expected pattern— extreme stress caused by a violent event, repeated challenges to the survivor's coping skills, and an overwhelming of those skills—the initial issues raised by male survivors in seeking their first postrape crisis intervention do not reflect a focus on crisis. Rather, such contacts often begin with a tentative question or comment that can be answered with the minimum personal intrusion by the intervener (Evans 1989). There are no absolutes regarding gender and personality in crisis, only an increased probability that the male survivor's outcry will include some traits that are attributable to gender socialization.

## Control of Intervention

Perhaps the most outstanding gender-related aspect of crisis intervention with male rape survivors involves the issue of control. Many survivors may substitute control of the crisis intervention process for a balanced interaction, which could increase the survivor's empowerment and improve his sense of mastery. Control mechanisms are varied but have identifiable patterns.

The male survivor may display an increased tendency to seek control of the disclosure contact. He may recognize that the problems presented by the traumatic event are beyond his control, but it is almost reflexive for many men to hide this fact even if they have contacted a counselor or therapist for intervention. This is difficult to differentiate from denial and, indeed, is a form of denial, which many men feel is expected from them by society. A male client can maintain control in several different ways, which are best detected by his choice of words.

While phraseology varies from person to person, I have compiled a list of some of the most often used phrases based on a review of male survivor disclosures through the Houston Area Women's Center Rape Crisis Program from 1985 to 1988. Crisis interveners who recognize control techniques need to empower the survivor without agreeing to the implied terms of statements meant to maintain short-term control at the expense of the survivor's attempt to gain true coping abilities. This tactic does not always require confrontation, but the intervener does need to address it. Interveners will recognize some client control avenues as legitimate expressions of anger, shame, or confusion. Reflecting on what they hear and not what was overtly expressed can be the most effective course in this situation.

Following are some phrases the client may use to exert short-term control.

**"Listen, I just want to get some information."** This approach is obviously limit setting. The intervener is expected to stay within narrow confines. This survivor response deflects attention from the survivor by forcing the intervener to do most of the talking.

**"I don't need a lecture from you."** The survivor who injects this type of statement has anticipated judgment of his actions, homophobia, or other negative attitudes from the intervener. Having set such a course, questions such as "Have you reported this to the police?" can elicit a response that the survivor knew before he contacted anyone that he would be "pressured" to report the sexual assault. One effective technique to help empower such a survivor is to explore sources of judgment in his life and establish his ability to make independent choices, even if they are similar to the advice of others.

**"This is only going to take a minute."** Few persons intending to disclose, discuss, emote, begin situational acceptance, and plan future actions after a sexual assault truly think that it will only take a minute. Establishing a time limit on the intervention does not always mean that the survivor intends to follow it, but it does indicate that the survivor wants to control the time frame in which it is addressed. There is nothing wrong with this, as long as the intervener points out that the focus of crisis intervention is not time but results. The contact can be as short or as long as the survivor wishes, but time is not so precious a commodity that it needs to be limited. As in many expressions of short-term control, this may reflect a fear that the survivor does not deserve more time from the intervener.

**"I don't know what kind of counselor you are."** One way for a survivor to limit the depth of disclosure is to limit the depth to which the intervener can go. Rather than suggesting that there will be limits to his self-disclosure, the survivor may concern himself with the fact that the intervener is a woman, a volunteer, or someone much younger or older than himself—in short, someone who is just different enough to have only limited expertise or compassion. While the intervener may share information regarding the negligible effects this may have on intervention (Atkinson, Ponce, and Martinez 1984; Evans 1989; Evans and Thomas 1989), there has been considerably more success in working around this barrier on an individual basis. "Do you feel comfortable with me?" is an important question for the intervener to ask. The negotiation that follows may result in a change of intervener or the survivor's acceptance of the present helper. Either way, the short-term control that serves as a barrier to outcry can be replaced with empowerment.

**"I want to talk about what somebody should do in this kind of situation and see if I'm right."** Another method of exercising disclosure control is for the survivor to enter the discussion with a preconceived interpretation of the assault, its effects, and, most importantly, how his response differed from the best possible course of action. The "what if" replay of a rape is a common reaction to this trauma. This self-judgment becomes more pronounced, as the certainty of failure is preferred to the uncertainty inherent in being a sexual assault survivor. The survivor may project his self-judgment on others (for example, he may say, "Most guys who get in this situation are really fags") in an attempt to avoid personal introspection by focusing on the defense of his hypothesis. Acknowledgment that the survivor's scenario is possible can be important as a starting point to help the intervener revise the survivor's viewpoint from a global or anecdotal one to one based on his personal and individual needs.

**"Let me ask you another question before I deal with what you said."** Obtaining information is one of the key ways in which a survivor may achieve empowerment and insight. This requires more than asking questions, however. It also requires processing the answers. A survivor can overcontrol crisis intervention through a series of questions that cannot have perfectly relevant answers for the survivor's situation. The intervener can, as many crisis advocates do, fall into the survivor's "Q & A" pattern and discuss sexual assault issues without ever really addressing the survivor's needs. The intervener must realize what is happening and gradually move back to the individual's perception of new information.

**"You poor thing, having to listen to so many sob stories."** A common reaction among sexual assault survivors is to apologize for burdening the intervener with their problems. In the outcry of many male survivors, this turns into a focus of interest that prevents discussion of the survival issues and promotes a 'I'm not like the other people who talk to you' denial that there are such issues. The expression of concern for the intervener is not, in and of itself, a control mechanism. It is important for the intervener, however, to monitor the object of the conversation to ensure that the survivor is not avoiding crisis management by focusing on the intervener.

**"You oughta have a dick shoved up your butt and see how it feels. You like it up there, huh? Do you?"** This control technique, particularly noted when male survivors have turned to female interveners, also has been used in male-to-male intervention situations. The expression of anger is important to recovery, but in some situations, anger can be used to reassert personal mastery by intimidating the intervener. Such statements also can be used to create a distinction that the survivor sees as a limitation of the legitimacy or expertise of the helper. It is particularly helpful to separate with the survivor anger directed at the assailant and anger vented on others. Validation of anger can be empowering, but the intervener's acceptance of inappropriate anger does not assist the survivor in finding coping mechanisms that will strengthen his support network and self-esteem.

**"This is what you should be telling people."** The survivor's ability to solve problems and find personal resolution after a rape crisis is an encouraging sign of recovery. Some survivors may have a gender-role expectation that they not only cope with their assault without difficulty but also express their anticipated competence. The survivor also may feel inferior to the intervener and use directive statements to increase his feeling of self-esteem. The intervener can address this by pointing out that it is not her or his role to direct crisis recovery and reassuring the survivor that he or she respects the client's status as a male and as a survivor.

## Presenting Issues in Crisis Intervention

The male sexual assault survivor will most likely focus on a particularly threatening issue or set of issues when seeking crisis intervention. Proportionately fewer male survivors may be expected to begin the intervention by expressing a thought such as "Something happened, but I don't know what I want to talk about." Presenting issues run along several lines: those that are concrete, such as medical, police, or legal concerns; those that are emotional, such as feelings of intense anger, fear, or guilt; and personal identity issues, such as sexual relations, homophobia, and relationships with others. Many other issues also will be encountered in crisis intervention, but issues that have particular relevance to male identity or gender socialization can be anticipated.

### Immediate Decisions Faced during Crisis

Concrete issues are, by far, the most often presenting concerns. These issues are most immediately addressed with information and referrals, but it is important to recognize the gender-related attitudes that shape the survivor's viewpoint. Fear is often expressed or implied in the presentation of these issues. Reassurance may be given that the survivor need not face these fears alone, but reassurance that "everything will be all right" needs to be scrupulously avoided.

Medical concerns can originate in a wide range of fears, the most prominent being the fear of contracting AIDS or venereal disease as a result of the sexual assault. The long dormancy of the HIV virus and the social stigmatization of regular AIDS testing can make this disease particularly haunting to male rape survivors. The clear unmanageability of the virus by the individual is sufficient to precipitate personal crisis even without consideration of the sexual assault (Gambe and Getzel 1989).

Crisis interveners deal with this health threat in a number of ways. Most interveners, whether they are rape crisis specialists or therapists, should make sure that they clearly understand how the virus is transmitted, what testing procedures are available, and where support services are offered in the community. Use of this information to suggest possible proactive steps by the survivor, such as using a condom, putting a test date on his calendar, and reading more about AIDS, can help make this a more manageable issue and reduce personal levels of anxiety. Exploring the survivor's attitudes toward AIDS is as important as providing information, since a survivor's resistance to testing or heterosexism/homophobia could result in denial of the facts about AIDS or an aversion to taking action. Concerns about venereal diseases, particularly herpes, also are commonly expressed. The referral to immediate medical care and testing needs without an examination of the survivor's beliefs may not be followed up by the survivor, and guilt or unresolved fears could continue to build despite crisis intervention.

Pain and bleeding also can produce fear and powerlessness in male survivors. A man who has rarely or never engaged in anal sex is likely to suffer intense pain and some rectal bleeding. The social stigma ascribed to anal penetration makes this symptomatology particularly difficult for the male survivor to face. Denial of anal penetration is common among both male and female survivors (Burgess and Holmstrom 1979). The survivor's fear about the extent of his injuries can, without medical assessment, grow into a crisis-provoking anxiety. Interveners are not in a position to reduce this anxiety except through referrals to medical care and through reassuring the survivor that such concerns are treatable.

Access to medical care is often closely linked to concerns about reporting the sexual assault. Because medical care is often provided through the rape evidence examination, many survivors may avoid both medical and law enforcement intervention. Reporting sexual assault raises a number of issues for survivors, who are aware that few promises can be made about the prospects of an arrest and conviction.

The prospect of turning to male-dominated law enforcement agencies at a time of gender anxiety and vulnerability does not appeal to many male survivors. This concern is particularly expressed by homosexual male survivors, some of whom reported rape only to be told that it could not have been sexual assault due to their sexual preference. This is, unfortunately, true of some rape crisis programs as well, where gender-socialized biases have prompted volunteers to refer men of either sexual preference to local gay men's organizations because they are unsure of the distinction between the rape of a homosexual and consensual homosexual relations. In one case, I witnessed a rape crisis advocate's decision to leave a male rape survivor on his own at a pay telephone after he had been pushed out of his assailant's car. The advocate decided that "if a man is that willing to talk about it to me, he was probably making up the whole thing."

In light of episodes such as these, urging the male survivor to report rape to local police is not necessarily anxiety reducing, and there is no reason to rest assured that the suggestion will be acted upon. Therefore, it is important to identify services or features of the local social support network that can give the male survivor some sense that he will have assistance in coping not only with the existing stresses of rape but also with the additional stresses of the reporting and court processes. Accompaniment through these processes by a trained advocate, follow-up calls to legal services, and concurrent therapy are all effective supports for the male survivor who reports a rape.

All the incentives in the world may not be enough to convince a survivor to report a rape, and he has a legitimate right to choose not to do so. The additional guilt, and possibly fear of the assailant, that may accompany this decision makes nonreporting just as challenging to the survivor as reporting. Crisis interveners need to respect the survivor's decision and discuss with him the consequences and the benefits of reporting and not reporting. The use of leading questions such as "What will you do about medical care if you decide to report?" can help a survivor regain personal control.

## Emotional Issues and Crisis

Another set of issues that may arise in survivor outcry center on emotions. Gender socialization interferes with men's expression of intense emotions, especially those associated with grieving, vulnerability, and helplessness (Johnson, Ellison, and Heikkinen 1989; Scully 1985; Viney et al. 1985; Whitaker 1987). These feelings, often misunderstood and unexpected, can overwhelm a male survivor and promote personal crisis. Interveners must, therefore, expect that strong emotions may be a presenting issue for the male sexual assault survivor.

The most common of these emotions is anger. Not only is anger the most gender-acceptable emotion, but it is also an understandable reaction to violent victimization. Anger for male survivors, as for female survivors, can be directed at a variety of targets. The rapist, significant other, family, friends, medical or police interveners, and crisis interveners all may be objects of this anger. Helping the survivor focus his anger and find appropriate channels for it is critial because anger can be externalized and destructive (Whitaker 1987) and because it is the emotion that male survivors have the most societal permission to express.

Fear is less likely to be the presenting issue unless there is a concrete concern to which it can be anchored, such as questions about AIDS or the reporting process. The expression of uncertainty and generalized fear can, because of gender expectations, make accessing of a support network more difficult. The crisis intervener who validates the expression of fear by men as healthy and acceptable can remove a potentially large barrier to problem solving and self-confidence.

Another presenting emotion after sexual assault is guilt. This is commonly expressed and is often gender related. Men who have been socialized to believe that they have control over themselves and their environment are paticularly vulnerable to feelings of guilt. Male physiology being what it is, it is possible for men to be manipulated to ejaculation during rape. Should it occur, this can result in a strong feeling of guilt and a sense of self-betrayal. Guilt that blocks a survivor's coping mechanisms is not assuaged by the words of absolution that interveners may automatically give. Many male survivors have reported, however, that such words are important to their decisions to address guilt through counseling or support groups, where effective work on guilt feelings is most prevalent.

An often misunderstood feeling expressed by male survivors in crisis is shame. Shame may be best explained as personal pain resulting from the feeling that something dishonorable, ridiculous, or indecorous happened because a person put himself into an indecent situation. It goes far beyond guilt in terms of its intensity and has often been cited by male survivors who have sought crisis intervention due to extremely high levels of personal distress.

Shame is both gender and culture based and often is related to the judgment of identifiable friends or family close to the survivor. Shame is most often associated in these situations with other males in the family, particularly the survivor's father, and heterosexism/homophobia has been linked to shame as a barrier to use of existing support networks. Such issues cannot be easily resolved, but intervention centering on this issue can be effective, especially if disclosure is role-played or the survivor imagines similar but undisclosed episodes among friends or family and discusses what his advice to them would be.

### Personal Identity Issues during Crisis

The male survivor in crisis also may seek intervention surrounding issues of personal choice, such as sexual practices, sexual preference, and use of his support network. The survivor's gender socialization usually has prevented him from closely addressing these areas in the past.

The sex drive is more central to the social identity of men than of women, and difficulties with sexuality can be more stigmatizing and crisis provoking for men (Tollison and Adams 1979). This may hold true not only for heterosexual men involved in long-term relationships (Mulvey and Dohrenwend 1983; Avery-Clark 1986; Weizman and Hart 1987), but also for unattached men (Beasley and Childers 1985). Sexual dysfunction may be the first postrape symptom of traumatic stress that the male survivor consciously recognizes. Should this occur, many male survivors feel forced into disclosure of the sexual assault by gender socialization. Often in our society, male sexual dysfunction is linked to overall competence, and survivors feel compelled to account for a decrease in arousal or performance.

Another serious concern is sexual traumatization resulting from survivor ejaculation. It is vital that male physiology be explained to the survivor and that the ejaculation be decoupled from the assault experience.

Lack of acceptance of a body-altering disease or trauma results not only is psychological trauma but also in somatic sexual dysfunction (Jensen 1986). Many male survivors who seek crisis intervention express the belief that sexuality, once depressed by rape, will not return. Such a prospect is extremely anxiety producing. Survivors may be reassured by information that postassault sexual dysfunction is not irreversible. Attempts to destigmatize sexual dysfunction also can be helpful.

Another deeply personal issue that provokes gender crisis is that of sexual preference. Central to the self-image of all survivors, preference is part of a person's gender identity and is shaped by gender socialization (Money and Ehrhardt 1972).

For the exclusively heterosexual survivor, rape may be the first male-to-male sexual contact in his life. Mixing the sexual and assaultive aspects of male-to-male contact causes many heterosexuals to suspect not only their gender responsibilities of self-defense but also their sexual preference. Nowhere is Money and Ehrhardt's hypothesis that we seek external validation for internal sexual drives more obvious than in the words of male rape survivors facing a crisis of sexual preference. "What was it that made him think I wanted this?" is a common theme of such concerns.

Many homosexual and bisexual male survivors face sexual preference crises as well. Past experience with anal or oral sex with men does not appear to lessen the trauma associated with sexual assault. It is important to note that homosexual survivors with sexual identity concerns also search for external indicators they may have given to the assailant promoting vulnerability or accessibility. Few gay survivors appear to see rape as a type of punishment for sexual preference, but the sudden emergence of male-to-male sexual violence promotes a fear of men in some survivors, seriously affecting healthy sexual function and relationships.

Survivors with sexual preference crises are, in many cases, actually dealing with sexual dysfunction crises. A discussion of the survivor's sexual history before and after the assault can be helpful. Distinctions between sex and rape can be most effectively drawn from the survivor, not provided in the form of information. Helping a survivor strategize and role-play actions that will reduce sexual anxiety and promote better understanding from significant others or sexual partners also can be effective.

Sexuality is just one of the areas in which male survivors may have difficulties communicating with those in their personal support networks. Crisis follows a decrease in personal coping skills and assets. Many problems seem to defy individual solutions. Men are socialized to believe that they can be emotionally competent and self-sufficient. Such socialization cuts men off from their natural support networks (Mulvey and Dohrenwend 1983; Sanders 1988; Scully 1985).

Many male survivors tell crisis interveners that they have no support network to which they can turn in order to talk about rape. They may feel, legitimately, that friends or family, even significant others, may be so disturbed about the assault that they will not be a source of support. Interveners should review all possible sources of support regarding rape recovery with survivors.

If current networks are not considered helpful, a survivor may be encouraged to develop new networks, including empathic but untapped friendships, rape survivor groups or services, and crisis hot lines. The intervener ought not to be overlooked as a source of support.

Although not all men are comfortable with self-documentation, the concept of a diary in which male survivors record their feelings and self-direction has been found to be an effective alternative to other supports. This and other ways to use incest specialist Sandra Butler's (1978) "internal mentor" for male survivors can be very helpful to survivors seeking to regain control and establish a source of support that reduces their feelings of helplessness.

These and other issues at the core of the survivors' personal identities can be intertwined with overwhelming emotions, physical concerns, and concrete issues regarding health or reporting issues. The complexity of needs for a male sexual assault survivor seeking crisis intervention is, fortunately, not reflected by an equally complex means of providing that intervention.

## Crisis Intervention Methodology

Men who survive sexual assault deserve the best interveners have to offer when they make the decision to share their needs in crisis. This is not, as we have seen, related to the intervener's gender or official capacity. Nor does it require the use of crisis intervention methods that are radically different from those that have proven successful with female survivors and with survivors of many types of trauma.

This section suggests some basic steps in crisis intervention, along with commentary regarding the special needs of "the blue-eyed Arabs" who survive sexual assault. The steps help the intervener to provide assessment, emotional support, information, male empowerment, and referrals. Three simple messages that can be given to all rape survivors, and their implications for male survivors, are discussed. Specific techniques of crisis intervention also are addressed, including problem identification, paraphrasing, reflection of feelings, summarization, self-disclosure, and confrontation. Finally, a case study in crisis intervention related to gender socialization issues is presented, including those intervention techniques and referrals actually used.

A survivor in crisis may be in any one of dozens of situations. He may be in immediate danger. He may be grappling with blinding rage a year after his assault. He may be suffering from flashbacks. He may be heterosexual, bisexual, or homosexual; young or old; of any ethnic group or societal background. The survivor has made the decision to share his crisis with you, the intervener, and upon initial contact, you know little about him.

You do, however, know about crisis for male survivors. The survivor is confused or unsure about what action to take. Personal issues appear larger than his ability to manage them. He feels helpless, and his self-esteem has taken a beating. In many cases, he is dealing with physical concerns related to rape or somatic anxiety. He is looking for assistance but wants support, not direction. He is tougher than he knows.

How can you find out who the survivor is, what his strengths are, and which problems have combined to produce severe disequilibrium? Many specific steps and techniques are available, but the crucial first step is to review the objectives of crisis intervention.

It is important to remember that the goal of crisis intervention is the interruption of the paralysis that the survivor is experiencing. This will help him reduce his level of anxiety and regain his sense of mastery over his life. To accomplish this, you must be nonjudgmental. This is often difficult to achieve, but you must do so.

Another component of successful intervention is nondirection. Counselors are socialized, as are men, to have all the answers. The survivor's feelings of competence and control disappear at the conclusion of the intervention if those feelings are not his own but a reflection of the confidence and control of the person he has turned to for help.

You also must take time into account. The suicidal survivor in crisis has a limited amount of time, sometimes minutes. An intervener who focuses on the immediate crisis situation and, with later opportunities, the precipitators and premorbid contributors to posttraumatic stress, is using time effectively. Intervention is, if nothing else, emotional triage. There will be other days for the discussion of the many other issues in question.

Finally, you must consider just what crisis intervention with rape survivors can and cannot achieve. Experience with male survivors has borne out the findings of Perl, Westin, and Peterson (1985) in working with female survivors. Crisis intervention is most effective in dealing with fear, anxiety, guilt, depression, and somatic complaints. Lesser but important gains can be made with phobias, social skills, and rape denial. Little or no immediate gains can be expected in the areas of sexual dysfunction or gender identity, areas in which socialization has been particularly pervasive. Each individual is different, of course, and each will be pursuing his own goals at his own rate.

### Crisis Intervention Hierarchy

Intervention with the posttraumatic stress disorder (PTSD) survivor is particularly effective when using a model with a hierarchy of steps to be taken by the intervener. These steps include assessment, emotional support, information, empowerment, and referrals. They are in a hierarchy because crisis intervention is a time-limited endeavor and it is useless to discuss empowerment before it has been determined that the survivor is safe and not injured. It is, therefore, highly advisable to take these in order.

**Assessment.** Determining the survivor's current situation and how serious it is may be the most important action taken. When contacting a crisis intervener, few survivors will begin by stating clearly their priority issues. It would be unfair to answer an office or hot line call from a survivor by asking, "What's on your mind?" and leaving the subsequent direction of the conversation up to the response. It is up to the intervener to find out, as quickly as possible, what threats there are to the survivor's coping mechanisms and to help him prioritize them. This can be done in short order by a three-tiered set of questions:

1. Assessing situations requiring immediate action
   a. What has happened?
   b. How long ago did this occur?
   c. Are you in a safe place? Do you feel safe?
   d. Are you hurt?
   e. Have you been taking any medications? What for?
   f. Have you been drinking or taking any drugs?
2. Assessing areas for crisis intervention
   a. What would you like to talk about?
   b. What are you feeling right now?
   c. Are you in emotional pain? Can you describe it?
   d. If you had to name the issue that is causing you the most pain, what would it be?
   e. Is there anything you are particularly afraid of happening or someone close to you knowing?
3. Learning about the man before you
   a. Tell me a little about yourself.
   b. How would you describe your personality to others?
   c. Who do you feel you can trust in tough spots?
   d. What kind of things were going well for you when you began to face the things you are facing now?
   e. What things were not going well?
   f. How have you dealt with problems in the past?

It is advisable to ask as many questions as you think are necessary from the first tier before moving on to the second and third. Persons in crisis may not be able to prioritize their needs and situation for the intervener, and they should not be held responsible for this. While many effective therapeutic intake formulas go from surface to personal information, rely on client prioritization, or reconstruct issues in a time-linear fashion, assessment during crisis intervention requires different rules. A New Hampshire colleague shared his experience when a man in crisis contacted him for an immediate appointment:

> The man I was seeing that day was somebody I had already talked to on the phone. He sounded somewhat nervous, but "all there." He came to my office and sat down. My questions started out in general lines . . . you know, "Can you tell me what has brought you here?" "Tell me a little bit about yourself." He kept fidgeting and holding his arm but answered my questions without any hesitation. Then he just passed out, went right to the floor. Blood was spreading on the carpet from his leg. We called the rescue squad. To make

a long story short, he had broken out a window and cut himself really deeply. He realized he wanted to live and called me to talk, without admitting what he had done. When I saw him in the hospital, he actually said he was too embarrassed by the suicide attempt to go to the emergency room or tell me. (Personal communication, 15 September 1989)

Making a priority-based assessment also gives the survivor some sense of the scale of his concerns, an understanding that often provides a survivor with his first feelings of insight and control since the onset of the crisis.

**Emotional Support.** It is in crisis that the prototypic men described by Haug (1987) and Scully (1985) come together. Haug found that men weave a moral fabric around business ethics or financial responsibilities, whereas women focus on their bodies. Scully believes that men in the grieving process, whose morals are centered on love, feel a traumatic loss yet are not given societal permission to express their loss, pain, fear, confusion, and anger. The helpers of men after rape and other traumas know that just because men do not normally express deep feelings, there is no reason to doubt that they possess them.

Providing effective emotional support also requires an assessment. First, the intervener needs to listen carefully to the survivor's words to determine his style of emotional expression. This can be easily tested through questions such as "It sounds to me as though you're angry. Is that how you'd describe it?" Society's gender rules for men often abolish explicit emoting in favor of more oblique statements.

The intervener can be of even more help by listening for the emotional component of all statements made by the survivor. All do not need to be reflected or addressed, but emotional support cannot be given if the intervener does not know where to find the emotion he or she knows is present. "I kind of have a problem with the thought that I might get VD" might mean anything from "I am scared that I might have AIDS or herpes" to "If I have been infected, how am I going to tell this to my lover?"

Emotions, once found and clarified in the course of intervention, can be nurtured by empathic and nonjudgmental comment. Crisis intervention is often the process of helping persons develop their own skills. Empowering and licensing men to find self-affirming ways to express their feelings may, in this framework, be "a life's work done in seven minutes," as one crisis counselor has put it. (Tina Prihoda 1987. Personal communication to the author, June 17.)

Proactive emotional support also is very important. Later in this chapter, basic messages that address some of the more universal emotional concerns of survivors and methods of reflecting feelings expressed by survivors are discussed. These messages seek to say "I care about you; I care about what has happened; I am not going away; you have a right to feel what you feel."

Particularly in the crisis hot line format of intervention, survivors may seek a number of very time-limited contacts en route to more substantive support services. If you have only sixty seconds to address a survivor's needs, that minute is well spent even if all you have to show for it is your knowledge of the survivor's current situation and his knowledge that you understand, care, and are available to him in the future. If more time is available, emotional support can be given throughout the interaction and should be one of the first items addressed in the last minutes of the conversation.

**Information.** Sir Edward Gibbon wrote, "New knowledge is a powerful antidote to indecision. In crisis, it is deliverance, be the news good or bad" (Gibbon 1914, 118). This observation, made of Timor's war in Anatolia, could have been made by any number of counselors to survivors in crisis.

Information is not to be confused with referral. It is simply sharing the knowledge of any source with the survivor. Many types of information are provided during intervention, including the following:

- Basic messages: "It isn't your fault you were raped"; "Men have a right to feel what they feel"
- Societal issues: why rape occurs, societal supports for rape, gender and rape myths
- Rape issues: rape trauma syndrome, issues of male sexual assault, sexualization of aggression, offender motivations and profiles
- Medical issues: injuries, examination procedures, sexually transmitted diseases, payment for services
- Legal issues: how rape is reported, police procedures, victim rights, the court process, trials, sentencing
- Survivor support: types of support and counseling, self-help techniques

Information is best shared in short bursts, each inviting the survivor's comment and assessment. Lectures for any period of time, even when the information is of key interest, are disempowering for the listener and may prove to be as overwhelming as the lack of information was earlier. An example of effective sharing might go like this: "The police may want you to go downtown to give a formal statement. Is that something you might want to do?" "Yeah, I might. What is that like?" The intervener gives another short answer.

Gender socialization makes many men particularly invested in the information-gathering process. In some respects, an intervener can encourage the survivor to participate in this process, perhaps by suggesting that he may want to take notes of the conversation. In other respects, the intervener may discourage it—for example, in the case of a survivor whose emotional needs are becoming critical but who is suppressing them through information gathering.

The intervener should be concerned with information exchange, as he or she wants to know how well the information is understood, how the survivor is using it, and how it affects the survivor's cognitive and emotional states.

**Empowerment.** Gender socialization has created many myths that are barriers to the expression and resolution of rape traumas. The intervener cannot undo these traumas in the limited time afforded him or her, but the intervener can help the survivor reframe his thinking on maleness as the need and opportunity exist.

The bottom-line question for men whose concept of masculinity is impairing them is this: What is a real man? The survivor may turn to male mythology for his answers, and the intervener may support, challenge, or add information in an effort to help the survivor find positive answers to this question and empower him to use this information in coping with crises. Socialization runs deep, and the intervener must anticipate resistance.

Commonly heard answers to the question "What is a real man?" often paint the portrait of a wounded and disempowered person, even without consideration of rape:

"A man isn't supposed to cry."

"Men don't let themselves get raped."

"A man can't let anybody know that he can't take care of himself."

"A man stands alone. He does what he has to do. If he fails, he dies."

"Men don't do all that touchy-feely stuff."

"So you're telling me," reflects the intervener, "that a man is responsible for whatever happens to himself and everyone around him. He can't feel. He can't cry. He can't talk. A real man who must decide between sexual assault and death by stabbing should fall on the knife, right?" Putting maleness in a new light is often accomplished through probing questions.

The different standards we apply to ourselves and others also may provide an avenue for intervention. The survivor ought to be able to name at least one man whom he admires. Through focused imagery, that man can be placed in the survivor's situation. The survivor could be asked if he would approve if that man cried, was angry, or felt vulnerable. The advice the survivor would give his friend after rape could be discussed and compared with male myths.

Not all men see the world through the lens of male control and omnipotence. Those who do, however, need to be told that real men cannot prevent rape; that men should be strong but that strength includes the strength to survive rape; that having guts does not mean seeking a bullet wound but being tough enough to face the emotions of rape trauma; and that being in control all the time is not, as Elizabeth Barrett Browning notes, "the mission of man, but the mission of gods."

Effective intervention with male survivors includes an assessment of gender attitudes that inhibit recovery. Confusion between power and empowerment can be addressed with information that may assist the survivor in crisis to recognize his strength and the value of that strength to real men seeking real recovery.

**Referrals.** Problem solving is incomplete without a thorough discussion of the tools the survivor can use in his future growth and recovery, as well as the supports that can assist him in avoiding future crises. Many interveners provide referrals immediately. In the instance of drug overdose or medical or safety concerns, this is highly appropriate. For the great majority of rape recovery issues, however, referrals ought to be the last area of exploration.

Two referrals are almost always called for: (1) yourself—make sure the survivor knows how and when to contact you again if appropriate, but remember to set realistic limits on contact; (2) a twenty-four-hour resource, preferably a rape crisis center. Other referrals can be made upon request. Empowerment begins with options, so it is advisable to make more than one referral of each type of support, such as therapists and physicians, whenever possible. Rape crisis centers and crisis help lines often have extensive and carefully screened referral lists. Agencies such as these can be a valuable and continuing resource to the survivor. No referral ought to be made to an agency or individual unless the intervener has considered the party's experience with male survivors and ability to meet his needs.

### Three Basic Messages

No matter what else transpires in a crisis intervention discussion, three messages are particularly appropriate. These messages are simple but address the major emotional and informational needs of rape survivors. They can be delivered anytime during intervention, either exactly as worded here or in whatever words the intervener finds most useful.

**You are not to blame.** The survivor is not responsible for his rape, regardless of what led to the assault or how he reacted to it.

**You are not alone.** The survivor is not the only man to survive rape. There are many others. The survivor will not face recovery alone. Even if he does not have any other persons he can turn to for support, he has the support of the intervener. In time, he will find others who share many of his concerns.

**No matter how bad it feels right now, you can and will survive.** The word *survivor* is a popular term for the victim of sexual violence and for good reason. It implies that the man who went through this experience possesses the special abilities to preserve his life and return to safety. Rape trauma is not necessarily a lifetime experience. Recovery is possible and begins with crisis intervention.

No matter what major themes interveners find in the lives of male survivors in crisis, the formulation and use of basic messages help them develop a focus that will not be lost in the myriad details, issues, and attitudes that arise during a time-limited interaction.

## Crisis Intervention Techniques

### Problem Identification

The intervener seeks to find out what is wrong through active listening and careful questioning of the survivor. Problems for the male rape survivor come in three varieties: precipitators of crisis, posttraumatic concerns, and inhibitors to action.

Precipitators of crisis are often related to decisions regarding presenting concerns, such as whether to report the assault or whether to seek a medical examination. Crisis points also are to be expected during recovery. The natural course of rape trauma syndrome includes changes in perception that present new challenges in emotional equilibrium. Even preparation for these changes cannot stop the feeling of fear and the sense of helplessness that result from the sudden onset of a new sleeping disorder or newly recognized phobias. Crisis also may be precipitated by changes in coping mechanisms. A survivor who has successfully coped with rape trauma in the past may turn to maladaptive strategies such as drug or alcohol use, promiscuity, dependence on telephone intervention, or venting anger on those in his support network.

External situations also may change, thus precipitating crisis. A survivor who loses his job, for instance, may question not only gender-based feelings of competence but also his ability to deal with his survival.

Often these precipitators are taken for crisis situations by the survivors. Through assessment, the intervener can evaluate the threat to the survivor's personal safety and coping ability that is posed by the precipitators. In many cases, these threats need to be addressed first but can be linked to the crisis throughout the intervention: "Bill, I understand that you are scared by your temper and the possibility that you may hurt your lover. Anger is a legitimate way to feel after sexual assault, but we can talk about how you can work on that anger in ways that will not add to your pain or hurt your relationship."

This type of linkage is particularly important for a survivor who focuses on a precipitator as a defense against facing survival issues.

### Paraphrasing

Returning the thought given to you intact, but in different terms, is the art of paraphrasing. When properly used, this skill is among the more appropriate in dealing with gender biases and promoting empowerment. Paraphrasing addresses the intellectual content of the thought, not the emotion behind it. Paraphrases ought to be briefer than the original statement and should reflect the central concern registered in that statement.

Paraphrasing may expose a misunderstanding between survivor and intervener and makes possible mid-course corrections that keep the interaction on track. An exchange in which corrective paraphrasing is used might go like this:

*Survivor:* In school I'm fine. It's just when I get home that things get crazy for me. I can't concentrate. I get really down, and nothing seems to help.
*Intervener:* So you feel depressed, especially when you are at home?
*Survivor:* No, it's really more like whenever I'm alone. If I didn't have so many people around me in my night class, I wouldn't go.

Since men are often conditioned to avoid expressing emotions, paraphrasing ought not to be used so much that it promotes this avoidance or undercuts the survivor's attempts to regain his sense of control. Knowing how much is enough is, as New York counselor Gary Schwartz has noted, "a matter of using your men's intuition" (Personal communication to the author, 19 April 1985).

### Reflection of Feeling

The description of emotions through give-and-take with a survivor is called reflection of feeling. Similar to paraphrasing, it involves listening for the emotional content of a statement or set of statements and reflecting that content. It, too, is a self-corrective technique.

An example might go like this:

*Survivor:* I feel like I'm gonna goddamn well explode, but I don't know who I'd go after. I can't describe it. It's like I want to hurt everybody I run into.
*Intervener:* It sounds as though you're dealing with a lot of anger, a kind of rage. Is it something like that?
*Survivor:* Oh, yeah. It's beyond angry.

Male survivors, disempowered to feel and express emotions, may intellectualize traumatic personal experiences, draining the description of its emotional content. The intervener, who is listening for the rational and emotional components of the narrative, can deal with each in its turn.

*Survivor:* They held me down . . . and there was some other man ten or twelve feet away, just watching. I didn't know him either. I wasn't sure what was going on, but I didn't want to be there for it.
*Intervener:* So at this point you were being pinned down by two men you had never met before?
*Survivor:* No, I never saw them before in my life.
*Intervener:* Did you feel helpless when they held you? It sounds like a pretty scary experience for anybody.
*Survivor:* I was scared all right. I thought I was going to die.

Some male survivors may lack a vocabulary of emotions. Many are socialized to avoid expressing their emotions in vivid terms. Interveners can listen for consistent understatements of emotional trauma or reliance on a few buzzwords or curses to identify male survivors who particularly need this kind of support. The intervener ought to avoid injecting his emotional response to the situation into this process. His or her empathy and modeling of emotional expression can give the male survivor a window into which he sees the effects of his own posttraumatic experiences and out of which he can vent his emotions.

### Self-Disclosure

Another technique for facilitating crisis intervention is the intervener's self-disclosure of personal information. Rare is the rape crisis counselor who has never been asked by a survivor, "Have *you* ever been raped?" In this case, the self-disclosure issue is met head-on in crisis counseling. In answer to that questions, Cassandra Thomas, Survivor Caucus director for the National Coalition Against Sexual Assault, advises, "We are together to talk about your rape and how you feel about it. Whether I have been raped may not be as helpful to you as knowing if I understand how it may feel to survive rape. And, yes, I hope I understand and can help" (Personal communication, 22 July 1986).

In some instances, self-disclosure can be a quick way to build an empathic bridge between the intervener and the survivor when time is limited. Self-disclosure actually begins when the intervener opens the door or answers the telephone. Their personal characteristics speak to survivors even when they are silent.

But self-disclosure, as many advocates of the sexual assault survivor attest, springs more from the heart than from any consideration of intervention formulas. It is, therefore, an area best explored by the intervener before the situation arises. How far is an intervener willing to go? Is self-disclosure something the survivor needs to build trust, or is it a means for the intervener to meet his or her personal needs? Once the values and parameters of self-disclosure are considered, the intervener need not fear probing questions from the survivor.

Disclosure of similarities need not always concern highly personal issues. Self-disclosure, especially by male interveners, can lessen the sense of isolation and gender alienation that can result from rape.

Self-disclosure comes in different forms, ranging from low to high situational impact:

- Disclosure of personal background: "I served in the army, too"; "I have two kids of my own"; "I have lived in that neighborhood"
- Disclosure of personal values: "I'd want to hurt him, too, in that situation"; "I'm gay, too"
- Disclosure of personal trauma: "I was gang-raped two years ago, and I never thought it would happen to me either"; "My lover died of AIDS; loss is hard to deal with"

Self-disclosure, for all its risks, may be important in male-to-male bonding during the intervention process. Sharing experiences of gender-role strains or limitations can be particularly effective with men in crisis (Prosser-Gelwick and Garni 1988).

### Confrontation

A maxim of rape crisis intervention may well be that interveners believe the survivor before they believe everything else. There are times that the problem-solving process can be jeopardized by conflicts that the survivor needs to resolve before intervention can be successful. Serious conflicts may call for confrontation of the survivor. These conflicts include the following:

- *Alcohol or drug impairment while seeking cognitive-based intervention.* A survivor who is impaired has legitimate needs but cannot benefit from intervention when under the influence of drugs or alcohol: "I want to talk with you about this, but I can't while you are drunk. We could get together when you haven't been drinking, okay?"
- *Contemplating retributional or other harmful acts.* Even extreme anger can be validated as part of the intervention process for male survivors socialized to "give as good as they get," but plans to act on that anger inappropriately may require confrontation or, in rare cases, interdiction:

"It's okay to be angry enough to want to kill him, but I'll never agree that it is okay to go do it."

- *Suicidal gestures.* Indications of suicidal intent or a gesture in progress may appear despite denials from the survivor and may appropriately become a focus of intervention: "Some of the things you have said make me think that you're considering killing yourself? Are you?"

- *Significant gaps between the survivor's words and his emotions.* The survivor may say he has no real feelings about his assault but has his teeth clenched in rage: "You say you are happy with your wife, but you seem to be very angry whenever we discuss your relationship."

In these and other situations, the needs of the client will not be met by the interveners ignoring indications of maladaptive responses to crises. Confrontation of the behavior is most effective when it is accompanied by expressions of empathy for the emotions that have prompted it—for example, "I can understand how hopeless the situation may seem, but suicide takes away all hope of changing it." Confrontation needs to be firm, but its object is not to force the survivor to surrender his right of independent action. The survivor has, through seeking intervention and disclosing serious conflict, involved the intervener in his behavior and may be seeking validation for his actions. Empathic but firm confrontation, followed by an exploration of alternative responses to crises, can literally be a lifesaver.

## Closure

Closure is a key step in crisis intervention, tying together the threads of disclosure and support, problems and solutions, into a conclusion. In time-limited crisis intervention, the need for closure is even more critical than in other counseling venues because the survivor may use crisis intervention as his only disclosure venue. Closure in crisis intervention includes a review of the following:

- The presenting complaint and the survivor's strategies for meeting the challenge presented by the situation
- Major life issues, such as rape trauma syndrome, mental health disorders, or barriers to communication and survivor strategies to deal with these issues
- The survivor's support network and the referrals that might augment them
- Changes in coping strategies for crises that the survivor may implement
- Basic messages of emotional support and empowerment

This review should not be a read-back of the conversation but should consist of the same paraphrases, questions, and reflections of feeling that have marked the intervention up to this point.

## A Case Study

The blending of crisis intervention steps and techniques, with an emphasis on gender barriers to coping and expression, is explored through the intervention provided to a male survivor in crisis.

"Greg" was a nineteen-year-old man who had been sexually assaulted by an adult family acquaintance when he was fourteen. He sought an emergency appointment after problems with alcohol resulted in a threat of dismissal from work. Greg stated that he was not sure why, but he felt that his drinking was related to his rape. He wanted to know if that was normal. He was asked why he felt his abuse of alcohol was related to his survival, and he said that he had not begun drinking heavily until approximately three months earlier and that his drinking seemed to escalate along with a general anxiety.

Greg expressed fear about potential unemployment. He talked about his boss and coworkers and stated his willingness to do "whatever it takes" to keep his position. Nonetheless, he was not confident that he would remain at the company, and he attributed his sense of helplessness to this possibility. His options for finding new employment and obtaining financial support until he found a job were discussed, and Greg decided to contact his parents to obtain short-term support if necessary. He said that he was now less anxious about the situation but was still concerned that it was the result of his drinking.

Greg was asked how often he drank, how much, and what conditions preceded his drinking. He responded that he drank six to eight beers on the two days a week he drank at all. He said he would drink more but could not afford to purchase more beer. He said he usually drank on weekend nights and had serious hangovers on Sunday and Monday mornings.

In exploring Greg's weekend activities, he talked about his participation in a flag-football league that met at a suburban softball park. He played in practices and games on Saturday and Sunday mornings. His feelings about the sport and his teammates were discussed, and although he proclaimed his enthusiasm for the activity, he seemed anxious and unsure of himself during this part of the conversation. This was pointed out to Greg, leading to a review of his interactions with men since his sexual assault. A history of intimacy avoidance with both men and women emerged. Greg said that he desired this and was pleased that his employer, a landscaping company, had employee parties and team sports. Greg said that he was shy and unable to express himself well and found that the football team and work were opportunities to feel like "one of the guys" and to interact with others socially.

Greg's gender identity was discussed. He said he saw himself as a "pretty tough guy" who could "take care of himself." Invited to give his impressions of his teammates, he began to express a mixture of admiration and feelings of inferiority. Greg wanted to "feel like they felt" and tried to join any activity that promised male bonding. But he also admitted to a sense of competition and differentness, which depressed him. The possibility was raised that Greg was drinking at night to relieve the tension and anxiety resulting from his interactions. Initially resistant to the idea, Greg talked about the special place he gave male friendship. This was compared to his needs after his sexual assault, and he decided that the two were linked.

Strategies for dealing with the drinking were discussed. Greg said he would consider participation in Alcoholics Anonymous if the drinking continued but was not prepared to begin attending until he determined whether he could stop drinking.

Coping strategies were reviewed at length. Greg was encouraged to use the rape crisis hot line, particularly on weekend nights, as an alternative to alcohol consumption. He was referred to a local incest survivors group, and future individual counseling sessions were scheduled.

Greg's gender identity and need for warmth and bonding were examined. The conflict between the suppression of his personal feelings and the need for love and affection were discussed. Also considered was the conflict Greg felt between his attraction to men and his fear of them, as well as the importance of exploring these feelings. He was reassured that his gender identity would not diminish if he concentrated effort on his rape recovery and found appropriate vehicles for self-expression.

Support networks for Greg were reviewed, and Greg decided to drop participation in flag football until he was prepared to participate without a high level of anxiety. He would, he decided, visit his parents during the coming weekend to avoid stresses that contributed to his alcohol abuse.

Greg was commended for facing a difficult set of problems and reminded that he had a right to assert himself and use the programs for which he had referrals.

Postintervention notes: Greg participated in an incest survivors support group and was a frequent caller to the rape crisis hot line for approximately four months. He did not return to company team sports but instead joined a health club. Greg's family was not open to his increased self-expression, and he was struggling with the development of alternative support networks six months after crisis intervention.

## Conclusion

Men face challenges to rape recovery that differ in many ways from those women face. Gender expectations that not only stigmatize male survivors but also result in barriers to coping with survival are among the challenges faced by those who care about them and want to provide support.

Our knowledge of these issues needs to be augmented by an understanding of the needs of different male populations in crisis, such as men who are gay (Lopez and Getzel 1984), bisexual (Wolf 1987), Native American (Kahn et al. 1988), black (Gary and Berry 1985; Gunnings and Liscomb 1986), or elderly (Lorensen 1985) or who have other important identifications.

Intervention with a male survivor may be a rare or a solitary disclosure of his sexual-assault issues. The time together is limited, and the future of follow-up support is uncertain. In this situation, interveners can help survivors prioritize, provide emotional support, inform, and brainstorm. Thinking of themselves as people who care and want to help, interveners seek survivors' self-empowerment so that crisis is not their only avenue for exploring the unacknowledged roles of men as nurturers, seekers of love, and vessels for many emotions.

For too long, interveners have ignored many of these survivors' needs, and their crises may be ours as well. Until we extend our feminism and its rapidly expanding support networks for disempowered women and children to our nation's men, the few who turn to help in crisis will be almost an oddity, a "blue-eyed Arab" whose ways are not completely understood. The rest will be following the example of T.E. Lawrence and seeking counsel in the wind.

# References

American Psychiatric Association. 1980. *Diagnostic and Statistical Manual of Mental Disorders,* 3d ed. Washington, D.C.: AMA.

Atkinson, Donald R., Fransisco Q. Ponce, and Francine M. Martinez. 1984. "Effects of Ethnic, Sex, and Attitude Similarity on Counselor Credibility." *Journal of Counseling Psychology* 31 (no. 4): 588–590.

Avery-Clark, C. 1986. "Sexual Dysfunction and Disorder Patterns of Husbands of Working and Non-Working Wives." *Journal of Sex and Marital Therapy* 12 (no. 4): 282–296.

Bart, Pauline. 1987. *Stopping Rape.* New York: Pergamon Press.

Beasley, L., and J.H. Childers. 1985. "Group Counseling for Heterosexual Interpersonal Skills: Mixed- and Same-Sex Group Composition." *Journal for Specialists in Group Work* 10 (no. 4): 192–197.

Borden, L.A., S.K. Karr, and A.T. Caldwell-Colbert. 1988. "Effects of a University Kape Prevention Program on Attitudes and Empathy towards Rape." *Journal of College Student Development* 29 (no. 2): 132–136.

Brown, P.C. 1984. "Legacies of a War: Treatment Considerations with Vietnam Veterans and Their Families." *Social Work* 37 (no. 3): 372–379.

Brownmiller, Susan. 1975. *Against Our Will: Men, Women and Rape.* New York: Simon & Schuster.

Burgess, Anne W., and L.L. Holmstrom. 1979. *Rape: Crisis and Recovery.* Bowie, Maryland: Brady.

————. 1985. *Rape and Sexual Assault: A Research Handbook.* New York: Garland.

Butler, S. 1978. *Conspiracy of Silence: The Trauma of Incest.* San Francisco: Blade Publications.

Dua, Jaggish K., and Helen M. McNall. 1987. "Assertiveness in Men and Women Seeking Counseling and Not Seeking Counseling." *Behaviour Change* 4 (no. 1): 14–19.

Evans, Mark. 1989. "Men as Direct Service Providers with Rape Crisis Centers." Paper presented to the Texas Association Against Sexual Assault, Houston, March.

Evans, Mark, and Cassandra Thomas. 1989. "Need for a New Respect: How the Women's Movements Support the Black Female Sexual Assault Survivor." Paper presented at the Annual Meeting of the South Central Women's Studies Association, Houston.

Frank, Jerome. 1972. "The Bewildering World of Psychotherapy." *Journal of Social Issues* 28: 27–43.

Gambe, Richard, and George S. Getzel. 1989. "Group Work with Gay Men with AIDS." *Social Casework* 70 (no. 3): 172–179.

Gary, Lawrence E., and Greta L. Berry. 1985. "Depressive Symptomatology among Black Men." *Journal of Multicultural Counseling and Development* 13 (no. 3): 121–129.

Gibbon, Edward. 1914. *The Decline and Fall of the Roman Empire.* Vol. 2. London: Methuen.

Gunnings, Thomas S., and Wanda G. Liscomb. 1986. "Psychotherapy for Black Men: A Systematic Approach." *Journal of Multicultural Counseling and Development* 14 (no. 1): 17–24.

Haug, F., ed. 1987. *Female Sexualization.* New York: Routledge, Chapman & Hall.

Hoiberg, Anne, and Brian McCaughey. 1984. "The Traumatic Aftereffects of Collision at Sea." *American Journal of Psychiatry* 141 (no. 1): 70–73.

Houston Area Women's Center. 1988. *Rape Crisis Program Resource Guide.* Houston.

Howard, J.A. 1984. "The 'Normal' Victim: The Effects of Gender Stereotypes on Reactions to Victims." *Social Psychology Quarterly* 47 (no. 3): 270–281.

Jacobson, Edith. 1975. "The Psychoanalytic Treatment of Depressive Patients." In *Depression and Human Existence,* edited by E. Athony and T. Benedek, 57–59. Boston: Little, Brown.

Jensen, Soren B. 1986. "Emotional Aspects in a Chronic Disease: A Study of 101 Insulin-Treated Diabetics." *International Journal of Rehabilitation Research* 9 (no. 1): 13–20.

Johnson, Richard W., Robert A. Ellison, and Charles A. Heikkinen. 1989. "Psychological Symptoms of Counseling Center Clients." *Journal of Counseling Psychology* 36 (no. 1): 110–114.

Kahn, Marvin W., Linda Lejero, Marion Antone, and Dorene Fransisco. 1988. "An Indigenous Community Mental Health Service on the Tohono O'odham (Papago) Indian Reservation: Seventeen Years Later." *American Journal of Community Psychology* 16 (no. 3): 369–379.

Katz, G., and M. Mazur. 1981. *Understanding the Rape Victim: A Synthesis of Research Findings.* New York: John Wiley.

Lawrence, T.E. 1938. *Seven Pillars of Wisdom*. Garden City, New York: Garden City Large Print Books.

Lopez, Diego J., and George S. Getzel. 1984. "Helping Gay AIDS Patients in Crisis." *Social Casework* 65 (no. 7): 387–394.

Lorensen, Margarethe. 1985. "Effects of Elderly Women's Self-Care in Case of Acute Hospitalization as Compared with Men." *Health Care for Women International* 6 (no. 4): 247–265.

May, Robert. 1986. "Concerning a Psychoanalytic View of Maleness." *Psychoanalytic Review* 73 (no. 4): 579–597.

Money, J., and A.A. Ehrhardt. 1972. *Man and Woman, Boy and Girl: The Differentiation and Dimorphism of Gender Identity from Conception to Maturity*. Baltimore: Johns Hopkins University Press.

Mulvey, Anne, and Barbara S. Dohrenwend. 1983. "The Relation of Stressful Life Events to Gender." *Issues in Mental Health Nursing* 5 (no. 1): 219–237.

O'Brien, Margaret. 1988. "Men and Fathers in Therapy." *Journal of Family Therapy* 10 (no. 2): 109–123.

Perl, Mark, Anne B. Westin, and Linda G. Peterson. 1985. "The Female Rape Survivor: Time-Limited Group Therapy with Female-Male Co-therapists. *Journal of Psychosomatic Obstetrics and Gynecology* 4 (no. 3): 197–205.

Prosser-Gelwick, Beverly, and Kenneth F. Garni. 1988. "Counseling and Psychotherapy with College Men." *New Directions for Student Services* 42 (Summer): 67–77.

Riger, Stephanie, and Margaret T. Gordon. 1983. "The Impact of Crime on Urban Women." *Issues in Mental Health Nursing* 5 (no. 1): 139–156.

Schurman, Paul G. 1987. "Male Liberation." *Pastoral Psychology* 35 (no. 3): 189–199.

Scully, Jean. 1985. "Men and Grieving." *Psychotherapy Patient* 2 (no. 1): 95–100.

Skord, Kenneth, and Brockman Schumacher. 1982. "Masculinity as a Handicapping Condition." *Rehabilitation Literature* 43 (no. 9/10): 284–289.

Smith, Ronald E., Charles J. Pine, and Mark E. Hawley. 1988. "Social Cognitions about Adult Male Victims of Female Assault." *Journal of Sex Research* 24: 101–112.

Steere, D.A. 1983. Bodily Expressions in Psychotherapy. New York: Brunner-Mazel.

Tollison, C.D., and H.E. Adams. 1979. *Sexual Disorders: Theory, Treatment, Research*. New York: Gardner Press.

Vander May, Brerda J. 1988. "The Sexual Victimization of Male Children: A Review of Previous Research." *Child Abuse and Neglect* 12 (no. 1): 61–72.

Viney, Linda L., Yvonne N. Benjamin, Alex M. Clarke, and Terence A. Bunn. 1985. "Sex Differences in the Psychological Reactions of Medical and Surgical Patients to Crisis Intervention Counseling: Sauce for the Goose May Not be Sauce for the Gander." *Social Science and Medicine* 20 (no. 11): 1199–1205.

Washington, Craig S. 1982. "Challenging Men in Groups." *Journal for Specialists in Group Work* 7 (no. 2): 132–136.

Weizman, R., and J. Hart. 1987. "Sexual Behavior in Healthy Married Elderly Men." *Archives of Sexual Behavior* 16 (no. 1): 39–44.

Whitaker, Leighton. 1987. "Macho and Morbidity: The Emotional Need vs. Fear Dilemma in Men." *Journal of College Student Psychotherapy* 1 (no. 4): 33–47.

Wolf, Timothy J. 1987. "Group Counseling for Bisexual Men." *Journal for Specialists in Group Work* 12 (no. 4): 162–165.

Zumkley, Horst. 1982. "Kausale Ambiquitat: Vorrangigkeit externaler ursachen?" (in German). *Psychologische Beitrage* 24 (no. 2): 224–241.

# 10
# Sexual Abuse of Boys:
# A Medical Perspective

*Carolyn J. Levitt*

T his chapter addresses the role of the physician examiner in child sexual abuse evaluations. The broad, culturally defined role of a physician encompasses the physical examination of a patient's body and discussion with the patient about intimate things in a private, trusting relationship. In applying this role to problems of child sexual abuse, a skilled physician examiner can gather valuable information about what happened while assessing physical and laboratory findings, providing any needed medical care, and addressing the questions and fears that typically arise for victims of sexual abuse. In many cases, the information gathered by the physician is a decisive factor that greatly influences what further intervention can and will occur for the child.

The increasing identification of young male victims of sexual abuse reflects the growing awareness and greater sophistication, of both professionals and the public at large, about signs and symptoms of sexual abuse. Several questions arise: Are boys victimized more or less frequently than girls? Are there cultural preconceptions and other factors that limit our ability to recognize abuse of male children? How does what we know about girls as victims apply to the victimization of boys, either in the patterns of victimization or in the typical responses of the child?

The assessment of physical findings is a critical part of the medical evaluation, and it has major forensic implications. The chapter includes a review of relevant literature and a discussion of the implications of McCann and associates' report of anal findings in a normal population (McCann et al. 1989). These findings make possible a more accurate determination of whether given physical findings are specific to sexual abuse.

The chapter also includes a detailed discussion of a protocol for the medical evaluation as well as a discussion of which laboratory tests and procedures are appropriate for specific presenting circumstances. Finally, there is a discussion of the fears and questions that are likely to trouble the child victim, such as fears about AIDS or homosexuality. Because children often do not articulate their fears, the physician is urged not only to be prepared to discuss these concerns but also to take the initiative in raising the issues. Helpful ways of discussing these sensitive issues are described briefly.

## Increasing Numbers of Young Male Victims

Medical centers evaluating large numbers of sexually abused children have noted a gradual increase in the numbers of male victims. Spencer and Dunklee (1986) report that the percentage of male victims in their series increased from 5 percent in 1980 to 14 percent in 1984. Reinhart (1987) reports that 16 percent of the victims in his 1983–85 series were male. In our experience at the Midwest Children's Resource Center (MCRC) at Children's Hospital of St. Paul, male victims increased from 14 percent in 1985–86 to 23 percent in 1988–89.

Based on statements from perpetrators, the actual percentage of male victims is thought to be much larger (Abel 1987). Some speculate that this is because males are less likely to report their own victimization. Reinhart (1987) compared the manner of disclosure of abuse of 189 male victims with a matched group of female victims. He found that the abuse was more often disclosed by a third party (with the victim later confirming) for the males (20 percent) than for the females (11 percent). Equal numbers of male and female victims had spontaneous disclosures and prompted disclosures. Also, only 10 percent of the cases involving male victims were reported as a suspicion without confirmation, as compared with 26 percent of the cases involving female victims. Perhaps the female is more stereotypically seen as the victim or suspicion is raised because of signs or symptoms more frequently related to the genital area of females than of males.

The increasing identification of male victims may be because younger males are being seen. They may be less likely to feel stigmatized by being a victim. The mean age of the boys in a series from 1979 through 1984 was 7.2 years (Spencer and Dunklee 1986). In a 1983 to 1985 series, the mean age was 5.7 years (Reinhart 1987). At MCRC, 58 percent of the boys seen in 1988–89 were ages 0 to 5.

We also are becoming more skilled at identifying abuse. Sgroi (1980) notes, "Recognition of sexual molestation in a child is entirely dependent on the professional's inherent willingness to entertain the possibility that the condition exists." Society now has recognized that the sexual abuse of children is happening in ever increasing numbers. Statements by these young abused children are being heard. Their behavioral symptoms and physical signs are being recognized by parents, day-care providers, and teachers. Specialists are now evaluating those children who show suspicious behavioral indicators but cannot disclose the abuse. These factors influence the incidence of reports from male as well as female victims.

## Physical Findings and the Need for a
## Medical Examination

Because the community needs an objective measure or a clear test of whether a child has been sexually abused, the physician is put in a particularly uncomfortable position when asked to examine a child for physical evidence of sexual abuse. The physician may or may not know the specific findings attributed to sexual abuse and may not know the true ranges of normal physical findings. Much of the pediatric literature describing these findings is purely descriptive—that is, consisting of one physician's opinion from his or her experience based on examining sexually abused and normal children but not actually studying them in a controlled fashion.

Hobbs and Wynne (1986) report that buggery is a common occurrence in England and describe physical findings of the anus that they frequently associate with these abused children. Are these physical findings specific for abuse? Are they perhaps part of a normal spectrum? Are they artifacts of the examination itself? Are they true physical findings but ones that also might be caused by other nonsexual abuse etiologies? Following the Hobbs and Wynne article, a number of articles appeared in *Lancet,* some supporting and some discounting reflex anal dilatation as a specific finding (see, for example, Roberts 1986; Bamford and Kiff 1987). The experiences involved sodomized male and female children. Higgs and Wyatt, two other pediatricians in Cleveland, England, used reflex anal dilatation to diagnose sexual abuse of many other children (Butler-Sloss 1987). Some of these findings correlated with the history of abuse and others did not. Within a short time, the vast numbers of children being diagnosed as sexually abused became overwhelming, and the methods of the physicians were questioned. There was a formal judicial inquiry, and the results of that have been published (Butler-Sloss 1987).

Many people in the general public and in the medical profession believe that physical findings must be present before sexual abuse of children can be documented. However, many acts that are clearly abusive and intimidating, such as fellatio, cunnilingus, and anilingus, rarely leave physical findings. Male victims most commonly experience penile-anal penetration (Spencer and Dunklee 1986; Reinhart 1987). In the Reinhart series, depending on the victim's age, anal penetration by a finger, penis, or object accounted for from 40 to 71 percent of the sexual acts. (Penile penetration accounted for most of these.) In the 0 to 2 age-group, oral-genital contact occurred more frequently (Reinhart 1987). Spencer and Dunklee (1986) reported that 78 percent of male victims experienced anal penetration. Of these cases, 53 percent were penetrated by a penis, 11 percent by a finger, 5 percent by a foreign object, and 9 percent experienced attempted penile penetration.

Considering these factors, one must ask what percentage of male victims are likely to have physical findings and what factors influence the recognition of those findings. Perianal bruising, scratches, or small submucosal hemorrhages and superficial fissures caused by forceful stretching heal rapidly and are present only if the boy is examined within a few days of the abuse. A still more complex question is whether physical findings, if present, are specific for sexual abuse. McCann and associates (1989) published anal findings in a normal population of 106 boys and 161 girls, whereas previous authors described findings noted as they examined a predominantly abused population (Spencer and Dunklee 1986; Reinhart 1987; Hobbs and Wynne 1986; Levitt 1986).

Reinhart (1987) reports that only 5 percent of the boys in his series had genital abnormalities, which included bruises, bite marks, erythema, rash, and urethral discharge. Abnormalities relating to the anus occurred in 29 percent of the boys, who had a total of seventy-seven abnormal findings. Some of them had two or three findings. It must be pointed out that the majority, the other 71 percent, did not have any physical findings documenting the abuse. Reinhart describes findings associated with acute and chronic injury. Nineteen of the thirty-two boys with acute findings had erythema of the perianal tissues. Four had bruises, three had lacerations, and three others had fissures. Of forty-five with chronic injuries, twenty-four had laxity of the anal sphincter, seven had scars, four had fecal soiling, three had skin tags, and four had irregularity of the anal orifice or thickening of the perianal tissues.

Spencer and Dunklee (1986) report that 68 percent of the male victims in their study had physical findings, including bruises of the penis or perianal area (7 percent), evidence of ejaculation (5 percent), perianal erythema (27 percent), rectal lacerations and fissures (11 percent), hyperpigmentation of the perianal tissues (10 percent), dilated perianal veins (4 percent), lax anal sphincter (3 percent), scars and skin tags (11 percent), and evidence of venereal disease (5 percent).

With the findings of McCann and associates (1989), the sexually abused population can be more accurately compared to the normal population. For example, dilated perianal veins or venous congestion, reported by others as a finding in sexually abused children, can be an artifact of the examination. These authors report that 73 percent of their normal subjects had perianal venous congestion at the end of the examination if kept in the knee-chest position for four minutes, 52 percent had the congestion if kept there for two minutes, and only 7 percent had it at the beginning of the examination. The knee-chest position may exaggerate this finding. Also, the examiner can inadvertently cause dilated perianal veins or heightened venous congestion and filling of venous lakes by occluding the venous return when his or her thumbs are placed over the ischium to spread the buttocks in order to examine the anus.

Levitt (1986) found that 40 percent of normal subjects had erythema, which seemed related to age because of diapering and perianal hygienic factors. Eleven percent of the normals had anal tags anteriorly in the midline, and 49 percent had anal dilatation up to 2 centimeters measured vertically in the midline. Anal dilatation greater than 2 to 3 centimeters was thought to be abnormal, particularly if the anus dilated immediately with initiation of the examination and there was no stool present in the ampulla. McCann and associates (1989) found no hemorrhoids in this normal population and felt that anal fissures with an adjacent tag were significant and suggested previous sodomy. They also felt that asymmetry of the anal orifice was abnormal.

In view of these new findings in the normal population, many of the physical findings in previous studies, such as erythema, dilated veins, and anal laxity, should be reinterpreted as perhaps being associated, but not diagnostic, findings. Specific physical findings highly suggestive of abuse are true bruising of the perianal tissues caused by extravasation of blood into the tissues, acute lacerations not explained by a specific history of trauma, true scars reflecting these healed lacerations, and immediate anal dilatation of 2 to 3 centimeters without feces present in the ampulla.

The presence of semen in the anus or a positive culture for gonorrhea or chlamydia taken from the anus also are clear indicators of anal abuse. The rest of the findings are probably nonspecific and can occur in both abused and nonabused children. However, the history provided by the victim relating to the signs and their symptoms may make them more specific. A boy may describe painful defecation following sodomy or blood on the toilet paper after wiping, and a fissure may be present at the time of the physical examination. This fissure may have been initiated by the sodomy and may be exacerbated by each bowel movement.

## The Role of the Physician

The myth that physician findings must be present to document child sexual abuse has been shown to be false by DeJong and Rose (1988). Sexual abuse of young children can be clearly documented based primarily on the child's history and the physical findings, or lack thereof, correlated to that history. DeJong and Rose reviewed 115 criminal court cases and found that there was no significant difference in the rate of felony convictions based on the presence or absence of physical findings of injury, sexually transmitted diseases, or semen. It was also somewhat surprising that the legal outcome did not appear to be affected by factors such as the child's age, sex, sexual act, relationship to the perpetrator, duration of the abuse, length of time from disclosure to trial, type of trial, and testimony of the examining or expert physician. Rather, the critical factor for a successful conviction was found to be the effective collection, preservation, and presentation of the child's history. Thus, physicians must pursue better methods of eliciting and preserving this valuable historic data from the child.

In our culture, most children have learned that it is the physician's job to examine their bodies when they are injured or ill, as well as during routine checkups. Therefore, it is natural for a boy who has been sexually abused to have a medical examination. It is an opportunity to document any physician findings, to provide any treatment needed to collect a detailed history, and to address fears and concerns the child is likely to have as a consequence of the sexual abuse.

Because of his or her role, the physician needs to be comfortable asking the boy what exactly was done to his body and how that made his body feel. Precise clarification of these sexual acts can be obtained through the combination of a medical history and medical examination, both of which are essential to a complete medical evaluation and accurate diagnosis.

Child sexual abuse is particularly difficult to prove because there are generally no witnesses, there are usually no physical findings, and children usually disclose long after subtle physical findings heal. Children are reluctant to talk about the abuse because of their own feelings of guilt or shame or their fear of reprisal by the perpetrator or a parent. When children do disclose, it is very important that they be questioned as soon as possible in a manner that does not alter the information they possess. To protect the child from further abuse, this history must contain enough descriptive information to validate that the abuse happened.

Because this history is so important, it is best to use a comfortable setting where the child can be interviewed alone, away from the influences of other adults. This setting must allow for the intimacy of the questions and the information that needs to be disclosed. John E.B. Myers, a professor of law, reminds physicians that the ability to protect a child frequently rests on how the physician questions the child and how thoroughly he records the history (Myers 1986).

A patient's statements to his physician are considered hearsay in a court proceeding but are often considered exceptions to the hearsay rule and allowed as evidence if the history is found to be reliable. The ability of the physician to recall the child's exact statement regarding specific sexual events and to remember whether the statement was made in response to a leading or nonleading question is very important in determining the admissibility of this evidence. The physician, therefore, must recognize his or her role in preserving this evidence through precise notes or audiotaped or videotaped records. Specific details about the child's demeanor and the spontaneity of the responses should be included. Notes also should be kept regarding any influence asserted by another individual or any incentive to invent or enhance the details of the abuse. The physician can use these records to refresh his or her memory at the time of a court hearing or trial months later.

# A Protocol for the Medical Evaluation

Because many sexually abused boys are either too young or are reluctant to disclose all the details of the abuse, it is best for the physician to review records documenting previous statements he or she has made to child protection or law enforcement investigators or the records of previous medical or psychological evaluations. A physician generally feels more comfortable speaking to the parent(s) prior to any medical evaluation to address the parent's concerns. Sometimes the parent's concerns are the same as the boy's, and sometimes the parent does not know about the suspicions or disclosure of the abuse. A brief discussion with the parent apart from the boy will help sort this out and provide the physician with some background, such as the setting in which the child might have been abused and to whom the first disclosure was made. If the boy has disclosed particular details to the parent, it is helpful to obtain this information quickly and not to invite detailed descriptions of the abuse, which can best be obtained directly from the victim.

Next the physician ought to interview the boy alone. It is helpful to begin by asking him questions that can be answered easily and can make him feel more comfortable about the interview and the examination. Depending on his age, he can be asked questions about family, friends, holidays, school, or vacations. Little boys do best describing where they live, where they sleep, who else sleeps at their house and where, and who is in their family. Gradually they can be asked where they were when the abuse occurred—that is, where in the house or outside it happened, where in the bedroom, and where everyone else was at the time. Young children have particular difficulty describing when things happened. Asking "where" questions helps these children define when the abuse occurred. It also eases the interview into the more specific and difficult questions about what happened.

Generally, boys seem to be shier and more embarrassed than girls about the abuse. They appear to need to be in charge of what happens to them and are uncomfortable in the victim role. Their disclosures are often minimized. They may test the reaction of the physician first by disclosing only parts of the abuse, and, with gentle encouragement, they will then go on to describe more serious aspects of it. At this time, the physician ought not to express anger toward the perpetrator or sympathy for the victim.

A boy may have acquired street names for the sexual anatomy and may have learned that it is disrespectful to use words such as *dick* or *pussy* when speaking to an adult professional. The use of anatomic drawings of a same-sex and an opposite-sex child clarifies the terminology and gives the boy an opportunity to hear himself say these forbidden words in a formal setting (Groth and Stevenson 1984).

The anatomical drawings can help focus the attention of boys who are distracted or hyperactive during the examination (Minnesota Department of Education 1989). If a boy is particularly shy, drawing circles around parts of the body or drawing lines from one part of the body to the other as he describes the sexual assault gives him the opportunity to convey very important information without actually having to verbalize it. Once the boy has provided the correct names for the anatomic parts and has indicated the sexual events on the drawing, he may become more comfortable disclosing more descriptive details regarding his own body.

They physician needs to question him specifically about exactly where on his body something went and how it made his body feel. If the child points to his mouth, genitals, or anus while describing a sexual event, the physician can ask him to demonstrate this on the drawing. The physician must ask how far back in the boy's mouth the penis may have gone, if it made him gag or vomit, and, if there was ejaculation in his mouth, how it tasted and what he did with it. The questions should be asked so that the boy provides explicit sexual information in his answer and is not influenced by the question. This precise history determines whether specimens should be taken from his mouth to test for semen or for sexually transmitted diseases or whether blood should be taken for serology for documentation of these sexually transmitted diseases. The boy can then provide the same precise history regarding what happened to the anus or genitals.

In taking a complete history, the physician is trained to do a review of systems to ask questions about related or possibly unrelated symptomatology. Sexual abuse of boys can be approached in the same way. To gain more information, a physician should ask a boy describing sodomy how that made his butt feel: Did it hurt at the time it was happening? Did it hurt when it was all done? Was there any bleeding on the toilet paper when he wiped his butt the next time? How did it feel to go poop the next time? Was there blood on the toilet paper when he wiped himself after going poop, and had that ever occurred before? Was there a spot that was particularly sore or stinging around his anus that could possibly have been a fissure or laceration from the sexual assault? Was there anything that the boy noticed coming out of his anus following the sexual assault?

Young children who are inexperienced in adult sexual practices often do not know about ejaculation and the characteristics of semen. A five-year-old male victim describing how it felt after he was sodomized by a teenage baby-sitter, when specifically asked whether anything came out of his butt, responded, "Yes, I had to pee and poop at the same time." When questioned further about where the pee came from, he said very clearly that it had come out of the other boy's penis. He disclosed this information rather matter-of-factly but clearly was amazed that both pee and poop came out of his butt.

The child also should be questioned specifically about any sores, bruises, bite marks, marks made by instruments, or discharge that might relate to the sexual assault. Questions about painful urination, painful defecation, constipation, fecal soiling, nightmares, and other fears should be addressed. Boys are often very worried about their penises. Many boys, particularly teenagers, will note pimples or plugged hair follicles (folliculitis) on the skin of the penile shaft and worry that this is herpes or perhaps even syphilis. Inquiring about the boy's specific fears and perhaps erroneous interpretations will help the physician to avoid missing subtle and perhaps normal physical findings that are causing the boy concern.

## Physical Inspection of the Boy's Body

The physician should explain to the boy that he or she needs to examine him and request that he show, using his own body, what precisely happened. A general physical examination should be done quickly to assess the boy's general health. Height and weight measurements, and the percentile that these represent for age, are always helpful in assessing general health. Any bruises, bite marks, abrasions, injury patterns, and imprints need to be documented photographically for the permanent record. Anything else striking about the medical examination should be described in detail in the chart. An anatomic drawing like the one used in the history can be used for documenting the nature and location of the findings in case the photographic equipment fails.

It is often helpful to ask a little boy to stand on the examining table so that he can be face-to-face with the physician. Then the physician can ask the boy to use his own penis to demonstrate what was done to it. Boys often pull on their own penises, hit them from side to side, squeeze them, or pinch them to demonstrate. Specific questions about the testicles and abuse of them need to be asked. Often the sucking of the genitals of a young boy includes both the penis and the scrotum, and this is done with varying degrees of gentleness or force that the child can recall and describe if questioned.

Inspection of the anus can take place either in the lateral position with the boy's legs drawn up against his abdomen, in the lithotomy position on his back with his legs spread apart, or in the butt-up position with his knees, head, chest, and/or elbows resting on the examining table. A decision regarding this position might be based on the boy's level of comfort with the examination, whether he is particularly shy or modest about having his genitals or anus exposed during the examination, and the specific history and nature of the physical findings.

The colposcope, which is actually a portable microscope with a camera attached and a light source for adequate illumination of the subject, is used extensively in child sexual abuse medical evaluations. A colposcope provides magnification in the range of five to twenty times, and the examining physician can use the resulting photographic documentation when consulting with another physician regarding the findings.

Fissures, anal tags, and anal dilatation may be seen in sexually abused boys but are not specific findings and do not necessarily indicate that the boy was abused. Acute anal lacerations without a history of accidental injury, perianal bruising that is true extravasation of blood into the tissues, and a large gaping anal opening (greater than 2 centimeters when examined without feces in the rectum) are indicators of anal sodomy. New or healed fissures, relaxed anal tone, anal tags with or without fissuring, and subtle scarring may be related to sodomy and need to be correlated with a precise history. Painful defecation or blood on the toilet paper following a bowel movement that occurred only following penile-anal penetration can be specified in the child's own history. Otherwise, fissures can occur spontaneously or with constipated, large bowel movements.

It is also important to note that penile-anal penetration and even fisting (the insertion of an entire fist inside the anus) can occur without damage to the anus and will result in normal physical findings at the time of colposcopic examination of the anus. Children, like adults, can learn to relax the anal sphincter to the proper stimuli, and various lubricants can be used.

The most accurate diagnosis of child sexual abuse includes a precise history documented by a careful examination during which the history is further clarified. To clarify the boy's definition of the sexual acts, the physician can perform a rectal examination that includes the penetration of the boy's anus by the physician's gloved and lubricated examining finger. The physician can ask him what he calls the buttocks or define that as outside and ask him to define whether the touch was at the anal opening or actually inside the anal opening as the finger enters the anus. This allows the boy to compare that sensation with the sensation of the abuse (Levitt 1986). Most children accept this as a medical examination and not an invasion or abuse of the body. The physician can explain that this is a routine part of the medical examination that will probably have to be done again as the boy gets older, particularly if other symptoms related to the genital-urinary or gastrointestinal tract occur.

## Laboratory Assessment

If the boy has been abused within seventy-two hours of the medical examination, specific laboratory tests must be performed to document the presence of semen. Beyond seventy-two hours, sperm are no longer motile, and acid phosphatase, a prostatic enzyme in the seminal fluid, has dissipated. However, dead sperm heads occasionally have been found vaginally and orally beyond the seventy-two-hour limit. A simple smear can be made on a glass slide from the specimens taken with an anal swab or the specimens taken from the oral mucosa, particularly along the teeth in the back of the mouth. This slide can then be sprayed with cytology fixative or hair spray, which is frequently available in physician's offices for fixing pap smears from female patients. These slides can be examined under the microscope by knowledgeable pathologists looking for sperm heads.

If the event occurred within the seventy-two-hour limit, it is best to examine the child in a planful way so that the specimens collected can be properly identified and protected through a previously established protocol. State crime labs often have specific rape kits for this purpose, and many hospital or forensic labs have set up, reviewed, and approved protocols for the collection of these specimens. It is not particularly uncomfortable for swabs to be collected from the anus. Generally, children are much more uncomfortable about having a throat culture taken than they are about anal or even vaginal cultures if the latter are done properly.

To spare the child some discomfort, it is recommended that cultures for sexually transmitted diseases not be obtained from all boys who are examined for sexual abuse. The specific history and the findings at the time of the examination help determine when these cultures should be taken. If there has been penile-anal or penile-oral penetration, cultures for gonorrhea should be obtained from the throat and the rectum and cultures should be taken from the rectum for chlamydia. Because it is often painful, the male victim's urethra should not be cultured unless there is a history of a sexual act that warrants it, a positive culture has been documented in the perpetrator, or the perpetrator is particularly at risk for that infection.

The medical examination and laboratory documentation for sexually transmitted diseases should not be seen as punishment and therefore a deterrent to the child's describing the sexual events. Serologic tests for syphilis, AIDS, and hepatitis B need not be done routinely unless they are epidemiologically indicated, the child is felt to be at specific risk because of the nature of the sexual act, or the perpetrator is unknown or belongs to a high-risk group, such as intravenous drug users, sexually addicted people with large numbers of contacts, and prostitutes. These blood tests can be done three to six months after the sexual assault.

## AIDS, Other Sexually Transmitted Diseases, and Homosexuality

The physician should assume that the child has fears and concerns that arise as a result of abuse. Acquiring sexually transmitted diseases, dying of AIDS, and becoming homosexual are typical fears confronting the male abuse victim. The physician should not assume, however, that the child will be willing or able to articulate all of these concerns on his own. Thus, the physician must anticipate these issues.

Many school-age children are now taught about AIDS (Minnesota Department of Education 1989), but they do not process and retain all that they learn, and what they do remember is often influenced by information from their friends and from the media. An eight-year-old boy being evaluated for abuse by a fifteen-year-old male baby-sitter had learned that AIDS comes from sex. He believed that if you had sex, you got AIDS, and if you got AIDS, you died. Since he knew he had had sex, he was worried that he would die. Many other boys have identical or similar fears regarding AIDS. These fears need to be addressed by the physician and either discounted because AIDS is so unlikely or dealt with during the laboratory assessment.

AIDS is very rare in sexually abused girls and boys for many reasons. Many children are just fondled or experience perianal or intercrural intercourse with or without ejaculation. These assaults are generally not brutal, and tissues are often not significantly injured. In addition, the virus is unlikely to be transmitted through one sexual act, and multiple sexual acts with deposit of semen inside the body is not a typical pattern. Catching herpes from the contact is much more likely.

The physician also must address the victim's fear of becoming homosexual as a result of the sexual act. Although it might be difficult to question a seven- or eight-year-old boy about his fears of homosexuality, addressing possible fears and educating the child in the process gives him some background information for the future when these fears may arise. For example, the physician could say something like the following: "Nothing that has happened to you will make you abnormal. There are some possible physical illnesses, but we can test for those. If the tests are negative, which we think they will be, you needn't worry anymore about them. Specifically, the fact that this boy put his penis in your anus does not mean that you will learn to like or prefer sexual relationships with men instead of women."

Even if a child is seven or eight, he can be told that "sometimes men grow up to love men more than they do women and want to do sexual things with men rather than with women but that sexual preference is definitely not a result of the sexual abuse experienced as a child." This type of discussion can, of course take place later with a therapist, but many children never see a therapist or discuss their fears with any knowledgeable professional or adult. They may suffer in silence.

## Conclusion

An increasing number of young boys are being reported and medically evaluated for suspected sexual abuse. This has prompted a rethinking of victimization and how sex-role expectations and stereotypes may interfere with the recognition of sexual abuse in young males. The role of the physician examiner in the evaluation of sexually abused male children includes several essential tasks:

1. Collecting and preserving a thorough and detailed history of the abuse as given by the boy
2. Conducting a physical examination that includes inspection of the boy's body for signs and symptoms of the sexual abuse and laboratory tests that are appropriate to the circumstances of the case
3. Assessing the significance of physical and laboratory findings, or the lack thereof, as correlated with the history provided by the boy
4. Providing any medical treatment needed
5. Discussing with the boy concerns about AIDS, other sexually transmitted diseases, and homosexuality in order to relieve unnecessary fears and misconceptions

# References

Abel, Gene. 1987. "Self-Reported Sex Crimes of Non-Incarcerated Paraphiliacs." In *Medical Evaluation of Sexually Abused Children,* a presentation of Project IMPACT, Brainerd, Minnesota.

Bamford, F.N., and E.S. Kiff. "Child Sexual Abuse." *Lancet* (no. 2): 1396.

Butler-Sloss, E. 1987. *Report of the Inquiry into Child Abuse in Cleveland.* London: Her Majesty's Stationery Office.

DeJong, A.R., and Mimi Rose. 1988. "Frequency and Significance of Physical Evidence in Legally Proven Cases of Child Sexual Abuse." *Pediatrics* 84: 1022–1026.

Groth, A.N., and T.M. Stevenson. 1984. *Anatomical Drawings.* Newton, Massachusetts: Forensic Mental Health Association.

Hobbs, C.J., and J.M. Wynne. 1986. "Buggery in Childhood: A Common Syndrome of Child Abuse." *Lancet* (no. 2): 792–796.

Levitt, C.J. 1986. "Sexual Abuse in Children: A Compassionate yet Thorough Approach to Evaluation." *Postgraduate Medicine* 80: 201–215.

McCann, J., J. Voris, M. Simon, and R. Wells. 1989. "Perianal Findings in Prepubertal Children Selected for Nonabuse: A Descriptive Study." *Child Abuse and Neglect* 13: 179–193.

Minnesota Department of Education. 1989. *Minnesota Student Survey Report.* St. Paul, Minnesota.

Myers, J.E.B. 1986. "Role of Physician in Preserving Verbal Evidence of Child Abuse." *Journal of Pediatrics:* 409–411.

Reinhart, M.A. 1987. "Sexually Abused Boys." *Child Abuse and Neglect* 11: 229–235.

Roberts, R.E.I. 1986. "Examination of the Anus in Suspected Child Sexual Abuse." *Lancet* (no. 2): 1100.

Sgroi, Susan. 1980. Referred to by Rolland Summit at the Minnesota Department of Corrections Sexual Victimization of Children Conference.

Spencer, M.J., and P. Dunklee. 1986. "Sexual Abuse of Boys." *Pediatrics* 78: 133–381.

# 11
# The Assessment Interview for Young Male Victims

*Paul N. Gerber*

J oining with families is very important when working with latency-age and adolescent children. We begin at intake, meeting and accepting these families where they are. We illustrate unconditional acceptance and respect and proceed in a manner that is respectful to all parties. We are particularly scrupulous about procedures when the abuser is one of the parents and is temporarily estranged or there is some suspicion by referral sources that a parent or a relative from the extended family has perpetrated the abuse on the primary client. Among the many statements and gestures we make to join with parents is to assure them that we see each member of the family as a consultant who can help us get to know the primary client better. We then ask them to accept us as their psychological and sociological consultants.

We try to offer an interview team comprising a male and female clinician at intake, primarily to allow the victim a chance to choose the gender of the person who will conduct his individual interview. Each member of the family is given a process chart (figure 11–1), and the full extent of the program is explained, with emphasis on the variety of options within the program as well as possible referrals to outside agencies when appropriate.

Individualized treatment planning is stressed, and we are careful to explain that each case will be handled by a clinician team comprising licensed social workers, family practice therapists, psychologists, and psychiatrists. We are careful to acknowledge that opinions in the mental health field vary and that the family will never be subjected to one person's opinion. We assure them that their case will receive ongoing supervision and reassure them about our commitment to openness concerning their input into treatment planning. The parents interview format is not discussed here, but it is as thorough and comprehensive as the victim interview format.

The PHASE (Program for Healthy Adolescent Sexual Expression) clinical team is highly skilled in the area of adolescent sexuality and family practice. The team has contributed significantly to the content of this chapter and the structure of the Male Victims Program. PHASE is part of Family Services of Greater St. Paul, Minnesota.

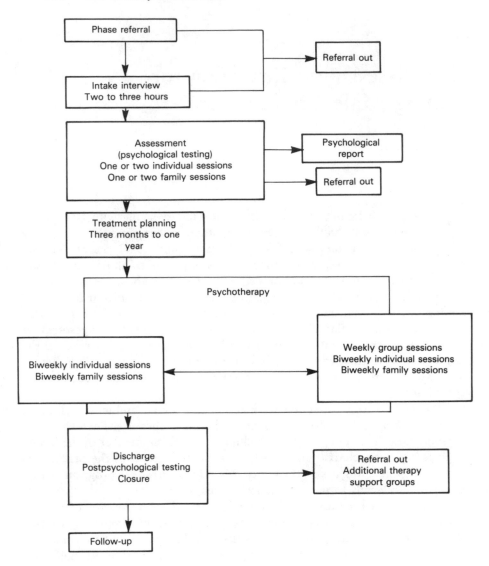

**Figure 11-1. Process Chart**

The initial posture with the primary client (the male victim) and his family is one of strategic compromise. The philosophy includes a belief that without a complete and detailed history, treatment planning cannot be comprehensive. Challenging cognitive distortions at intake or nearly in the assessment process has the potential to impair disclosure. We must be extremely mindful of the nomenclature used. Ultimately, we can guide clients to verbalize their experiences at the bottom of a power dynamic. Initially, terms such as *violate* rather than *violent* or feeling *confused* rather than *abused* may better fit their realities.

Boys who are sexually abused often experience a confusing mix of emotions and thoughts about their experiences. Initially, they may not be able or willing to define the sexual events as abusive. There may be a reluctance to express any feelings at all about what happened or how they feel toward the abuser. The interviewing clinician must be sensitive to the client's perceptions, psychological vulnerabilities, and resistance. A safe structure that facilitates the sharing of his experiences by a pace-lead methodology will be most helpful. The following condensed guidelines are suggested for those conducting the initial assessment interview of sexually abused male youth. These guidelines are incorporated as a cover for the Male Victims Program intake interview form when it is disseminated through workshops or requests by mail.

1. Restate for the client who you are and what is going to take place in the individual interview. This conveys respect and enhances the atmosphere of safety. The clinician also might share some thoughts on his or her philosophy about working with youths. Specifically prepare the client for a series of questions necessary to help you better understand how he thinks and feels about a variety of things in his life. Indicate that the approach will be historical and will cover sexuality, family, relationships, and life issues. Be clear about the issues of data privacy and mandatory reporting. Provide the parents with a copy of your state's client's bill of rights.

2. Let the client know that you are aware of concerns about an individual or individuals having been inappropriate with him. Indicate that some questions will relate specifically to those experiences. Be creative in expressing your comfort and openness in hearing his reality.

3. Inform the client that if he experiences embarrassment or other strong feelings in response to certain questions, he has a choice as to how much information he will share. This empowers the client and facilitates rather than inhibits openness. Incorporating teaching to dispel myths and fears about sexuality is particularly helpful in reducing shame at this juncture. The teaching style should be age-appropriate, graphic, and yet respectful.

4. While the interview format is structured, it is extremely important to remain flexible within the structure. If the client is resistant to discussion of certain topics, temporary shifts to a less distressing area will quell his anxiety and enhance trust. A return to the difficult material later will prove more productive. While the questions are numbered, full discretion as to order is left to the interviewer.

5. At the termination of the interview, the clinician should acknowledge any obvious struggles and offer praise for specific interludes of openness and

courage. Most important is to convey a sense of hope that the victim will be given the support he needs to ("heal," "process," "understand," "overcome," or "work through") his sexual abuse experiences. Reassure the client about confidentiality.

The series of questions for intake (see appendix) are a guideline for building a foundation for comprehensive treatment planning and assessment reports. Interviewers must word and frame questions in a manner that melds with their own personality and comfort levels. Boys are well aware of why they have been referred. I did not endorse allowing the client to raise the issue of sexual abuse. It has been our experience that while the client-initiated approach is viewed as respectful, often the reactive therapists themselves appear to be shameful or avoidant. The client's interpretation will surely retard or prohibit full and accurate disclosure. When using the proposed questionnaire, modify words in keeping with the youth's level of intellectual functioning and vocabulary, particularly as it applies to the use of slang terminology.

Having the intake interview outline in hand does not guarantee an accurate disclosure of all the client's sexual experiences, regardless of whether they might be categorized as aberrant, normative, variated, or deviated. This questionnaire is an ineffective tool if the clinician is uncomfortable with his or her own sexuality and is not well grounded experientially in working with sex-specific issues, particularly as they relate to the age-group and gender of the client.

Children and adolescents are far too perceptive to be disarmed by a lot of sophomoric rhetoric about mutual respect and acceptance. A singsong voice and head-bobbing affirmations will do little to dislodge a recalcitrant youth. Conversely, a poorly executed or contrived projection of self will be perceived as pomposity or bombasticism, which will immediately result in the client's discounting the clinician as being insincere and unprofessional. Finally, as stated earlier, confrontation during intake and assessment is simply bad strategy. Intake and assessment is a fact-gathering process, with the details gleaned being integral to the development of a treatment plan. Challenging cognitive distortions are appropriately placed in the treatment process.

A perfect contrast to the posture in intake and assessment is the posture in a game of poker. Rather than the clinician's maintaining a poker face, he or she should be able to exude self-confidence, a general investment in and affection for children and adolescents, and a solid sense of competency. This cannot be a charade but must be representative of the clinician by a force of personality that is a projection of self. It is important to let the client know about the clinician's age, expertise, academic accomplishments, and street wisdom if it is genuine. This can be done with some humility and humor, and it will not take the client long to tally the score: "I'm seven; he's forty-seven. I'm in seventh grade; he's got eight years of college. I'm afraid to talk about sex; he's talked to hundreds of boys my age about sex. He's streetwise, and he's a boy, too."

Probably one of the greatest advantages a clinician has is extensive knowledge about sexual behaviors. Many behaviors that are relatively common in the general population are feared to be deviant. For example, we learn that boys are very curious about their bodies starting early in childhood. Being familiar with the smell or even taste of a variety of body fluids, including sweat, urine, feces, ear wax, mucous, saliva, and seminal fluid, are things to which children and adolescents could readily attest if provided the proper context within which to make the disclosure. Additionally, being familiar with all parts of their bodies through other sensations such as sight and touch are relatively common. This is the sort of knowledge that can be used strategically.

Once a child has agreed to be completely honest, the clinician can assert that while the commitment is probably heartfelt, upon being confronted with certain questions, the boy's spirit will weaken. At that point, it might be wise to tell the client that you are going to ask a series of questions that you do not want him to answer. You can explain that you do not want answers because he will probably be dishonest about them. You can then ask a long series of questions, including the following:

1. What did it feel like the first time you put your finger or crayon or pencil inside your ("butt") anus?

2. Can you tell me how difficult it was to position yourself near a mirror so you could see what your ("asshole") rectum looked like?

3. Can you describe how your ("cum") seminal fluid tastes?

4. When did you first become familiar with how your ("butt") buttocks smell(s)?

Continue to disallow any responses or reactions. It is strategic to explain that in the course of your taking sexual histories, you have ascertained that sometime between age three and the current age of your client, all children are extremely curious about their bodies and in total privacy have experimented in all the ways just described and sometimes many more. Further, because they have done those behaviors in absolute privacy, they have no idea as to whether the behaviors are okay or weird. Explain that it is highly likely that those behaviors might never have been discussed and would have remained one of those gnawing, unanswered questions about their sexuality. Let the client know that he is fortunate enough to have an enlightened and uninhibited mentor who can put his fears to rest.

At that juncture, I usually advise the client that most of the kids I have worked with have ultimately acknowledged that they have done most of those things or other very similar things. Furthermore, those kids all readily admitted that they were embarrassed and ashamed about those behaviors and never dreamed that they would admit to having explored their bodies in such a manner.

Inevitably, the current client will admit to a number of the items listed when asked generally, "Are you good for five out of seven?" The clinician can seize this opportunity to praise the bravery of the disclosure and honesty, which neutralizes the majority of the defensiveness. This kind of normalizing and neutralizing strategy can apply to much more aberrant or deviant experiences or behaviors that are disclosed during the remainder of the interview. The most effective strategy involves stating what should by now be the obvious, which is that the interviewer knows the answers to many of the questions before he or she ever asks them. A young client once announced to his parents at the end of the intake interview, "You know that guy can look right inside my head." Taking a lead from my client, I have often stated, "It's almost as if you have a window in your head and I'm looking into it." This is also a great place to talk about building a therapeutic relationship that is predicated on honesty.

As the intake interview continues to uncover a variety of sexual behaviors and experiences, it is important to continue to neutralize shame by affirming the client's bravery and candor, as well as assuring him that his experiences are not unique and are shared by many boys both younger and older than himself. Catastrophizing or pathologizing his continued disclosures is tantamount to disaster with regard to his sense of safety and well-being in the therapeutic setting. Making sure that the boy knows that dozens of boys before them have made similar disclosures has a rather normalizing and neutralizing effect. Specific case examples often make that assertion more genuine. Continued acknowledgment and praise in regard to his bravery and honesty remains integral throughout the process. Occasional explanations of the interrelationship between intimacy and honesty will further the bonding process with the client.

This approach is effective with a wide variety of clients between the ages of ten and nineteen. It requires that the clinician have and project clear sexual boundaries. It is important to remember the idiosyncratic nature of each client's life experiences. In an approach that is this powerful and proactive, the clinician must be particularly sensitive to the client's perceptions, psychological vulnerabilities, level of intellectual functioning, and ego strength, as well as a variety of other factors that may necessitate modification of this approach. Modification also will be necessitated if the proposed approach does not fit the clinician's personality. Conversely, we tend to minimize the resiliency of children.

While the intake interview questionnaire proposed here may be a helpful tool, it should be obvious that much about presentation, style, projection of personality, and even theatrics cannot be set forth in outline form. Like any tool, it can only be used effectively when paired with skill.

# Appendix:
# Male Victims Program

---

**Intake Interview**

Name _____ Date _____

D.O.B. _____ Interviewer _____

A. *Family/Social History*

1. (Hand-sketch genogram). Ask for some historical data about each family member (adoption, chemical dependency, placements, or divorces). Who are you closest to? Least close to? How do family members get along with one another? Who fights with whom?

   Delving into the client's perceptions of his nuclear and extended family is often quite revealing. Well-masked family problems become evident during the dialog. To enhance participation in constructing the genogram, a flip chart can be used and the client can participate with some of the drawing and writing.

2. What do you like best about your family? What kinds of things do you do with your family? What's the biggest problem in your family? Who does the disciplining, and how is it done? What responsibilities do you have at home?

   Focus on discipline can uncover physical violence within the home. These questions can help discern if the family system is matriarchal or patriarchal in structure or if the child is parentified because of inadequacies in either or both parents.

3. Have you ever experienced any significant loss, like through a death, disappearance, or moving away?

   Because of the abstract nature of the meaning of death and what follows death, latency-age children and adolescents have distinctively different reactions. Interviewers can begin to ascertain if the child has grieved the loss of the significant person or is in the grieving process. The client's being separated or protected from the abuser also may be experienced as a loss, and grieving may need to take place.

4. Outside of your parents, are there any other important adults in your life? What is special about these adults? What do you do with them?

    Questions about important adults provides information about how interactive the client is with adults, particularly in relation to how involved or uninvolved the parents may be in monitoring these relationships. Inquiries can lead to disclosures of additional abuse or the existence of surrogate parents. Pseudosocialized adolescents, often rejected by their peers, tend to gravitate toward adult relationships.

5. Do you have a best friend? How often do you see your friends? What do you like to do? Are your friends mostly girls or guys? Have you ever "gone with" anyone or "dated"? How often do/did you see each other?

    Inquiry about friends will be one opportunity to examine the client's abilities in peer relationships. Unfortunately, isolated children tend to describe best friends who in reality have very limited relationships with the client. Germane are the types of play or activities that occur with friends, the gender of the friends, and disparities in ages.

6. Is there anything you would like to change about your social life or your friendships?

    Children and adolescents do not often voluntarily report wanting to make major changes in their social lives. Particularly among adolescents, there seems to be some stigma attached to acknowledgment of problems within their social lives. They fear being viewed as unacceptable ("nerds," "geeks," or "burnouts").

B. *Behavioral History*

1. In general, how has school gone? How do you get along with teachers? Ever have any problems with skipping? Ever been in detention or suspended? Are you in any special programs (advanced or learning disabled)? What kinds of grades do you get? Are you involved in any school activities?

Questioning about school provides further insight into peer relationships and how supportive or interested the family is in the client's life outside the home.

2. Were there any behaviors that people were worried about before this happened? Have you ever gotten in trouble before?

   Framing a question focused on the concerns of others can provide insight into a client who may be experiencing parents as controlling, rigid, or hypercritical. Conversely, it can disclose the fact that the parents have legitimate concerns respectfully brought to the client who discounts or minimizes the information.

3. Have you ever seen a therapist, social worker, or doctor in the past? Have you ever been in any kind of therapy or treatment, groups, or family counseling? Are you on any medications and, if so, for what?

   A client's perception of difficulties with other helping professionals can help the interviewer avoid similar pitfalls. Reasonable exposure can help alert the interviewer to a youth who may be oppositional or avoidant or who covers with psychological jargon. This information can allow you to get a view of health problems. In the event that some of the prior professional help has been in response to a similar or the presenting issue, releases can be obtained to ensure some continuity in the process.

4. Have you ever gotten drunk? When? How often? Have you ever used pot? Speed? Downers? Coke? Crack? Acid? Other? Are you concerned about your use? Have you ever experienced any negative consequences because of your use?

   Clients have tended to be quite candid about their patterns of using/abusing chemicals. Because the interview is not a chemical dependence assessment, they tend to be very specific about quantities, frequency, and their physical and emotional reactions to the given substance. This is an area where information gathered may be cause for referral for a formal chemical dependence evaluation. Actively using chemically dependent clients need their dependence problems resolved before entering therapy.

C. *Sexual History*

1. Where did you learn about sex? Where did you learn the most about sex (school, friends, siblings, parents, books, magazines, or movies)?

Is sex discussed in your family? How? By whom? What messages do/did you get about sex at home?

Sex is not an open topic in most homes. When parents profess being open about sexuality, their child often describes the discussions as being limited to biological functioning, particularly as it relates to pregnancy. Unfortunately, latency-age children and adolescents tend to be misinformed and underinformed.

2. What are your earliest recollections of experiences you had or things you saw that may have been sexual?

Often, children have pathologized exploratory, sexual things they have done with their own bodies or similar things that they have done with other children during latency years. Naive curiosity and experimentation often constitute "secrets" for children and adolescents that need clarification.

3. Can you give me a narrative history about sexual experiences following your earliest memory (masturbation, onset of puberty, or sexual interaction with peers)?

Discussions about a client's general sexual history is a less threatening way to begin discussing sexuality than focusing on the abuse experiences. At this juncture, it rests with the given talents of the interviewer to exude comfort, dispel shame, and temporarily normalize deviations in order to enable the client to be open about his reality.

D. *Abuse Reactive Behavioral History*

1. When people have been the object of inappropriate sexual behavior, they sometimes have a tough time coping with all the feelings that they have. As a result of the abuse or as part of trying to cope, people may experience some changes in themselves or in their behavior. What changes, if any, have you noticed? Have you noticed any changes in the way you get along with others?

These are good transition questions to move the client from the standard sexual history questions to those about the active abuse experience. This data also will give the interviewer some sense of how reactive the client is.

2. Sometimes people close to victims have trouble coping with their feelings. Do you feel people are treating you differently since they learned you were abused?

Shame is an extremely difficult emotion for youths to describe. Victims often describe a sense of being soiled, exposed, or alienated, as if the abuse had left a telltale physical mark.

3. Have you been feeling down or wanting to spend a lot of time alone? Have you had any thoughts of hurting yourself or running away? Have you engaged in other risky or dangerous behaviors?

The sense of alienation becomes so pronounced for some clients that they begin to feel a sense of hopelessness. Make specific inquiry to separate self-debasing behaviors from suicide ideation or suicide attempts. Consider the symptoms for dysthymia, clinical depression, and posttraumatic stress disorder.

4. Any changes in your sexual behaviors? Do you feel this experience has affected how you feel about being sexual with someone? How are you feeling about your body?

This approach can often elicit some attitudinal issues spawned by the abuse experiences. Some people fear they cannot participate in consensual sex with a peer. Others fear they will attract exploitive partners and be revictimized. Self-loathing, playing out in body image issues, also can result from sexually abusive experiences.

E. *Sexual Abuse History*

1. You are here at the clinic today because of concerns that someone has been sexual with you in an inappropriate way. Can you describe what happened? Feel free to use whatever words you are comfortable with to describe body parts and the sexual acts.

The sexual abuse history, like the family history and the social history, is germane to the continuity of the assessment. Life does not begin or end with the sexually abusive experiences; they simply become one of the linked events in the client's life. Guarded responses might hint about what kind of coping mechanisms came into play that might bar accurate recall, such as disassociation, repression, or retrograde amnesia. For the most part, it has been our experience that there is significant recall and that the primary barrier will be shame. In the event that the offender was significant in the client's life, fear may cause the client to minimize or deny.

2. What was this person's relationship to you (parent, stepparent, relative, stranger, or neighbor)? Was this someone you cared about? Did

you feel he or she cared about you? How did this person show you he or she cared?

Emotional attachment with the perpetrator and a sense of loss relating to the disclosure tiein to the myth of complicity and internalized homophobia. Feelings of this nature may not be disclosed during the early stages of intake or assessment.

3. Was there anybody else around when it happened? Was anybody else involved? Do you think anybody else knew? Did you tell anyone?

Inquiry about the involvement of others may identify individuals who failed to protect the child or enabled the behavior with complicity or passivity. Others may have acted as co-conspirators. In the event that the offender is a parent, sibling, or extended family member, the client may have disclosed to someone significant in the system only to be further unprotected, ignored, or poorly advised.

4. Where did it usually happen (car, house, barn, or woods)? Do you know exact locations (street addresses, owner's name, or business logos)?

Environmental factors, combined with the actual experiences, also may relate to a variety of therapeutic issues. Details of this nature may be very germane to criminal or civil legal proceedings.

5. Did the person make any threats or use physical force? Did the person offer you money, drugs, or other things to be sexual with him or her? Did the person do strange things to scare you? Did the person have you join him or her in other unusual activities?

Establishing the use of coercion or violence, subtle or otherwise, is important because these factors are prognosticators for the intensity and duration of treatment. Check for pseudosatanic, satanic, or ritualistic abuse without use of leading or contaminating verbiage. Do not be seduced by these issues. There is both public and professional hysteria about these issues that can distract clinicians from their primary tasks.

6. How long ago did it begin? How long did it continue? How often did it happen? Where did it happen?

Age of onset, duration, and frequency are significant prognosticators as to the intensity and duration of treatment. This information also can be a predictor for learned deviant arousal.

7. How was this person sexual with you? Did he or she have you take off your clothes? Were you touched? Where on your body did the person touch you? Did he or she touch you with (hands, mouth, penis, or object)? Did the person have you touch him or her with (hands, mouth, penis, or object)?

> Gathering specific information as to the types of sexual contact, whether or not there was penetration, and what other related behaviors occurred often generate memories that are paired with significant shame. Myths of complicity and internalized homophobia are often exacerbated by whether or not the child was eroticized to the abuse and how participatory he views himself. This information often relates directly to the level of anxiety and trauma.

8. Besides sexual contact, were you involved with (video, pictures, other kids, bathing, eliminating waste, pornography, or animals)? Did the person show you pictures, videos, or movies?

> While some clients may find inquiry about pornography, use of animals, or the elimination of waste curious or bizarre, these factors appear as part of sexual abuse scenarios with some regularity. Knowledge about specific acts may better inform the interviewer as to the need for a medical examination. Pornography is also known to be a common instrument in covert presexual conditioning. Pornography will be used to lower the inhibitions or eroticize the child or adolescent.

9. Has anyone else ever been sexual with you in an inappropriate way (adults, relatives, older kids, or baby-sitter)? Has anyone ever paid you to be sexual with him or her or offered you special gifts?

> Clients also report abuse by yet other adults or older adolescents. Particularly with adolescent males, one is better off posing the question "Who is the oldest person you have had sex with?" rather than "Has anyone else sexually abused you?" This may uncover an adult or adolescent female being sexual with a latency-age or young adolescent male in her case.

10. How did people become aware of the abuse? What happened when people found out? How did you feel? Was there anybody you could talk with about this? Why did you feel you could say something to this person? What was his or her reaction? Who in the family knows? What has been their reaction to finding out? How much have you been able to talk about this with your (parents, brothers, sisters, grandparents, aunts, or uncles)?

Often well-meaning parents and concerned others can make statements that will be interpreted as blaming. Statements and behaviors also could be interpreted as signs of abandonment and revulsion. This provides data for the educational aspects of the family therapy, as well as some instructions for immediate reparative work.

11. Was this reported to the authorities? Were you interviewed by (police officers, social workers, therapists, or lawyers)? How have these experiences been? Did you make formal statements?

Mandatory training has greatly sensitized law enforcement officers, social workers, and medical practitioners who are involved in the early investigation, assessment, and examination of abuse victims. Often clients misunderstand how important the involvement of these professionals is. Conversely, you can validate the child's reality as to the feelings of invasiveness these inquiries spawn. If a formal statement has been made, it may later become evident that the client initially overreported or underreported, which will complicate future interactions with the system.

12. When was the last time you saw a doctor for a physical exam? Have you had any worries about your body? Any problems with wetting or soiling? Have you noticed any physical changes since the sexual contact? Have you noticed if it hurts or burns when you urinate or defecate? Any bumps or sores on your penis, mouth, or anus?

Due to the epidemic proportion of certain sexually transmitted diseases, this question is clearly on point. Unfortunately, diseases such as chlamydia or HIV are relatively asymptomatic. One also must be mindful of other physiological symptoms of sexual abuse, such as enuresis and encopresis.

13. Have there been any changes in your eating or sleeping habits? Any dreams or nightmares that concern you?

Night terrors, nightmares, recurring dreams, and insomnia are found among male victims of sexual abuse. If these issues are disclosed early in the assessment process, special focus on them can escalate healing.

14. Guys and girls usually have a number of feelings about someone being sexual with them in this way. Sometimes the feelings are mixed, and sometimes they are very clear. Can you describe what feelings you had about this happening to you (during, after, or now)?

Allowing the client to describe his reality about his sexual experiences can be revealing on a variety of fronts. The fabric resulting from the weave of abusive and nonabusive sexual experiences is a critical piece.

F. *Closure Information*

1. Do you have any questions about today?

2. Do you have any questions about what happened to you?

3. Do you have questions about sexuality in general?

4. What would you like to have some help with? What do you think it would be helpful for you to talk more about?

5. Do you have any fears or concerns about getting help with this?

G. *Interviewer's Impressions*

1. Did the client appear to be (open, cooperative, dissociative, passive, repressed, projecting, suicidal, rageful, self-mutilating, or depressed)?

2. Is the client appropriate for extended assessment and treatment planning? Would referral out or discharge be more appropriate at this point in time?

3. Would additional projective testing or a psychiatric interview be in order as part of the extended assessment? Is a medical examination warranted?

4. Can you make a diagnosis or provisional diagnosis at this point?

5. Did you do some psychological testing at intake, or is current testing readily available?

# 12
# Female Perpetrators of Sexual Abuse:
# A Feminist View

*Charlotte Davis Kasl*

**M**y interest in writing about female perpetrators of sexual abuse was ignited at the United Nations Decade of Women Conference in July 1985. I presented a workshop titled "Incest: Connections to Spirituality, Sexuality, and Imperialism," which included a small segment on covert and overt sexual abuse by females drawn from my nine years of clinical experience. I was unprepared for the intensity of the responses. In most cases, women expressed gratitude, saying that the information hit with a sudden jolt of recognition that opened the door to understanding some of their struggles. One woman said, "I've always known I had all the symptoms of an incest survivor, and finally I know why." A few others said we should not be talking about female perpetrators because it lets men "off the hook" and they will use the information to obscure the extent of male-perpetrated sexual abuse.

Diana Russell joined me for a portion of the workshop and presented data drawn from her study of 930 women who had been sexually abused. Russell's data on sexual abuse by females differs greatly from my clinical observations. Her study showed that less than 1 percent of female abuse survivors are abused by women, while my estimate from clinical observation ranges from 15 to 25 percent.

Subsequently, I asked numerous therapists in Minneapolis who work with survivors of childhood abuse what percentage of their clients had been abused by women. The answers ranged from 10 to 39 percent. The highest incidence of people surviving female sexual abuse occurred in male perpetrators.

I would like to thank the following people for input into this chapter: Shirley Carlson, who helped gather the initial data; the Upper Midwest Sexual Abuse Consortium, a group of more than one hundred women and men who work in all areas of sexual assault and abuse; Mic Hunter on the prevention section; and the clients I have worked with in the past thirteen years who have played a big part in bringing the issue of sexual abuse by females to my awareness. Adapted from a paper presented at the First International Congress on Rape, Jerusalem, Israel, April 1986.

Subsequent data I gathered on childhood histories of men, which appear in my book *Women, Sex and Addiction: A Search for Love and Power*, suggests that a large percentage of men who become sexually addicted have experienced both overt and covert sexual abuse by their mothers, female relatives, baby-sitters, and older females as well as abuse by males. In response to my book, numerous men, both clients and friends, have confided that they were abused by women and had not spoken about it because of the shame they felt.

I believe that there are several explanations for the discrepancy between Russell's data and clinical observations. First, until very recently, sexual abuse by females has been a taboo subject. Through social custom and emotional aversion, both perpetrators and victims have felt prohibited from speaking out about it. When something is taboo, most people relegate the associated experiences to their subconscious to protect themselves from self-knowledge that conflicts with society's norms. To speak out is to challenge the rules under which our society is organized. If knowledge does touch the conscious level, a person will usually maintain silence for fear of being ridiculed and misunderstood.

The second reason has to do with definition. Sexual abuse by females is often illusive and difficult to define. Descriptions cannot always be extrapolated from definitions of abuse by males. Men cannot smother children against their breasts. Men do not usually walk around in sheer nightgowns flirting with their children or with deliverymen who come to the house. Women do not have a penis they can use to penetrate a male. Very often it is covert or involves sexually intrusive behavior such as bathing a male child when he is old enough to bathe himself, giving him enemas, commenting on his growth of pubic hair, or walking around seminude in the presence of the child and getting a sexual high from seeing him stare or become sexually aroused.

While a man may remember childhood incidents that elicited shameful or repulsive feelings from sexually loaded interactions with his mother or other females, it may not compute mentally that it was sexual abuse. In fact, it may take months or years of therapy before he makes the connection between the inappropriate sexual intrusions of childhood and his adult dysfunctional or abusive relationships.

Defining sexual abuse by females is in the embryonic stage, and it will be a while before there are some widely accepted criteria. Until there is sufficient education and awareness, researchers and people in the helping professions may not know how to ask appropriate questions. And, of course, clinicians, whether or not they have been abused by a female, will need to confront their stereotypes and prejudices before they will be open to hearing their clients speak about the subject. In addition, as of 1990, the mass media have not brought the subject into the open, which is fundamental to a mass cultural change in attitude that will help lift the taboo.

For all these reasons, it is highly unlikely that a male or female asked directly on a questionnaire or in an interview whether he or she has been sexually abused by a female would say yes. The person would be unaware of the abuse or unable to remember it, or he or she would not define sexually loaded childhood experiences with a female as abuse, even though these experiences may have elicited intense shame, rage, fear, and guilt. Thus, the magnitude of the problem is simply not yet known. And whatever the percentage may turn out to be—3 percent or 20 percent—the task is to break the taboo, become aware of the needs of both victims and survivors of sexual abuse by females, and start working toward prevention.

## Women's Uneasiness in Discussing Female Sexual Abuse

As women, our self-image is challenged when we open our eyes to abuse by other women. It destroys the myths about the innocence of women and thus about ourselves. It may bring to the surface internalized hatred of other women and raise issues about our own sexual fantasies, obsessions, or behaviors.

As the subordinate group in a patriarchal culture, women do not want to give information to men that may be used against them. This fear has been reflected in the fact that female perpetrators are more likely to face severe cultural prejudice. Unlike men, their parental rights are often terminated, and social service workers are more likely to see them as irredeemable. While teenage male perpetrators are often seen as victims, teenage females are treated in a more punitive way. Another fear is that men will attempt to assuage their guilt and obsure the preponderance of male sexual abuse by saying, "But women do it too."

Women fear incurring the anger of other women who may believe that by exploring sexual abuse by females, we are apologists for men. There is also a fear that men will possibly coopt the subject or be recognized as the authorities and neglect to include a cultural analysis that takes power differences between men and women in account. It is crucial that sexual abuse by females not be seen as simply parallel to male abuse. A deep understanding of female and male socialization and power dynamics within the culture is crucial to any discussion of the subject.

The examination of female abuse may raise buried feelings that women have about their own parenting, sexuality, and capacity to abuse—problems that women are taught to deny. For a clinician, this subject can raise painful countertransference issues. To make a therapeutic bond with female perpetrators or their victims, however, it is necessary to be conscious of our own internalized belief system and repressed experiences. This can be both threatening and painful because it requires a strong commitment to self-exploration and vulnerability.

## Reasons We Need to Talk about Female Sexual Abuse

We need to explore female perpetrators of abuse because they exist. Without knowledge and understanding, we cannot help perpetrators and their victims to heal. As one female therapist said, "What's wrong with saying, 'Women do it, too'? It's true! As feminists we need to tell the truth, and we need to reach out to these women." By focusing on the infrequency of female perpetrators cited in numerous studies, we overlook both the victimizers and the victims.

Another reason to talk about sexual abuse by females is that it can eventually help women in their own empowerment. Female abuse mirrors women's pain and rage, which women are conditioned to deny. They turn it inward, thereby neutralizing much of their potential for power. As one therapist said, "Let's get honest here. When I'm victimized, I always get even somehow. As a woman, I've learned to perpetrate in covert ways. We don't ever get victimized without perpetrating in return." In other words, the anger has to go somewhere. Therefore, by looking at our own capacity to victimize others, we also can see the magnitude of our victimization.

## Cultural Factors Relevant to Men

Little boys are socialized to think of themselves as little men at a very early age. They are taught to disdain the vulnerability of being small, needy, and powerless over treatment by care givers. As one man said, "As a tiny child I kept hearing 'Don't be a baby, grow up, take it like a man,' as if there was something shameful about being a little boy. But I *was* a little boy." This results in little boys burying their psychological neediness and eventually being vulnerable to older females who, tapping into a boy's unconscious need, use him for their own sexual needs. The boy is unable to compute that this is abuse because, after all, if he was a man at age eight or twelve or fourteen, he was peer of the older stepmother, baby-sitter, or mother, so it must have been his choice to participate in sexual games or intercourse.

Male macho conditioning includes being both invulnerable to and in charge of women at all times. Therefore, acknowledging being abused by a woman feels demeaning and shameful. This creates a double bind: If a man denies being abused or does not talk about it, the shame harbored inside takes on a life of its own, often leading to violence, addiction to sex, and sexual perpetration of others; yet telling someone feels equally shameful. For men who have internalized injunctions not to be aggressive or angry, the rage gets turned inward, resulting in depression, emotional numbness, and self-hatred. In both cases, men usually maintain silence rather than risk being the target of ridicule or disbelief, which would threaten their core identity—a person who is supposed to be invulnerable and in control. Homophobia plays a subtle part at this point because if a man says a woman hurt him sexually, he may be called a sissy or a queer.

Men are often conditioned to think of sex as an erotic, pleasurable experience that can be separate from a bonded, intimate relationship or even caring about the persons they are with. "If it feels good, hey what's the problem!" Thus, when a boy of fourteen is seduced or sexually stimulated by a woman of thirty, it may never cross his mind that he was exploited. When I saw the movie *The Last Picture Show,* in which a woman probably in her thirties has sex with a teenage boy, it never occurred to me that this was a form of sexual exploitation. Yet such abuse is a repeated theme among sexually addicted men and male perpetrators of abuse.

Evans and Schaefer (1987) conducted a study that reflects how submerged our awareness of sexual abuse by females is. The experimental group comprised one hundred women who had completed treatment for chemical dependence at the Chrysalis Treatment Program for Women in Minneapolis and had maintained their sobriety. The control group was matched on a number of demographic variables. While the groups reported no significant differences in the amount of childhood sexual abuse, 25 percent of the women who had completed treatment and maintained sobriety reported having been sexually abused by a female, as opposed to 0 percent of the control group. This matches the observations of numerous therapists working with male perpetrators and female survivors—that is, that people are usually unaware of having been sexually abused by a female until they encounter some form of treatment or therapy and that awareness of having been sexually abused by a female is often kept at bay through chemical abuse.

## Defining Sexual Abuse by Females

Definitions of female sexual abuse need to come from clinical observations and from those who have been victimized. People who have been silenced by a taboo can provide a rich source of information. If clinicians and researchers project their ideas of what constitutes abuse onto their clients, they may give clients conscious or unconscious signals to avoid the topic, or limit what they say, and thus unwittingly perpetuate the abuse by denying the inner reality of the persons they are attempting to help. It is crucial that clinicians listen to clients with a well-attuned ear and an open mind. What were the childhood sexual experiences that elicited shame, pain, rage, and fear? How are early sexual experiences currently being reenacted with a partner or a child? For example, if a man felt loved or important as a child when an older woman was sexual with him, he may not experience an internal prohibition against using his daughter for his sexual gratification or seeing her as a peer.

Definitions of sexual abuse must be broken down using terms such as *overt abuse, covert abuse, sexual violation, boundary crossing,* and *ignorant parenting.* This is important for two reasons. First, the term *sexual abuse* should not be a catchall phrase that will eventually become meaningless. Second, a broad definition of abuse helps people identify behavior patterns that result from sexual trauma. This helps to validate the victim's pain and grief as a starting point for healing. In my experience, it is the victims of covert abuse who most often feel that their pain is not valid and who tend to minimize it.

Definitions of abuse must be based on both the external objective criteria and the victim's subjective experience. For example, Larry and Jim, two brothers who were sexually abused by their mother, reacted very differently to a similar experience. On separate occasions, their mother had driven each of them out to a motel far from home and threatened to leave them there if they did not play certain "games" with her. For Jim, the threat was terrifying, so he "consented" to her sexual requests. Recounting this episode brought back the terror of being overwhelmed along with the fear of abandonment that had had a profound impact on his life. Larry had thought that his mother was stupid to make such a threat and had said, "Go ahead and leave me; I don't want to be at home anyhow," whereupon his mother ceased her request, took him out for lunch, and eventually drove him home.

Another aspect of the definition problem is that the term *penetration* is often used as a definition of criminal sexual contact by a male perpetrator. When the offender is a female, it may be that the victim actually performs the penetration. When an adult woman has intercourse with an adolescent, however, she is the offender even if he penetrated her. Therefore, definitions need to consider who has the power, what the motivation is, and whose needs are being met either overtly or covertly. For example, a teenage boy receives a totally confusing message if the sexual act is supposedly for his sexual education or benefit but the older female is getting a secret high from her sense of power and motherly role.

Another consideration concerns power in the relationship. Who has the power is often far more relevant to the consequences of the sexual abuse than actual age differences. A research criteria of a five-year age difference as a prerequisite for sibling abuse can miss many incidents of sexual abuse. Under certain circumstances, a child can experience the trauma of sexual abuse by a sibling of the same age or even younger. For example, one therapist I interviewed cited the case of an older mentally retarded child who sexually abused a younger sibling. In another situation, a boy abused a sister who was only one year younger, not a criterion for abuse in some studies. Because he was treated as the little prince of the family and she was the object of ridicule and humiliation, she felt that she could not fight back, talk about the sexual abuse, or get angry at him. She had internalized her programming as an inferior female who deserved abuse, and he had internalized his belief that he had the right to use her as he pleased without fear of retribution by his parents.

With all the complexities of definition, we may never come to a set of absolute criteria for what constitutes sexual abuse by females. But if we listen to the stories of men who have been abused or men who perpetuate abuse, become sexually addicted, or maintain a victim role as an adult, we gain insight into the patterns of abuse. The one criteria that remains constant is the survivor's own account. If a given experience results in shame, guilt, or rage and leaves a lasting negative impact on the survivor, it can be considered abuse.

## Some Related Data on Adolescent and Adult Male Perpetrators

Shirley Carlson, who has done extensive work with male perpetrators, kept data on sixty male perpetrators over a period of four years (see chapter 12 in volume 2 of this book). Using "hands-on" definitions only—that is, overt sexual abuse—she found that over 90 percent of the men reported being victims of childhood sexual abuse by a male and/or a female. Of the men who graduated from the program, 39 percent acknowledged sexual abuse by a female. Those entering the program rarely mentioned being sexually abused by a female. This supports the theory that length of time in therapy—aware therapist, I might add—is an important variable in uncovering sexual abuse by females.

Walter Bera, a therapist at a treatment program for teenage male sex offenders, reports that of three hundred male clients seen at the agency over a four-year period, 20 to 25 percent were sexually abused by females, very often teenage baby-sitters (Bera 1985). A whopping 62 percent reported getting the idea for the abuse from pornography.

These studies suggest several variables to be considered when doing research. First, it is crucial to ascertain whether subjects reporting abuse have been in therapy and, if so, for how long. Second, did the therapist ask questions about childhood sexual abuse by a female? If so, what were the questions, and when and how were they asked? Third, was the therapist knowledgeable about and sensitive to issues of sexual abuse by females?

## Motivation of the Perpetrator and Effects on Victims/Survivors

A given act can have many meanings. Part of the trauma and resulting feelings of shame and rage that become internalized relate to the motivation and emotional state of the perpetrator. Was the abuse conscious, sadistic, compulsive, ritualistic, or unconscious? Did it stem from poor parenting skills, curiosity, anger, or ignorance?

Following are three examples of an external behavior—giving enemas—that was carried out with different motivations and thus had extremely different effects on the boys involved.

In one case, a man reported that his mother gave him occasional enemas when he was a child. They had been prescribed by a doctor in his presence, been administered as the physician had suggested, and ceased when the physical difficulties abated. He remembered being a little embarrassed when his mother inserted the syringe, but she respected his privacy and laid a towel over him. He also remembered having a pleasurable sensation during the enema, which is not abnormal. When he talked about them, he seemed neither in denial nor upset. Sometimes experiences reported as unimportant events turn out to be buried traumas, but in this case, the enemas did not appear to be a problem.

A second man reported that his mother started giving him daily enemas because of "doctor's orders," which he had not heard. The boy reported an uneasiness at his mother's seeming delight in being told to give the enemas. "Now, Charlie, come on, it's time for your enema." She also asked constant questions about his bowel movements and hovered over him as he ate, reminding him constantly that he needed lots of fiber so he could have a good bowel movement. The mother started to experience a sexual rush while administering the enemas and became compulsive in giving them long after the apparent need was gone. Thus, the enemas became sexually abusive as the mother used them for her own compulsive sexual gratification. The crucial factor for Charlie was the intense feeling of shame related to the enemas and his increasing aversion to having them, as well as to being near his mother. He started to tune into his mother's emotional state and avoid her when he perceived an "enema mood" coming on. To compound the confusion, he felt guilty for avoiding his mother—"You're supposed to love your mother"—and on occasion he felt sexually aroused by the enemas. Thus, the mother's obsession about enemas was passed on to her son, who found himself thinking about the experience, feeling a jumble of shame, attraction, aversion, physical pleasure, and ambivalence about being the object of his mother's attention.

Another confusing event that entered the picture was when Charlie overheard his father questioning his mother about the enema bag in the bathroom and she said she used it for herself. He felt both shame and a sense of vindication. So it *was* a secret, and there *was* something wrong with it. Thus, his mind connected together sexual stimulation, intrusion, aversion, deceit, and powerlessness. Later, as an adult perpetrator of sexual abuse, it took nearly a year in therapy before he could connect the repeated enemas with his mixture of attraction, rage, and ambivalence toward his victims whom he abused anally.

In a third situation, a mother gave enemas both for punishment and for no apparent reason. It was as if she was attempting to clean out her own shame by giving her son, Eric, enemas. He became merely an object for her use. In this case, the mother's use of enemas was ritualistic, abusive, and sadistic. Without warning, Eric's mother would take him in the bathroom, tell him to take off his pants in front of her, and lie down. He remembered that her eyes seemed remote and glazed over and he always experienced fear and shame. Sometimes the enemas lasted for over an hour and became very painful as she prodded his rectum with the enema device. She would say things like "Now that's a good boy, lie still. Mommie is getting you all cleaned out."

On other occasions, when he was late getting home, she would flash anger and say, "Come on Eric, we'll have to clean you out now." His tears went ignored, and he learned to go numb during these rituals. Sometimes, after he had gone to bed, he heard his parents arguing about enemas. As he lay in bed, he was overwhelmed by fear. Often, after the argument had subsided, his mother would come in and carry him to the bathroom for an enema ritual. He would lie there hoping his father would come in and stop her, but he never did.

Sometimes, much to his dismay, he would have an erection against his mother's leg during the enema and would feel mortified when, shortly thereafter, he heard his mother's heavy breathing. Eventually he became aware that after an erection and a period of his mother's heavy breathing, she would often stop the enema. Thus, he had the control to stop the enema by having an erection that sexually stimulated his mother. This was a case of psychological and physical rape, with the child left feeling overwhelmed by guilt and shame. It was an extremely traumatizing form of sexual abuse. When, after several years in therapy as an adult, Eric started to talk about the enema rituals, he was overcome by nausea and then intense rage. Eventually he experienced both rage and grief at being used for the narcissistic needs of his mother and having been abandoned by his father.

## Types of Sexual Abuse by Females

The danger of categorizing types of abuse is that it is easy to say that one kind of abuse is more serious than another. In reality, a complex web of factors work together to create a child's belief system and view of the world. All abuse is serious and leaves emotional scars. The categories presented here are an attempt to identify some different types of abuse based on factors such as intensity, motivation, good role models apart from the family, and the child's temperament.

The following criteria were derived by Shirley Carlson in chapter 12 of volume 2. I have added examples from my interviews with sexually addicted males and male clients. Sexual abuse by women falls roughly into four categories, which Carlson describes as the four levels of abuse:

1. *Chargeable offenses,* such as oral sex, intercourse, masturbation, fondling, or sexual punishments. An example of a sexual punishment is fondling a child until he has an erection and then whipping him with a belt.

2. *Less flagrant offenses,* such as voyeurism, exposure, seductive touching, sexualized hugs, kissing on the mouth in a sexual way, extended nursing that satisfies a sexual need of the mother, or flirting with a male child possibly to shame or make her husband/partner jealous. Examples of exposing include deliberately attempting to sexually arouse an adolescent son by wearing transparent lingerie in front of him, particularly in the absence of the father, or undressing in a seductive way in front of a male child. Voyeurism would include sexual obsession with an adolescent son's sexual and physical development. The mother might repeatedly comment on his big muscles, his pubic hair, and his changing voice and be obviously sexually intrigued by him. In these cases, the son has to set limits on his mother's sexual energy and starts to feel shame about his sexuality in the presence of his mother. He is confused, feeling both flattered and ashamed.

3. *Invasions of privacy* in a sexual area of the body. This may include enemas, bathing together, washing the child beyond a reasonable age, obsessive cleaning of the foreskin, squeezing pimples, intrusive questions about bodily functions (particularly bowel movements), or any such activity in which the adult is using the child to fulfill a sexual or erotic desire. Examples also include an adult aunt or family friend at a family gathering stimulating an adolescent boy sexually by rubbing the back of his neck, cuddling up to him as one would a peer, bringing jokes about sex into the conversation, or behaving in a flirtatious way. At the time, it may feel exciting to an adolescent male, but it often results in confusion, which is compounded if the boy's parents observe the situation without making any comment or seem to enjoy and encourage it.

4. *Inappopriate relationships* created by the adult, such as substituting the son for an absent husband, sleeping with him, unloading emotional problems on him, or using him as a confidant about personal or sexual matters. In these forms of abuse, the child is forced to occupy an inappropriate role, such as father, lover, husband, or peer. Sometimes a male child is expected to contribute money—that is, be a provider—for an alcoholic mother (or

father) who will not work. Or he may have to protect his mother when she is battered or raped by her partner or others. Sometimes a mother who feels insecure will constantly ask her young son's advice because she feels unable to make decisions on her own. All of these situations create immense feelings of failure and shame because the child can never provide enough money, give adult advice, or stop someone from physically abusing his mother.

According to Carlson's data, 31 percent of the men who completed a long-term sex offender program had experienced the first form of abuse. When the second form of abuse was added, the proportion of male perpetrators who were sexually abused by women rose to 50 percent. Nearly all the clients had experienced some form of sexual intrusion listed in the third and fourth levels.

It is impossible to know to what extent these forms of abuse contributed to the perpetrating behavior of these clients. For the most part, these men were subjected to many other forms of abuse and neglect, such as sexual abuse by males, physical abuse, exposure to pornography, presence of incest in the home, and alcoholism. We can, however, explore some effects reported by these clients.

1. *Internalizing the shame and guilt of the offending female.* The client shames himself, believing he attracted the sexual behavior of his mother or another female. He does not understand that the role of the parent is to block sexual activity between the parent and the child even if the child initiates such behavior. He may feel guilty because he became sexually aroused, had an erection, or lusted after his mother. He may consider himself to be the aggressor because she had him lie on top or because he performed the penetration. He may feel guilty about having looked at his father's pornography, or he may feel guilty for having looked at his mother and felt sexually aroused when she was nude or partly clothed.

2. *False feeling of power.* The client does not know that these sexual behaviors constitute abuse. He thinks they were about being special or being macho. This false belief becomes part of the offender mode because it promotes incest as a normal and desirable behavior. The client may stay "in love" with his mother and continue a delusional relationship throughout his life while he sexually abuses his daughters, sons, or other minors.

2. *Feelings of worthlessness.* The client believes that he can be used, abused, loved, and discarded. He may continue this pattern by getting into relationships with female sex addicts. His feelings about being used often escalate to the point of violence. He may act this out in numerous ways, such as rape, battering, stealing, and other antisocial behaviors.

4. *Betrayal and abandonment.* The man harbors tremendous hurt and pain beneath his defended exterior. The child within him is crying, "There

was nobody there for me. I am not worth loving. If I am not wanted sexually, I am worth nothing."

5. *Rage.* Even though the man may appear to be compliant and passive, there is a deep underlying core of rage with no outlet. He does not understand the source of the rage and may attempt to rationalize it by blaming his victims.

6. *Fear and insecurity.* Like any sexual abuse victim, this child was an emotional orphan, abused by one or both of his parents and not protected by the other. As an adult, this man is tremendously needy and tries to get these needs filled in a sexually controlling or aggressive way.

7. *Conflict and ambivalence about sex and women.* This extraordinary ambivalence is played out through being at once dependent on women and rageful toward them. While it is impossible to separate the effects of cultural conditioning in forming negative attitudes toward women, the frequency of sexual abuse by females in the history of perpetrators and sexually addicted and violent men is compelling.

To expose the prevalence of sexual abuse by females is to put a magnifying glass over our culture. We are forced to see some very discomforting flaws. The damage done by our narrow social conditioning leaves women feeling powerless over their lives and men in a state of denial about their dependence and vulnerability. The result is confusion, jealousy, rage, and grief, which are often acted out in the sexual arena, too often with children. The macho man and the sweet, subservient woman are but charicatures of people, both missing important attributes of a complete, integrated human being. Thus, men and women emotionally and sexually slug it out, trading sex for security, sex for nurturing, sex for love. Women overtly seek security and too often bury their needs for self-actualization and social power. Men can openly seek power but are conditioned to use sex to get the nurturing and comfort they have been conditioned to deny needing.

Women, socialized to roles of passivity and dependence, are taught to believe that men are superior and that a woman is not complete without a man. When a woman does not receive care and nurturing from her partner, she often looks to her son to meet these needs, seeing him as a man rather than as a child who needs her care protection, and guidance. Because our culture has sexualized intimacy to a large degree, these relationships often involve overt or covert sexuality.

## Prevention

### Education

People need to learn about childhood development starting in elementary school. What are reasonable expectations of a child of three, eight, or twelve?

What kind of touch is okay, and what is not okay? As part of public education, I would love to see all boys and girls spend some time providing supervised care for younger children at a nursery or credible day-care establishment.

Children should have sex education so they will not try to answer their own questions by exploring or victimizing a younger child. Older siblings who sexually abuse a younger brother or sister often are attempting to educate themselves.

Another aspect of education is to teach children about appropriate touch. What is caring touch? What is confusing touch that might feel sexual, pleasureable, and shameful? All children need to learn that they have a right to say no to touches and kisses that do not feel good. They need to learn about masturbation at an early age so it will not be associated with something dirty, and secretive. Children need to understand that pleasurable senstions in the body are natural and normal.

Parents need to learn about emotional and physical boundaries with their children. Children have a right to closed bedroom and bathroom doors—both theirs and their parents'. If a mother undresses or bathes with the door open, a child is often left without the choice of seeing her nude. A care giver helps a child develop autonomy and internal power by respecting his or her right to have control of how he or she is touched or kissed. It is not a personal rejection if a child does not want a hug or a kiss. The parent who says "Give me a kiss" and then looks hurt and wounded when the child refuses is asking the child to prostitute his or her integrity for the parent's emotional needs. And while dos and don'ts can be a starting place, there is no way to give parents a complete list of all possible problem situations. This comes with awareness, education, openness in talking about sexuality, and learning appropriate boundaries. The parent who feels comfortable with his or her body and sexuality will probably give the clearest positive signals to a child.

### Raising Inner Awareness

Starting at an early age, people also should learn to read body language. This is crucial in parenting. This education begins by helping children recognize happy faces, sad faces, and scared faces; noticing feelings; and being aware of having a relaxed or tense body and having physical sensations with the body. They are then able to apply this knowledge as adults. I have often observed a parent playing roughly with a child—tickling him or her to the point of tears, kissing him or her, blowing bubbles on his or her stomach, enveloping him or her—while the child's face contorts, he or she begins to cry, or his or her body goes stiff. The parent, immersed in his or her own needs, appears oblivious to the most reliable feedback a child can give—facial expressions, verbal cues, and body language.

Parents and care givers need to develop enough inner awareness to realize whose needs are being met in interactions with children. Am I "allowing" my young son to sleep with me every night because I'm lonely? Do I stop him from visiting his friends because I would feel alone without him or because I am jealous of the pleasure he derives from his friends? Am I asking him for his opinion becauses I am afraid to be a responsible adult? Do I flirt with my son's friends to bring some light into an unhappy life or to assuage the pain of encroaching wrinkles or the suffering from a dead marriage? To appraise himself or herself, an adult needs permission to explore his or her inner world, feelings, fears, and inadequacies.

There need to be groups where parents can talk about sexuality—their personal concerns as well as questions they have about relating appropriately to their children. I remember one such meeting I attended with a group of parents who ran an alternative school in the 1970s. We shared our fears and asked for input from each other. One man said he sometimes got an erection wrestling with his son. He talked about his reaction, which was not to feel ashamed or to disconnect emotionally from his son. We talked about taking pictures of nude kids in the bathtub, how to get feedback from the kids about their feelings, what kind of sex play was allowable in each other's houses, and what the kids were doing with pornography in someone's house. How did we feel about it? It was a wonderful gathering—open and nonshaming—as we helped each other find answers to our questions. I wish all parents could have access to such groups in public schools and in the community. Too often parents repeat the damaging behavior of their parents because no one ever taught them anything else. One woman was taught by her mother to rub her baby boy's penis if he was restless or had a hard time going to sleep. Until she was in a supportive parenting group, she never questioned the behavior, which was a chargeable offense.

Many parents who I counsel are eager to learn about boundaries and appropriate behavior. They are also willing to learn appropriate questions to ascertain their child's feelings and reactions to their behavior. Other parents feel more threatened. Because of their insecurity, guilt, or shame, they constantly defend their behavior. Any criticism or suggestion is seen as a personal attack. For them it may take a while to break the ties of loyalty with their parents and to consider new ways of relating to their children.

## Cultural Consciousness

We need to develop a cultural consciousness that we are all in this life together. We are all parents of the next generation, and we are all role models of what it is to be an adult. As men and women, we need to stop pointing the finger at each other and start learning from each other. By sharing our internal experience and becoming vulnerable to each other, we pave the way to understanding. Only then can we join in an effort to slow the tremendous momentum of increased childhood sexual abuse. Men and women both need to take responsibility for their sexual behavior and to be held accountable. Wherever there is denial, there is also shame, pain, and isolation. The first step to healing is to admit there is a problem.

To prevent childhood sexual abuse, there must be equality between men and women. As long as a power imbalance is maintained, the antagonism, frustrations, hurt, and anger spill over onto children. Men maintain their power position through rape or threats of rape or abandonment, and women use sex for reward and punishment or become seductive with men as a covert way of expressing anger. Women must be granted equal access to power, money, safety, and decision making in our culture. Men need the psychological right to cry and be vulnerable. If men take a share of the responsibility for child care, not only will they learn to care for children, but they also will come closer to the child within themselves.

To accomplish this, boys must be taught from an early age to care for and bond with children. This starts with play activities, toys, dolls, and attitudes in the home. When men learn to feel competent and comfortable around children, they are likely to enjoy them in an appropriate way—not as objects or possessions but as fascinating, vulnerable little people. One result of men's bonding with children is that they will be more likely to take a stand in creating safety, care, good education, and protection for children.

We do little to help men feel close to their children. In fact, there is something of a cultural taboo that says young boys should not care for children and develop kindness and sensitivity. Consider the following: When you think of a baby-sitter, what is the image that comes to mind? A teenage girl or boy? What images come to mind when you picture a fourteen-year-old girl baby-sitting to a seven-year-old boy? Do you imagine her reading a story to him, being kind and friendly? What do you picture when you think of a fourteen-year-old boy baby-sitting an eight-year-old girl? Do you think something is probably wrong with that boy—that he is gay, he is a sissy, or he wants to sexually abuse her? Yet, as one man said, "I was never abused by a man. I was abused by two female baby-sitters."

Exploring sex-role stereotypes and attitudes toward children is one way to challenge our cultural values. While this type of exploration initially results in shock, pain, and discomfort, the ultimate rewards can be a profound change in the relationships between men and women and a reduction in childhood sexual abuse.

We need to open the Pandora's box of females who sexually abuse in the spirit of love for all people concerned. The goal is to heal both the child who is wounded and the woman who perpetrates the abuse. If we do not face up to the fact that women can and do sexually intrude upon, exploit, and abuse male children, then we can never explore women's parenting skills and feelings about sexuality. We deny that many women feel lost, overwhelmed, and ashamed about their lack of parenting skills and their sexual confusion.

This exploration must be done in the context of our understanding of patriarchy and its inequities. It also must be done in the spirit of openness to seeing what we do not want to see, to feeling what we may fear within, and eventually to loving all people in a deeper way.

## References

Bera, W. 1985. "A Preliminary Investigation of a Typology of Adolescent Sex Offenders and Their Family Systems." Master's thesis, University of Minnesota.

Evans, S., and S. Schaefer. 1987. "Incest and Chemically Dependent Women: Treatment Implications." *Journal of Chemical Dependency Treatment* 1 (no. 1): 141–173.

## Suggested Reading

Kasl, Charlotte. *Dear Therapist: Through the Voices of Survivors.* Minneapolis: Castle Consulting, Inc., 1986. Copies available by writing to P.O. Box 7073, Minneapolis, MN 55407.

———. "A Feminist Perspective on Female Sexual Abuse." Paper presented at the First International Congress on Rape, Jerusalem, Israel, July 1986.

———. *Women, Sex, and Addiction: A Search for Love and Power.* New York: Ticknor & Fields, 1989.

McBean, Anne. "Another Secret Out in the Open: Female Sex Offenders." *Innovation and Inquiry in Family Sexual Abuse Intervention,* Spring 1987, 1.

Russell, Diana. *The Secret Trauma: Incest in the Lives of Girls and Women.* New York: Basic Books, 1986.

Sterne, M., S. Schaefer, and S. Evans. "Women's Sexuality and Alcoholism." In *Alcoholism: Analysis of a Worldwide Problem,* edited by P. Golding, 421–425. Lancaster, England: MTP Press Limited, 1982.

# 13
# Female Sexual Offenders

*Ruth Mathews*
*Jane Matthews*
*Kate Speltz*

Although social awareness of sexual abuse increased greatly in the 1980s, the female sexual offender has been virtually invisible. Viewing females as perpetrators of sexual abuse, perhaps parallel to viewing males as victims, challenges traditional cultural stereotypes. Females are thought of as mothers, nurturers, those who provide care for others—not as people who harm or abuse them. Since, historically, females have been viewed as noninitiators, limit setters, and anatomically the receivers of sexuality, it is difficult for some to imagine a female sexually abusing others.

Limited formal information is available on female offenders, and the existing writings on the topic have been descriptive and exploratory. While it is acknowledged that more research is needed and research efforts on female offenders have been limited (such as by sample size), consistent patterns that suggest types of female offenders are emerging.

In general, female offenders victimize both males and females, although it appears that certain subtypes of female offenders specifically target males (Faller 1987; Mathews, Matthews, and Speltz 1989; McCarty 1986). Studies on female offenders have not yet made further differentiations regarding the impact of sexual abuse on male versus female victims.

## Summary of Existing Research

Studies and papers recently have begun to identify and describe incidents of sexual abuse perpetrated by females (Brown, Hull, and Panesis 1984; Faller 1987; Mathews, Matthews, and Speltz 1989; McCarty 1981; McCarty 1986; Wolfe 1985). A few studies have explored the prevalence of sexual abuse by women, as well as the characteristics of women who rape and sexually abuse children. In addition, typologies of female offenders and treatment strategies specific to working with female offenders have appeared in the literature and at professional conferences (Faller 1987; Mathews, Matthews, and Speltz 1989; Mathews 1988).

## Prevalence of Female Sexual Offenses

The prevalence of sexual abuse perpetrated by women is an issue of debate, and the limited research available to date is inconclusive. As early as 1979, Groth began speculating that sexual victimization by women is more frequent than the small numbers (1 percent in his samples) might indicate. Groth (1979) and others (Justice and Justice 1979; Plummer 1981) note that the types of sexual offenses perpetrated by women are possibly more incestuous in nature, more difficult to identify, and, due to the female's relationship with the victim, less likely to be reported.

Plummer (1981) speculates that adult female-to-child sexual activity is more hidden because of the expectation that women have bodily contact with children and because the existence of sexuality in women is denied. Justice and Justice (1979) suggest that mothers engage more frequently in types of sexual activities that are less likely to get reported, such as fondling, sleeping with a son, caressing him in a sexual way, and keeping him tied to her emotionally with implied promises of a sexual payoff. Groth (1979) says that the sexual offenses of females are more incestuous in nature, and, therefore, a woman's children are more reluctant to report sexual contact.

The most comprehensive estimates currently available on the prevalence of female sexual abuse have been compiled by David Finkelhor and Diana Russell (1984). Based on their review of the American Humane Association and the National Incidence Studies of sexual abuse victims, they found that approximately 24 percent of sexually abused males and 13 percent of sexually abused females were victimized by females either acting alone or with an accomplice. In approximately 42 percent of the cases of male sexual victimization and 54 percent of the cases of female victimization by females, the female offender was acting in the company of others. Although from these percentages it would appear that females more often abuse males, since many more females were victimized, female offenders were actually involved in victimizing females more frequently than males.

## Motivations for Abuse

In an attempt to understand why and how females sexually offend, researchers have begun to explore characteristics of female offenders, their lives, and the crimes they commit (McCarty 1981; McCarty 1986; Wolfe 1985). In 1987, this author and her colleagues (Mathews, Matthews, and Speltz 1989) conducted an exploratory qualitative study on sixteen adult females referred to outpatient treatment for adult female sexual offenders (Genesis II, Minneapolis) to gain greater understanding of the dynamics involved when females sexually offend. The research involved interviewing and testing (the Minnesota Multiphasic Personality Inventory [MMPI], Family Adaptability Cohesion Evaluation Scale [FACES], and the Tennessee Self-Concept Scale [TSCS]) the women at various stages of treatment and presents the most comprehensive information regarding adult females' motivation for abusing.

During the initial (intake) interview, the women were asked, "Why did you commit the offense(s)?" and "How do you understand your behavior now?" Thirteen of the sixteen women stated that the major factors were either prior or present abuse or dependence on or rejection by males. Seven women were manipulated into sexually abusing by their husbands. All reported that their dependence and fear, and their husbands' threats and physical abuse, were major reasons for their involvement:

> I was sexually abused as a child from quite young on up, until I was a teenager. Some of the same things that I did to my children, some of the inappropriate boundaries, of growing up, of thinking, came from my family. (Irene)

> I didn't want my husband to leave me. I didn't want to be alone. He always threatened to leave: "Do what I say." (Jenny)

> I didn't want to be there. He wanted me there. . . . Why? I had to. Didn't say no when I should of. He hit me to make sure I did. (Nancy)

Nine of the women described themselves as needy or in a low period at the time they became involved in the abuse. They reported needing acceptance, attention, and closeness; having unmet needs and low self-esteem; and being isolated. Feelings of anger, revenge, power, jealousy, and rejection toward people other than their victims were listed as reasons for abusing by seven of the offenders.

The majority of the women reportedly viewed their own and other children as safe targets for these displaced feelings. Four of the women believed that their acts were expressions of love, three saw them as love for the victim, and one saw them as love for her husband. Although all (n = 11) of the women who had initiated some of the sexual abuse they were involved in acknowledged either arousal or fantasies involving their victims, the majority stated that arousal was not a main motivating factor. They reported that their fantasies mainly involved imagining that their victim(s) was the perfect adult man. Only one of the women projected any blame or responsibility for the abuse onto the victim.

## Female Rapists and Child Molesters

Additional research efforts have focused primarily on subgroups of female offenders. In researching female rapists, Brown, Hull, and Panesis (1984) studied twenty cases from the files of the office of the Massachusetts Commissioner of Probation. They found that the female rapist knew her victim as either a family member, friend, or acquaintance. In 23.5 percent of the cases, the female offender abused male victims. Grier and Clark's (1987) study of incarcerated female offenders (n = 13) also revealed a higher frequency of female victims. Only two of thirteen female offenders victimized males (stepson and son). The offenders' involvement in the abuse varied from planner to passive spectator and included luring, restraining, forcing compliance, or being sexual with the victim.

McCarty (1981) found in his study of seven convicted women rapists in the New York State Prison System that the females were psychologically unstable at the time of their offenses. In addition, McCarty (1981) and Grier and Clark (1987) found that in nearly all (nineteen of twenty) of the females' crimes, at least one male accomplice was involved. All three studies (Brown, Hill, and Panesis 1984; Grier and Clark 1987; McCarty 1981) suggested that force or violence was often used before, during, or after sexual contact by either the female or her male co-offender.

Grier and Clark (1987) report that incarcerated female offenders often were unaware of the consequences suffered by their victims. In general, the women perceived themselves as "competent and having a sense of self worth" (p. 10). Their lack of self-dissatisfaction, preference for self-focus, lack of victim empathy, and rationalization of offending behavior reflect little motivation for change. Quite possibly, these factors are critical in determining disposition (treatment versus incarceration) and are more characteristic of an incarcerated population.

In contrast, Marvasti (1986), after reviewing five cases of incestuous mothers, came to the following conclusions:

1.  The sexual abuse perpetrated by females within an incest dynamic was usually nonviolent.

2.  With one exception, the women themselves, not the victims, reported the abuse.

3.  The sense of power and authority, which is explained as a psychodynamic factor in father-daughter incest, was not substantially present.

4.  There was no finding of psychosis in the cases involving mother-son incest.

McCarty (1986), in her study of twenty-six incest mothers in the Dallas Treatment Program, was able to begin differentiating subtypes of incestuous female offenders, which she labeled the independent offender, the co-offender, and the accomplice.

## Preliminary Typology of Female Sexual Offenders

Some authors (Mathews, Matthews, and Speltz 1989; Mathews and Ray-maker 1987; Faller 1987) have been involved in treating a cross section of female offenders on an outpatient basis and have developed similar typologies of female offenders, which include incest offenders. Faller (1987) studied forty female offenders, three of whom were adolescents, in Michigan. At Genesis II, we have worked with an additional fifteen women since completion of the research on sixteen adult female offenders (Mathews, Matthews, and Speltz 1989). In addition, along with Raymaker, we have worked with approximately twenty adolescent female offenders at the Program for Healthy Adolescent Sexual Expression (PHASE) in Maplewood, Minnesota (Mathews, and Raymaker 1987). Based on our work with both adolescent and adult female sexual offenders at Genesis II and PHASE, as well as the above research efforts, we have developed a preliminary typology of female sexual offenders (table 13–1). The typology includes three main categories in which the female acts alone and two categories in which the perpetrator is frequently in the company of others. The four most frequently found types of female offenders are described in the following sections in order of their frequency.

### Intergenerationally Predisposed Female Offender

This category of female offender is predominant in adult as well as adolescent and child clinical populations. Almost half of the adolescent offenders and half of the adult female offenders we have worked with at PHASE and Genesis II cluster within this category. Johnson's (1989) child female perpetrators (ages four to thirteen) also predominantly fall within this category. Others have described this offender type as the single parent (Faller 1987) or the independent female offender (McCarty 1986).

Most characteristic of this female offender is her history of severe sexual and physical abuse as a child and the similarities between the abuse she has

**Table 13–1**
**Preliminary Typology of Female Sexual Offenders**

| *Self-Initiated Offenses* | *Accompanied Offenses* |
| --- | --- |
| Intergenerationally predisposed (child, adolescent, and adult) | Male-coerced (adolescent and adult) |
| Experimenter/exploiter (adolescent) | Psychologically disturbed (adult) |
| Teacher/lover (adult) | |

suffered and perpetrated. More than in any other category, this offender tends to choose female victims rather than male victims, though often the choice of victim is determined by availability. Adult offenders generally abuse their own children or someone they identify as close to them. Similarly, child and adolescent offenders tend to abuse relatives, foster siblings, or neighbors—someone in close proximity with whom they have a relationship. The victims' ages vary and frequently are similar to the age at which the perpetrator herself was first sexually victimized.

Unlike other types of female offenders who are either caught in the act or reported, these adolescent and adult females tend to self-report their victimization of others in the course of treatment or therapy. As Groth (1979) speculates, at times their victims will deny or refuse to talk about the sexual abuse, possibly due to their close relationship with the perpetrator and their emotional or physical reliance on her (for example, she may be a single parent or an idolized relative).

The sexual abuse these females initiate is generally tied to their own victimization. The abuse tends to be either a reenactment of their own victimization or the result of a learned adult-child deviant arousal pattern, boundary confusion, and/or thinking errors. The involved sexual behaviors are often ritualized and compulsive, and they occur frequently over an extended period of time, especially when the victim and offender reside together. The number of victims is few if the female has constant access to them.

The offending female's tendency is to engage the victim in behaviors similar to those into which she was forced. The sexual acts include kissing, fondling, oral sex, exposing, and penetration. It is fairly common for the perpetrated sexual behaviors, particularly of adolescents in this category, to be more aggressive than the abuse the perpetrators suffered. This is possibly due to unresolved issues and feelings regarding their own victimization.

Both adolescent and adult offenders in this category generally approach treatment with a great deal of shame and/or defensive oppositionality. The latter appears to be related to the female's generalized lack of trust stemming from her early victimization. A primary issue facing this group of offenders is the resolution of their own sexual victimization. Like many victims of sexual abuse, these women have a history of extensive family of origin stressors, boundary confusion, poor concentration, verbal and physical aggression, stealing, running away, low ego strength, poor self-confidence, low self-esteem, fears, daydreaming, and extensive fantasizing. These offenders are often very self-destructive. They frequently abuse alcohol and drugs, exhibit many symptoms of depression, are generally socially isolated, are not self-sufficient at the time of their offending, and have poor reality testing.

*Case Example.* Fran lived with her daughter and two sons. When the children were between the ages of four and nine, she initiated sexual contact with them. She described that, at the time, "my boyfriend wasn't giving me enough sex." She felt "neglected" by him and "isolated from friends and others." All the incidents took place when she was "high" on pot, but she did not abuse her children every time she was high.

Although Fran initiated sexual contact with all of her children, her daughter resisted and was not abused. In discussing the sexual abuse of her sons, Fran stated that she never used force: "If they said no, it would end." The pattern of abuse with each boy was essentially the same. It consisted of Fran asking her son if he wanted to "mess around." He would pull his pants down, and she would fondle him and rub his penis up and down on her vulva.

Fran discouraged penetration by telling her sons no when their "penises would slip" into the opening of her vagina. As the boys grew older, they tried to penetrate her, and although they would sometimes succeed, she would quickly have them pull out. The abuse continued for seven years and occurred every three to six months with the older son and every six months with the younger son. Fran "knew it was wrong" and "felt guilty." She initially told the boys not to tell or they would be taken away from her. As the abuse continued, however, Fran's guilt increased. After the last incident with her oldest son in 1986, Fran was greatly bothered. She said, "I sat down and did some serious thinking. Possibly it was bothering the kids. I put myself in their shoes, thought they and I needed some help. They wouldn't talk with me about it. I thought it bothered them to have a secret."

Shortly thereafter, Fran entered chemical abuse treatment, and while there, she told her counselor about the sexual abuse. She said, "I told the boys that I told so we could get help. I asked them how they felt. They said they still loved me and that they thought talking about what happened would help."

## Male-Coerced Female Offender

This is the most frequent type of female offender reported in adult clinical research populations (Faller 1987; Mathews, Matthews, and Speltz 1989; Mathews and Raymaker 1987; McCarty 1986). As Faller (1987) points out, the abuse perpetrated by this group often occurs in polyincestuous family situations. In general, the females in this category are coerced into sexually abusing predominantly their own children by their significant male partners. Adolescent females at PHASE (n = 3) also have been identified in this category. Two were coerced into sexually abusing a peer-aged female by an older brother/stepbrother and one was pressured into having oral sex with her little brother by a female peer. In addition, at Genesis II we have identified adult females who have been coerced into sexually abusing peer-aged females. McCarty's (1986) incest co-offender falls into this category.

The abuse generally begins with either the husband, boyfriend, or older brother abusing the victims. Along with Faller (1987), we have found through reports by victims, male co-offenders, and female offenders that males dominated and abused these female offenders in many areas of their lives.

These women typically had a troubled childhood during which they were sexually abused. They often performed poorly in school and were shunned by peers. Few have been employed outside of the home. Many have been neglectful parents, and some have physically abused their children (Mathews, Matthews, and Speltz 1989; McCarty 1986).

We found that many of these women have been sexually abused and battered within their significant relationships. Often the female offender's husband, boyfriend, or person coercing her has been physically abusive or at least intimidating to her prior to her being coerced into the sexual abuse.

The women in this category have been extremely dependent and isolated and evidenced low self-esteem. One woman described herself as "not being a whole person unless there was someone else with me. That's pretty much what it's been like for a long time. There had to be a male in my life; otherwise I would think I was nobody" (Marie).

The women's psychological profile on the MMPI* (extremely low K, low 5, low ego strength, elevated 4, and elevated MacAndrews) suggests a person who tends to be passive and nonassertive. She is angry and has tendencies toward antisocial behavior. Because forming emotional attachments may be difficult for her, most of her relationships are shallow and one-dimensional. She has very low self-esteem and has difficulty believing that people can care for her. She also has an elevated risk for substance abuse and dependent relationships.

Due to these personality characteristics, when the woman is enlisted into the sexual abuse, she feels that she has no choice but to participate. At times, she is beaten and threatened with physical abuse. The male also may threaten to leave her if she does not participate. Because of her extreme dependence, the woman may describe fearing that her world will end if she is separated from her husband or boyfriend.

These women have expressed a belief that they would never have sexually abused another person if not coerced. Once introduced into the pattern of sexual abuse, some of them will begin initiating sexual abuse without the male being present. It appears that the male chooses the victim and that both sexes are victimized.

---

* *Editor's note:* The K scale is a measure of the subject's test-taking aptitude. A low K is sometimes due to the belief that one is unable to cope with problems, or a deliberate attempt to give a poor impression or to exaggerate one's faults. Scale 4 is the Psychopathic Deviate scale. An elevated 4 scale is often associated with people who are irresponsible, aggressive, socially inadequate, not dependable, or having marital problems (Duckworth 1979; King-Ellison Good and Brantner 1974). An elevated MacAndrews scale can indicate that the subject has an addictive disorder.

*Case Example.* Kris was married to a man who had a history of sexually abusing children. Before their first child was born, Kris's husband started physically and verbally abusing her. This abuse continued until after their third child was born. Kris stated that she became suspicious about her husband's sexual involvement with their children. She reported confronting him. His response was denial of the sexual abuse. He later suggested that they play a family sex game. When she resisted, he threatened to beat her and forced her to participate.

Initially, they played a version of spin the bottle that forced the children to undress, allowed Kris and her husband to touch the children, and required that the children touch them. Physical abuse as well as sexual abuse was part of the game, since the children were sometimes spanked when they did not want to participate. According to Kris, the sexual abuse eventually consisted of oral sex, fondling, touching, penetration, forcing the children to be sexual with one another, and having the children witness adult sexual contact.

Kris progressed from being a forced participant to being an active participant: "I was unwilling at first. But then it seemed like [with] all the threats my ex-husband made, I was afraid he was going to hurt me so I did it willingly, even though I knew it was wrong. But then after a while, it got to the point where I liked it."

### Female Offenders Who Predominantly Abuse Males

Males are specifically targeted by the next two types of female offenders unless the offender's sexual preference is same sex. Approximately half of the adolescent females referred to PHASE fall in the first category, labeled experimenter/exploiter. An increasing number of adult females referred to Genesis II have been identified as falling into the second category, described as teacher/lover. Both of these subgroups of offenders choose to be sexual with much younger males. In general, these males are under the females' care but are not related to them (for example, the female is a baby-sitter or foster mother).

**Experimenter/Exploiter.** This offender tends to be sixteen years old or younger and generally chooses a young male child (six years old or younger) as her victim. The abuse usually takes place while the adolescent is baby-sitting the child. Often the female will fondle the child, have oral contact with his penis, or have the child touch her breasts and vagina, suck on her breasts, and attempt intercourse. This is usually a one-time event and is characterized by detachment, no intimacy, and low emotionality, as the offender seems to be unaware of or denies sexual arousal.

These females often act disgusted and anxious when talking about their bodies, sexual feelings, and sexual relationships. Typically these females are very naive and fearful of sexuality and have had no prior sexual experiences. At times, the adolescents have expressed a belief that "if I allow myself to get sexually aroused, I won't be able to protect myself and say no to sexual advances by peer males." The girls express a fear of being raped, which also seems to be an obstacle to their feeling safe in exploring their sexuality. Their concerns regarding sexual acceptance are often reflected in their scores on the Millon Adolescent Personality Inventory (MAPI). In addition to sexual concerns, the MAPI also describes the adolescents as sensitive, with a tendency to be self-depreciating and socially detached, and possessing few social skills.

Frequently, parents describe these girls as somewhat nervous, with a tendency to withdraw from peer interactions. Their lack of social confidence and fear of sexuality appear to be reflected in their choice of young male victims whom they view as safe. Within the confines of a baby-sitting situation, they have authority and control over the child.

*Case Example.* Julie, age 13, was baby-sitting for her neighbor's two-year-old son. As she was changing the little boy's diaper, her mind flashed to a scene she had seen in a movie that involved two adolescents in bed having intercourse. Within the past few months, she had heard her girlfriends talking about sex and began to wonder what being sexual would be like.

Julie decided to take off her clothes and rub her body against the boy to see if she could have that same feeling she saw the adolescents in the movie having. When nothing happened, she decided to try some of the things she heard her girlfriends talking about. She began to touch the boy's penis, then suck on it. Eventually she started to rub her genitals. Suddenly she got scared, stopped, and got herself and the boy dressed. Because the boy was so young, she thought he would never tell.

The next day, the boy's mother observed him rubbing two dolls together and calling out Julie's name. The mother reported this to child protection, and when questioned, Julie shamefully admitted to her actions.

**Teacher/Lover.** This offender becomes sexually involved with generally vulnerable teenage males at a time of relationship dissatisfaction or conflict with peer-aged significant others. The abuse is described by these females as a "love affair," and it is often very difficult for them to understand the negative impact of their behavior on the victims.

The male victims (primarily ages eleven to sixteen) of these women are often a stepson, a foster son, a resident of a treatment center where the female works, a friend of one of her children, a neighbor, or a young friend. If the abuse victim is the woman's own son, it is very likely that the woman was an abuse victim within her family of origin. The young male victims often come from dysfunctional families and have a history of acting out, involvement with the criminal justice system, and placement outside their homes.

During a time in which the female's intimate relationships with her spouse or boyfriend is failing or troubled, she finds comfort and acceptance from a young male(s) with whom she has fairly regular contact. Initially, she befriends this naive or troubled boy. She gets involved in discussing his problems, providing for his needs, and wanting to rescue him. Gradually she begins to share more and more of herself because involvement with him is a welcome escape from her present or past relationship conflicts. She begins to lose perspective, viewing the boy more and more as a peer and herself as newly in love. The women describe riding bikes, driving around in cars, and running around drinking with these boys as if they were teens themselves. Eventually caring for these young males develops into sexual attraction. Often these females sexually fantasize about these males and use projection as a defense mechanism.

Psychological testing (MMPI elevations on 4 and MacAndrews scales) reveals some defensiveness and a denial of the reality of the offenders' actions and those of others. These women find it difficult to acknowledge flaws in their character and behavior. Members of this subgroup usually minimize the negative impact of their behavior. They may be very angry, but that anger tends to be acted out rather than expressed moderately or assertively. There is a strong likelihood of chemical abuse or dependent relationships.

*Case Example.* As a young woman, Ann had been involved in numerous abusive relationships with male peers. In the early 1980s, she decided not to tolerate further physical or emotional beatings and chose to live unpartnered with her two preadolescent sons. One day, in approximately 1983, one of her son's friends (age fourteen) came to visit:

> He came down and I met him and talked to him and all of this. . . . I knew I started feeling some kind of fondness. . . . He came back in the summertime. And I started getting to know him a little bit more . . . it was something. I took him grocery shopping with me, and he'd carry the groceries home. If I wanted to get rid of an old couch, he'd carry it out to the dumpster. He was a big help—not financially. At night, when my kids were sleeping, when nobody was around, he started flirting, started giggling and things. And I made a pass at him. And he says "nope." And then he went back to school. . . . And he came at Christmas time and says, "[Ann], I'm a man. I'm ready." . . . We had sex. And then he went back to school and came home again in the summertime. And things started to progress off and on. . . . But we had an affair, a love affair.

## Additional Subtypes

Several other subtypes of female offenders have been cited in the literature, including the female rapist (previously described), the incestuous female accomplice, and the psychologically disturbed or psychotic female perpetrator. McCarty (1986) describes the accomplice (19 percent of her sample), who is of average intelligence and often employed outside the home. Similar to the male coerced offender, she has a strong need to be taken care of, which takes precedence over her children's needs. Although these women did not directly sexually abuse their children, their "roles in enabling the abuse were so extensive that law enforcement officials treated them as offenders" (p. 448). The victims were most often the women's adolescent daughters.

Faller (1987) reports a type of offender that she classifies as psychotic (7.5 percent of her sample). She describes this female as suffering from out-of-control libidinal impulses. "In an attempt to organize them, she develops a delusional system which also provides justification for the sexually abusive behavior" (p. 14). The psychotic perpetrators in her sample all abused female children (daughters and a niece).

## Treatment

Female sexual offenders can benefit greatly from treatment if they are amenable and motivated. Although the subject of treatment is beyond the scope of this chapter, issues relative to treatment of female perpetrators' victims are discussed briefly. It is the authors' belief that the victim, his family (if a child), the offender, and her family can benefit from therapeutic services.

### Adolescent Female Offenders

When an adolescent female abuses someone outside her home (experimenter/exploiter and some predisposed offenders), the offender and her family often have some relationship with the victim and his family (neighbor, relative, or friend). This being the case, it is often helpful in the healing process for the offender (possibly with her parents present) to apologize to the victim and/or his parents (via a letter, phone call, or face-to-face meeting). The victim's and/or his parents' wishes should dictate whether this reconciliation occurs and in what form.

When adolescent females are involved in perpetrating within the family (predisposed), it is imperative that the family be involved in the treatment process to assess the family's level of functioning and to prevent additional victimization. The female offender needs to be removed from the home if she is at risk to reoffend or if the victim is traumatized by her presence. It is important that the parents hold the adolescent accountable for her behaviors, protect the victim, and establish healthy boundaries within the family. Accepting responsibility for the abuse, understanding its impact on the victim(s), resolving issues motivating the abuse, and apologizing to family members are imperative if the female offender is going to return home. Reconciliation does not require that the victim forgive the offender.

*Adult Female Offenders*

Similar procedures are recommended for adult female offenders who abuse outside the home (teacher/lover, predisposed [usually those without children]), especially if the offender is fairly well known to the victim and/or his family or the offender is likely to come into contact with the victim.

When an adult female abuses her own children, it is crucial that she and her family be involved in family therapy in addition to individual treatment if it appears likely that reunification will occur. In cases of mother-child incest (predisposed and male coerced), the children often are placed outside the home because there is no nonabusive parent available. At Genesis II, we have found it very beneficial to begin family therapy as soon as the offender takes full responsibility for her behavior and the victim's therapy is stabilized. It is therapeutically beneficial to the victim if the offender takes responsibility for her abusive behavior and gives her children permission to talk about what happened and their feelings.

For example, Olive had four children, who were placed in foster care and therapy after the sexual abuse by her and her husband was discovered. After two years of therapy, her children had made little therapeutic progress regarding the abuse. Eventually, a family therapy session was scheduled for Olive and her children. During the session, Olive described what she remembered occurring and encouraged the children to talk about what they recalled and how they felt about it. Within two months, the children opened up in therapy and revealed years of additional abuse.

Family therapy also gives the professionals an opportunity to assess the family's functioning to ensure that the family has learned appropriate boundaries; that the offender(s), not the victim(s), takes responsibility for the abuse; that the victim(s) feels safe within the family; and that protection plans are in place so that further victimization will be reported.

## Comparison of Female and Male Offenders

Wolfe (1985) studied a sample of twelve female sex offenders assessed in an outpatient program specializing in the evaluation and treatment of male and female offenders. In comparing this population with male offenders, she found the following similarities and differences:

1. Fifty percent of the women worked in concert with another adult, something rarely seen among male offenders.

2. Some females excused their behavior on the grounds of dependence, a rationalization rarely heard from a corresponding male population.

3. Females used denial, projection, and minimization as defenses, just as did male offenders.

4. Both male and female offenders rarely used physical force as opposed to coercion.

5. Male and female offenders were more likely to victimize a family member rather than someone outside the family.

Mathews, Matthews, and Speltz and Faller (1987) have reported similar findings but have viewed women's dependence on males quite differently. Rather than an excuse used to rationalize their behavior, these authors describe this dynamic as rooted in cultural male dominance and a reality in the lives of female offenders. As described earlier, many of the male-coerced offenders experienced being beaten, sexually abused, and dominated by their husbands or boyfriends. In general, adult female offenders have extreme feelings of inferiority and are nonassertive with men. The Genesis II womens' MMPI profiles suggest that most of the female offenders had a very traditional, socially stereotypical view of women (low 5*) and very little development of their own identity or self (extremely low ego strength).

Several adult female offenders at Genesis II made statements that reflected this dependence and lack of ego strength:

> I didn't care for myself . . . so dependent on male approval . . . needed a man all the time. Thought that's how life was supposed to be . . . waiting on him, being around the house. (Lisa)

> I wasn't a whole person unless there was somebody else with me. That's pretty much what it's been like for a long time. There had to be a male in my life; otherwise I would think I was nobody. Now I'm working on being important to myself. (Marie)

> Yeah, it's really different. . . . It's not me, it's another person in there, when I compare to the way I used to be. It's just different—every feeling with people is different. I can talk, say more what I feel. Say a lot more. I feel like a different person that way. I can get as angry or as frustrated or whatever, and no way. I can't never see myself doing that again. I feel more equal with people. I don't put everybody up on pedestals. I don't know what I was, but not a person. (Bonnie)

---

* *Editor's note:* Scale 5 originally was a measure of masculinity and femininity. Low scores with women subjects suggest a high degree of identification with the traditional stereotypic feminine role, including submissiveness and passivity (Carson 1969). Very low scoring women have been described by King-Ellison Good and Brantner (1974) as having "masochistic passivity."

Additional differences between male and female offenders have been found in clinical diagnoses and in consideration of sexual offense charges. Male sex offenders are often diagnosed as having paraphilias or an antisocial personality disorder (Metzner 1988). Female offenders more typically are diagnosed with personality disorders of the dependent, borderline, passive-aggressive, or avoidant types.

Cultural stereotypes, perceived power differentials, and presentations of male and female sexuality appear to influence what is considered a sexual offense, as indicated in discussing the teacher/lover. Few female offenders appear in clinical and research populations for exposing, stealing men's underwear, making obscene phone calls, or window peeping. Do females not engage in these nontouch types of behaviors, or are they not considered offenses when committed by females, or both?

Possibly, as in the case of cross-dressing (for example, women wearing men's dress shirts in television or print advertisements), some of these behaviors are perceived differently and may even be culturally sanctioned or encouraged (consider, for example, men's entertainment magazines and phone sex lines). One can further question how these cultural differences affect the female offender's victims, especially the male victim.

## The Victims

The victims of adult male-coerced and predisposed offenders are most often the women's own children. Most victims are negatively affected by the abuse, although the degree of trauma varies (Faller 1987; Mathews, Matthews, and Speltz 1988). Many children who are sexually abused by their mothers also are neglected and/or physically abused within their families. Although these other forms of abuse make it difficult to determine the specific source of the consequences to the victims, these other forms of abuse highlight the adverse family conditions to which these children are subjected.

In Faller's (1987) study (87.5 percent of offenders in these two categories), victims were affected in numerous ways. They often were under-socialized, had severe problems in interpersonal relationships (58.7 percent) and in sexual acting out (58.7 percent; problems included excessive masturbation; being sexual with toys, animals, and peers; and sexual aggression toward children and adults), and had problems in school (40.4 percent of school-age children were in special classrooms, special schools, or behind a year or more in school). Children who were sexually abused outside the home or placed in foster care when very young had fewer problems with interpersonal relationships. The vast majority of the others had problems with attachment. They tended to be affectionless, unempathic, manipulative, and aggressive. Differences between male and female victims were not reported.

Children victimized by their mothers are often placed outside the home, since there is usually no nonabusive parent available for child care (Faller 1987; Mathews, Matthews, and Speltz 1988). Whether this placement is experienced as a relief of trauma, it is an additional adjustment that the child must make. Faller (1987) found that 71.1 percent of the children placed in foster or residential care experienced multiple placements and 12.7 percent of those were further sexually abused in foster care. At Genesis II, we found that in cases (n = 3) where children were placed with a father or stepfather, two of the fathers had been accused of sexually abusing their or other children (unsubstantiated at the time of placement), one was actively chemically dependent, and all were reportedly noncompliant in previous therapeutic interventions.

Based on our clinical work at Genesis II, we have found that, in general, children victimized by both parents (male-coerced) over an extended period of time were most severely traumatized by the abuse. Generally, in the course of treatment, the adult male-coerced female offender divorces or separates from the male offender. Often the male offender minimizes or denies the sexual abuse, has served some time in prison, and, in some cases, has been deemed untreatable. Therefore, if these families are reunified, usually the father is not in the home. This transition has appeared to be especially difficult for male children within the family.

In general, the victims of the experimenter/exploiter are young male children, and the victims of the teacher/lover are young teenage boys. In both situations, there is an age and power differential between the male victim and the female offender. The offender is usually a nonrelative in a position of care giving. These types of abuse appear to be experienced and/or viewed differently than those in incest situations. The boundary betrayal of the mother in the incest situation affects the child's primary bond(s) and has a clear cultural message regarding wrongfulness.

Our cultural double standard legitimizing and eroticizing sexual activity between younger males and older females (for example, the movie *Summer of '42*) makes it difficult for these male victims to identify the sexual behavior with these females as sexual abuse. Due to this cultural scripting, male victims tend to deny the effects of this type of abuse. In addition, therapists, other professionals (for example, those in social services and criminal justice), family, and friends who join in this denial by not perceiving this behavior as abusive either negate the male victim's reality or support his denial.

This double standard also makes it difficult for the teacher/lover to see the wrongfulness of her sexually inappropriate behaviors. The experimenter/ exploiter and the teacher/lover are probably two of the most underreported types of abuse perpetrated by females. Would intercourse between a thirty-year-old male and a fifteen-year-old female be considered sexual abuse, even if the female was willing? What about a willing fifteen-year-old boy and a thirty-year-old female?

In cases of adolescent females abusing young male children, the abuse dynamics might appear to be clearer. But are adolescent females being identified, adjudicated, and treated specifically for sexual crimes at rates that are proportional to those of adolescent male offenders? Are their male victims getting treatment that is comparable to that of female victims? Are males similarly affected by these types of abuse?

One victim of a teacher/lover described his experience this way:

> When I was a young teen, I had a sexual relationship with a woman twice my age. At the time, I thought it was great. We were in love. She taught me things that were beyond belief. At the time, I thought I was her lover. Now, as a middle-aged man, I realize I was a victim.
>
> Approaching subsequent relationships from the standpoint of that first relationship was disastrous. All relationships, until my more recent marriage, ended in failure. My marriage has been a constant struggle. I expected my lovers to recreate those fantasy-like sexual encounters. What I thought was so great and flattering years ago has haunted me like a cancer.

Many of the teacher/lover offenders have described their male victims as willing and desirous. Some have viewed the young male as initiating the offense. At the time of the offense, few see the adolescent boy as vulnerable, even though most of the victims were separated from their families and in treatment or placement for behavioral problems. Although most teacher/lover offenders describe their victims as boasting about their sexual relationships with the offenders, they also describe acts of anger and revenge by the adolescents (for example, threatening to expose the sexual involvement if not given money or calling the offender names in front of peers). The abuse appears to be confusing to the victims and anger producing. Quite possibly, we will not know how these males are affected by female sexual abuse until cultural double standards that romanticize younger male–older female relationships and describe males as dominant and in control of sexual relationships change.

## Conclusion

Relatively little is known about the female offender and, more specifically, about her victimization of males. Most of the research on the topic has been conducted only since 1985 and has focused on profiling adult female perpetrators. Through these limited research efforts, tentative portraits of different types of female sexual offenders are emerging. The female rapist (sexual aggressive), predisposed, male-coerced, experimenter/exploiter, teacher/lover, accomplice, and psychotic offender types have been identified and described.

More research on the child, adolescent, and adult female sexual offender is needed. Further development and expansion of the above typology of female offenders will help in understanding the dynamics of female-perpetrated sexual abuse. Studies regarding treatment, prognosis, and outcome are lacking, and there is no known longitudinal research on female offenders.

Little is known regarding the impact (short and long term) of female-perpetrated sexual abuse on male and female victims, although it appears that the effects are mediated by the male victim's relationship to the offender and the type of offense. Research on female offenders has not addressed these issues directly. Perhaps the research and writings on male victimization in this book can help us better understand male victims' experiences when abused by female offenders.

As our cultural awareness of male victimization and female offenders increases, traditional sexual stereotypes will continue to be challenged. Likewise, as perceived power differentials between males and females are confronted, our perceptions of females as offenders, males as victims, and what is considered sexual abuse possibly will change. As our knowledge of these populations increases, it is hoped that we will be able to identify and treat male victims of female offenders more effectively.

# References

Brown, M.E., L.A. Hull, and S.K. Panesis. 1984. *Women Who Rape*. Boston: Massachusetts Trial Court.

Carson, R. 1969. "Interpretative Manual to the M.M.P.I." in *M.M.P.I. Research Developments and Clinical Applications*, edited by J. Butcher, 279–296. New York: McGraw-Hill.

Duckworth, J. 1979. *M.M.P.I. Interpretation Manual for Counselors and Clincians*, 2d ed. Muncie, Indiana: Accelerated Development.

Faller, K. 1987. "Women Who Sexually Abuse Children." *Violence and Victims* 2 (no. 4): 263–276.

Finkelhor, D., and D. Russell. 1984. "Women as Perpetrators: Review of the Evidence." In *Child Sexual Abuse: New Theory and Research*, edited by D. Finkelhor, 171–187. New York: Free Press.

Grier, P., and M. Clark. 1987. "Female Sexual Offenders in a Prison Setting." Unpublished manuscript, Behavioral Science Institute, Inc., St. Louis.

Groth, A.N. 1979. *Men Who Rape*. New York: Plenum Press.

Johnson, T.C. 1989. "Female Child Perpetrators: Children Who Molest Other Children." *Child Abuse and Neglect* 13 (no. 4): 571–585.

Justice, B., and R. Justice. 1979. *The Broken Taboo*. New York: Human Sciences Press.

King-Ellison Good, P., and J.P. Brantner. 1974. *A Practical Guide to the M.M.P.I.* Minneapolis: University of Minnesota Press.

Marvasti, J. 1986. "Incestuous Mothers." *American Journal of Forensic Psychiatry* 7 (no. 4): 63–69.

Mathews, R. 1988. "Female Sexual Offenders." Presentation to the national training conference of the National Task Force on Juvenile Sexual Offending: *Imple-*

*menting an Intervention Continuum for the Youthful Sex Offender,* Long Beach, California, November.

Mathews, R., J. Matthews, and K. Speltz. 1989. *Female Sexual Offenders: An Exploratory Study.* Orwell, Vermont: Safer Society Press.

Mathews, R., and J. Raymaker. 1987. "Preliminary Typology of Adolescent Female Sexual Offenders." Unpublished manuscript, P.H.A.S.E. Program. East Community Service, Maplewood, Minnesota.

McCarty, D. 1981. "Women Who Rape." Unpublished manuscript, P.H.A.S.E. Program, East Community Service, Maplewood, Minnesota.

McCarty, L. 1986. "Mother-Child Incest: Characteristics of the Offender." *Child Welfare* 65 (no. 5): 447–458.

Metzner, T. 1988. "Evaluating Programs." Presentation to the conference on Adjudication and Disposition: *Adult and Adolescent Sex Offenders.* Project Impact, Brooklyn Park, Minnesota, February 3.

Plummer, K. 1981. "Pedophilia: Constructing a Psychological Baseline." In *Adult Sexual Interest in Children,* edited by M. Cook and K. Howells. London: Academic Press.

Wolfe, F.A. 1985. "Twelve Female Sexual Offenders." Presentation to the conference on Next Steps in Research on the Assessment and Treatment of Sexually Aggressive Persons (Paraphiliacs), St. Louis, Missouri, March.

# Index

Abused children. *See* Boys, sexual abuse of; Child abuse; Children, sexual abuse of

Acquaintance rape, 61, 63

Adult abusers. *See* Offenders, sexual

Adult victims, of child sexual abuse: behaviors of, 144, 145; emotional problems of, 115–117, 124–125, 144, 145–146; and offending history, 119, 150, 153; psychiatric problems of, 114–115, 145–146; and sexuality, 117–120, 144, 145, 183–184. *See also* Victims of sexual abuse

Advocacy. *See* Victim advocacy

Age, and definition of sexual abuse, 125, 126, 264–265

AIDS, and abuse victims, 203, 211, 237, 238

Antonelli, Judith, 20

Aristotle: on patriarchy, 23

Battered child syndrome, 6, 90

Battered women's movement, 7–8, 10

Boys, sexual abuse of: and age of victim, 125–126, 228, 233, 234; data collection methods on, 94–96, 127, 139, 181–182; definition of abuse, 92, 93; duration of, 122; and long-term effects, 8, 10, 35, 114–115; prevalence of, 3, 89, 90, 137, 228; and reporting of, 91–92; research on, 89, 96–100, 105, 107, 126, 187–188; and sex of offenders, 123, 173, 260, 264; and types of abuse, 229, 230, 260, 268; and use of violence, 124–125.

*See also* Prevalence estimates of male abuse

Boy victims, of sexual abuse: behavioral reactions of, 106, 108, 178; case studies of: (Anon.), 266–267; "Greg," 220–221; "Joe," 81, "Nick," 157–168, "Sam," 81–82, "Timothy," 168–171; emotional reactions of, 108–110, 138, 243; outreach for, 113; physical effects of, 110–111, 124, 230, 231, 235; and relationships to offenders, 123, 124; sexual identity of, 111, 177, 238; and sexuality of, 111–113, 157; and social support mechanisms, 179, 180. *See also* Male (adolescent and adult) survivors, of abuse

Castration, 15

Child abuse: and advocacy efforts, 5, 6, 7, 8; norms of, 9–12, 19; prevalence of, 3, 34, 90; reporting of, 3; sanctioning of, 14, 25, 27; and social change, efforts of, 8, 10, 39, 41–42; and social service professionals, 7; types of, 264, 267–270. *See also* Children, sexual abuse of; Prevention of child abuse

Child abuse movement, 41, 89–90

Child Abuse Prevention and Treatment Act, 6

Childbearing, early beliefs about, 20, 21

Child molestation: film treatment of, 53–54; and victims in film, 53, 54, 55–56, 67

# About the Contributors

**Maria Capra** is a graduate student working toward a master's degree in child development in the Department of Family Studies at San Diego University. She has completed the Interdisciplinary Child Abuse Graduate Training Program and has extensive knowledge in the area of physical and sexual abuse. She is the director of a research project on survivors of childhood sexual abuse and their interpersonal relationships, co-counselor for Daughters & Sons United in the senior high school age-group, and an interviewer for a research project involving sexually abused children.

**Mark C. Evans** is a veteran of the U.S. Army's infantry, Ranger and Special Forces. He has been involved in rape crisis intervention since 1985. He is currently a rehabilitation counselor at New Mexico Highwatch in Ossipee, New Hampshire, and is pursuing a doctorate in social psychology through the Union Institute in Cincinatti, Ohio.

**Paul N. Gerber, M.A., L.I.C.S.W.,** has two decades of criminal justice experience as a Special Agent for the Minnesota Crime Bureau and eight years of clinical practice combine to give him a unique perspective as an author, lecturer, and psychotherapist. Currently, he administers an outpatient program for adolescent and latency-age male victims of sexual abuse. He also works with adolescent sex offenders at the Program for Healthy Adolescent Sexual Expression (PHASE).

**Jane F. Gilgun, Ph.D.,** is an assistant professor in the School of Social Work at the University of Minnesota in Minneapolis.

**Charlotte Davis Kasl** has a Ph.D. in counseling psychology. She is a licensed consulting psychologist, healer, and the author of *Women, Sex, and Addiction: A Search For Love and Power.* She has written many articles and conducted numerous workshops on addiction, sexuality, codependency, incest, childhood abuse, and spirituality in the United States and abroad. She is currently writing the book, *Many Roads, One Journey: Twelve-Step Programs in an Age of Diversity.*

**Lisa Marie Keating** is a graduate student in the Department of Family Studies at San Diego State University and is working toward a master's degree in child development. She has completed the Interdisciplinary Child Abuse Training Program and has extensive knowledge in the area of family violence, specifically the effects of physical punishment on children. Her experience in family violence includes co-counselor for Daughters & Sons United in the twelve to fourteen-year-old age-group, director of a research study on parental use of physical punishment and children's self-esteem/locus of control, and interviewer for a research study involving sexually abused children.

**Carolyn J. Levitt, M.D.,** is a practicing pediatrician in St. Paul, Minnesota. She has been a consultant to the Ramsey County Child Abuse Team since 1972. Over the past nine years, Dr. Levitt has interviewed and examined more than three thousand children for documentation of sexual abuse. She, along with Sandra Hewitt, developed the Midwest Children's Resource Center, a diagnostic and treatment facility for victims of child abuse. Dr. Levitt was elected to the Executive Committee of the newly established section of the American Academy of Pediatrics on child abuse and neglect and serves as the liaison member to the provisional committee on Child Abuse and Neglect of the Academy. She also serves on the Executive Committee for the National Network of Child Advocacy Centers. She is an ad hoc reviewer for the *Journal of Child Abuse and Neglect* and the journal *Pediatrics*. Dr. Levitt is collaborating with a group of medical experts to develop a teaching atlas of normal and abnormal genital and anal findings documented by colposcopic examinations.

**Ruth Mathews, M.A., L.P.,** is a licensed psychologist who received her M.A. in psychology from St. Mary's College in Winona, Minnesota. She is currently completing requirements for her Ph.D. in psychology at the Saybrook Institute in San Francisco. She is coordinator of the Program for Healthy Adolescent Sexual Expression (PHASE) and is co-developer and therapist for the Genesis II Adult Female Sex Offender Program. Mathews has been involved in research on female sex offenders, adolescent sex offenders, and the role pornography plays in the crimes of adolescent male sex offenders. She is a member of the National Task Force on Juvenile Sexual Offending.

**Jane Matthews, M.A., L.P.,** received her B.S.Ed. from Southeast Missouri State College and her M.A. in psychology from St. Mary's College in Winona, Minnesota. As a licensed psychologist, she has worked with adolescent and adult male sex offenders and their victims and families in residential and outpatient settings for over ten years. She is co-developer and therapist for the Genesis II Adult Female Sex Offender Program. She also has a private practice in Minneapolis. Matthews also has been involved in research on adult female sexual offenders and the reunification of incestuous families.

**Peter E. Olson, Ph.D., L.P.,** completed his Ph.D. in 1987 at the University of Minnesota. He is a licensed psychologist and has counseled in private practice in Minneapolis since 1980. His work with sexually abused children dates back thirteen years. Aside from his clinical work and research on sexual abuse, Dr. Olson also has conducted research on chemical dependence treatment efficacy and affectional/sexual preference. His interest in family-of-origin problems, affect disorders, behavioral problems, abuse, sexuality, and men's issues has led him to conduct workshops and to keynote conferences for mental health professionals and social advocates.

**Fran A. Sepler, M.A.,** is the executive director of the Crime Victim and Witness Advisory Council and the Crime Victims Reparations Board. Previously, she served as the child sexual abuse specialist for the Minnesota Department of Public Safety. She also served as the supervisor of nonresidential licensing for the Department. She has a master's degree in public administration and was an original member of the State Interagency Team on Child Abuse and Neglect. Former chair of the Minnesota Incest Consortium, Sepler was a primary actor in the development of radio station WCCO's acclaimed Project Abuse, which broadened the public's awareness of child sexual abuse. Through her professional affiliations, Sepler has represented the interests of victims of child abuse, sexual assault, and other crimes in the Minnesota legislature for the past nine years. She served as co-chair of the Minnesota Attorney General's Task Force of the Prevention of Sexual Violence Against Women and is involved in implementing the recommendations of the task force. She received an award from Minnesota governor Perpich for her work on the task force.

**Kate Speltz, M.Ed.,** received her B.S. in psychology from St. Mary's College in Winona, Minnesota, and her M.Ed. from Boston University. In 1986, she received a Bush Foundation Leadership Fellowship to study Public Policy at the Lyndon Baines Johnson School at the University of Texas–Austin. As executive director of Genesis II, Speltz was instrumental in developing the Female Sex Offender Program. Currently she is grants coordinator for the Minnesota Office of Drug Policy, administering the Federal Bureau of Justice assistance grants program.

**Jim Struve, M.S.W., L.C.S.W.,** is a licensed clinical social worker. He received his M.S.W. from Atlanta University and has extensive training in family therapy. He is in private practice with Metropolitan Psychotherapy Associates in Atlanta, Georgia, where he approaches therapy from a profeminist perspective. Struve provides general psychotherapy, including individual, couples, and family therapy for adults and adolescents, as well as specialized services regarding trauma (including sexual abuse), sexual identity, eating disorders, and compulsive exercise.

**James W. Trivelpiece, M.Ed.,** is a therapist working in community mental health in Moscow, Idaho. He completed a master's degree program in counseling and human services at the University of Idaho and comes to the field with expertise in community organization, recreation, and student personnel services. In his undergraduate work, he dabbled in fine arts and cinematography before completing a bachelor's degree in psychology.

**Anthony J. Urquiza, Ph.D.,** is a child clinical psychologist at the Child Protective Center and Clinical Faculty at the University of California Davis Medical Center. As a psychologist, he has extensive clinical experience with children, adolescents, and adults in a variety of inpatient and outpatient settings. His primary clinical, research, and publication interests center on family violence of all types, the treatment of sexually abused children—with a specific focus on the sexual victimization of males—the development of children's sexuality, ethnic minority populations, and mental health psychodiagnostic issues as they relate to child maltreatment. Additional clinical and research interests include homeless children and families, mental health assessment of foster care children, and the use of physical punishment of children.

# About the Editor

**Mic Hunter, M.A., M.S., L.P., L.M.F.T., C.C.D.C.R., N.C.A.D.C.**, is licensed both as a psychologist and a marriage and family therapist and is certified as a chemical dependence counselor (reciprocal). He is also a national certified alcohol and drug counselor. Currently he is in private practice in St. Paul, Minnesota. Prior to this, he was employed by several outpatient mental health centers and chemical dependence treatment programs. His formal education includes an undergraduate degree in psychology from Macalester College in St. Paul; a master of arts degree from St. Mary's College in Winona, Minnesota; a master of science in education/psychological services from the University of Wisconsin–Superior; and completion of the University of Minnesota's Alcohol/Drug Counseling Education Program, the Program in Human Sexuality's Chemical Dependency and Family Intimacy Training Program, and the Intensive Post-Graduate Training Program at the Gestalt Institute of the Twin Cities. He started his doctoral studies at the Minnesota School of Professional Psychology in the Fall of 1990. In addition to articles for other helping professionals and the general public, Mr. Hunter is the author of *Abused Boys: The Neglected Victims of Sexual Abuse* and *The Twelve Steps and Shame*. He also is co-author of *The First Step for People in Relationships with Sex Addicts*. His current project is a book on the identification and expression of emotions.